The Mambi-Land

NEW WORLD STUDIES
Marlene L. Daut, Editor

The Mambi-Land

OR

ADVENTURES OF A *HERALD* CORRESPONDENT IN CUBA
A Critical Edition

James J. O'Kelly

Edited by Jennifer Brittan

University of Virginia Press
Charlottesville and London

University of Virginia Press
© 2022 by the Rector and Visitors of the University of Virginia
All rights reserved
Printed in the United States of America on acid-free paper

First published 2022

978-0-8139-4692-4 (hardcover)
978-0-8139-4693-1 (paper)
978-0-8139-4694-8 (ebook)

9 8 7 6 5 4 3 2 1

Library of Congress Cataloging-in-Publication Data is available for this title.

Cover art: "Grupo de insurrectos en la Manigua," from *Historia de la insurrección de Cuba, 1869–1879*, by D. Emilio A. Soulère (1879). (Wikimedia Commons)

Contents

Foreword, by Peter Hulme   vii

Introduction   xvii

Chronology of James J. O'Kelly in Cuba   xlix

Editor's Note   liii

The Mambi-Land, or Adventures of a *Herald* Correspondent in Cuba   1

Prologue to *La tierra del mambí*, by Fernando Ortiz   215

Acknowledgments   265

Bibliography   267

Foreword

I FIRST came across the title of *The Mambi-Land, or Adventures of a* Herald *Correspondent in Cuba* around twenty-five years ago, when I was beginning to do research on travel writing about Cuba. It sounded interesting but there was no copy in the UK, so it was not until a visit to the Library of Congress in Washington, DC, a few years later that I got to see it. I remember reading the first page and being immediately hooked. I spent the next two hours photocopying the whole book.

In those early years of the century, information about O'Kelly was not easy to come by, but I eventually realized that, although he was not at that time well remembered in Ireland, in Cuba he was a figure of some repute for having written one of the very few eyewitness accounts of the Ten Years' War (1868–78), the first war for Cuban independence. Originally appearing in Philadelphia in 1874, *The Mambi-Land* was translated into Spanish and published in New Orleans in 1876, in Cuba twice in 1887, in Puerto Rico in 1888, and then again in Havana in 1930 with a prologue by the leading Cuban intellectual of the day, Fernando Ortiz, who had done serious research on O'Kelly's life, including interviewing James's artist brother Aloysius in New York. This Cuban interest continued with the 1930 edition republished in 1968, 1990, and again in 2001.[1]

As so often happens, there turned out to be a number of people becoming interested in James J. O'Kelly at about the same time that I was. Niamh O'Sullivan had been working for some years on a critical biography of his artist brother, Aloysius; Owen McGee was uncovering O'Kelly's Fenian history; and Jennifer Brittan—editor of this critical edition—had started a PhD in Literature at the University of California, Santa Cruz, which included a chapter on *The Mambi-Land* read from an inter-American perspective.[2] The University of Michigan Library soon published a facsimile of the original English edition of *The Mambi-Land;* and Ireland's largest trade union, SIPTU, published extracts from the book, using the occasion to reaffirm Irish–Cuban solidarity, a point underlined when flowers were laid on O'Kelly's grave in Glasnevin Cemetery in Dublin on June 4, 2009, at a ceremony organized by the SIPTU Solidarity with Cuba Forum. The Cuban ambassador Noel Carrillo placed a wreath in fulfilment of Fernando Ortiz's prediction that "some day Cubans will lay flowers there, remembering him with affection and gratitude."[3] Then, during his official visit to Cuba in 2017, Irish President Michael D. Higgins discussed O'Kelly in his survey of Irish–Cuban links for the keynote address he delivered at the sixth biannual conference of the Society of Irish Latin American Studies.[4] On the Cuban side, it is clear that the appreciation of *The Mambi-Land* stems from O'Kelly's own warmth towards the Cuban peasants he encountered in the east of the island, easily associated with the *fidelista* experience of the late 1950s. In Revolutionary historiography the Ten Years' War, started in 1868, is seen as the beginning of a struggle for independence only fully achieved in 1959.[5]

Twenty years ago, James J. O'Kelly appeared as a figure every bit as hazy as the land he describes at the beginning of his book. His outline is much clearer now, even if many of the details remain obscure. The two traditions to which he clearly belongs are those of war journalism and Irish republicanism.

Within the long and honorable tradition of war journalism, O'Kelly fits into the category of "special correspondent," a group that flourished in the years between the US Civil War and the start of the Second World War. Typically, these "specials" would be given roving commissions by their newspapers: following their noses to the trouble spots of the world, usually writing long pieces that went deeper than day-to-day reporting, and often patching those pieces together into travel books, as O'Kelly did with *The Mambi-Land*. Often interviewing and even advising high-ranking politicians and soldiers, the specials' international experiences and contacts became highly valued. Three figures whose careers overlapped with O'Kelly's provide points of comparison. George Augustus Sala (1828–1895) learned his trade with Dickens's *Household Words* before beginning a long stint with the *Daily Telegraph* covering the US Civil War. He would go on to interview Abraham Lincoln, Emperor Napoleon III, and Garibaldi, among many others. His emphasis on narrative, background color, and investigative depth marked a step towards modern journalism. Sala's only deep commitment, however, was to his bohemian lifestyle, with a particular penchant for flagellation, and he never put himself into the kinds of dangerous situations that O'Kelly seemed to relish.⁶ Richard Harding Davis (1864–1916) was, like Sala, also a novelist, but he courted danger in South Africa, Greece, Cuba, and Belgium, and was praised by Theodore Roosevelt for using his revolver when US troops were under fire during the invasion of Cuba in the summer of 1898.⁷ The closest match is probably Emile Joseph Dillon (1854–1933), also Irish, and an even greater linguist than O'Kelly. Dillon—who, like Sala, wrote for the *Daily Telegraph*—became an associate and friend of the Russian politician Sergei Witte, and on occasion put himself into serious danger, as when he disguised himself in order to report on the Turkish massacres of Armenians in 1894–95. Dillon's long account of President Álvaro Obregón, the result of several months of travelling with him through Mexico, has parallels with O'Kelly's interview with Céspedes in its sympathetic portrayal of a revolutionary figure—a journalistic trope still extant in the second half of the twentieth century in Herbert Matthews's interview with Fidel Castro.⁸ Any of O'Kelly's three major expeditions to war zones—eastern Cuba, the US frontier, and Sudan—would give him a prominent position in the history of war correspondence. Taken together, they give him a strong claim as its pre-eminent practitioner.

O'Kelly's papers were destroyed by his wives and later by his cousins, on the basis that they were too incriminating to keep. Since he mostly liked to work undercover, personal details are often hard to verify, and large swaths of his activities are still shrouded in mystery. There is, however, no doubt that James Joseph O'Kelly (1842–1917) led an adventurous life. A brief sketch can only scratch the surface.⁹

Born in Ireland in 1842 into an artistic family on his mother's side (the Lawlors), and educated in London, Dublin, and Paris, O'Kelly's lifelong commitment was to Irish independence. As early as 1860 he allied himself with the Fenian movement, joining the Irish Republican Brotherhood (IRB) alongside his friend John Devoy and beginning a long career of running guns into Ireland. In order to gain military training he enlisted in the French Foreign Legion, seeing service in Algeria and Mexico (in the latter as part of the forces of Emperor Maximilian). After a disastrous battle in 1866, O'Kelly led the remnants of a French force across the US border and into New Orleans, from where he travelled to New York to meet exiled members of the IRB. Back in London in 1867, he found the Fenian movement weakened by internal divisions and riddled with informers. As a result, he distanced himself from a planned rebellion which he judged premature. In 1868 he became secretary of the IRB's Supreme Council, began work as the London correspondent for the *Irishman*, and started what would be two years as the leading IRB arms agent in Britain.[10] In 1870 he volunteered on the French side in the Franco–Prussian War and attempted to recruit a brigade of Irish volunteers. In financial straits and with police surveillance tightening, O'Kelly moved to the United States in 1871 to write for the *New York Herald*. He worked first as drama critic and then as war correspondent, immediately making his name by obtaining a long interview with General Phil Sheridan, a man notoriously distrustful of reporters but who was won over by O'Kelly's charm and military knowledge, and then an even longer exclusive with the French anarchist and Communard Henri Rochefort after he escaped from imprisonment in New Caledonia.[11] O'Kelly's knowledge of French was the key factor here, and the resulting friendship between the two men helped the Irish cause get a good hearing in radical French circles. O'Kelly's adventures in Cuba followed in 1873, with his reports to the *Herald* about his successful search for the president of insurgent Cuba, Carlos Manuel de Céspedes, quickly turned into *The Mambi-Land* (1874). The warm reception of the book consolidated his reputation as an intrepid war reporter. Meanwhile, he also moved in New York artistic circles, acting as his brother Aloysius's international agent.

Another scoop resulted from O'Kelly's close relationship with Emperor Dom Pedro II of Brazil, whom he accompanied from Rio de Janeiro to San Francisco and escorted throughout his 1876 tour of the United States.[12] Immediately, however, O'Kelly was called away to report on the aftermath of the Battle of the Little Big Horn, in which Lakota, Northern Cheyenne, and Arapaho forces had annihilated five companies of the Seventh Cavalry Regiment of the United States Army under the command of Lieutenant Colonel George Armstrong Custer. O'Kelly's thorough investigation, in articles published without a byline, probably constitutes his most sustained and impressive piece of journalism.[13] It was then, in October 1876, that O'Kelly became a US citizen.

In 1875, O'Kelly had married Harriet Clarke, a singer and sister of Joseph I. C. Clarke, his fellow Fenian and colleague at the *New York Herald*. However, two years later it came to light that O'Kelly had previously secretly married Edith Gertrude Bowes, a 17-year-old girl with whom he had a baby. In a blaze of damaging publicity, Harriet was granted a divorce and O'Kelly resigned from the *Herald* and moved to Paris, where he resumed his relationship with Edith. She died in childbirth, the baby did not survive, and their son, Jamie, died soon afterwards. It was around this time, in Paris, that O'Kelly first met Charles Stewart Parnell.

In New York O'Kelly had belonged to Clan na Gael, an Irish organization which Devoy managed to radicalize, notably through the success of the daring 1876 *Catalpa* expedition to rescue Fenian Irish prisoners from the British penal colony in Western Australia. Back in Ireland, O'Kelly worked to persuade Devoy and other Clan leaders that, while continuing to prepare for armed revolution, the Irish republican movement should call for an Irish nationalist parliamentary party to be established at Westminster. This was the basis of the Clan's "new departure" proposals published in the Irish press in November 1878, an alliance between Clan na Gael, Parnell's Home Rule Party, and the Land League, which was fighting to abolish landlordism in Ireland and to enable tenant farmers to own the land on which they worked. In 1880 O'Kelly unsuccessfully tried to persuade the Clan and the IRB to arm the tenants. Resigning from the Clan and under Parnell's patronage, O'Kelly was elected as MP for County Roscommon on a Land League ticket. Always with an eye toward stretching the resources of the British Empire, he urged support for the Zulus in 1879.

In 1881, along with Parnell, now his close ally, O'Kelly was imprisoned for seven months for his Land League activities. Soon after his release he became a member of the central committee of the Irish National League (established in October 1882), and was effectively the Parnellites' chief spokesman on British foreign policy in parliament. Then, in 1884, working for London's *Daily News* and in conjunction with his brother Aloysius, an illustrator for the *Pictorial World*, O'Kelly covered the uprising of Mohammed Ahmed ibn 'Abdullah, the self-proclaimed prophet and nationalist military leader known as "the Mahdi" in Sudan. Operating out of Cairo (he spoke Arabic), working alongside Egyptian nationalists, and writing anti-British articles for the *Bosphore Egyptien*, O'Kelly again demonstrated his international credentials. In still-mysterious circumstances, he led an expedition into the desert which was thought lost for several weeks.[14] One of Aloysius's illustrations is drawn as if from behind the Mahdi's lines, and it is indeed possible that is where the brothers had been. This was probably the high point of what Niamh O'Sullivan calls "an imaginative Fenian internationalism which sought to extend anticolonial activities beyond the confines of Ireland."[15]

O'Kelly's position as a member of the British Parliament, now for North Roscommon, did not prevent his examination by the Special Parliamentary Commission investigating the supposed criminal activities of Parnellism, which had been formed after an 1885 report in the *Times* based on forged letters.[16] Undeterred, he designed a plan to blow up the

British fleet off the west coast of Ireland during their summer maneuvers. He also persistently intervened in the case of the Cuban revolutionary José Maceo (brother of Antonio Maceo), who had been detained by British authorities in Gibraltar.[17]

In the 1892 general election, the anti-Parnellites highlighted O'Kelly's anti-clericalism and the scandal of his divorce in order to undermine his campaign. He narrowly lost his seat, but regained it in 1895, after which he was returned unopposed until his death. His parliamentary career, however, was dogged by financial difficulties and ill-health.[18] Predictably, he held strong pro-Boer sympathies during the South African War (1899–1902) and hoped that the Irish revolutionary movement might be able to capitalize. Finally, in keeping with party policy, he advocated support for the Allies during the First World War, an action that surprised his old friend Devoy, who remarked that this was the first time the two men had strongly disagreed on political matters. By now very ill, O'Kelly maintained silence regarding the Easter Rising, and died of pneumonia in London on December 22, 1916.

The *Times*'s obituary called O'Kelly an "Irish Soldier of Fortune," which, though probably not meant kindly, was not wholly inaccurate.[19] During O'Kelly's lifetime the term was associated with the fictional hero Robert Clay from Richard Harding Davis's 1897 novel, *Soldiers of Fortune*, which was made into a successful film in 1913. Clay was a man of business and principle, notionally above political intrigue but with strong military instincts. However, when Davis wrote *Real Soldiers of Fortune* in 1907, his prime exhibit was the young Winston Churchill, who in South Africa had, like O'Kelly, combined journalism and fighting, even though neither would have appreciated the comparison.[20] Both Churchill and O'Kelly covered the Mahdist Revolt and, while there is no evidence that they met on that occasion, they later crossed swords in the House of Commons. However, whereas a soldier of fortune will go where the adventure leads, O'Kelly was always guided by his political commitment to Irish nationalism, whether in Cuba, Sudan, New York, or Paris: he always positioned himself alongside British enemies, whereas other specials would have either played patriotic roles or taken sides in conflicts that did not immediately affect Britain or the US. That is why Fernando Ortiz's assessment is the more accurate one: "While unquestionably bold in his behavior, O'Kelly's advice was always carefully weighed rather than impulsive or rushed. No rash adventurer, he was a soldier, entirely an old soldier, and a cool calculator of the enemy."[21]

Although much of O'Kelly's journalism was unsigned, his work can usually be identified and reconstructed. However, his political work, with the obvious exception of his parliamentary career, was mostly underground, a matter of false identities, ever-shifting addresses, and messages written with disappearing ink. This makes it very difficult to assess his importance. His military training, more extensive than other prominent Irish nationalists of his time, led to technical knowledge of weaponry, but also to an appreciation of military tactics. His instincts were always against gestural rebellion, and in favor of creating the circumstances in which an uprising could stand a chance of success. If "England is engaged in a great war that will strain her resources," O'Kelly wrote to Devoy, "seizing some critical moment [we will] attack her with all our power."[22] As a hard-headed man with a military background, who eventually saw the need to build a broad movement through constitutional means, O'Kelly can perhaps ultimately be seen as pointing to the path finally taken by Irish republicanism in 1994.

Peter Hulme
Sedbergh

Notes

1. As *La tierra del mambí, o aventuras de un corresponsal del 'Herald' en Cuba*, trans. Nicanor Trelles (New Orleans: Imprenta de P. Marchand, 1876); [unknown translator], *El Cubano* [Havana], 3 May–12 October, 1887; trans. Ricardo García Garófalo (Santa Clara: n.p., 1887); trans. E. C. (Mayagüez: Tipografía Comercial, 1888); (Havana: Cultural, 1930); (Havana: Instituto del Libro, 1968); (Havana: Editorial de Ciencias Sociales 1990 and 2001). These last four all use the translation by García Garófalo and feature the prologue by Fernando Ortiz. One of O'Kelly's *Herald* articles (31 January 1873) had been immediately translated into Spanish to appear in Rafael María de Labra's *La abolición de la esclavitud en el orden económica* (Madrid: Imprenta de J. Noguera, 1873), 440–44 (*The Mambi-Land*, 30–42). Fernando Ortiz refers to this in his *Los negros esclavos* [1916] (Havana: Editorial de Ciencias Sociales, 1996), 471.

2. Niamh O'Sullivan, *Aloysius O'Kelly: Art, Nation, Empire* (Dublin: Field Day Publications, 2009); Owen McGee, "O'Kelly, James Joseph," *Dictionary of Irish Biography*, ed. James McGuire and James Quinn, vol. 7, (Cambridge: Cambridge University Press, 2009), 601–03; Jennifer C. Brittan, "Movable Locations and Geographical Accidents: Small Hemispheres in the Inter-Americas," Ph.D. in Literature, University of California, Santa Cruz, 2010; Jennifer Brittan, "A Foreign Correspondent in the Mambi-Land: James J. O'Kelly's Fugitive Cuba, Fernando Ortiz's Irish Mambí," in *Studies in Travel Writing* 15, vol. 4 (2011): 377–392;

and Peter Hulme, "James J. O'Kelly at Jiguaní," in *Cuba's Wild East: A Literary Geography of Oriente* (Liverpool: Liverpool University Press, 2011), 17–72.

3. See below, pp. 262–63.

4. Michigan Historical Reprint Series, 2006; Manus O'Riordan, ed., *Irish Solidarity with Cuba Libre* (Dublin: SIPTU, 2009); "Irlanda y Cuba: Desde un pasado con luchas complejas y solidaridades hasta un futuro de posibilidades compartidas," Discurso Magistral por parte de Michael D. Higgins, Presidente de Irlanda, Colegio Universitario San Gerónimo, Universidad de La Habana, Cuba, 17 February 2017: https://www.dfa.ie/media/embassymexico/newsandevents/Key-note-address-at-the-Society-for-Irish-Latin-America-Studies-ESP.pdf [17.2.2019].

5. See Fidel Castro, "Ceremony marking centennial of Cuba's struggle" (La Demajagua, 10 October 1968) http://lanic.utexas.edu/la/cb/castro.1968/1968 1011 [24.1.2007]; and *Casa de las Américas*, 50 (1968), "La guerra del 68."

6. See Peter Blake, *George Augustus Sala and the Nineteenth-Century Periodical Press: The Personal Style of a Public Writer* (Farnham: Ashgate, 2015).

7. See Arthur Lubow, *The Reporter Who Would be King: A Biography of Richard Harding Davis* (New York: Scribner, 1992).

8. E. J. Dillon, *President Obregón—A World Reformer* (London: Hutchinson & Co., 1922); Herbert L. Matthews, "Cuban Rebel Is Visited in Hideout," *New York Times*, 24 February 1957, 1.

9. See O'Sullivan, *Aloysius O'Kelly*, and McGee, "O'Kelly, James Joseph," for the best accounts of his life, both of which I draw on here. O'Kelly wrote about his early life (up to 1867) in a series of newspaper articles in the *Irish People*, from 16 September 1899 to 1 December 1900, under the title "The Dawn of Fenianism: Some Reminiscences of a Great National Movement." Also important are his letters to his friend John Devoy in *Devoy's Post Bag, 1871–1928*, eds. William O'Brien and Desmond Ryan, vol. 1 (Dublin: C. J. Fallon, 1948).

10. For background, see Owen McGee, *The IRB: The Irish Republican Brotherhood, from the Land League to Sinn Fein*, 2nd ed. (Dublin: Four Courts Press, 2007).

11. On O'Kelly's work for the *Herald*, see Paul A. Townend, "A Cosmopolitan Nationalist: James J. O'Kelly in America," in T. G. McMahon et al., eds., *Ireland in an Imperial World: Citizenship, Opportunism, and Subversion* (Cambridge: Cambridge University Press, 2016), 223–43; and Gera Burton, "'For the Sake of the Pen—to Defy the Dangers of the Sword': James J. O'Kelly's Adventures in American Journalism," conference paper at *Connections and Contacts*, Canadian Association for Irish Studies, Université Laval, Quebec City, 13–16 June 2018. For background, see Terry Golway, *Irish Rebel: John Devoy and America's Fight for Ireland's Freedom* (New York: St. Martin's Press, 1998).

12. See the Portuguese translations of O'Kelly's articles in Argeu de Segadas Machado-Guimarães, *D. Pedro II nos Estados Unidos. As reportagens de James O'Kelly e o Diário do Imperador* (Rio de Janeiro: Editôra Civilização Brasileira, 1961).

13. See James W. Wengert, *The Custer Despatches: The Words of the New York Herald Correspondents in the Little Big Horn Campaign of 1876* (Manhattan: Sunflower University Press, 1987).

14. See Niamh O'Sullivan, "Lines of Resistance: The O'Kelly Brothers in the Sudan," *Éire-Ireland* 34, vol. 1 (1999): 131–56.

15. O'Sullivan, *Aloysius O'Kelly*, 3.

16. "Ireland—Special Commission (1888) Report," *Hansard* (21 March 1890), HL Deb vol. 342 cc1357–497.

17. See Steve Cushion, "Las reclamaciones de James J. O'Kelly al parlamento británico por la fuga de José Maceo hacia Gibraltar," in *Maceo en el tiempo: acción, pensamiento y contexto histórico*, ed. Jorge Renato Ibarra Guitart (Havana: Editorial de Ciencias Sociales, 2015), 255–68.

18. On O'Kelly's relationship with Parnell and his parliamentary career, see Carla King, "A 'Whig Rebel'? The Parliamentary Career of J. J. O'Kelly (1845–1916)," *Studia Hibernica* 39 (2013): 103–35.

19. "Death of Mr. J. J. O'Kelly," *Times*, 23 December 1916, 9.

20. Richard Harding Davis, *Soldiers of Fortune* (New York: Charles Scribner's Sons, 1897); Richard Harding Davis, *Real Soldiers of Fortune* (London: William Heinemann, 1907).

21. See below, p. 255.

22. *Devoy's Post Bag*, vol. 1, 410.

Introduction

> Dim, mystic, and clothed in awful shadows, there floats on the edge of the American continent an unknown country.
> —James J. O'Kelly

IN LATE 1872 the *New York Herald* named James J. O'Kelly as its special correspondent to Cuba, sending him to the island to cover what would later be known as the Ten Years' War for independence from Spain (1868–78). O'Kelly was tasked with crossing Cuban lines, locating insurgent camps, and interviewing the president of the Cuban Republic, Carlos Manuel de Céspedes. The domestic and foreign press dubbed O'Kelly a "second Stanley," comparing his mission to find Céspedes to *New York Herald* correspondent Henry Morton Stanley's 1871 discovery of David Livingstone in central Africa. O'Kelly became a political lightening rod and household name in 1873 when imminent threats (arrest, court-martial, execution) served as the organizing crises for the *Herald*'s near-daily reporting on Cuba and fueled the paper's relentless (and unsuccessful) calls for US intervention in support of the Cuban rebels. For the book that followed, *The Mambi-Land, or Adventures of a* Herald *Correspondent in Cuba*, O'Kelly assembled edited versions of his eighteen dispatches to the *Herald*, some written in the remotest imaginable places in the Cuban interior. *The Mambi-Land* constitutes one of the first book-length accounts of the war, and when considered in the broader context of the *Herald*'s reporting on Cuba, this text provides a window on a decisive, though generally overlooked, period in US–Cuba relations.

Cuba did not achieve independence in either the war of 1868 or the Little War (Guerra Chiquita) that followed in 1879–80. The war that ended Spanish rule in Cuba began in 1895 and ended in 1898, also the year of American intervention and the beginning of a US occupation that would last until 1902. The Spanish-American War of 1898—the American victory that drove Spain from Cuba—is far better known in the United States than the previous decades of anticolonial struggle on the island. Shifting attention from 1898 to the Ten Years' War constitutes, as historian Ada Ferrer notes, "a challenge not only to the revolution's invisibility in American historical consciousness but also to its centrality and coherence in Cuban national memory."[1] The war *was* central to American national consciousness, if only briefly, as the constant attention to Cuba in the *New York Herald,* the most widely circulated newspaper of the time, makes clear.[2] A large readership followed O'Kelly's mission in Cuba, even as the Spanish–Cuban press insisted that James J. O'Kelly was not Henry Morton Stanley, that Cuba was not Africa, and that what happened to O'Kelly was not major news. During O'Kelly's five and a half months on the island, including forty days in rebel camps and sixty days in Spanish prisons, the *Herald* reprinted commentary on the correspondent from fifty domestic and international newspapers, marshaling quotes as evidence of a press and public invested in the fates of both the man and the rebel republic. As papers predicted the possible political fallout of O'Kelly's execution, New York City's Bowery Theatre opened its 1873 summer season with *Cuba Libre, or O'Kelly's Mission*—a wildly popular show, if we can trust the *Herald*'s review. The play follows O'Kelly in Spanish Cuba, in rebel territory, and finally in prison, where he remains through the defining moments of the war, released just in time to witness the Cuban victory. What a refreshing diminishment of the imagined role of the United States in Cuban independence![3]

Herald publisher James Gordon Bennett Jr. may have expected O'Kelly's assignment to be a catalyst for US intervention in Cuba, and in this sense O'Kelly anticipates the so-called "newspaper war" of 1898.[4] But calls for intervention meant something different in the early 1870s and the O'Kelly–*Herald* archive tells its own story, providing insight into the period of US Reconstruction (1863–1877).[5] The *Herald* made Cuba not simply *the* foreign policy issue of the time, but a question vital for defining the United States in the post–Civil War moment. A *Herald* editorial welcomed former Union Army commander Ulysses S. Grant into a second term as president with the declaration, "We in America have felt that the Cuban policy of General Grant was the weakest and most reprehensible feature of his administration"—strong words, given the party divisions, sectional tensions, and violence of this moment, particularly in the South.[6] Relations between the United States and Cuba were intensifying, with increasingly active colonies of Cuban nationalists in the United States, American involvement in liberating expeditions, and a nationwide African American campaign to end slavery and colonial rule in Cuba. The *Herald* hailed newly enfranchised African American activists as embodying the ideals of American republicanism; and, through its critique of American non-intervention in Cuba, the paper became a platform for conversations about continued American investment in slavery. The O'Kelly–*Herald* archive invites attention to the international contexts and contradictions of US Reconstruction. But O'Kelly's book belongs just as much to Cuba and its popular accounts of a struggle for independence that extended from 1868 to 1959, and beyond. Just as O'Kelly was fading from public memory in the United States, his book began a second life in Cuba.

A Second Stanley: The *Herald* Special Correspondent in Cuba

> The adventures of HERALD correspondents during the last two or three years are as marvellous as anything in the annals of travel.
> —*New York Herald*, 26 May 1873

To create a second Stanley, the *Herald* needed a perilous assignment in an unmapped region, racialized danger, and the search for a missing person. Or a missing republic. How did Cuba, already familiar to Americans from early and mid-nineteenth century travelogues, become, in O'Kelly's words, an "unknown country"?[7] A *Herald* editorial reads, "For a long time Cuba had been a mysterious land." This "long time" was five years. The newly unknown country was the independent republic hidden in the eastern interior—a country within the colony. The editorial continues:

> We knew that there was a revolution or some kind of military trouble; at least that there were fighting parties moving up and down the Island of Cuba—some carrying the flag of Spain, others a flag representing the Cuban Republic. In New York we had a large Cuban and Spanish colony whose members fought the battles of their country through the newspapers, in the hotels and clubs on Fifth avenue and Broadway. This colony being a noisy aggregation of ladies and gentlemen, given to assembling in public and addressing long letters to newspapers on the wrongs of Cuba, it so happened that the revolution occupied a large share of public attention. . . . It was difficult to understand. We could not give it a history, a topography, or even a geography. (19 Nov. 1873, 6)

The problem went beyond a lack of reliable information on the nationalist insurgency. To survive, the rebel republic had to be itinerant, "constantly moving from point to point," as O'Kelly will report in *The Mambi-Land* (*ML* 62).

There was public interest in the rebellion in Cuba, and finding it was sure to prove nearly impossible—both essential ingredients for the *Herald*'s next major serialized adventure story. The paper hooked readers by presenting Carlos Manuel de Céspedes as the next Dr. Livingstone: "We regard it as important now to discover the true condition of the revolutionary army and the actual state of affairs on the Island of Cuba as it was to discover Livingstone" (1 Dec. 1872, 8). The *Herald* already had a special correspondent in Cuba at this point, A. Boyd Henderson, who had returned abruptly to the United States just before O'Kelly's departure. He claimed to have met Céspedes (having crossed Cuban lines), but his story was doubted and later discredited. Brilliantly self-interested, the *Herald* made a story out of the search for a second "scoop of the century." Readers followed other papers' coverage of the *Herald*'s mission "to Stanleyize the Cuban question," as the *Portland Oregonian* and others framed it (15 Jan. 1873, 5). When the news arrived that O'Kelly had found the rebel army in the remote interior, the *Herald* was quick to identify this success as the equal of its predecessor: "It will stand fitly beside the achievement performed by Mr. Stanley in the heart of Africa" (19 Mar. 1873, 6).

O'Kelly's résumé for the job of *Herald* special correspondent to Cuba included military training, support for anticolonial uprising, sharpshooting chops, biting wit, and all-around knack for survival. He was born in Dublin in 1842 to a family unusually populated with artists and political radicals, and by eighteen was a member of the Irish Republican Brotherhood. Young Fenians were encouraged to gain military training as preparation for the struggle to end British rule in Ireland, and, like his lifelong friend John Devoy, O'Kelly joined the French Foreign Legion, serving as a volunteer soldier in Algeria and in French occupied Mexico. As Peter Hulme's foreword in this edition makes clear, O'Kelly's extraordinary professional and personal life provides no shortage of stories for biographers—impressive, and sometimes outrageous. He was arrested in 1871 for smuggling arms into Ireland. By one account, he had guns "stashed inside religious statues and transported across the Irish Sea."[8] Joining the many Fenian émigrés to the United States, he fled to New York and took a job with the *New York Herald*. Before becoming the *Herald*'s "second Stanley" in late 1872, O'Kelly was an art editor, drama critic, and general reporter with a silent role in the paper's encoded reporting on Fenian activism in the United States and Europe.[9] Crucially, he had also distinguished himself as a reporter capable of securing difficult interviews.[10]

The *Herald*'s choice of Cuba for its next periodical coup had the added benefit of further establishing the paper as a leading voice in international abolitionism.[11] The paper's investment in Livingstone—a fierce critic of the East African slave trade—paid moral dividends. Stanley gained authority as an abolitionist in his own right and the *Herald* promoted its now-famous correspondent by announcing a first public lecture in the United States, titled "Life in Central Africa and the Horrors of the Slave Trade" (4 Dec. 1872, 3). Pairing Livingstone and Céspedes as similarly dedicated abolitionists, the *Herald* identified "the abolition of slavery" as "the corner stone of the insurgent constitution for Cuba" (15 Dec. 1872, 8). Sending a special correspondent to Cuba then represented a logical continuation of the *Herald*'s work on the global stage. Famously, Céspedes began the war by freeing all enslaved people on his sugar plantation and inviting them to join the fight for Cuban independence as citizens. Surely the Cuban leader would recognize a *Herald* agent as a powerful ally in the fight to end slavery. Or so Bennett presumed: "Doubtless the hope was in the mind of Cespedes that the success of the HERALD commissioners in Cuba would be as good an omen to the cause he served as the triumph of Mr. Stanley in Africa had been to Dr. Livingstone and the cause he wished to advance—the abolition of slavery as well as the discovery of the headwaters of the Nile" (17 June 1873, 6). This editorial does not mention Livingstone's support for British colonial expansion in Africa or the many ambiguities in the Cuban Republic's position on slavery. As Ada Ferrer explains, "in the revolutionary manifesto that outlined the objectives of the rebellion as a whole, Céspedes expressed only a 'desire' for abolition. This abolition, moreover, would be gradual; it would indemnify owners; and it would occur only after the successful conclusion of the war."[12] The constitution of 1869 made all inhabitants of the republic free citizens, but amendments led to a system of forced and unpaid labor for *libertos* ("the liberated") that persisted in various forms throughout the war.[13] O'Kelly makes condemnation of slavery an early and major focus of *The Mambi-Land*. And yet, as readers may note with surprise, he does not discuss abolition in his interviews with insurgent leaders.

O'Kelly arrived in Cuba four years into a war for independence that began in October of 1868 on Céspedes's sugar plantation, La Demajagua, outside the southeastern city of Manzanillo. In what would become known as the "Grito de Yara," Céspedes, the thirty formerly enslaved people on his plantation, and a small band of rebels declared an armed struggle to end Spanish rule in Cuba. The war's geographical base remained *Oriente,* or eastern Cuba, where economic disadvantage fed dissatisfaction with colonial policy, although the struggle had support and recruits from across the island. For much of the nineteenth century, uprisings of the enslaved and separatist conspiracies had threatened the colony's racial and political order, and native-born Cubans (creoles) had lobbied without success for tax and tariff reform, power in local governance, and

Figure 1. Portrait of James J. O'Kelly from the *Daily Graphic,* 10 April 1873, 4. (Courtesy of Thomas Tryniski, fultonhistory.com)

representation in parliament. By 1868, the rebels generally supported the abolition of slavery and either independence or annexation to the United States. The rebels looked to the post–Civil War United States as a natural ally in the fight to end both slavery and colonial rule in Cuba. In chapter three of *The Mambi-Land,* O'Kelly presents a harrowing portrait of life under slavery on a sugar plantation east of Matanzas, while also noting the changes forced on slavers by the near-cessation of the illegal transatlantic slave trade and the diminishing supply of enslaved laborers on the island. With slave labor scarce and expensive, planters were turning to the indentured labor of Chinese people, which O'Kelly describes in a withering critique as "the new slave-trade" (*ML* 39). Before the Civil War, the United States held a majority interest in the transatlantic slave trade, with predominantly American ships supplying Cuban and American markets.[14] Once outlawed in the United States, this form of slavery could not last long in Cuba.[15] When O'Kelly approaches owners of plantations using slave labor, he tends to present himself as an Irish gentleman or a French speaker, since American affiliations earned him no advantage. Finding little affection for Americans in Spanish Cuba, he draws a pointed conclusion: "the slaveocracy in Cuba look on America as the chief cause of all their misfortunes" (*ML* 41–42).

The rebels would soon make a similar complaint. The issue concerned

FIGURE 2. Portrait of James J. O'Kelly by Aloysius O'Kelly. (Courtesy of Frank Tarpey and Barry Feely, King House, Boyle, Co. Roscommon, Ireland)

belligerent rights, a subject to which representatives of the Cuban republic, military leaders, and *Herald* editorials return with Sisyphean persistence. The fate of the rebellion hinged considerably on the United States granting the rebel army belligerent status, along with the legal rights of war that would follow. The Spanish insisted that the insurgents were too few in number to qualify, and argued that as bandits and brigands they could not claim rights of war. The rebels required official recognition as belligerents to access the loans needed to finance the war, deploy commissioned naval vessels at sea, and guard against charges of piracy for boats running the Spanish blockade. A Cuban captain arriving in New York after one such resupply mission underscored Céspedes's hope for official status, describing it as "the winning of half the battle" (*NYH* 27 Mar. 1873, 3). Withholding this recognition amounted to de facto support for Spain. This helps to explain efforts to manage American perceptions of the insurgency, with both sides using the American Civil War as the default point of reference. Sympathizers decried the Spanish as the party of slaveholders, while the Spanish cast Cuban separatists in the role of the seceding Confederates.

Consider two examples from early and late in the O'Kelly archive.

Shortly after O'Kelly's arrival in Cuba, Captain General Francisco de Ceballos likens O'Kelly's request to cross Cuban lines to a desire to "go to the Confederate camps" (*ML* 18). This analogy did the job of presenting the insurgents as secessionists who needed to be reintegrated into the whole, rather than a people seeking independence from a colonial power. Almost a year later, the *Herald* printed lengthy portions of a letter to President Grant from Manuel de Quesada, the Cuban republic's representative abroad, appealing to Grant to recognize the Cuban insurgency. Quesada addresses "erroneous impressions," namely that Cubans hold "the same relations to the Spanish government that the seceded States did to the government of this Union." No, says Quesada, "the Cubans fight to abolish slavery, the South fought to preserve it." The American Revolutionary War provides the better analogy, he suggests: "Cubans have the long since admitted right or independence belonging to every oppressed colony, as proclaimed in 1776 by the fathers of this country" (*NYH* 8 Dec. 1873, 4). While Grant expressed sympathy for the Cuban republic much along these lines, his administration never formally recognized the insurgency, which ended in 1878 with neither independence nor the abolition of slavery.[16]

The *Herald* tried to tip the scales using one lone adventurer. With a romantic mission and bad odds, O'Kelly would gather a sympathetic public and lead it into the heart of the insurgency—if he could find it. He would have been sobered by the great gusto with which the *Herald* and other papers anticipated his death, whether from a stray bullet or Spanish court-martial, sure that it would prompt the American government to act in favor of the insurgency. Initially he planned to travel east through the center of the island but was forced to turn back before reaching the central interior city of Camagüey, where he had hoped to find the famed insurgent commander Ignacio Agramonte. *The Mambi-Land* describes O'Kelly then traveling by steamer from Cienfuegos to eastern Cuba, where, apart from a brief stint with a Spanish battalion, he strikes out alone into the outer reaches of Spanish Cuba, failing repeatedly to find the rebel camps. At one point, faced with militarized plantation outposts and "dark, impenetrable woods," O'Kelly wields his machete in an unsuccessful attempt to hack a pathway to the rebel republic (*ML* 63). After a second arrest, Spanish authorities bar O'Kelly from traveling in the region, except with Spanish troops, and warn him of "stringent orders to the outposts and scouts to shoot" him if he is caught returning from Cuban lines. When a mysterious letter offers him an escort into insurgent territory, he makes first contact with rebels "in the very centre of Spanish posts extending for leagues in every direction." Reaching their camps proves less a matter of border crossing than scaling the "almost perpendicular slope" of a mountain. He asks us to picture it: "Imagine a *caballero,* with heavy riding-boots, spurred, a long machete, which insisted on getting between his legs, hanging at his side, with other *impedimenta*" attempting a climb "only possible by gymnastics" (*ML* 103–4). Well into the next day, O'Kelly arrives in an insurgent camp having lost his horse and a good share of his provisions.

O'Kelly covers considerable ground in *The Mambi-Land,* meeting Máximo Gómez and Calixto García—the latter a key figure in all three Cuban wars for independence—before traveling to Cuba's seat of government, located temporarily in Jiguaní, one of "the wildest and most uncultivated portions of the island" (*ML* 160). He marches for weeks with Céspedes and documents life in the camp of Modesto Díaz before beginning his journey back to the Spanish outposts with a guard of twenty men. While "sleeping at the very muzzle of Spanish guns," O'Kelly approaches the Spanish lines close to Manzanillo (*ML* 176). He bequeaths his machete to Calixto García and walks into town, where he presents himself to authorities and is promptly arrested, jailed, and threatened with summary execution. *Herald* editor Bennett all but declared war on Spain. The *Herald* reported public demand for American military action to save or avenge O'Kelly, noted an emergency mass meeting of Cubans in Key West and an appeal to President Grant by Cubans in New York, and printed sections of a letter from Céspedes to his wife on matters including O'Kelly's imprisonment (9 April 1873, 9; 10 April 1873, 3). The American ambassador to Spain, General Daniel Sickles, requested clemency for O'Kelly, reminding Spanish Foreign Minister Emilio Castelar that O'Kelly "represented the same journal which had so much distinguished itself in the discovery and relief of Dr. Livingstone."[17] This was Sickles's best defense for a newspaper and correspondent so clearly hostile to Spanish rule in Cuba. O'Kelly's sojourn came to a fitting end months later when he was released from prison in Madrid in time to meet a visitor to the city, Henry Morton Stanley.[18]

One thing most distinguishes O'Kelly's book from his earlier dispatches to the *Herald:* his toponym "the Mambi-Land." Even the term "mambí" is scarcely present in his original reports, the first mention being in reference to an unruly horse. O'Kelly recounts traveling east of Matanzas to the province of Villa Clara, where he secures a place for the night, only to realize that the hotel owner is a "captain, or general or something." Needing a quick cover, he poses as a slaver *in prospectu,* whereupon the obliging man supplies him with a horse and an escort to a local sugar plantation. Neither proves particularly friendly: "The horse procured me was a small native animal, rather restive, but, as I found afterwards, good to go. From the manner he conducted himself I am under the impression that he was a *mambi* to the core, and, mistaking me for a Spaniard, endeavored to get rid of me" (31 Jan. 1873, 4). For insurgent territory, O'Kelly mainly uses the term "Cuba Libre." When writing the book, however, he exchanges "Cuba Libre" for the "Mambi-Land," which he describes as the preferred term of "those who dwell within its confines" (*ML* 3).

O'Kelly's use of this toponym does more than establish him as an insider. This racially inflected term fits with O'Kelly's role as a "second Stanley," conjuring an Africa in the Cuban interior. Anti-independence and pro-slavery factions characterized the insurgency not as a nationalist movement but as a race war, equating the end of colonial rule with the "Africanization" of Cuba. The Spanish leveraged the same fears in the colony of Santo Domingo (present-day Dominican Republic), where the term "mambi" originated. In designating all nationalists "mambises," the Spanish implied that the rebels were predominantly black.[19] O'Kelly also uses the term to play on anxieties, present in both Cuba and the United States, that the rebel army was almost entirely composed of "negros sueltos," or fugitive slaves. The original frontispiece for *The Mambi-Land* depicts O'Kelly's first contact with a rebel, a black man with a gun, an image chosen to spark fascination and concern. Americans on both sides of the color line took an interest in the Cuban conflict, in part because an upset of the racial hierarchy in Cuba could have implications at home.

Proponents of Cuban independence also had to work against the popular belief that racial homogeneity was a precondition of nationhood: an argument that would be used twenty-five years later to justify the American occupation of Cuba. O'Kelly arrived on the island sharing this view. The following statement appears in one of O'Kelly's early dispatches to the *Herald,* but is absent from the book: "On account of the conflicting interests of race it appears to me impossible that Cuba could avoid an internecine conflict in case she succeeded in establishing her liberty, unless by attaching herself to some stronger Power. The choice would seem to be, then, either to remain under the Spanish flag or to enter the Union" (9 Jan. 1873, 4). O'Kelly begins using the term the "Mambi-Land" following his discovery of a racially integrated Cuban republic already established in the island's interior. A romantic revolutionary at heart, O'Kelly suggests that the war and the difficulties of life in the forest transformed the Spanish creole and the formerly enslaved into republicans and models of masculinity. "Shoeless, blanketless, in many cases without coats, often with a piece of ragged linen doing service as a uniform," he writes, "these men support the hardships and fatigues of an unequal struggle with a patience and courage that have seldom been equaled and never excelled." O'Kelly continues, "If we would respect the Cuban character we must see it here in the camps. Between the men in the field and the effeminate race of the towns there is a separation so wide and so distinct that it is difficult to believe they are of the same blood." "The change has been made in the war," O'Kelly concludes (*ML* 130). O'Kelly's reference to blood is significant: his story of transformation betrays the degree to which he makes fitness for self-governance a test of whiteness, measured in degrees. According to O'Kelly's metaphorics of skin color, the war made Spanish creoles white, and black men brown: "About one-third of the fighting men are white, and the majority of the other two-thirds are of color other than black, all shades of brown predominating." Rather than predicting civil war, O'Kelly presents republican Cuba as a model of postwar reconstruction. "The most perfect equality exists between the white and colored races," O'Kelly hyperbolizes, "the officers taking precedence by rank, and although the majority of the officers are white, a very large proportion are colored" (*ML* 130). While falling short of "perfect equality," Cuba did have a racially integrated army "unique in the history of the Atlantic world."[20] The US military would not desegregate until the mid-twentieth century. Contrast O'Kelly's utopian vision of raceless fraternity, soon to become a cornerstone of Cuban nationalist rhetoric, with Theodore Roosevelt's discontent with the mixing of black American soldiers among his own "Rough Riders" during the 1898 battle of San Juan Hill.[21]

Order, efficiency, and racial integration prevail in O'Kelly's descriptions of settlements and rebel camps in the Mambi-Land. He Africanizes the territory of the insurgency, but not to trigger white anxieties. Quite the opposite. The racialized space of the Mambi-Land becomes the Cubans' proving ground. As he describes hidden communities surviving for years in remote mountain regions, O'Kelly gives his guerrilla soldiers the republican values of the maroon: autonomy, economy, and self-reliance. This blurring of identities is most apparent in his description of "strong Spanish columns ... hunting like bloodhounds the ill-armed and wretchedly-supplied soldiers of the Cuban republic" (*ML* 62). O'Kelly aims to outrage with this image of republican soldiers treated like fugitive slaves. The Spanish are the army of the slaveholders, he reminds his readers, while contrasting the progressive ideology of the post–slavery republic with the anachronism and brutality of the slaveholding colony. For O'Kelly, the maroon and the republican soldier fuse into the figure of the transracial patriot.

The O'Kelly Archive

> O'Kelly era un mambí del separatismo antibritánico.
> —Fernando Ortiz

The Mambi-Land has messy borders. First, there are O'Kelly's original eighteen dispatches to the *New York Herald*, published between December 30, 1872, and November 20, 1873. Bennett responded to each dispatch with a detailed editorial, and more often than not O'Kelly's stories appeared alongside other reporting on Cuba. O'Kelly was in the news even during the quiet stretches between dispatches. In fact, discussion of O'Kelly picked up when he was most silent—during the seven weeks he spent in insurgent camps and two months in Cuban prisons. The *Herald* introduced a regular column called "The Press on the Arrest," reprinting and responding to commentary from newspapers at home and abroad, from the *Paducah Kentuckian* and the *Boston Globe* to the *London Morning Post*. O'Kelly became a talking point for leaders of the insurgency, representatives of the Cuban Republic, and the Cuban press. All told, O'Kelly was speculated about, defended, excoriated, or mentioned in almost 150 editorials, interviews, and notices.

Wasting no opportunity to draw attention to its correspondent, the *Herald* often juxtaposed commentary on O'Kelly from opposite sides of the Cuban question. In one example, two New York papers—the pro-Spanish *El Cronista* and the pro-Cuban *La Independencia*—squared off on the page (12 Mar. 1873, 7). Later, the *Herald* printed a translation of what at first seems to be a death notice for O'Kelly in *El Cronista*. O'Kelly would have appreciated the wit of this piece, if not for its prevailing chill. First we read: "The following are the terms upon which the HERALD's second ambassador has gone to Cuba." These "terms" include: "He is to be killed in that island and the fault is to be thrown on the Spanish volunteers," followed by, "[His] children are to be educated at the expense of the HERALD until they graduate at Five Points or Sing Sing." The final term regards the inscription on O'Kelly's mausoleum. The eye is drawn first to this text, set apart and bordered in black: "JAMES O'KELLY. Died heroically in the service of Mr. JAMES GORDON BENNETT, and to give satisfaction to a lot of (Cuban) rascals" (8 April 1873, 5).

The O'Kelly archive begins weeks before O'Kelly's first dispatch, when Bennett started drumming up support for a *Herald* expedition to Cuba to be led by a "second Stanley." The number of news items on Cuba in the year of O'Kelly's mission is quite staggering: over five hundred. Consider, for example, the burst of reporting following O'Kelly's January 31 dispatch. First, the paper covers a meeting of the Cuban Anti-Slavery Committee of New York, which calls to action "the 4,000,000 who have so recently partaken of the fruits of freedom," stating "we cannot rest while slavery and the slave trade exist at our very doors." This leads directly into an advertisement for the sale of enslaved people, taken from the Havana-based *Diario de la Marina*, complete with names, descriptions, and prices. The final item on the page, "Exciting News at Key West," reports $13,233 raised in a fundraising campaign for the Cuban cause, with donations including watches, rings, and clothing. The piece concludes: "The Cubans speak with gratitude of the NEW YORK HERALD for espousing the cause of 'Free Cuba,' and admire the indomitable courage of its correspondents," mentioning O'Kelly by name (1 Feb. 1873, 5). Another lengthy article on Cuba occupies the next page, and all of this even before the threat to O'Kelly's life. For access to the O'Kelly archive, see this edition's companion website at www.okellyarchive.com.

Returning *The Mambi-Land* to its original context, namely *Herald* reporting on Cuba, yields unexpected benefits. Readers in the O'Kelly archive may find the Ten Years' War and US–Cuba relations triangulated—sometimes compellingly—with other big stories of the time. Research does not generally pair President Grant's action-allergic approach to Cuba with his simultaneous career-damaging obsession with annexing Santo Domingo—an important reminder that Grant was not opposed to American intervention in the Caribbean.[22] The O'Kelly archive also encourages comparative perspectives on race relations. O'Kelly's accounts of integrated Spanish and Cuban troops, black officers, and the joint struggle against colonial rule and slavery unfold alongside stories of increasing racial tension and violence in the American South. Finally, the *Herald*'s self-promotion included cataloguing the heroics of several special correspondents understood to be continuing the legacy of Henry Morton Stanley; although it was O'Kelly alone who was championed by name. Editorials praise *Herald* "Stanleys" abroad covering the war in Cuba, and at home covering the Modoc War, a conflict in California and Oregon between the Native American Modoc people and the US military from late 1872 to 1873. This pairing of two *Herald* "Stanleys" embedded among hostile forces suggested false analogies between the Spanish and the Modoc. The Modoc align more closely with the Cuban rebels, as both opposed colonial powers. While Havana's *La Voz de Cuba* does not make this point, it does use the Modoc War to ridicule the United States's self-appointment as the moral watchdog of the hemisphere. Bennett reproduces the argument: "The *Voz de Cuba* has been criticizing the recent encounter between the Modoc Indians and the United States troops. It thinks that 'this Indian war wounds humanity in its noblest sentiments, and is a real scandal to this century of humanitarian sensitiveness.' The same organ also insinuates that President Grant needs instruction in the means of civilizing the Indians, instead of exterminating them, and obscurely hints that a good moral effect might be exercised over us by the sending forth of correspondents from Europe to spy out what is passing in the Indian Territory." Bennett then offers a rebuttal so witless it does not bear repeating (28 Jan. 1873, 6).

O'Kelly was likely the person most involved in, but least aware of, the unfolding newspaper war. Once behind Cuban lines, he learned that insurgents brought newspapers into the camps, including the *New York Herald*. Rebels may well have had copies of O'Kelly's columns before he did. Cuban newspapers in Havana, New York, and Key West printed translations of O'Kelly's columns, including *El Republicano, La Revolución de Cuba, Diario de la Marina, La Independencia,* and *El Cronista,* sometimes accompanied by lengthy editorials. When Spanish officials arrested and court-martialed O'Kelly, they surely anticipated big headlines and forces mustered on both sides of the political divide.

Tracking O'Kelly's influence and legacy requires attention to his parallel lives and afterlives in Spanish-language accounts of his time in Cuba and translations of his work. Some of his adventures were first described by others more practiced at getting word off the island. While Bennett waited for news from O'Kelly, Céspedes sent letters to his wife in New York detailing O'Kelly's detention in Palma Soriano, his arrival at the seat of government, and the plan to escort him across Cuban lines. The first Spanish translation of *The Mambi-Land* appeared in New Orleans in 1876, followed by several additional Spanish editions in the late 1880s in Cuba and Puerto Rico.[23] *La tierra del mambí* made its formal entry into the Cuban canon in 1930, featuring a prologue by renowned scholar Fernando Ortiz. This present edition of *The Mambi-Land* contains the first English translation of Ortiz's prologue.

Ortiz's introduction to *The Mambi-Land* forms part of a tradition in Cuban historiography that traces the nation's independence to struggles predating the US intervention of 1898. The 1930 edition of *The Mambi-*

land was reissued (with Ortiz's prologue) in 1968 for the centenary of the Ten Years' War, which Fidel Castro claimed was the "spiritual and ideological predecessor" of the 1959 revolution. Connecting "the first anticolonial uprising in 1868 to the revolutionary present of the 1960s," Castro emphasized a long Cuban Revolution or "one hundred years of struggle."[24] Ortiz's introductory framing for O'Kelly's book represents both a historical and a geographical intervention, in the sense that Ortiz uses O'Kelly's biography to pivot Cuba away from the United States. First, Ortiz clarifies that "O'Kelly was Irish and not born in the United States, as some people have suggested."[25] Readers may be surprised that a prologue to a book on Cuba's Ten Years' War would devote so much attention to the author's career as an Irish nationalist. But this background provides Ortiz with a more appealing context for O'Kelly's mambí sympathies than do his ties to the *New York Herald* or the United States. He finds historical precedent for O'Kelly in examples of Irish participation in abolitionist and separatist movements in Cuba, from famed anti-slavery crusader Richard Robert Madden to the four Irish members of the infamous mid-nineteenth century filibustering expeditions of Narciso López. Finally, having drawn analogies between the independence movements in Ireland and Cuba, Ortiz names O'Kelly a "*mambí* del separatismo antibritánico." With this expanded definition of "mambí," Ortiz argues for O'Kelly's inclusion in "biographical dictionaries of Cuba" and connects Cuba to anti-colonial movements worldwide.[26] Through the figure of this Irish mambí, Ortiz has Cuba look out across the Atlantic, rather than to its neighbor to the north.

While not all details from O'Kelly's life fit Ortiz's portrait of a global anti-imperialist, O'Kelly did understand the Irish nationalist movement as part of a larger struggle to end British colonial rule.[27] As Ortiz notes, he smuggled arms into Ireland while advocating (unsuccessfully) for Spanish military action to retake British controlled Gibraltar. Much to his regret, he failed to persuade the Fenian leadership to lend material support to actions against British imperial power in Afghanistan, Egypt, and South Africa. In 1895, twenty-three years after his sojourn in the Mambi-Land, O'Kelly was writing about another war for independence in Cuba. At this point O'Kelly was a member of parliament for Roscommon North and a reporter on foreign affairs for the *Irish Daily Independent,* the leading Irish voice in support of Cuban independence. O'Kelly provided insider information about mambí strongholds, wrote a tribute to Antonio Maceo after the general's death in 1896, and was reportedly working on a play, now lost, called *A Cuban Rebel.*[28]

The 1930 Cuban edition of *La tierra del mambí* appeared in the same year as another of Ortiz's projects, also published in the Libros Cubanos series under his direction—a first Cuban edition of Alexander von Humboldt's *Ensayo político sobre la isla de Cuba* (*Political Essay on the Island of Cuba*), originally published in French in 1825. Ortiz uses the first Spanish translation of the text, from 1827, which had been banned in Cuba mainly due to Humboldt's critique of slavery. In his afterword, however, Ortiz focuses on the least reputable translation of Humboldt's essay—John Sidney Thrasher's *The Island of Cuba*, published in New York in 1856. Thrasher's English translation sparked controversy and condemnation by Humboldt himself, as Thrasher silently removed material—most notably the section on slavery—in order, Ortiz argues, to produce a text less ideologically out of step with Thrasher's own "Preliminary Essay."[29] As Ortiz explains, Thrasher was a pro-slavery lobbyist for annexation who had been an American journalist in Cuba as well as, allegedly, Narciso López's Havana correspondent, known as "El Yankee." Ortiz's edition includes Thrasher's notes and a first Spanish translation of Thrasher's essay. Thrasher and O'Kelly must have become counterpoints for Ortiz, with O'Kelly's third chapter, on slavery, reminding him of the material missing from Thrasher's text. In aligning the Irish nationalist O'Kelly with a mobile anti-colonialism, Ortiz further orients him away from American and American-backed annexationists of the mid-nineteenth century. Reading Ortiz, one might forget that O'Kelly was known by his detractors as chief of the *Herald filibusteros*.[30]

"Fear of Herald 'Filibusteros!'"

> The HERALD now calls its foreign correspondents "Commissioners." The next thing they will be wearing livery and will be denominated Ambassadors or Ministers Extraordinary.
> —*Rochester Express,* 11 February 1873

James J. O'Kelly left for Cuba without any mention in the *New York Herald*. On the contrary, the paper still seemed to be interviewing candidates for the role of its "second Stanley." The paper began the month with the announcement, "We may require the services of many who have the pluck and energy to undertake bold adventures, and as we believe the volunteer always makes a better soldier than the conscript, we shall give a fair consideration to all who may apply to us for the honor of enrolment in the HERALD expeditionary army" (1 Dec. 1872, 8). Within days the

Herald reported "3000–4000 volunteers" and began dedicating entire pages to profiling these motley recruits, reprinting "offers to enlist," and transcribing interviews curated for humorous effect (4 Dec. 1872, 4). Recruits ranged from former Union officers to bakers and saloon workers. One describes himself as "born a Louisianian, reared a cosmopolitan" (8 Dec. 1872, 10). Most applicants expected to be judged on their military strategy and mettle, rather than their potential for newspaper reporting. Some claim no journalistic ability or ambition whatsoever. Instead, more fundamental challenges take precedence, like how to land a *Herald* army on the island and cross into rebel territory. Two recruits suggest hot-air balloons. Another recommends technological marvels like "submarine armor," "explosive pills," and noiseless gunpowder (6 Dec. 1872, 5). We can only hope that Timothy Fitzdoodle was joking when he proposed luring the Spanish into trenches and "pouring large quantities of hot champagne on them" (8 Dec. 1872, 10). "My plan is to disguise myself in male attire," declares another volunteer on the same page: "I do not want to lead the insipid life of the average American woman. . . . Give me a trial. Send me to Cuba, and you'll see if I do not become a female Stanley."

As the tally of recruits topped six thousand, the *Herald* translated and printed furious responses from the Spanish–Cuban press, spotlighted with headlines like "FEAR OF HERALD 'FILIBUSTEROS!'" (1 Jan. 1873, 4). The term "filibuster," synonymous for many with pirates, referred in this context to companies of mainly US and Latin American privateers who launched military operations to free Cuba from Spanish rule.[31] O'Kelly describes Cuban reaction to the so-called *Herald* expedition: "It was seriously believed among the people here that the 6,000 volunteers who wanted to die for the HERALD were coming out in real earnest" (1 Jan. 1873, 5). A publicity stunt, the *Herald* expeditionary army ensured a stage for O'Kelly and demonstrated broad support in the United States for the Cuban rebels. The *Herald* pushed for American intervention in Cuba, pointing to this farcical army as evidence of an American public at odds with Washington on the question of Cuba. The Grant administration's continued nonrecognition of the rebels further embittered Bennett's relationship with the president, and even more so with Secretary of State Hamilton Fish. Early in 1873 the *Herald* published an interview with Fish, who, when asked to explain the administration's position on the rebels, stated, "there is no more reason now than there was three years ago for giving belligerent rights to a party of insurgents who have no seat of government, at least none that can be found" (8 Jan. 1873, 3). Cue O'Kelly. We can understand much of the *Herald*'s reporting on

Cuba as working to dismantle the administration's argument for denying official recognition of the rebels. In addition to finding Céspedes, the *Herald* had to change perceptions about the nature and limits of the rebel territory.

Spain did not regard the rebel strongholds as real territory. In referring to "the wildest and most uncultivated" regions of the interior as the "Mambi-Land," O'Kelly gives the rebellion a specific, bounded geography, and his own adventure story an ideological and formal center (*ML* 160). Consider the difference between O'Kelly meeting Céspedes at the "Forest Headquarters of the Cuban Government" (16 Apr. 1873, 5), as announced in the *Herald,* and at the "White House in Cuba Libre," as O'Kelly later describes it.[32] With this shift from the literal to the symbolic, the republic gained legitimacy and measurable territory. No longer a "homeless and wandering Republic," Cuba becomes a country within the colony (16 April 1873, 8).

"Alone, among the bookmakers, have I visited the forbidden region," O'Kelly writes (*ML* 4). When O'Kelly revised his original dispatches, he lengthened his description of the rebel camps such that the Mambi-Land takes up more space and occupies the physical center of the book.[33] Distorting the geography of the insurgency, which was based in the eastern provinces, O'Kelly gives the impression of a region deep in the domestic interior, encircled by Spanish outposts. "Like the fabled garden of the Hesperides," he writes, "the frontiers of the Mambi-Land are guarded by monsters ready to devour the rash intruder" (*ML* 4). Here O'Kelly casts himself as the *Herald*'s Hercules, making Céspedes the golden apple. Classical myth and reality meet awkwardly for a moment when Céspedes offers O'Kelly an unherculean return journey: an escort to Jamaica. O'Kelly chooses the more dramatic option of returning to Spanish Cuba, explaining: "It appeared to me better to accept all the risks of my mission and so place my testimony beyond question" (*ML* 148).

Céspedes's alternative exit route for O'Kelly would not have surprised the *Herald*'s readers, since foreign ports (Kingston, Key West, New Orleans, Colón) figured prominently in the paper's coverage of the Cuban struggle for independence. Once again, the *Herald* attempted to tip the debate concerning belligerent rights towards the Cuban rebels, in this case by redefining what counted as rebel territory. The US minister to Spain, Caleb Cushing, used the rebels' insularity to justify their nonrecognition, explaining that "one of the serious objections heretofore to recognizing the belligerency of the insurgents has been the fact of their being shut up inland, and having no access to the sea by means of any fortified position.

With such a port as Manzanillo, if they can hold it, they will have the first great element of government, which heretofore they have not possessed" (8 Apr. 1873, 5). Bennett was not going to wait for that possible outcome. He responded instead by identifying surrogate ports in the broader hemisphere. When Costa Rica followed many of its Central and South American neighbors in declaring support for the Cuban rebels, the *Herald* reported this news in terms of its practical implications for the insurgents: "Costa Rica possesses Port Limon in the Caribbean sea, which can now be used for liberating expeditions and other objects by the patriot Cubans, and the whole littoral of the Caribbean from Yucatan, in Mexico, down to Venezuela, now has ports open to ships and expeditions employed on behalf of Cuba Libre" (22 June 1873, 13). With this sweeping vision of open ports, the insurgents seemed decidedly less "shut up inland." And in documenting the complex itineraries of these liberating expeditions, the *Herald* connected covert landing points in eastern Cuba to a network of ports in the circum-Caribbean and on the eastern seaboard of the United States.[34] The *Diario de la Marina* called the *Herald* the "organ of the filibusters." Quoting the *Diario* and claiming this title, the *Herald* treated the hemispheric careers of Cuba's blockade runners as an integral component of the insurgency, including the famous *Edgar Stuart* and the ill-fated *Virginius* (21 Apr. 1873, 3).[35]

The *Herald*'s coverage of a particular *Edgar Stuart* expedition shows how O'Kelly's and Bennett's maps of the Cuban struggle intersect. The steamer departed New London, Connecticut, in April 1872, bound for Key West, Florida, with supplies for the rebels and over fifty mainly Cuban men. After two failed landings and a stop in Colón, Panama, the boat came ashore in eastern Cuba in late December, shortly after O'Kelly's arrival on the island. Over a month later, O'Kelly met members of the landing party in the insurgent camps, just before some of them embarked on a thirty-hour journey to Kingston, Jamaica, in a dugout canoe, accompanied by Cuban Congress member Antonio Zambrana.[36] (This gives us a sense of the journey home that Céspedes had in mind for O'Kelly.) When Zambrana arrived in New York at the end of March, a *Herald* interviewer immediately asked if he had information about O'Kelly, who had been behind Cuban lines for weeks. Zambrana reported he was safe but warm in his "woolen clothing" (26 Mar. 1873, 3). The established routes and friendly ports that brought news of O'Kelly to New York locate the bounded rebel territory of O'Kelly's Mambi-Land within a larger geography of insurgency.

Filibustering is "a textual-military process," Rodrigo Lazo writes, noting the close connection between military plotting and publishing.[37] One of the *Herald*'s most stunning attacks on American nonrecognition of the insurgency starts with an editorial titled "How We Administer Impartial Justice to Cuba." Thus began a series of articles on New York City shipyards building or refitting gunboats for Spain, in violation of neutrality laws. "Armed and equipped at this port," we read, "these gunboats steamed down New York Bay with a silent benediction from our rulers at Washington" (1 Feb. 1873, 6). A week later the *Herald* detailed the extraordinary history of the *Bazan,* formerly the Confederate privateer *Chickamauga* (9 Feb. 1873, 5). The gunboat was built in London in 1864, sold to Mexico after the US Civil War, and then bought by a Spanish naval agent in New York. Readers would have drawn an uncomfortable parallel between England's supplying gunboats to the Confederacy and the United States's doing the same for Spain in its war against the Cuban rebels. Only a few years earlier, in the Alabama claims, the United States had demanded and eventually won financial restitution from England for a similar breach of neutrality.

Herald interventionism reached a fever pitch following O'Kelly's imprisonment and court martial. With its correspondent under threat of death, the *Herald* published a map of "Insurgent Cuba" flanked by a column of explosive headlines (see fig. 3). Gone is the sense of sealed-off rebel territory accessible only to a "second Stanley." At a glance, the map seems to allocate all of the eastern provinces to the rebels. Tiny Spanish and Cuban flags do a half-hearted job of demarcating territory, and, in showing "the District Traversed by the Insurgents," the map emphasizes the rebels' mobility rather than their enclosure.[38] Meant for military strategy instead of mystification, the map marks O'Kelly's travels and place of imprisonment with a prosaic functionality. Outraged and spurred to action, the *Herald*'s public would have sized up this island boxed in on the page—noting its vulnerable coastlines, squinting at those almost-indiscernible flags.

The *Herald* failed to lead an American intervention in Cuba. However, the paper was remarkably successful in establishing its own autonomy, influence, and central role as a better representative of American public opinion and republican cosmopolitanism than a US government that was constrained by narrower national interests. The *Herald* was tireless in its self-mythologizing. "Independent journalism," Bennett claimed, "started with the HERALD" (16 Mar. 1873, 8). What better advertising than the following, from Kentucky's *Louisville Ledger:* "the NEW YORK HERALD, rising by regular gradations from a morning newspaper to an institu-

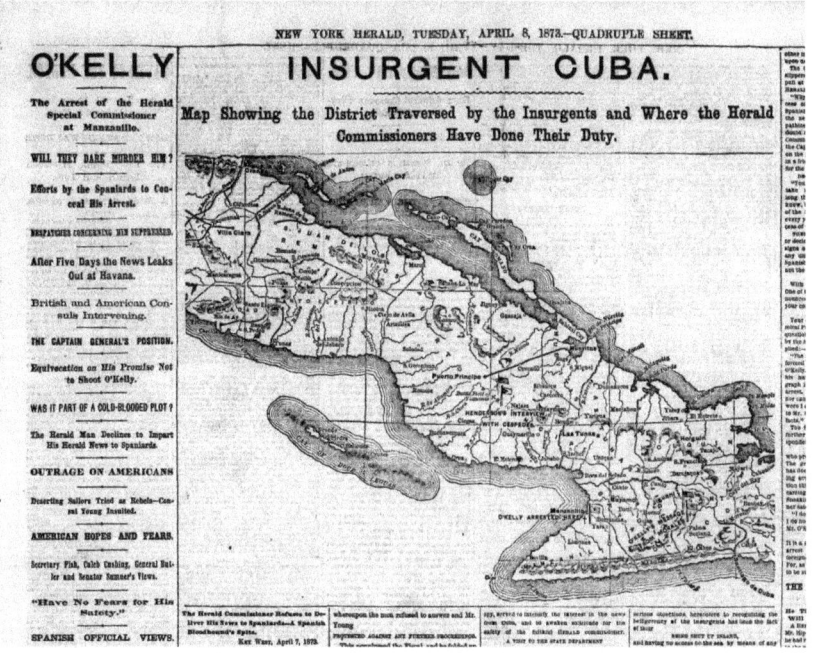

FIGURE 3. Detail of full page on O'Kelly's arrest in the *New York Herald*, 8 April 1873, 5. (Courtesy of the Chronicling America collection, Library of Congress, control no. sn83030313, reel no. 00271743828)

tion, has at last become a government" (quoted in *NYH*, 15 Feb. 1873, 7). When the *Herald* spoke for the United States, promising war with Spain if O'Kelly was shot as a spy, the *Austin State Journal* assured Bennett that he would have the domestic press behind him: "Such a spectacle of a combined press has never been known since the discovery of the art of printing" (quoted in *NYH*, 1 Mar. 1873, 6). Support for the rogue *Herald* became sympathy for the Cuban cause.

Expecting little support from the US diplomatic corps in Cuba, Bennett created his own *Herald* equivalent, renaming O'Kelly the "Special Commissioner" to Cuba (30 Dec. 1872, 4). Bennett goes so far as to suggest, laughably, that O'Kelly would make an effective peace broker (18 Feb. 1873, 6). The paper's bombast aside, O'Kelly paints a damning portrait of consular officials in Havana, claiming they served only personal commercial interests. Among the so-called "shopkeeping representatives of the British lion," O'Kelly singles out acting British Consul General John V. Crawford, writing that Crawford's personal investment in slavery made him a poor advocate (13 June 1873, 10).[39] "For all practical purposes he is one of the black band," O'Kelly writes (*ML* 202). O'Kelly's suspicions were well founded: "the Crawford family had indeed had a long involvement in the Cuban slave trade."[40] This was true of many American diplomats in Cuba, going back to the late eighteenth century. Historian Stephen Chambers notes that "foreign diplomatic posts were frequently handed to the relatives and allies of wealthy merchants, who expected to receive commercial information and public protection for their foreign investments."[41]

The O'Kelly archive raises questions about American foreign policy after 1865, and points to transbellum investment in Cuban slavery. As the Monroe Doctrine continued to serve the purpose Chambers established it did in the antebellum period—namely, to protect the interests of Northeastern business elites profiting from the Cuban slavery economy—the antebellum imperative that Cuba remain Spanish persisted into the 1870s.[42] Characterizations of the United States as an abolitionist power emerged during Reconstruction, and persist today. However, key figures in the O'Kelly archive present yet another argument for a more accurate understanding of American economic investment in slavery. 1865 mattered little to Bennett, for example, who, when reviewing foreign policy stretching back to 1826, found that the American government was "absolutely responsible for the reign of slavery in Cuba during the last forty-six years" (*NYH* 1 Feb. 1873, 6). He refers here to the United States's record of actively supporting Spanish colonial rule in Cuba.[43] Bennett then interprets the US nonrecognition of the Cuban rebels as the state safeguarding the economic interests of an American elite. Manuel de Quesada suggests the same in his 1873 letter to President Grant: "Between the interests of certain American merchants and the duty of recognizing Cuban belligerency the balance was inclined in favor of the former." Quesada negotiates for recognition with the promise that the Cuban Republic would lift "duties paid on the sugar and tobacco" and open Cuba to unrestricted importation of goods from the United States. These measures would, he says, "more than recompense" the United States "for the losses consequent on passing from slave to free labor" (*NYH* 8 Dec. 1873, 5). Quesada's logic is clear: moral imperatives follow the market. In bargaining for recognition, he cuts straight through the Grant administration's frothy condemnation of Spain for delaying abolition in Cuba.[44]

Cuban Contexts of US Reconstruction

> The four million negroes here, who are now moving in behalf of five hundred thousand of their race enslaved in Cuba, could furnish a large army if they were free to go.
> —*New York Herald*, 30 December 1872

The *Herald*'s coverage (and shaping) of American popular opinion on the war in Cuba, and their urgent calls for intervention, form part of the paper's larger efforts to redefine the American nation following the Civil War. By representing broad American support for the Cuban rebels, the paper replaced sectional divisions with a united American public at odds with Washington over the fate of a foreign nation. The *Herald* printed headlines like "The South for Cuba" and "Colored Men for Cuba," but used different strategies to appeal to what were undoubtedly different publics. While covering Southern resistance to Reconstruction governments and explosions of racial violence—most notably the April 1873 riots in Colfax, Louisiana, which Eric Foner describes as "the bloodiest single instance of racial carnage in the Reconstruction era"—the *Herald* pivoted in its critique from federal policy in the South to foreign policy on Cuba.[45] The *Herald* would use other articles to leverage the moral politics of Reconstruction, underscoring the abolition of slavery as the cornerstone issue of the war in Cuba. The paper emphasized Cuba's place in the unfolding story of African American civil rights, stressing the potential influence of the black voting bloc and encouraging African American interventionism by framing activism as acts of black citizenship.

Many articles in the O'Kelly archive describe the mobilization of African Americans lobbying for both civil rights at home and the end of slavery in Cuba. In the same month that O'Kelly sailed for Cuba, Rev. Henry Highland Garnet and other prominent African American abolitionists and civil rights activists established the New York-based Cuban Anti-Slavery Society.[46] The committee resolved to draft an appeal to President Grant for American diplomatic recognition of the Cuban rebels, which it presented in a personal meeting with the president and printed in the *Herald* (1 Feb. 1873, 5). African American activism came under scrutiny by pro-Spanish factions in the city, with the *Herald* reporting that "paid Spanish spies" had infiltrated the committee's inaugural meeting and distributed a circular addressed "to the Colored Citizens of the United States" by the editor of the *El Cronista* (14 Dec. 1872, 10). The *Herald* then called for a united black voice and voting bloc on behalf of the Cuban insurgency:

> we call again upon the four million of emancipated blacks of the United States to prosecute in every city and town of the Union the agitation which they inaugurated recently in the Cooper Institute for an active diplomatic intervention on the part of our government in behalf of the liberation of the four hundred thousand slaves of Cuba; for in the united voice of the colored voting element of the United States, seven hundred thousand strong, there is a power in behalf of liberty to the slave which cannot be disregarded at Washington. (20 Jan. 1873, 4)

This triumphalist vision of African Americans exercising power from within the system, as citizens, affirms American democracy at work. But the *Herald* also thought beyond the ballot box in an editorial that imagines four million African Americans "moving in behalf of five hundred thousand of their race enslaved in Cuba." The message is clear: "They could furnish a large army if they were free to go" (30 Dec. 1872, 4). What a stunning contrast to fear campaigns that conjured nightmarish images of a race war erupting in Cuba and spreading to the United States.

Cuba constitutes an important focus of black Reconstruction even as it does not neatly fit into this temporal container. Before the end of the US Civil War there were already calls among African Americans to take the fight to end slavery beyond national borders, and the war would remain unfinished for some African Americans, who pointed to the persistence of slavery in Cuba and elsewhere in the hemisphere.[47] The New Orleans-based *Black Republican* addressed its constituents: "We have great work to accomplish before we can rest satisfied. There are thousands of our brethren now upon the island of Cuba, wearing the yoke of bondage, and they too must be free."[48] Support for Cuba forms an integral part of the history of black political participation during Reconstruction. The formation of the Cuban Anti-Slavery Society in New York marked the beginning of a nationwide African American solidarity campaign, with support and leadership from towering figures like Frederick Douglass, William Wells Brown, and Governor P. B. S. Pinchback, a Union Army veteran and the country's first African American governor. In its meeting with President Grant, the committee brought a petition with up to 500,000 signatures collected at "religious gatherings, Emancipation commemorations, and Fifteenth Amendment ceremonies, among other settings."[49] Tracing the scope and priorities of black Reconstruction requires attention to joint strategies to advance equality at home and the abolition of slavery in

Cuba. Consider, for example, meetings of the Convention of Colored Men in Washington, where a speaker supported a shared focus on "Civil and Belligerent Rights" with the claim that "the two really constituted but one subject" (11 Mar. 1873, 7); or, in Louisiana, where urgent matters included electoral fraud, Ku Klux Klan violence, and the continued existence of slavery in Cuba.[50]

Cuba is not often thought to figure in news stories about issues in the Reconstruction South, like the black labor shortage. And yet, the *Herald* reprints an article from Chattanooga, Georgia, with the title "Wild rumors from African Quarters in Georgia—Five Thousand Negroes Alleged to Have Been Shipped to the Antilles to Reinforce the Republican Regiments." The article begins: "The negroes here and at various other points of this State, of Alabama and Tennessee are greatly excited over current reports that allege the probable destination of large numbers of the able-bodied men of their race who have been sent off enveloped in a shroud of mystery." The convoluted explanation that follows reveals white anxiety about the newfound mobility of African Americans in the postwar period. As the story goes, African Americans were being diverted from the fields to the ranks of the Cuban revolutionary army. "Emissaries of the Cuban Republic," posing as labor agents, promised African Americans work on sugar and cotton plantations in various parts of the South, only to spirit them away to Cuba (25 Feb. 1873, 5). Cuba could only be leveraged in this way to discourage black flight because the war was part of African American consciousness in the 1870s.[51]

These "wild rumors" originated in a white South that was less sympathetic to the Cuban insurgency than the *Herald* suggests. One of the *Herald*'s strategies to muster support for intervention seems designed to appeal simultaneously to American self-importance and Southern discontent. Despite having exposed the economics behind American inaction, the *Herald* pushed the more inflammatory story of a United States in thrall to Spain. After O'Kelly reported that he could be killed by colonial authorities for crossing Cuban lines, the *Herald* responded with the following: "Our diplomacy has been marked by a subserviency to Spain and a harshness towards the struggling Cubans at once humiliating to us as a nation and inconsistent with our republican principles" (7 Feb. 1873, 6). The editorial continues: "Shoot Mr. O'Kelly as a spy, and a subservient State Department would be but a reed in the way of the storm of indignation that would sweep over the United States and declare war against the assassin Power." Reinforcing this idea of a rogue public united, the *Austin State Journal* imagines O'Kelly's death bringing the nation together, with "all parties, sects, creeds and shades . . . one as the sea in thundering the voice of a nation roused to revenge" (*NYH* 1 Mar.1873, 6). Amy Kaplan will similarly describe the 1898 Spanish-American War as "the final antidote to Reconstruction, healing the conflicts of the Civil War by bringing together blue and gray on distant shores."[52] In the immediate postwar period, when the *Herald* characterized the Grant administration as "subservient" to Spain, the paper recast the relationship between Washington and the American South. As long as the focus was on Cuba, it was the federal government—and not the South—that was submitting to an outside power.

In 1873 the United States was nowhere near going to war with Spain, but interventionism in the early 1870s cannot simply be regarded as a rehearsal for 1898. In this postwar moment, intervention meant an end to US investment in Cuban slavery, and, for some, the next step in an unfinished Civil War. While unquestionably hawkish, the *Herald* pushed primarily and persistently for American diplomatic recognition of the rebels and remained unequivocally opposed to the US annexation of Cuba. A *Herald* editorial reads: "We do not want Cuba as a State or Territory of the United States" (13 Nov. 1873, 6). We can, however, look to the O'Kelly archive for an early effort to imagine what will be known by the mid-twentieth century as the West Indies Federation. The *Herald* advocated for a "Republic of the Antilles" eighty-five years before West Indies Federation would begin its short career as a union of British Caribbean colonies, an experiment premised on what Bennett believed in 1873: "England is prepared to cast off her colonies" (3 Dec. 1873, 6). He explains:

> Our statesmen will learn . . . that the formation of a Republic of the Antilles is not an impracticable scheme; that it may be promoted by the recognition of Cuba as a free and independent Power accompanied by a positive renunciation of all ideas and desires for an extension of our territory by annexation. . . . We may find in England a colaborer [sic] in the work of establishing independent republics over the whole American Continent where provincial governments now exist, if we can only succeed in removing from her mind the erroneous impression that we desire to absorb all outlying States in our own confederation. (16 April 1873, 8)

This editorial frames, and was undoubtedly influenced by, O'Kelly's interview with Calixto García, published in the same issue of the *Herald*, with the headline "England's Confederation Plan." A later editorial returns to the subject, stating: "Our true policy is embraced in the gradual building up of a cordon of independent, self-sustaining, but allied republics, south and north of us, with the United States as the head and guardian of the confederation" (13 Nov. 1873, 6). With this, Bennett adds to a long tradition of representing hemispheric American space through the geo-formal topography of the archipelago. He brings his own reconstructed nation into hemispheric focus, using a defining feature of island space—self-containment—to suggest a shoring up of national differences. What results is an island chain of independent republics with the United States as the undisputed regional power. Bennett's vision of a US-led hemisphere is bound up with the US foreign policy of "no annexation in the tropics." His proposed empire without annexation anticipated white supremacist aversion to what would later be called the United States's "negro empire" in the Caribbean and Pacific.[53]

The O'Kelly archive expands and challenges what we think of as the geography and cultural significance of Reconstruction: it points to a trans-bellum investment in slavery on the one hand, and a key international context of black Reconstruction on the other. While *The Mambi-Land* presents a rare firsthand account of the Ten Years' War, the broader archive reminds us that this conflict was as much about Cuba's relationship with the United States as the insurgent colony's relationship with Spain. This was a moment of intense—often acrimonious, sometimes instructive, and always lively—exchange between Cuba and the United States. Figures like Carlos Manuel de Céspedes, Calixto García, and Manuel de Quesada shaped American understanding of both the war and US–Cuba relations, through both the letters they sent for publication in the *Herald* and their interviews with O'Kelly. As O'Kelly faced the daunting prospect of leaving the Mambi-Land, he tells us: "More than once I was inclined to abandon the idea of returning to New York. It seemed so much safer to merely send on the letters by the *laborantes* and join the Cuban forces" (*ML* 176). In a sense, he does stay. As his memory fades in the United States, he begins an afterlife in Cuba. Translated into the revolutionary historiography of Cuban nation building, the "second Stanley" becomes the Irish mambí.

Notes

1. Ferrer, *Insurgent Cuba*, 6.
2. Douglass, *The Golden Age of the Newspaper*, 90.
3. For the *New York Herald*'s review of the play, see "Bowery Theatre—O'Kelly's Mission," 20 May 1873, 6. At least one other theatrical production that year centered on the war in Cuba—*The Spaniards*—produced by Josh Hart at the

Theatre Comique. This play also ends with victory for the Cubans (see "Musical and Dramatic Notes," *New York Herald,* 17 Feb. 1873, 3). For all *Herald* reporting on Cuba and O'Kelly from December 1872 to December 1873, see this edition's companion website at www.okellyarchive.com.

4. As a war correspondent and self-styled "rash adventurer," O'Kelly anticipates later celebrity journalists in Cuba like Richard Harding Davis, Stephen Crane, and Harry Scovel. However, O'Kelly distinguishes himself from these later figures by the depth and detail of his engagement with Cuban rebels and his support for Cuban self-government.

5. The period of US Reconstruction is so named for the national project to reintegrate the former southern Confederacy into the Union and to end slavery. Historians have typically dated Reconstruction from the end of the Civil War to 1877, when the last federal troops withdrew from South Carolina, Louisiana, and Florida. Here I use Eric Foner's periodization of Reconstruction as beginning with the Emancipation Proclamation in 1863. See Foner, *Reconstruction: America's Unfinished Revolution, 1863–1877.*

6. "A Spanish View of the Cuban Question—America Arraigned for Her Perfidy and Covetousness," *New York Herald,* 25 Mar. 1873, 8; *New York Herald* hereafter cited parenthetically with the abbreviation *NYH.*

7. *Mambi-Land,* 3, hereafter cited parenthetically with the abbreviation *ML.* The *Mambi-Land* contributes to a well-established tradition of travel writing on Cuba. At least 18 travelogues were published by Americans traveling in Cuba between 1850 and 1870 alone. See Harold F. Smith, "A Bibliography of American Travellers' Books about Cuba Published before 1900," *The Americas* 22, vol. 4 (1966): 404–12. O'Kelly stands out for his support for Cuban independence.

8. O'Sullivan, *Aloysius O'Kelly,* 8.

9. Townend, "A Cosmopolitan Nationalist," 228.

10. For a more detailed biography of O'Kelly, see Peter Hulme's foreword in this edition. Also see O'Sullivan, *Aloysius O'Kelly;* Owen McGee, "O'Kelly, James Joseph"; and Townend, "A Cosmopolitan Nationalist."

11. James Gordon Bennett Jr. distinguished himself from his father and *Herald* founder, who sided with the Union during the Civil War but did not support the abolition of slavery.

12. Ferrer, *Insurgent Cuba,* 22.

13. Ferrer, *Insurgent Cuba,* 27–28.

14. See Horne, *Race to Revolution,* 9, 62. For increased transportation of enslaved Africans to Cuba during the Civil War, see Horne, 106.

15. While curtailed, the trade did continue. A US Navy report from 1870 estimated that at least 40,000 enslaved people were transported annually from Africa. In 1876, British officials noted the ongoing participation of American ships in the transportation of enslaved Africans. See Horne, *Race to Revolution,* 106, 11.

16. The Ten Years' War ended in February 1878 with the Pact of Zanjón and was followed almost immediately by the *Guerra Chiquita* or Little War (1879–1880),

led by Calixto García. See chapter 15 of *The Mambi-Land* for O'Kelly's interview with Calixto García.

17. Quoted in Townend, "A Cosmopolitan Nationalist," 224.

18. O'Kelly does not describe the circumstances of this meeting but does state that he "received many attentions" from the "celebrated correspondent" (*NYH* 19 Nov. 1873, 5).

19. For more on the origins and significance of the term "mambí," see Fernando Ortiz's prologue in this edition.

20. Ferrer, *Insurgent Cuba*, 3.

21. Kaplan, *Anarchy of Empire*, 126.

22. See Eric Love's excellent analysis of Grant's failure to persuade the Senate to ratify the Santo Domingo annexation treaty in *Race over Empire*, 27–72.

23. The first Spanish translation of *The Mambi-Land* (New Orleans: Imprenta de P. Marchand, 1876) was by Nicanor Trelles y Santoyo. Trelles contributed to the pro-independence newspaper *La Voz de la Patria* (New York, 1876–1877), sometimes under the names "Yara" and "Hatuey." Most Cuban editions (1930, 1968, 1990, 2001) use the 1887 translation by Ricardo García Garófalo (Santa Clara, Cuba: n.p.). García Garófalo was a journalist, lawyer, and Marxist organizer in Santa Clara, Cuba, before moving to New York in 1891, where he worked with José Martí. He provided legal counsel to Antonio Maceo in Costa Rica before moving to Mexico City in 1892. See Jorge Jesús García Ángulo, *Ricardo García Garófalo y su pensamiento social: Una perspectiva inédita desde la Cuba colonial* (Riga: Editorial Académica Española, 2012). For a more complete publication history, see Peter Hulme's foreword.

24. Ferrer, *Insurgent Cuba*, 6.

25. F. Ortiz, "Prologue," 218.

26. F. Ortiz, "Prologue," 232, 217.

27. Ortiz has trouble accommodating some chapters in O'Kelly's life, including his campaigns as a volunteer soldier for France in Algeria and Mexico. In one dispatch from Cuba, O'Kelly opines that Spain should give up the island and turn its attention to Africa, and Morocco in particular (*NYH* 6 Aug. 1873, 4).

28. Maume, "'Cuba, the Ireland of the West,'" 30.

29. See Fernando Ortiz, "El traductor de Humboldt en la historia de Cuba," in *Ensayo político sobre la isla de Cuba* by Alexander von Humboldt, trans. Adrián Valle (La Habana, 1930). For an English translation, see Vera M. Kutzinski, "Humboldt's Translator in the Context of Cuban History," *Atlantic Studies* 6, vol. 3 (2009): 327–43. Also see Vera M. Kutzinski, "Translations of Cuba: Fernando Ortiz, Alexander von Humboldt, and the curious case of John Sidney Thrasher," *Atlantic Studies Literary, Cultural and Historical Perspectives* 6, vol. 3 (2009): 303–26.

30. My thanks to the anonymous reader of the manuscript for drawing my attention to Ortiz's simultaneous work on a Cuban edition of Humboldt's *Political Essay* and the 1930 edition of *La tierra del mambí*.

31. The term "filibuster," as Rodrigo J. Lazo explains, "comes from the Dutch vrijbuiter, or free-booter, and was modified into the French flibustier and the Spanish filibustero, which became common in the seventeenth century as an epithet for pirates who plundered the Spanish West Indies" (94).

32. Précis of chapter 16, *The Mambi-Land* (Philadelphia: Lippincott, 1974): 239.

33. Chapters 12–14, 27, and 28 are original to *The Mambi-Land*. Chapters 25 and 26 are much expanded versions of *Herald* dispatches.

34. Some of these surrogate ports lacked the sanction of their governments—those in the United States and the British West Indies, for example.

35. The *Virginius* was an American ship captained by former Confederate naval officer Joseph Fry and contracted by Cuban rebels to bring men and supplies to the island. The so-called "Virginius Affair" began with the Spanish seizure of the ship on 30 October 1873. Fifty-three crew members were executed in the weeks that followed.

36. For *Herald* coverage of the expedition, see 8 Jan. 1873, 7; and 14 Jan. 1873, 3.

37. Lazo, "Los Filibusteros," 89.

38. The map tracks two *Herald* commissioners in Cuba: O'Kelly and his predecessor, A. Boyd Henderson. The map marks "Henderson's Interview with Cespedes" as south of Puerto Principe. Henderson would later admit to fabricating this interview.

39. A British subject but a *Herald* correspondent, O'Kelly appealed to both British and American consular officials for help.

40. Hulme, "James J. O'Kelly at Jiguaní (1873)," 61. For more on consular involvement in the O'Kelly case, see Hulme, 60–62.

41. Chambers, *No Gain but Gain*, 24–25. Also see Horne, *Race to Revolution*, 11, 62–63.

42. Chambers shows how the Monroe Doctrine of 1823 protected US involvement in the illegal transatlantic slave trade, as well as merchants primarily from the Northeastern US profiting from Cuba's slavery-based economy. Describing Cuba as "a uniquely central driver of U.S. economic development and foreign policy in these early national years," he explains support for continued colonial rule rather than Cuban independence or annexation to the US, writing, "the creation of an informal American empire in Cuba depended on the simultaneous survival of the Spanish empire. . . . Americans invested in the island had no interest in anything that might upset the balance of slave and flour imports and sugar, coffee and specie exports" (11, 67, 68).

43. For example, Bennett writes, "in 1826, the South American States plotted to seize the island, with the intention of manumitting all slaves, [and] our worthy President, John Quincy Adams, cried, 'Hands off!'" (1 Feb. 1873, 6).

44. According to historian Richard H. Bradford, President Grant was more inclined to grant the rebels belligerent status than business-minded Secretary of State Hamilton Fish, who "favored the interests of Americans who had invested

in sugar and slaves." Bradford further explains that "the 'hard-money elite' of upper-class Northeasterners in both parties fought Cuban recognition" (14). For more on Fish, see Love, *Race over Empire*, 38–40.

45. Foner, *Reconstruction*, 437.

46. For a more detailed account of African American support for the Cuban insurgency, see Paul Ortiz, *An African American and Latinx History of the United States*, 71–94. Cuban leader Antonio Maceo acknowledged Rev. Henry Highland Garnet's importance to the struggle by requesting a meeting during a visit to New York in 1873.

47. See Leary, "Four Million Freedmen and One Bronzed Body."

48. Quoted in Ortiz, *An African American and Latinx History*, 74.

49. Ortiz, *An African American and Latinx History*, 75.

50. Ortiz, *An African American and Latinx History*, 82.

51. These rumors of black abduction to Cuba tapped into and repackaged anxieties originating after the Emancipation Proclamation that formerly enslaved people could be resold into slavery in Cuba. See Guterl, *American Mediterranean*, 147. Enslaved people were, in fact, "decoyed to Cuba." See Horne, *Race to Revolution*, 8.

52. Kaplan, *Anarchy of Empire*, 141.

53. Love, *Race over Empire*, 8. Hamilton Fish suggested a similar alternative to annexation when President Grant lacked support in the Senate for his proposal to annex Santo Domingo (Horne 62). For more on ties between racism and anti-imperialism in the post–Civil War period, see Love, *Race over Empire*.

Chronology of James J. O'Kelly in Cuba

1872
December
14	Departs New York City on the *City of Havana*
19	Arrives in Havana
20	Writes first report for the *New York Herald* (published 1 January)
22	Petitions Captain General Ceballos for a safe conduct pass (refused)

1873
January
14	Arrives in Santiago de Cuba (returned from Cienfuegos, Las Tunas, Sancti Spíritus)
15	Writes from Santiago de Cuba (after marching with San Quentin battalion)
20	Writes from Santiago de Cuba
29	Released from detention in El Ramón

February
1	Writes from Palma Soriano
5	Writes from Santiago de Cuba
19	Leaves Santiago de Cuba for insurgent lines
20	Reaches "Encampment of Cuba Libre"
26	Reaches headquarters of Calixto García

March
3	Marches with troops led by Calixto García to Cañadon, four miles from Jiguaní
6	Arrives at the camp of Carlos Manuel de Céspedes

l *Chronology*

10	Writes from the "Residence of the Government, Cuba Libre" (interview with Céspedes)
12	Marches with Céspedes and presidential guard towards region of Guisa
19	Arrives with presidential party in camp of Modesto Díaz (Guá)
24	Leaves with Modesto Díaz for Spanish outposts
31	Arrives in Manzanillo, arrested and taken to Fort Gerona

April

1	Writes from Fort Gerona prison, Manzanillo
4	Awaits assembly of military tribunal for trial
29	Arrival of British gunboat *Plover* in Manzanillo

May

7	Transferred to Fort Morro Prison, Santiago de Cuba
21	Embarks for Havana
25	Arrives in Havana, imprisoned in La Cabaña
30	Sets sail in the *Antonio López* for Santander, Spain

June

18	Imprisoned in the Cárcel Nacional, Santander, Spain

July

11	Arrives in Madrid, released on parole

September

25	Arrives in Gibraltar

Cast a glance over the map of Cuba. Its average width is 48 miles. Let us fancy a body of land between two coasts, placed at less distance than New York is from Philadelphia. In the intervening space, with a length of several hundred miles, place as many forests and mountains as may be wished.... There exist to-day 20,000 patriot troops on a war footing, stationed throughout the Eastern and the Camaguey States and a part of Cinco Villas.... Let your Excellency compare this enthusiastic and increasing body of men with the 4,000 troops to which the dismayed and disheartened army of Washington was reduced before the great foreign reinforcements and supplies were received, and from this an approximate idea of the strength of the Cubans can be formed.

—General Quesada to President Grant, 1873

Editor's Note

THIS IS the first English-language edition of *The Mambi-Land* since 1874. What follows is the complete text, excepting chapter headings, modified only to avoid inconsistencies in formatting and spelling or to aid readability through minor adjustments to punctuation. Misspellings of words in Spanish remain, including missing accents, although this edition does provide corrections to some proper names in the footnotes. Footnotes also clarify moments of temporal confusion as O'Kelly moves between real time and retrospective narration.

The Mambi-Land

OR

ADVENTURES OF A *HERALD* CORRESPONDENT IN CUBA

James J. O'Kelly

1 The Mambi-Land

Dim, mystic, and clothed in awful shadows, there floats on the edge of the American continent an unknown country. Mirage-like, it looms up at intervals on the horizon in gloomy grandeur; and, when its form and general features seem about to reveal themselves, it fades away from the vision and leaves only indistinct impressions behind. But it fades not forever: again it appears, and the evidences of its existence are perceptible to the senses. This mysterious country is the Mambi-Land. It is hid from our view by the war-clouds which obscure its frontiers and veil its territory from the gaze of the outer world. The clash of arms and the thunder-roar of guns that come borne on the winds, mingled with shrieks of battle and anguished cries for help, assure us that the dim and indistinct country is no dream-land, but the abiding-place of men with the same instincts, hopes, and passions as ourselves. The land of the Mambi is to the World a shadowland, full of doubts and unrealities. It is a legend, and yet a fact. It is called by many names, yet few know where begins or ends its frontier. Spaniards call it the Manigua, or Los Montes, Americans talk of it as Free Cuba, and those who dwell within its confines, Cuba Libre, or the Mambi-Land.* It possesses no cities, no pomps, no splendors; it is bathed in sunshine, and yet bedewed with tears, often tears of blood. Indistinct it rises on the horizon, phantom-like it fades at the approach of the traveler, who yet feels and knows that its territory surrounds him on every side. Only in the depths of the silent forest does this mysterious land take tangible form and express itself in organized communities. Its limits may be vaguely marked by the shores of Cuba; for even in the Spanish strongholds the dominion of the Mambi is spread over Cuban hearts. There are two Cubas, Spanish and free Cuba, or Mambi-Land. The slave-holding, sugar-producing Queen of the Antilles, with her legions of fierce *voluntarios,* has become commonplace, while the vague,

---

*Nomenclature matters, as O'Kelly suggests that while Americans acknowledge the insurgent republic (calling it "Free Cuba"), the Spanish refer to rebels and rebel territory, and use the terms "los montes" ("the mountains") and the pejorative "la manigua" ("swamp" or "jungle") to suggest an "uncivilized" enemy.

4 The Mambi-Land

unvisited territory of Cuba Libre is full of romantic interest.* Few from the outer world have crossed its shifting frontier, so full of unknown perils and awe-inspiring mystery. Like the fabled garden of the Hesperides, the frontiers of the Mambi-Land are guarded by monsters ready to devour the rash intruder. The dragon of the fable has been replaced by the *voluntario,* the soldier, and the executioner; but the crime of passing beyond the forbidden confines is not the less rigorously and savagely punished. Death is the doom decreed by Spanish law against whoever dares to cross the borders of the mystic Mambi-Land. Some have doubted its very existence, and declared it to be a creation evoked from the rank imagination of an evil-working race called *laborantes.*† Before me no impartial witness from the outside world had ever crossed the mysterious frontier to lift up the cloud that hid from view the strange land. Alone, among the bookmakers, have I visited the forbidden region; moved and dwelt among the inhabitants of the silent forests, the new nation growing into life; partaken of their cheer, joined in their revels, assisted at their deaths, accompanied them to battle, and witnessed their constancy in defeat, their exaltation in the moment of victory.

In the following pages I shall present to the reader an account of the difficulties and dangers encountered and overcome on my way to the Mambi-Land, and faithful pictures of the habits and modes of life of the dwellers in the woods. They will be seen in their leaf-covered huts and in their camps, employed in the labors of peace and war. They will tell to the reader, in their own words, their hopes, aims, and resolution. What I saw and heard will be passed in panorama before the reader, until he shall see the unknown land grow up in form and color to his mind's eye; and he shall behold, through the leaves of this book, as through the foliage of the forest, glimpses of life in the Mambi-Land. Why I went on the perilous expedition to discover the semi-fabulous Cespedes and his Mambi legions; how I lived among them; and how, a prisoner in the hands of the Spaniards, I was snatched by a saving Providence from the edge of the grave, will be told simply and without exaggeration.

Towards the close of the year 1872, the New York *Herald,* wishing to

---

*O'Kelly's later description of the Spanish volunteer corps ("voluntarios") as "almost wholly made up of Peninsulars, or immigrant Spaniards" (14) applied more to western, urban areas. When in remote regions in Cuba's eastern provinces, he contrasts Spanish soldiers with creole "volunteers, made up of a hybrid collection of all colors and conditions" (87).

†The term "laborantes" referred to civilian conspirators, mainly in urban areas.

throw light on the Cuban insurrection, sent a correspondent to Cuba, with orders to see Cespedes, the President of the Cuban Republic. The correspondent found the mission so hazardous and full of danger that he abandoned it.* Mr. James Gordon Bennett then intrusted the mission to me, with the following characteristic instructions: "Go into the Cuban lines, see Cespedes and other important leaders, give a fair account of their position, and bring back reliable information of the prospects of the insurrection; draw upon the office for whatever funds you may need."†

My course of action was left free. It was understood that I was to succeed. It mattered little what the cost should be so that I saw Cespedes or his successor, and furnished the *Herald* with the required information about the Cuban insurrection. My first care was to visit Madame Cespedes, and endeavor to glean from her some information as to the whereabouts of her husband. But, though willing to give me every assistance, she could only furnish the vaguest hints as to the regions in which he was likely to be found. Other Cubans were applied to, with no better success; and, except good wishes and some letters of introduction to the generals commanding in the field, the Cubans in New York could give me no aid. Introductions to sympathizers in Cuba were not to be thought of; and so it would be necessary to grope my way into the insurgent camps, which existed somewhere, but no one knew exactly where. My preparations were soon completed, and on the 14th of December, 1872, I embarked on the *City of Havana* for Cuba.

The mail steamer swung out into the river about four o'clock P.M., amid the waving of handkerchiefs and kissing of hands that usually accompany temporary separations. There were some tears shed by a few extremely sensitive or lachrymose people, who either could not help it, or thought it was the proper thing to do; but, for the most part, the scene was gay and lively. There were touching scenes also; for, among the passengers, were invalids going south, as a last resort; and, as their anxious friends bade them good-by, with words of encouragement and cheer, it was only too evident that there existed an underlying sentiment that the parting would

---

*The predecessor O'Kelly mentions is A. Boyd Henderson. Henderson claimed to have crossed Cuban lines and met Carlos Manuel de Céspedes, publishing details in the *Herald* on 19 Dec. 1872, 3. His story is discredited in April of the following year, when Céspedes tells O'Kelly that Henderson fabricated the story of their meeting (*NYH* 16 Apr. 1873, 5).

†O'Kelly refers to James Gordon Bennett Jr. (1841–1918), then owner and editor of the *New York Herald*.

be an eternal adieu. It was curious to notice the fleeting expression of pain and sorrow passing over the faces of the assistants in these scenes, and the brave endeavors made to conceal the truth from the sufferers. But the greater number of the passengers were of a different type—people who looked forward to the trip as a means of pleasure or profit. These chatted gayly, and seemed rather to enjoy the fuss their friends were making about them, and some were even so ungrateful as to look upon their friends as bores.

The evening was calm and the harbor was bathed in moonlight, and consequently most of the passengers were on deck to watch the receding shores of native land. The shore looked misty and indistinct in the cold, clear moonlight. Here and there the twinkling light from the distant windows called up pictures of the happy home-life we were leaving behind. It is impossible to find anything more delightful than New York Bay on such a night. We had left Sandy Hook behind us, when steam was let off, and the speed of the vessel began to slacken. We knew that the pilot was about to leave us. We crowded the side of the vessel to see him descend into his mysterious little boat, and charge him with our final adieus to native land. It is the work of a moment: he drops over the vessel's side, sliding down into the frail-looking boat that is waiting to receive him, and is rowed away into the ever-deepening shadows, until he becomes a speck, and finally is lost to our sight. Just at this moment we pass pilot-boat No. 7, looking like a fairy craft in the moonlight. Her lines are sweeping and graceful, and the cordage and rigging are so clearly defined in the silver light of the cold moon that they seem like a delicate web. It was just one of those pictures that nature makes, full of admirably-combined effects—broad, yet delicate and suggestive.

One by one the passengers retired, and I was left alone to contemplate the beauties of the night; above, the clear sky with its millions of twinkling stars; below, the phosphorescent sea, bathed in moonlight, and flecked with the foam of our gallant sea-horse, that plowed onward, panting and straining every nerve, overcoming every obstacle and carrying us gallantly on our moonlit way.* At last I was forced to turn into the little state-room, and coiled myself up on a narrow shelf that appeared to me to be not more than five feet long. It was covered with a faultlessly white counter-

---

*O'Kelly mentions in his first dispatch to the *New York Herald* (dated 24 Dec. 1872) that he spent his first evening on the *City of Havana* in the saloon reading Charles Dickens's 1842 *American Notes for General Circulation*. Dickens ends this travelogue with a critique of American slavery. Writing thirty years later, O'Kelly begins his travelogue with a critique of Cuban slavery (chapter 3).

pane, on which stood out in bold relief, in red letters, the words, "City of Havana." The horribly monotonous motion of the screw prevented my going to sleep for some time, but tired nature gave way and I dozed off. At length morning dawned, but let me draw a veil over the occurrences of this day. Suffice it to say that Scotch ale, brandy-and-water, and other resources were called upon in vain. The decks were deserted except by a few of those men who seem to have been intended by nature for seagulls or porpoises. They look into your stateroom with provoking coolness to assure you that it is splendid weather, only a little fresh, and advise you to get up and walk about a little.

The third day out sees most of us on deck; no one inclined to admit he has been sick, but only a little squeamish, you know. We had already left behind the bleak northern clime, and the day was warm as in our summertime. We seemed to glide through a palpitating sea of molten glass, the balmy air producing that exquisite, sensuous feeling which is only felt in the neighborhood of the tropics, and enabling us to bear the monotony of the sea-voyage with equanimity, for here the sense of life is pleasure enough. On Thursday morning the coast of Cuba looms up in the distance, seen vaguely through the morning mist. Over the dark, shadowy, purple-tinted outline of the coast rise immense piles of cumulus clouds grand and impressive, that threaten to pass over us in storm before we reach the port; but, as the sun shines out, dissipating the mists and bathing the aerial regions in vaporous hues, the cloud-masses sail along the sky and reveal the deep, clear azure of the firmament. My confidence returns, and I go into my stateroom to make final preparations for disembarking. We were nearer to Havana than I imagined; and, long before the last strap of my trunk had been buckled, the grim mass of the Morro Castle had come clearly into view. It is an imposing-looking structure, and evidently very strong. It is mounted with heavy Dahlgren guns, and is, from situation and solidity of construction, a very formidable work. It is situated on the left of the harbor as we enter. On the right the Batteria de la Reina, a semi-circular fort on the opposite side of the harbor's mouth, affords it efficient support. Both works are dominated by an important fort behind the Batteria de la Reina. The lighthouse is on the left of the port, and bears on it in large letters the inscription, "O'Donnell, 1844."*
As we pass it the harbor opens to our view. It is narrow at the entrance,

---

*Leopoldo O'Donnell y Jorris (1809–1867) was captain general of Cuba in 1843 and the figure responsible for the massacre, imprisonment, and exile of thousands of both enslaved and free people of color in response to the alleged conspiracy known as "La Escalera" (1844). He was prime minister of Spain in 1856, 1858, and 1865.

but, as we proceed, it widens into a sheet of water, irregular in form, of considerable extent. On all sides low ranges of hills protect it from the violence of the winds, so as to render it a remarkably safe anchorage.

The narrow passage is defended at intervals by old batteries, that recall the time when the Spanish flag swept the southern seas in all the haughty pride of unchecked conquest. Today these batteries but too truly reflect the changed fortunes of the Iberian nation. The old stones remain, but grown gray under the influence of time. The ravages of age are only made the more noticeable by the efforts of the moderns to conceal them. New cement has been placed in the interstices, and the old brass guns that were young in the days of King Philip peep out from the crenelated batteries with a senile curiosity and impotence. They, however, give to the place an air of antiquity that more than compensates the traveler for their want of efficiency.

The city lies to the right as we enter, on a flat tongue of land, between the harbor and the open sea. Above the mass of houses rise towers and lofty steeples, the whole jumbled together, presenting a scene unrivaled in picturesque effect. The square, solid houses, painted yellow, and green, and blue, rise up in exquisite confusion, in which ever-varying gradations of light and shade, commingling with brilliantly contrasting color-effects, give to the scene a brightness and joyousness we never find in northern climes. In the view of Havana there is much of the East. The monotony of the architecture is somewhat relieved by the varying height of the houses, which are painted to suit the fancy of their owners. For this purpose a kind of distemper is used. The prevailing color is dirty yellow, relieved by green, brown, blue, or red. White, with appropriate relief, is not uncommon. Brilliant colored awnings also shade the streets, and give them a bright and gay appearance. The shops, too, are open, no doors or glass being used, and the rich merchandise piled up within catches the eye of the passerby. The sight is not dazzled by an eternal blistering white. So well is the sunlight absorbed by those colors that one can look about, even when the sun is at its height, without the sensation of being blinded.

The interior slopes of the lower hills, on whose summits the lines of fortification are continued, are clothed with verdure; here and there little clusters of white houses with red tile roofs, and some sparsely planted trees in their vicinity, present a picturesque effect that is perfectly delightful. But what adds more than perhaps anything else to the charm of the harbor, are the lumbering passenger-boats, that seem to belong to another age. These boats resemble somewhat a rude kind of gondola, but are propelled by sails: they have only one mast, which supports a square sail, by which the boat is principally managed. The velocity with which these craft dash about is absolutely marvelous.

As soon as we had cast anchor a cloud of these boats came scudding round us, and it was a beautiful sight to see them moving about in ever-changing groups, offering every instant new combinations of color. They are of all sizes, forms, and colors, according to the owner's sense of the aesthetic; but the most lumbering and weather-beaten are unquestionably the most picturesque.

The port officers were at breakfast when we arrived, so there was plenty of time to enjoy all the beauties of the harbor, as it was nearly two o'clock in the afternoon when the permit to land arrived. In the mean time a Spanish mail steamer entered, having on board a number of soldiers and civilians. The expedition with which these were attended to and landed contrasted strangely with the cavalier manner in which mere Americans were treated. Those of our passengers who had influence on shore were allowed to land by special permit; but those who were not so fortunate were obliged to remain until the official stomach had been satisfied.

Even a Spanish official cannot well remain at breakfast all day, so the looked-for permit arrived in its own good time. Then the group of little boats that had been moving round us suddenly swarmed toward the ship's gangway, and their occupants, who were strong and rather hard looking Spaniards, set up a babel of appeals for employment.

As we shoved off from the vessel's side, we were enjoying, by anticipation, the novel sights upon which our eyes were soon to dwell, while the black prophet of the party shook his head with evil forebodings of what was to happen to us in the custom-house. While all were in this happy frame of mind, an incident occurred which was nigh having a fatal termination. Our boat was heavily laden with baggage, and carried six passengers, one being a lady, in addition to the two Spanish boatmen. We were scudding before the wind at a fair rate, when a man-of-war's boat, propelled by a dozen lusty arms, appeared rowing directly across our course. It was impossible for us to stop or to change our direction with sufficient rapidity to avoid a collision; so we held on, the sailors shouting to the man-of-war's crew to change their course. The latter, however, paid not the slightest heed, but rowed down with a sweeping stroke. The position became critical, as it was evident that a collision was imminent. Our sailors shouted and gesticulated with increased energy, and, at the last moment, the Spaniards backed water not an instant too soon; for, in spite of the frantic efforts of our boatmen, the prow of the man-of-war's boat struck ours on the quarter heavily and made her reel. The lady of the party only escaped injury by jumping up from her seat just in time to escape being struck by the colliding prow. In the stern of the Spanish boat a nabob of an officer was seated, whose white hair ought to have been a guarantee against such an outrage; but the hidalgo sat quietly and unconcernedly by, as if it were a matter of sublime indifference to his decorated soul whether or not some half-dozen mere civilians were sent to the bottom. Before we landed we were treated to another sample of official insolence by having our boat thrust back to allow some uniformed swell to pass before us—an incident that cost us half an hour of struggle before we could regain our lost place.

My first care, after depositing my luggage at the San Carlos Hotel, was to seek Mr. Price, the resident correspondent of the *Herald,* who introduced me to General A. T. A. Torbert, the American consul-general, who received me kindly, but seemed to think that, in view of the state of public feeling, there was very little chance of obtaining permission to visit the insurgent camp, without which, he expressed the opinion, it would be a very hazardous and very foolhardy undertaking to attempt to pass the Spanish outposts.* General Torbert was reserved and cautious in the expression of his views, and evidently wanted to keep out of any unnecessary complications with the authorities. He excused himself from accompanying me to the Captain-General, but gave me a letter of introduction and recommendation, saying that it would be well to see his Excellency at once, and return to inform him what answer had been given to me.

The distance from the consulate to the palace of the Captain-General was traversed in a few minutes, and I found myself in one of the spacious apartments of the Palacio de Gobernacion. An officer in full dress, decorated and *aiguiletted,* was in waiting. He had laid aside his sword, and was engaged in conversation with a gentleman who, I afterwards learned, was an aide-de-camp in mufti. His Excellency was engaged on important business; but, as soon as he was disengaged, my letters were presented. There was time to look around and examine the portraits of former Captains-General. But the study lacked interest, from the fact that the names were not given, though the dates of their holding office were marked on each frame. The most striking, and, to me, interesting, were the portraits of O'Donnell, de Rodas, and Valmaseda, the latter a fierce and by no means very intelligent-looking man. O'Donnell occupies the place of honor over the door of the antechamber; and, unless the painter flattered him very much, he was one of those men who, once seen, leave

---

*O'Kelly refers to the *Herald*'s correspondent in Havana, Leopold A. Price.

their image impressed on the mind forever. The portraits are, however, execrably painted, evidently by some local genius. The examination of this interesting collection of historical portraits was soon interrupted by the officer with the golden aiguillettes informing me that his Excellency the Captain-General would receive me. On entering the grand *salle de reception,* I saw, coming towards me, a distinguished-looking man of some fifty summers, dressed in military uniform. Mr. Price, who accompanied me, introduced me to General Ceballos as the correspondent of the New York *Herald.* He bowed politely, but coldly. After the exchange of the usual civilities, the object of my visit was explained, and a shade of displeasure and annoyance passed over his face. It was, however, transient, as his Excellency, during this interview, exhibited a marked and almost chivalrous courtesy.

In answer to my request for a safe-conduct, to enable me to pass freely through the Spanish lines, and protect me should I fall into the hands of the Spanish troops while among the insurgents or in their district, the Captain-General answered, "It is impossible. I was anxious that a true account should be given to the world, and, when a former correspondent arrived here, I gave him every facility to see for himself the exact state of the insurrection. He was furnished with letters of recommendation to the commanding generals in the districts which he wished to visit; and in all cases he was well received and offered every facility to acquaint himself with the condition of the insurrection. He was treated with all the attention that could be paid to a *niña bonita,* a beautiful girl; yet, after all this, he deceived me and misrepresented the situation.*

"I regret that you did not come first; you could then have had all the facilities, but now it is different. So much dissatisfaction has been caused by the proceedings of your predecessor, and the unfounded reports which have been spread relative to his personal safety, that I should expose myself to misconception if I should again place myself in a position to be deceived. You come recommended; but your predecessor also came recommended as a reliable and honorable man; but yet he deceived me, after all my kindness and attention, when I had treated him as though he were an ambassador. With these circumstances fresh in the public mind, I cannot accept the responsibility of recommending you to any of my subordinate officers. If I had only myself to consider, I would do so with pleasure; but I cannot consent to do anything that might tend to weaken

---

*Captain General Ceballos refers to A. Boyd Henderson. See note above on p. 5.

respect for authority, or that would make it appear that I can be used as a toy."

"I acknowledge that your Excellency's position is a difficult one; but—"

"No, my position is not difficult. I command here, and am obeyed implicitly in all parts of the island."

This unfortunate phrase seemed to annoy the Captain-General very much; and, though I pressed him to give me a simple military pass, he was firm in his refusal, at the same time expressing his regret that the peculiar circumstances of the case, and the tone of the public mind, prevented him according a request that otherwise it would give him much pleasure to grant. In conclusion, he said—

"I cannot accept the responsibility of giving you any authority, for the reasons that I have already explained; besides, you might be wounded or killed by a shot from behind the stump of a tree, and we would then be charged with the responsibility of your death. I will not, therefore, expose myself to the danger of further misrepresentation. You are, however, at liberty to travel wherever you wish at your own risk. You can go to Puerto Principe, Santiago de Cuba, or wherever else you like, and will not be interfered with; but I cannot give you any papers to protect you, or any special authorization of any kind. The *visé* of your passport will suffice to enable you to pass through the country with perfect safety."

It was evident that, unless my application could be supported from more influential quarters, no special protection would be granted; and, unwilling to prolong uselessly the interview, I made my bow to his Excellency and departed, but with my mind made up to try again.

Whoever goes to Havana in search of the beautiful will be disappointed. Like other painted beauties, it looks best at a distance, and fails to improve on closer acquaintance. The streets are narrow, dirty, and ill paved. Footpaths, scarcely ten inches wide, furnish the only security from the *volantes* and *victorias,* which dash about in the most reckless manner, without the slightest regard to the safety of foot passengers. In the dry season the stench is dreadful, and when it rains the streets are converted into small rivers, owing to the want of proper drainage; yet the city has the harbor on one side and the ocean at the other. It is situated in an admirable position to allow the drainage to be carried into the ocean, but the little that has been done in the way of sewage has been made to empty into the harbor, converting it into a large cesspool. The prevalence of disease during the heated term is largely due to this cause.

Club life prevails to a large extent in Havana, and has exerted an unfavorable influence on the character of the inhabitants. Havana is essentially a male city. The ladies are in a hopeless minority. At first sight this would appear to increase their influence, but the contrary is the fact. Native ladies never go out unaccompanied, as they would be exposed to insult. Foreign ladies sometimes defy the native prejudice; but, in the end, are obliged to conform to the rule, or expose themselves to annoyance and even insult. The life of a woman must be unbearably monotonous. They go to church in the morning, and in the evening drive out to hear the music on the Prado, or go to the opera. On the Prado it is very rare to see a lady, even accompanied, taking walking exercise; they remain in their carriages and chat with their gentlemen friends, or partake of ices and sherbets, which are brought from the brilliant cafés in the neighborhood. The Prado is the great centre of amusement. Here are grouped within sight the beautiful *Casino Español,* so sadly celebrated, the Albisu Theatre, the Louvre, the Tacon Theatre, where operas are given. The Tacon is a very large house of pretentious appearance. It looks gay and bright at night, when tier above tier of boxes are crowded with gayly-dressed ladies, powdered, rouged, and made up generally to kill. They look like a collection of tropical birds of brilliant plumage, while the gentlemen, dressed in dark coats and black stove-pipe hats, who occupy the parterre, which is reserved wholly for their use, look like a flock of huge crows, especially when the curtain drops, and they rise *en masse,* put on their black hats, and pour out into the cafés and halls until the warning-bells call them back to their places. A custom also prevails which has long been banished from our stage: between the acts gentlemen go behind the scenes to chat with actors and actresses.

The population of Havana is made up of Peninsulars, or Spaniards, who hold in their hands all political or administrative power; Creoles, or white people born in the island; and free colored people, slaves, and Chinamen.*
Between the Peninsulars and the Creoles there exists an intense but suppressed hatred. It does not, however, appear on the surface, as the Creole has been thoroughly cowed by the bloody examples made in the beginning of the insurrection. Most of the old Cuban families left Havana after the massacres in 1869 at the Villanueva Theatre and the café of the Louvre.†
The mere suspicion of sympathy with the insurrection at that period was

---

*"Creole" is not an exclusively white category. When touring a slave plantation in chapter 3, O'Kelly remarks that "nearly all the children, are Creoles, with unmistakable evidence of the mixture of white blood in their veins" (37).

†On 22 January 1869, voluntarios stormed the Villanueva Theatre in Havana and killed some ten members of an audience gathered to watch Juan Francisco Valerio's *Perro huevero aunque le quemen el hocico,* a Bufo theater production critical of Spanish rule in Cuba.

sufficient to expose the unfortunate Creoles to the vengeance of the infuriate volunteers. Acts of violence are rare now, because the necessity for them has passed, but the terror and hate they inspired remain. Nothing can exceed the detestation of the Creoles for the Peninsulars, and though the Cubans of the large towns dare not attempt any hostile demonstration against Spanish power without exposing themselves to massacre, in secret they plot to aid the men in arms, and to accomplish the overthrow of the Spanish power. A constant correspondence is maintained between the insurgents and the *laborantes* in Havana and other large cities. The troubles in Spain give the conspirators, or *laborantes,* hope that in the end Spain will be obliged to relax her grasp from sheer exhaustion. This hope enables them to bear with patience the oppressive rule of their Spanish enemies. They are firmly convinced that the triumph of the Cuban cause is assured, "mañana o mañana pasado"—that is, the Spanish tomorrow—sometime in the future. This belief is founded on the successful resistance of the men in the Central and Eastern Departments during the past six years, and the knowledge that thousands of armed Cubans have lately deserted from the Spaniards and joined their patriot brothers in the field. The strength and organization of the volunteer battalions, which are almost wholly made up of Peninsulars, or immigrant Spaniards, render any attempt at insurrection in cities like Havana, Matanzas, Cienfuegos, or Santiago de Cuba a very hazardous experiment. Among a hardier race the effort would be made, but the Creoles of the large towns are wanting in the fierce energy that builds up barricades. The climate and an indolent mode of life have combined to render the Cuban of the city effeminate, and he is certainly no match for the hardy and industrious immigrants who compose the strength of the volunteer battalions. The Peninsulars are chiefly natives of the northern provinces of Spain, and, so far as physical energy and courage are concerned, are perhaps the hardiest and most resolute of the Spanish race. In great part they are made up of the same class of men as we send to the gold fields; bold, unscrupulous, fierce, and energetic men, thirsting to become rich, and not over-scrupulous how they reach their end. These men are supported by the armies and moral aid of Spain, and rule the indolent Creoles with a hand of iron. Though considerably in the minority, even among the white population, their compact organization, and their concentration in the large cities, render them masters of the situation. The Creoles are carefully disarmed in the cities, and a widely spread system of espionage, combined with prompt, and even savage, punishment of suspected treason, holds the Creole population in such terror that organization for revolt within the Spanish lines is well-nigh impossible. It is not, however, so much the fear of death for themselves as the dread of exposing their families to outrage and ruin, that restrains the Cuban, who, though lacking in the stubborn energy of the northern peoples, possesses a latent courage and constancy not surpassed by any race of men. Whoever is conversant with the history of the Cuban struggle cannot doubt this apparently contradictory characteristic. The Creoles are polished in their manners, hospitable, and generally well educated. In this they contrast favorably with the Peninsulars, who, as a class, are generally very ignorant; a fact which renders their rule more galling to the Cubans, who see themselves excluded from all places of honor and profit by the sturdy immigrants, who look on the island as a gold-digger might on his claim, as a place to be exploited for his sole benefit. The white population of the island does not exceed 700,000. Of these about 180,000 are Spanish immigrants, the immense majority of whom are men capable of bearing arms. The remainder of the population is made up of blacks, colored people, slaves, and Chinamen, numbering in all over 600,000. The slaves and "apprenticed" Chinamen are set down, on good authority, at 300,000.* The insurrection has had the effect of concentrating the slave and apprenticed classes principally in the Western Department, which has prospered at the cost of the Central and Eastern Departments, ruined by the war.

In order to understand why it is that the *vomito* and other pestilences are so deadly in Havana, it is only necessary to pass through the streets. When it has not rained for some time the stench is absolutely overpowering, and there are some quarters where even the tropical tempests are unable to purify the atmosphere. Very little effort seems to be made by the *ayuntamiento,* or town council, which is composed of Peninsulars, to promote intelligent measures of sanitary reform. As a result of this indifference, a considerable proportion of the population is swept off every year, the immigrants being the chief sufferers. When the *ayuntamiento* meets two ropes are drawn across the street where the council chamber is situated, to prevent the traffic from disturbing the wiseacres in their deliberations. If we except the sole duty of imposing taxation, I do not see what these people have to do, except, perhaps, to agree among themselves as to the distribution of the pickings. Report says that most of the taxes find their way into the pockets of the councilmen. As there is no public

---

*The 1861–62 census puts the enslaved population at 368,550, and the Asian population at 34,050. See Rebecca J. Scott, *Slave Emancipation in Cuba: The Transition to Free Labor, 1860–1899* (Pittsburgh: University of Pittsburgh Press, 2000): 7.

opinion here, no liberty of the press or of speech except by the will of the authorities, these abuses remain without remedy. The people seem to be content if they are let alone; and, so long as they are not too inquisitive, and confine themselves strictly to their business, the governing classes do not interfere with them.

Unwilling to leave Havana without making another effort to obtain permission from the government to visit the insurgent lines, I wrote the following letter to the Captain-General:

HOTEL SAN CARLOS, December 22, 1872.

TO HIS EXCELLENCY THE CAPTAIN-GENERAL:

YOUR EXCELLENCY,—The gracious reception accorded to me on the occasion of my first interview with your Excellency, and the kindly sentiments you were pleased to express, encourage me to request that you will reconsider your refusal to grant me a safe-conduct, or military pass. In the following letter I propose to submit to your Excellency the reasons that to my mind appear sufficient to justify you in adopting this course. I am deeply sensible of the irritation that the failure of my predecessor on this mission to avail himself of the opportunities and facilities procured for him by your Excellency. Whatever fault has been committed in this connection is the fault of an individual, for which neither myself nor the journal which I represent can be held responsible. Had he fully performed the task which he accepted voluntarily, my presence here would be unnecessary. If, therefore, your Excellency has reason to be discontented, Mr. Bennett also has reason for dissatisfaction. The object of my visit, as explained to me by Mr. Bennett, is to examine, without prejudice or partiality, into the state of the insurrection, and through the columns of the HERALD to make known to the world whether the statements put forward by the Spanish authorities, or those advanced by the insurgents, represent more accurately the existing state of affairs. For this purpose, and in order to present fairly both sides of the question, I have been instructed to visit the insurgent camps as well as the Spanish lines. In order to be able to do this with greater facility, I have applied to your Excellency for such protection as would prevent the minor officials throwing obstacles in my way, or the Spanish outposts stopping my free passage through the disturbed districts; in fact, such a recognition of my position as a neutral as would prevent my being mistaken for an emissary of the insurgents in case I should encounter outlying parties of the Spanish troops.

Belonging to a people by whom the remembrance of old alliances with Spain is still warmly cherished, I claim to be free from the prejudices that are too often entertained by northern peoples against the Spanish nation; and I have come here in the full confidence that I shall have to deal with brave and honorable men.* There is, in my mind, no fear that any Spanish soldier will degrade himself by becoming an assassin, and I comprehend fully your sensitiveness lest some unforeseen accident should lay the Spanish cause open to the suspicion of being stained by what would be a crime against civilization.

For myself, while comprehending and appreciating your caution in declining to expose yourself to the danger of misconception, I cannot accept the justness of your deductions. Availing myself of the express permission you assured me would be given to my passing freely through the island at my own risk, I will endeavor, by favor of that permission, to carry out the mission which I accepted in New York, even should the special protection which I seek be refused me. Should the event—which you foresee as among the contingencies of that mission—unfortunately befall me, then, indeed, the authorities are more likely to be censured for not having granted the facilities of the case, and for having, by this refusal of a safe-conduct, given my undertaking an appearance of hostility, which, in reality, is foreign to it. I would not have dwelt on a question that, after all, is of so strictly personal a nature, but for the emphasis your Excellency laid on this point during our interview.

The broader and more important considerations which must influence your Excellency's final decision are those which touch the honor and the interest of Spain.

It is impossible to ignore the fact that the civilized world desires to know how it happens that an insurrection, which the Spanish authorities proclaim to be of no importance, continues unsuppressed after four years of armed conflict. If, as we have been assured, the insurrection has been reduced to the last extremity, and has no longer the sympathy of any large class of this community, it is for the interest of Spain that the representative of an independent and neutral journal should be able to place before the world an unbiased statement of the Cuban question. The insurgents, through their sympathizers in New York, have already promised to the HERALD correspondent every protection and facility once he enters their lines; and if the Spanish authorities refuse, on their part, to allow the examination to be made, or if they throw obstacles in the way, universal public opinion will argue that they have some interested motive for the adoption of such a course. The fact that my predecessor, through fear of assassination or of the *vomito,* abandoned his post, will not be accepted as

---

*Here O'Kelly refers to historical alliances between Ireland and Spain. See Ortiz's prologue, 217–18, 229–32.

sufficient explanation, in view of the fact that one of the editors of the *Herald* has presented himself to take the abandoned post.

For myself I have but one desire, and that is to fulfill honorably the mission intrusted to me. I wish to leave no effort untried to obtain all the assistance and information that will help me to form a correct judgment before I record it. If the authorities, by the appearance of discouraging my mission, prevent me from obtaining that full and broad view of the situation which it is my wish and aim to obtain, they must not blame me if my conclusions and deductions become partial from the want of that very information which they refuse me the facilities to acquire. Before my departure from New York, a telegram was received by Mr. Bennett from Admiral Polo, the Spanish Minister at Washington, promising that he would use his good offices with your Excellency to procure for me the assistance of the authorities in Cuba.

Requesting the honor of an early reply, I beg to subscribe myself your Excellency's obedient servant,

JAMES J. O'KELLY

THE CAPTAIN GENERAL'S REPLY

HAVANA, December 24, 1872

SR. DON JAMES J. O'KELLY:

DEAR SIR,—I have received your polite letter which you have been pleased to direct under date of the 22d instant, inviting me to reconsider the causes which hinder me from granting you a safe-conduct to visit the enemy's camp, which you solicited in the interview which I had the pleasure to concede to you. It is easy to understand how pertinent these reasons must appear to me when they overcome my desire to grant your wishes.

As you remark opportunely in your letter, this is an affair of a personal nature, and easily granted. For this reason, independent governments and their legitimate representatives deny or concede permission to go and remain in the enemy's camp—a thing against the established practices of war—but, what is much more generally observed and regular, to permit, in their own army, the presence of foreigners with a private or official character. The denial, when it is given, does not give cause for unfavorable interpretations, as you state in your letter; because, then, the government of the United States would not have denied its permission, as it did in the last civil war, to Spanish officers to visit the Federal camps, when solicited by the representative of the Spanish nation in Washington. It was not then the object to go to the Confederate camps to declare to the world if the generals and Confederate authorities circulated false reports, or if their assertions were worthy of credit, as you say you pretend to do in respect to us, by order of the proprietor of the NEW YORK HERALD, but solely to study professionally the interesting incidents of that war.

Such pretensions, so clearly manifested, cannot by any means be assented to by the first authority in this island; nor can he sanction so offensive and unfounded a doubt.

The pretensions of your predecessor were less absolute; and therefore I granted him the permission to accompany our columns, and even to visit some of the rebel bands, as he did in one of the two departments not yet pacified. But for motives which he undoubtedly understands, the attentions he was the object of as a guest, and the subject of a friendly government, he thought himself in danger when he enjoyed the most perfect security, under the banner of Spain; and this belief appears to be sufficient cause to excite public opinion against the authorities and respectable corporations, attributing to them the intention to exercise over his conduct and opinions a reprehensible pressure. What would it have been if he had fallen a victim to the undisciplined hordes to which to-day the insurrection is reduced; or if, in some encounter, a Spanish soldier had not recognized him as a pacific and neutral person? Fortunately, he finds himself in his own country, and he can say what he ought to or wishes; but a second rehearsal cannot be permitted, nor your unusual pretensions; nor, admitting your good faith, the species of violence which, apparently, you intend to exercise, judging from some of the paragraphs of your letter, as, in Spain, whatever has the air of intimidation cannot be tolerated.

As I have already had the pleasure to tell you verbally, you will be furnished with an ordinary passport to travel throughout the island, as could be done by any Spanish subject or stranger; and be assured that you will not be molested, nor will your trip be fruitless, as in our towns you can acquire news relating to the insurrection by consulting the thousands of the surrendered, who fight in our ranks or live quietly in their homes, pardoned by the Spanish government. Any other course you adopt must be understood to be at your own risk.

I have had the satisfaction to answer your letter; but this condescension I could not repeat, because you already must understand that it is not customary that the authorities explain to private individuals, respectable as they may be, the motives of their conduct or the foundation of their opinions.

I am your attentive servitor,

FRANCISCO DE CEBALLOS.

2   Cuban Travel

THE LETTER of the Captain-General dissipated all hopes of being able to carry out amicably my mission. It was now evident that every difficulty would be thrown in my way, and the prospect was not at all cheering. It was not possible to turn back without dishonor, and, though it should cost even life itself, I would have to visit the Cuban camp, learn the state of the Mambi-Land, and see Cespedes, or, if dead, as reported by the Spaniards, his successor.

My word had been given to accomplish this, and, at whatever cost, it should be done. I had counted on being able to convince the authorities that advantages would accrue to Spain by the true state of the insurrection being made known by an independent and impartial witness, but their insensate pride rendered reasoning impossible, and forced me from the outset into a position of hostility to the government of the "Ever-Faithful Isle." At the time of my arrival in Cuba my knowledge of the people and the island was imperfect and crude, as is common in the outside world.

The pictures of the struggle, and of the men who have sustained it, persistently drawn by the Spanish press, had made that impression on me which statements constantly repeated and apparently well founded never fail to make, even on the most thoughtful and cautious minds. It had not occurred to me that a system of persistent misrepresentation was relied on by the Spanish party as the most effective way to deprive the Cubans of all outside sympathy. It appeared to me that not only would the authorities be willing but eager to have the truth made known by a witness whose impartiality could not be affected by partisan feeling. But this supposition proved unsound, and, instead of aid and encouragement, I encountered suspicion and hostility, and every obstacle was thrown in the way of a successful accomplishment of my mission. The foreign residents, and even many Cubans, advised me, with provoking unanimity, to abandon the enterprise as impracticable. It is not cheering at the outset of an undertaking to be assured by everyone whose opinion merits attention, that failure is inevitable, and that the road to be pursued leads to death. The many unavoidable dangers which would attend an attempt to penetrate the Cuban lines were recited with Munchausen-like exaggeration, until the dreadful stories told on every hand made me feel really uncomfortable about the probable issue of my undertaking. The pictures drawn were so black and hideous, that the surrounding civilization seemed all a sham, and the inhabitants cannibals masquerading in more or less civilized costume. Respectable men assured me that not alone was my life in danger from the *Negros Sueltos,* or Cuban Swamp Angels, and brigands who infest the roads, but that even the soldiers and officers of the contending parties would not hesitate to dispose of me in order to rob me.*

The universality of this opinion most astonished me. No distinction among parties was made, and men holding Spanish commissions have warned me on no account to trust myself with a small detachment of Spanish troops, unless specially recommended to the commander by the superior authorities. The opinion was general that if I ventured with a small squad I would be murdered on the road, as a ready excuse would be found by alleging that the party had been attacked, and the *Herald* correspondent killed by accident.

Now, without attaching too much importance to these exaggerated statements, it was impossible not to be somewhat influenced by their constant reiteration. Still, as there was no means of abandoning honorably the enterprise, it was necessary to make the best of a bad position, and go on at all hazards, trusting to the chapter of accidents to come out successful. In order to obtain a thorough acquaintance with the country and the people, and at the same time acquire by personal observation exact knowledge of the condition of the insurrection, I resolved, if it were possible, to go down through the center of the island, so as to encounter Agramonte.† It was evident that no trust whatever could be placed on the reports or circumstantial accounts of the inhabitants, whose Oriental imagination led them to exaggerate, often unconsciously, every fact

---

*Readers may be surprised by O'Kelly's odd translation of "negros sueltos" as "Cuban Swamp Angels" rather than "runaway slaves." O'Kelly may be likening the mambises to members of North Carolina's infamous Lowry gang, dubbed the "Swamp Angels" by the *Herald* (see, for example, *NYH* 5 Jan. 1873, 6). The gang, comprised mainly of African Americans and Native Americans and led by Henry Berry Lowry, began a guerilla war in 1864 to resist conscription, enforced labor, and intimidation by the Confederate Army. The gang operated until 1872, targeting members of the white upper class and postwar white supremacist power structures.

†Key figure in the Ten Years' War, Ignacio Agramonte y Loynáz (1841–73) was, by O'Kelly's arrival, major general of the Cuban forces of Camagüey. He served briefly as secretary of the Cuban Congress but resigned in 1869 due to clashes with Céspedes. Agramonte was killed at the battle of Jimaguayú on 11 May 1873, whereupon Máximo Gomez took his place as commander of the central troops.

connected with the insurrection. Sometimes only half the truth was told, at others most ingenious stories and theories were invented to bias my judgment. Fortunately, both Spaniard and Cuban carried exaggeration so far that almost from the moment I set foot in the "Ever-Faithful Isle," my suspicion was aroused, and I resolved to advance nothing on the faith of what others told me. It was the more necessary to exercise caution, because the Spanish party were strongly convinced that my mission to Cuba was not so much to throw light on the state of the insurrection, as to injure Spain in the public opinion of the world, by distorting the evils of the situation, and so afford an excuse for the interference of foreign powers in the affairs of the island. It was vain on my part to disclaim any such intention. With a simplicity quite charming, all classes of Spaniards were fully persuaded that the New York *Herald* was the obedient instrument and mouthpiece of the Cuban *laborantes* in the United States. It would be illiberal to blame too severely this mistaken notion, because these people have not the slightest conception of what is meant by "Free Press" and "Independent Journalism," and they think a newspaper must of necessity be the organ of some party. The extremely sharp people saw in the *Herald* correspondent a secret agent of the United States government. It was useless to decline the great honor sought to be thrust upon me, and in despair I abandoned the effort, and allowed the clever people to imagine me a relation of his Majesty the Brother to the Sun if so disposed. If this mistaken notion created deeper suspicion and more marked dislikes, it probably had its counterbalancing advantages by casting over me in some sort the shadow of Columbia's giant shield.

When the Captain-General finally announced his decision not to aid or allow me to pass to the insurgent lines, I endeavored to discover the much-talked-about *laborantes*, to try if they would not help me to pass the frontiers of Cuba Libre. It was difficult and very delicate work approaching these people, who lived in daily terror of discovery by the authorities. The slightest proof of treasonable correspondence would ensure their summary execution; but one or two ventured to see me; they confined themselves, however, to throwing out vague hints, which left me in exactly the same state of uncertainty as before. Nothing was to be gained by staying in Havana, so I applied for a *cedula*, or permission to travel. An unexpected difficulty arose. It was Christmastide, and the government employés gave themselves holidays, so I was obliged to wait their good pleasure for several days. On the expiration of the time named, I again applied to the Consul-General for my papers, but was informed that the police authorities would sign no papers for four days longer. This was too much for my patience, so I told the Consul-General that if he would kindly *visé* my passport, I would go on without waiting for the *cedula*. He advised me not to adopt this course; but, as I was resolved, he returned my passport with his *visé*. And next morning saw me on the way to the Mambi-Land.

Ten minutes before six A.M. a small ferryboat, built on the American plan, left the pier close to the San Carlos Hotel, and in a few minutes deposited her passengers on the western side of the harbor, close to a long, low, brick building. This was the railway station. In the five minutes occupied in the passage across, I had ample opportunity to note the features of the strange scene. The cabin was lighted by lamps that threw a faint and sickly light over the passengers, who were of many races and colors. There were planters and their slaves, shrewd businessmen, and curious travelers, jumbled together, and all forming a strange, weird picture under the flickering light of the oil-lamps. For the most part the negroes and Chinese carried with them bundles, which probably contained all their worldly goods. They appeared to be wretched beings, ignorant and degraded to the last degree, without a spark of that manly independence which is so marked a feature of the working classes in free countries. A few favored coolie servants preserved their appearance as rational beings; but the field hands furnished evidence in their persons of the brutalizing influence of slavery in its worst forms. The colored men on board the little ferryboat were the first specimens of plantation slaves I had seen, and the impression they made on my mind was very unfavorable to the system—an impression further acquaintance with this sad subject intensified.

As we moved slowly out of the plain but neat little station, the morning sun was smiling through dark, drifting clouds. The air was raw and somewhat chill, and it seemed as if Dame Nature had not quite made up her mind whether or not she would weep through the morning as she had done through the night. But, in the end, old Sol coaxed her to dry up her tears, and the dark shadows which obscured the fair face of day were swept slowly across the sky, to give place to light, vaporous clouds, bathed in brilliant sunlight. Gradually the dark masses faded into gray, then melted into silver, tinged, at intervals, with roseate hues, or a sudden burst of sunlight changed the pale gray of the silver clouds, as by touch of a fairy wand, into one vast expanse of golden waste, fringed by dark, threatening, cumulus clouds, lurid red, like evil giants frowning at the loveliness and beauty of the scene which God had prepared for man.

In the warm, mellow sunlight of a tropical clime, the green of the waving trees refreshed by night tears, and new-bathed in the morning dew, acquired intense brilliancy, and the crystal drops, still nestling on the leaves, sparkled like diamonds in the sun. It was Sunday, and the fair scene was not disfigured by the presence of a slave. It was nature in all her bountiful magnificence, freed from the dark shadow of grasping and cruel man. In the distance, the dark forms of the trees that fringe the fields seemed like huge sentinels keeping watch and ward over the harvest. Could I for a moment have forgotten that these fields of waving verdure had been made fruitful by the tears of men, and the sweat and blood wrung from human beings under the cruel lash of relentless taskmasters, I would have experienced greater pleasure in contemplating the wondrous fertility of this land of perennial growth. Seasons can scarcely be said to exist, for while the cultivator cuts down one crop another is springing up from the ever-fruitful earth. Over such a land one might be pardoned for growing enthusiastic, and certainly the patriots are right in thinking it well worth fighting for.

So the ever-changing beauties of the sky continued as we swept onward in the track of the iron dragon, that puffed and snorted as though he would annihilate space. On either side of the track groves of palm-trees rose gracefully from the green cane-fields; groups of *bohios,* or native huts, with their thatch of palm-leaf, dotted the country, and lent picturesqueness and interest to the scene. Their position was, generally, happily chosen, down in glades and valleys, in small patches of cultivation, where the banana and a little corn seemed to be almost the only crops grown. These were the houses of the natives, who, philosophers in their way, think it better to enjoy life than to die rich. Hence they prefer cock-fighting to the labors of the field, and so long as their immediate wants are supplied care little how the world wags. Generous, good-natured, and improvident, they are true sons of this glorious land, where open-handed nature would shame a niggard race. Some moralists would persuade us that man was made to labor and to weep, but the Cuban thinks he was destined to be idle and to laugh. For my own part, I think the Cuban is right; and it must have struck most people that the men who preach about the duty of labor avoid hard work as much as possible.

At all the railway stations we met groups of wretched-looking negroes and Chinamen. It was difficult to make out what they were about, as they seemed to have no definite business. The puzzle was soon solved by a fellow passenger, who informed me that, as it was Sunday, the negroes and coolies were permitted to attend at the station, in the hope of earning a few cents by carrying passengers' luggage, if the chance should occur.

A more important feature of the journey was the appearance at every station of two soldiers of the *guardia civil,* who passed through the train, looking after suspicious persons. Colored people and coolies were constantly compelled to exhibit their permit to travel; and, in several cases, men were arrested on account of some irregularity in their papers. Nor were the white passengers altogether free from molestation, though the attention of the authorities was due, in their case, to political rather than social causes. My appearance was evidently considered peaceful, and no questions were asked me. A young man seated near me, evidently a Cuban, did not escape so well; he was reading, and this circumstance, no doubt, marked him for suspicion. In Cuba, a man who reads is held to be dangerous, and authority keeps its eye upon him. In the present case, however, there was nothing in a book. The *guardia civil* examined carefully the young man's *cedula,* and finding it was all right on one side, turned the other for examination, at the same time scrutinizing closely the suspected person. At last, to my great relief, the *cedula* was handed back without comment, and the soldier left the car. No one spoke to, or went near, the young man after this occurrence, nor was there made openly the slightest remark. Some of the passengers looked at one another, as if to invite some reference to the incident, but no one ventured to speak. After a good run of four hours we arrived at Matanzas, where the train stopped half an hour to enable the passengers to breakfast. In a *fonda,* or native hotel, close to the station, a really good breakfast was provided, and the neatness and promptitude of the service contrasted favorably with the discomfort of American and European railway restaurants.

Leaving Matanzas, the line of railway sweeps into the interior, and for some time we passed through valleys of circular formation, bounded by low hills. As we advanced these hills decreased in elevation, and finally seemed to be swallowed up by the plain. The fertility of the land increased at every league, and patches of forest were no longer met with in proximity to the railway. On either hand extended fields of sugar-cane—vast expanses of waving verdure, broken only by the noble form of some lonely palm tree, which seemed to nod its tufted head in response to the obsequious bowing and flutter of its lowly but graceful companions of the field. It would be futile to attempt with words to paint to the eye of the imagination the scenic beauties, the gorgeous color, the wealth of form, that passed in panorama before me.

Bomba, the point of junction for the lines of Cardenas and Matanzas, is situated in the midst of this beautiful country. Here the train delayed an hour, and there was time and ample opportunity to observe the motley crowd gathered on the platform. It was composed of men of all nations, and formed a pretty fair representation of the population. The majority was made up of negroes, coolies, and soldiers. It is astonishing how many of the latter class are to be seen. Wherever one turns a uniform looms in sight. Most of them seem to be going on a campaign, and many bear traces of former hostilities; still, they look game, but no doubt most of them are sighing for the time when they will go back to *La Vieja España*—if ever, which in most cases is doubtful. It is impossible to avoid thinking how much better it would be if these strong fellows would turn their machetes to peaceful uses, instead of hacking human creatures to pieces. But so long as the Spanish people can be persuaded that patriotism demands the holding of Cuba against the wishes of the population, and the maintenance of the slave-master's power, it is idle to hope for peace. The Spanish immigrants, hardy, industrious, and brave, but ignorant and fanatical, look on the Cubans with suspicion and contempt. In the large towns the Creole population is certainly physically inferior to the hard-working immigrants, and seem to lack the decision and vigor of character of the Peninsulars. The cause of physical degeneration among the Creoles is not due so much to climatic influence as to the neglect of athletic exercises, and the abandonment of the ruder labors to the colored races. Slavery has degraded labor and made it distasteful, but there is no foundation for the idea popularly entertained that white men cannot work in this climate. Athletic sports are not patronized by the people, who prefer to amuse themselves in the bullring, the concert, and the ballroom. As a result, their bodies have lost the rude strength which only labor, or manly exercise, can retain among a people.

    The negroes form the hardiest and most vigorous part of the population. Even brutal treatment, and insufficient nourishment, seem incapable of breaking down their iron constitutions. Exposed to the heat of the sun and to the inclemency of the weather, their happy nature lifts them above their misfortunes. The free colored people avoid field labor, and are to be found in the towns employed in many trades, but chiefly as coachmen, postilions, and servants. They exhibit the same fondness for dress and display for which they are noted in the United States. They appear to be quiet and orderly members of the community. From the moment we left Bomba until we reached Alvarez, a little *pueblo* on the edge of an extensive forest, the only incident worthy of note was the passage through a new town which had been christened Colon, after the great discoverer of America. It is a neat and prosperous-looking place, resembling so strongly an American town that I was at first inclined to think it was an American colony. Most of the houses are constructed of wood, with verandas in the

American style, but many of the buildings are of stone. Two important structures in course of erection particularly attracted my attention, and on inquiry I found they were the Governor's house and the barracks. This showed me at once that it was only American in outward appearance, for had the spirit of our republican institutions penetrated the community, they would have built a schoolhouse instead of a barracks. It is deserving of remark that during my traveling in Cuba I saw no traces of anything which could claim to be a public school, in the American sense. The few claimants to the distinction of being schools are simply places where children receive only an elementary education.

Nothing is more noticeable to an American than the complete absence of books in the houses. It is only in the very best houses that even a small collection of works can be found, and, except in very rare cases, these collections have not the slightest pretension to be called a library. Anxious to get a glimpse into the mode of thought of the people as seen in their songs, I endeavored to obtain a small volume of Cuban melodies, but to my surprise no collection of national songs existed. There were a few published in sheets, but this was all.

Soon after we left the promising town of Colon behind the character of the country began to change. The soil appeared less rich and less carefully cultivated. The *fincas* no longer extended to the horizon, and the clustering *bohios,* with their groves of banana and patches of sugarcane and corn, came once more prominently into view. The country gradually became more wooded, until we reached Alvarez, which is situated on the edge of a forest and within the region of hostilities. Up to this point the *guardia civil* had performed the duty of gendarmes, and were neatly and tidily dressed in their holiday suits. They were in all cases armed with the machete, a kind of cutlass peculiar to cane-growing countries; and I had become so used to their visits that they excited no more attention. The train had stopped a few minutes, and I had satisfied myself that there was nothing to be seen, when, suddenly, my attention was attracted by a heavy tramping, and a tremendous clanging of spurs and ringing of sabre; my first impression was that the *commandatore* from the opera had broken loose, and was practicing his awful stride in a moment of forgetfulness. As the noise came closer, I ventured to look around, and just at my elbow was a soldier, with rifle-carbine at the support, sabre at his side, and *cartouchière* filled with cartridges, booted, spurred, mustached, and, in fact, looking generally grim and ferocious. He spoke not a word, but scanned carefully the faces of the passengers; arriving at the end of the car, and finding no fit subject for ball-practice, he turned on his heel and strode out in the same silent and terrible manner in which he came in. When that apparition of an old ironsides was gone, I experienced a feeling of relief, for he looked like a person that would shoot on the slightest provocation. It required no ghost to tell me the signification of the sudden change in the equipment and manner of our soldier visitor, and I was not astonished in the least when a communicative neighbor informed me deprecatingly that there were *algunos partidos* about. On consulting an excellent map of Cuba, published in 1869, I found that in that year this very point marked the limit of the Cuban insurrection; so that, after six years of war, waged, as the Spaniards assure us, with success, the insurrection covers the same ground, though in this district it has certainly diminished in power. It was strange, however, to find it covering the exact ground it did six years ago. This was the very information I proposed to gain in passing through the center of the island. The Spaniards claim to have reduced the Cinco Villas to order, and, so far as holding possession of the towns and dispersing the larger bands, they have done so; but many small detachments still hold their ground, and nothing like the security which we look for in a civilized country in a state of peace exists. The insurrection never obtained control of this department, because the nature of the country is unfavorable to the only mode of war which the Cubans can successfully practice against the better armed and disciplined troops of Spain. The bands have, therefore, been exposed to more difficulties, and have not been able to assume the proportions reached in the Central Department; but they are sufficiently numerous to make traveling unsafe, and to render it necessary for Spain to garrison every little point at all exposed to attack. However small the number of these partisans may be, they render considerable service to the cause of the insurrection, by making it impossible for the Spanish troops to concentrate their whole strength in the Central and Oriental Departments.

We found the station at St. Domingo, where the line of railway on which we had traveled terminated, filled with a curious throng, that embarrassed the free movement of the passengers, who were engaged in frantic efforts to buy tickets and obtain possession of their luggage in order to reship it for Las Cruces. With a view to augmenting the confusion, the officials refused to take the paper currency of the country, and such as were unprovided with *plata,* or coin, were engaged making frantic appeals to the clerks to charge the difference, and not cause the unfortunates to lose the train. In most cases this was done, but not until the officials made the mere public understand how much they owed to the "condescension" of their lords and masters—the railway clerks. The same farce was renewed at Las Cruces, where we were again obliged to have our luggage transferred, and, of course, had to pay the clerk a consideration for his goodness. The railway cannot derive a revenue from this reshipping of luggage much in excess of the salary of the officials charged with the bureau, and to my mind the only reason for its existence is to force the passengers to submit to petty annoyances and vexation of spirit, all for the good of their souls or otherwise. At last, when the shadows of evening were closing rapidly over the way, we reached Esperanza, a village next to Villa Clara; but what it was like could not be made out through the gloom that surrounded us. It was a name of good augury; conferred, no doubt, by some unhappy swain who had been doomed to make this long and wearisome journey. Night comes so rapidly in these climes, that, though we stand in the shadow of night, the distant horizon is still lighted with the gorgeous hues of the setting sun.

In my experiences of many lands, I have never seen anything more beautiful than the scene between Esperanza and Villa Clara. In its characteristics it was Eastern. In the distance the sun had dipped beyond the horizon; but the clouds were still bathed in his golden beams, the sky looking like a field of molten gold, with just the suspicion of a crimson tinge permeating it. Light drifts of dark clouds, the forerunners of the night, barred the yellow of the firmament, and strove to eclipse its glory, while the heavy masses of dark-purple clouds, tinged at their edges crimson red, flushed with the conflict and victory over day, marched on irresistible. In the fading light, the tall and graceful forms of the tufted palms looked like the spirits of past ages watching sadly over scenes of former glory. Except the puffing of the engine and the monotonous whirl of the wheels along the iron rails, the silence was unbroken; for the few passengers who remained were tired out and reposed half-somnolent on their seats, so the spectacle could be enjoyed without interruption from prattling companions; the desolation of the landscape being only broken by the solitary palms, for all other objects had become confounded with the earth in the night-gloom. The richness and glow of the sky recalled the Orient lands, and it required little effort to fill the voids with the ruins of cities of the past; unconsciously I was engaged in this work of construction, when the train stopped with a shock, and my neighbor, starting up, exclaimed, "Ya estamos en Villa Clara."

3 Slavery

WHEN THE train at Villa Clara came to a stand-still, with a shock that recalled me from the contemplation of past glories to the necessity of attending to such vulgar cares as the safety of one's baggage involves, I found myself set down on the outskirts of what appeared in the starless night a large village. A small crowd of irrepressible *muchachos* were gathered at the station, waiting, like so many jackals, to pounce on the passengers' luggage. After a good deal of pushing and elbowing and shouting, the pack was driven off; and my worldly goods intrusted to the care of a pair of strong urchins, each one of whom, in his greed, desired to hold sole control, although together they found it difficult enough to convey my camp equipage to the hotel to which a fellow-passenger had recommended me. It was situated in the center of the town, for, as soon as the first palm-covered huts were passed, a comparatively well-built and pleasant little town, boasting of gas-lamps and sidewalks, the latter frightfully irregular and more dangerous than convenient, presented itself. The hotel, like all hotels in this country, was rather a *fonda,* or inn; but the love of high-sounding names is so engrafted on Spanish human nature, that it is proof against the arrows of ridicule. Owing to the perfect indifference to the comfort of their passengers exhibited by the railway officials, it had been impossible to procure anything to eat from early morning, so my first care was for dinner. The proprietor was engaged playing billiards, but heroically left the game to attend on his guest. Some pointed questions relative to the plantations of the neighborhood aroused the fellow's curiosity; and being a captain, or general, or something of the sort, of volunteers, he tried to worm out of me my business, and what my motives were for visiting the island. When he had tired himself asking questions, he was convinced that his guest was a young man with plenty of money and a laudable ambition for nigger-driving. Under this impression his heart opened, and he professed himself my very devoted servitor.

Horses and a good guide were ordered to be in waiting next morning, *muy temprano,* to conduct me to the principal *finca,* or plantation, of the neighborhood. The *muchacho* of the hotel awoke me before the sun had well risen to take my coffee; this duty performed, I prepared for the road. The horse brought for my use was a small native animal, rather restive, but, as I found afterwards, good to go. From the manner he conducted himself, I am under the impression that he was a Mambi to the core, and, mistaking me for a Spaniard, endeavored to get rid of me. Finding the plunging business would not do, he tried what a sharp run along the road would effect, but at last gave up, and conducted himself in a somewhat reasonable way. Rain had fallen for many days, and the roads were in a wretched condition. We had scarcely crossed a picturesque old stone bridge that spans a deep gully, at the bottom of which flows a stream of water that the natives dignify with the name of a river, when we found ourselves navigating through puddles and stretches of morass, in which we frequently sunk almost to the saddle-girths. For a few hundred yards the ground, though muddy, was somewhat level; but we had not been riding a quarter of an hour when a morass, stretching away across the road, blocked further progress. I was obliged to pull up while the guide went forward carefully, as if sounding a ford, to find a reasonably convenient passage. After a good deal of splashing about, he made his way across without sinking any deeper than his horse's knees—an achievement which I had the good luck to imitate successfully. Bad as this passage was, it was by no means the worst, as before long we were obliged to quit the roads and ride in the bush, or in the fields skirting the highway. We had been dodging about in this way for about three-quarters of an hour, now on firm land, now traversing pools of water, and sometimes tumbling into holes in the most unexpected localities, and only escaping broken necks by keeping a sharp look-out and a tight rein. One of these obstructions had delayed me an unusual length of time behind my guide, whom I always allowed to be well ahead of me, when an accident occurred that was nearly putting me *hors de combat*. My guide was a taciturn old soldier, who never condescended to speak unless addressed, and then he replied with military precision and brevity. I do not think that he once turned his head to see whether or not I had succeeded in following him through the maze of sheep-tracks, bushes, pools of water, and mud-holes through which he led me. In setting out, I had ruffled his temper by insisting on shortening my stirrups, and riding cross-country style, much to his disgust—the Cuban mode being to have the stirrup-leather long, and the toe pointing gracefully to the ground like a thirteenth-century swell. I had soon, however, reason to be thankful for my obstinacy.

The guide had ridden far ahead. After passing one of the many morasses, in order to regain on him, I struck spurs into my horse. At first the animal was inclined to dispute my authority, but having given expression to his feelings in a few vicious plunges, he rushed off at a good pace. A sudden turn in the track, which passed at this point along a field, brought us into very broken ground, and I had only time to gather up my reins when the horse stumbled, and, in spite of my efforts to hold him up, went down head foremost. Fortunately, I came down on my feet, but before I could completely free myself he rolled over, crushing my leg but very slightly. The softness of the ground had saved both myself and the horse from any serious injury, so I remounted and joined the guide, who had chanced to look back just as my horse fell, but had not stirred one inch. When I rode up, he asked, in a perfectly cool and unmoved manner, "Ha V. recibido daño?" Assured in terms equally brief that I had not hurt myself, he relapsed into silence, that was not broken until he reached the outer gate of the plantation to which we were bound. We entered without any ceremony, riding up to a large mass of buildings standing almost in the center of the plantation, which extended for miles on every side. Here we were fortunate enough to find all the superior officials at breakfast, in the shadow of a great shed which protects the machinery from the weather. It was delightfully cool, as the shed was open on all sides, allowing the air free passage without creating any perceptible draft. The usual invitation to partake, which is always tendered by the Spanish race to whoever enters when they are at their meals, having been declined on the ground that we had already eaten, the object of my visit was explained to the *mayor-domo,* who expressed himself delighted at the chance of being of some service. While waiting for the meal to be over, I had an excellent opportunity to notice the dozen or so of slave-drivers who were gathered around the table. For the most part they were vigorous, semi-military looking men, with faces indicating sternness. With one or two exceptions, there was nothing strikingly brutal in the expression of their faces, while in some instances there was an open frankness about their look that consorted badly with the vile profession of the men. They were seated around a large deal table, on which a number of dishes of the country were placed, and the rough plentifulness of the board reminded one of feudal times. For the most part these men were rudely clad, and, in some cases, their linen was not remarkable for its cleanliness. Nearly all were travel-stained, having sat down to the table as they arrived from the fields. In spite of the roughness of their exterior, there reigned, however, among them all the polished courtesy of the old *régime*. It was amusing to watch the punctilious attention paid to each other by this somewhat rude looking group—rugged in feature, coarse in attire, but with the innate refinement of the Latin races, which not even the barbarous habit of thought engendered by slavery could wholly eradicate. Booted and spurred, with the formidable machete hanging at their sides, these men looked like beings called back from the barbarous days of chivalry by some magician's wand to contrast with modern ideas and progress, as seen in the complicated machinery in whose shadow they were breakfasting.* There was something so opposed to the spirit of liberty and thirsting after progress and justice which distinguishes the nineteenth century in this scene, that I am not sure that I did not pinch myself, just to be certain I was not dreaming.

As soon as breakfast was concluded, the director of the plantation ordered one of the black slaves in attendance to saddle his horse, and in a few moments we were jogging through the grounds, which were divided by well laid out roads to facilitate the conveyance of the cane to the mill. Our first visit was made to the buildings used by the slaves. In the distance, raised up on piles, were what appeared to me huts, but on closer inspection they were discovered to be small and unfit for human habitation. These were the storehouses in which the slaves were permitted to keep whatever corn they raised in the patches of land set apart for their use. Underneath each hut were sties occupied by pigs of various sizes and conditions. These animals were "bought" by the plantation for the maintenance of the employés. The use of the word "buy" in the transaction must, however, be looked on as a euphuism. A purchase of this nature was made in my presence, in this wise: One of the superintendents of the estate called out a woman's name. Almost immediately a wretched-looking creature advanced to where the superintendent was standing, and, taking up a position of absolute subservience, with head bowed and eyes cast down, awaited in silence the further wishes of the superior being before whom in spirit she was prostrated. She had not long to wait. A pig was wanted; she had one ready to be killed; it was to be delivered up, and, in return, she would receive two dollars. The poor creature curtsied awkwardly, mumbled an assent, and the "purchase" was completed. Not far from those houses we came upon an open shed, on two of its sides were placed narrow planks, on which a couple of old negro women were busy placing a number of tin platters, each one filled

---

*O'Kelly remarks here on the "complicated machinery" used in Cuban sugar production. Cuban planters had fully mechanized sugar mills well ahead of their counterparts in the US South. By the mid-nineteenth century, Cuba was the largest supplier of sugar to the US market, and overall production reached nearly one quarter of global supply. See Anthony E. Kaye, "The Second Slavery: Modernity in the Nineteenth-Century South and the Atlantic World," *Journal of Southern History*, 75.3 (2009): 627–50.

with what appeared to me boiled maize. This was the breakfast of the slaves, who leave the fields at eleven o'clock. There was no sign of spoons, and it is reasonable to suppose the mode of disposing of the boiled corn was the same as that adopted by a number of naked urchins, who were busy in the kitchen diving into the pots, when, much to their disgust and confusion, we appeared on the scene. They were engaged kicking up a jolly row over their feast, evidently not caring a straw for the old women, when the shadow of the superintendent was cast in front of the shed. Suddenly the noise ceased, and the little ones crept stealthily away, until the voice of the man of power riveted them to the spot. An authoritative "Ven aqui!" brought a few of the young scamps to us. The poor children looked frightfully guilty, as if to eat corn out of a pot were a crime deserving very severe punishment; so they shambled towards us, too much afraid not to come, but not at all certain of the kind of reception that awaited them. For the most part they were fine, healthy children, and, in spite of the horribly degrading influences by which they were surrounded, bright and intelligent looking; quite as much so as white children under similar circumstances would have been. There was only one lesson taught them, and, young as they were, they already knew it by heart. It was not to be good or virtuous or honest, but to fear and obey the master, if they would avoid the whip. There was something irresistibly comic in the expression of those faces, smeared with the corn, which they had eaten out of their hands; for their spirits, though bent, were not yet broken by the knowledge of their abject and hopeless condition. Dismissed by a wave of the hand, the troop of youngsters disappeared with alacrity, and we pursued our way to the sleeping-quarters of the slaves. There were on the estate one hundred and fifty human chattels, including some twenty children. The greater number were men, most of them natives of Congo, one only being a coolie, who, contrary to the representations made about the traffic in Asiatics, was treated in every respect in the same way as his sable companions in misfortune.

The sleeping-quarter of the slaves is a low, square structure, entered on the side facing the mills by a gateway which leads to a large courtyard, or open space, around which the sleeping-rooms are placed. It is a one-storied structure, divided into five apartments—two small and three large—which were occupied in common. Nominally the females occupied different apartments, but as there was free intercommunication, and no recognition of the marital relation, the state of morality can be imagined. At night all the slaves are locked in this building, and an armed guard mounts sentry to see that none escape.

In my character of nigger-whipper *in prospectu,* all these details were treated in an exhaustive manner. The organization of the slave system is admirably adapted to give the largest possible amount of labor at the smallest possible cost. If the aim of existence were to obtain the greatest amount of work out of the human race, without regard to the happiness of individuals here, or their fate hereafter, no system could be better devised to obtain this result than the one adopted on these plantations. At four o'clock in the morning the slaves begin their labor in the fields, and, under the eye of the task-master, who moves about on horseback, armed with a whip which, in New York, would expose a bullock-driver to the anger of the humane Bergh, continue to work until eleven in the day, when they return to the frugal meal we have already seen in waiting for them. Through the scorching heat of the day men and women are kept steadily at their post until ten o'clock at night, when they return to their prison to snatch some rest to enable them to go through on the morrow the same monotonous course of toil. During the summertime necessity for labor is not so great, and the master is content to exact only twelve hours' sweat from his unfortunate bondsmen. Such is the uncolored and unexaggerated statement made by the taskmasters themselves; and the pictures of misery and suffering it calls up vividly to the mind must arouse the indignation of every heart in which there dwells a particle of humanity or of love of justice. The plea upon which bad men have sought to justify this abomination—that without the system of slavery it would be impossible to work the plantations with profit to the capitalist—is false. And even if it were not, can men be so lost to honor and all sense of right as to admit that a few men, for their own advantage, have the right to inflict untold suffering on their fellow-man, and reduce him to a state of degradation little, if anything, removed from the brute? But the system has not even this defense. The planters grow enormously rich, and become millionaires at the expense of the tears and misery of the wretches who toil for their benefit. That such a system can be permitted to exist among men pretending to be civilized is an outrage on the common conscience of mankind. When one sees the representatives of this abomination kneeling before the altar of the God of Christians, he must regret the thunderbolts of the grand old gods of the past, who, the poets tell us, smote in their indignation such criminals.

After a sharp ride through extensive fields of cane, it would have been easy to forget everything but the wonderful beauty and fertility which surrounded us, if it were not for the erect and soldier-like form of the slave-driver. At his side hung the long, formidable machete, and the ornamented handle of a dirk peeped out from his girdle. These realities reminded me constantly that the peace and happiness were only on the surface. During the ride, this man told me that from time to time some of the slaves escaped into the woods, but that in the majority of cases, not being able to obtain food, they were obliged to return and give themselves up to the authorities, by whom they were sent back to their masters. It is certainly astonishing that the slaves do not rise and kill their persecutors. Slave and freeman alike are armed with the terrible machete, which at will can be used as a weapon as well as an instrument of cultivation. Scarcely any of the employés on the plantation carried firearms, the moral effect of their authority being sufficient to prevent any serious resistance on the part of the slaves. The Chinamen are by no means as tractable as the negroes. They are revengeful, and are looked on as dangerous. This is due to their superior intelligence, and their keener sense of the wrong done to them.

On our return from the fields oranges were produced, and proved grateful and refreshing after the sharp ride in the sun. As soon as the slaves had finished their feed, for it would be a misuse of language to call it a meal, they were mustered in front of the machine-shed. Each one brought his tin platter, and placed it in the general heap. The platters being counted and found all right, the men and women were divided into squads, and assigned to various duties. If I had never known anything of slavery but what I saw in the few minutes that parade lasted, there was enough to make me a determined abolitionist for life. Not that any act of violence or brutality was committed, for no such occurrence took place, and I am quite willing to believe, as the directors assured me, that corporal punishment of a severe nature is very seldom inflicted on the slaves. It is not necessary, however, to ascribe this gentleness to any considerations of humanity, but simply to the fact that it is more dangerous to punish the slaves now, because, in order to escape the inhuman lash, even these degraded beings sometimes have latent enough of the spirit of manhood to make them fly to the woods, where they become the most terrible and the most implacable enemies of the white man. They wage a war in which quarter is neither asked nor given. As an able-bodied slave is worth fifteen hundred dollars, and is becoming dearer every day, the running away of a slave inflicts serious injury on the master; besides, it is almost impossible to replace him, as the demand surpasses, by ever so much, the supply. Knowing this, it did not much surprise me when the director asserted that, except in extreme cases, it was not the custom on the estate to resort to severe corporal punishment. It would be impossible to paint in words the forlorn and hopeless look of the slaves as they stood in a half-circle before the director and his assistants. The clothing of men and women alike was made out of a coarse stuff used in the manufacture of coffee-bags. The men's garments were sometimes intended to represent pantaloons. The covering of the women was still more simple. It consisted in a kind of loose gown, which, in most cases, fell only a little below the knee, being fastened round the waist with a rude cord. There seemed to be little or no difference in the amount of work expected from the women or the men, and, indeed, at first sight, it was not easy to discover any difference of sex. For the most part, the slaves on this estate are Congo blacks; but a number of them, and nearly all the children, are Creoles, with unmistakable evidence of the mixture of white blood in their veins. In the older slaves, all traces of human intelligence had almost disappeared, and their labor seemed to be performed mechanically, under the direction of the overseers. In the faces of the women not a vestige remained of the softness and gentleness of character which we look for in those whose destiny it is to be the mothers of men; beneath the lash of the overseer's whip all thoughts and feelings planted by Heaven had been crushed out, the light of love extinguished, and the being whom God created for a noble end reduced to the level of a brute of the field, whose only use was to minister to the base passions and avaricious greed of a master.

View slavery from whatever side we may, we shall be able to perceive nothing but moral turpitude as its immediate result. Trampling all laws human and divine underfoot, we shall see the slave-master and his assistants handing over their own flesh and blood to this terrible life of degradation, and exposing their own children to the lash of the task-master.

That this terrible crime against humanity is committed daily can be seen in the color of the children born on the estates, and who, because they are not so white as their fathers, are condemned to slavery. A system capable of so deadening the best feelings of our nature as to change human beings into monsters, must be regarded by all honorable men as accursed. In presence of this awful wrong the church is silent, because the slaveholder is rich and powerful. True to its conservative instincts, it is on the side of order, as represented by the rich, chivalrous slave-driver, who sells his own child into slavery, or hands his daughter over to satisfy the caprices of some new master. It is only when the poor and weak are unjust that the modern church can thunder. Not a word is uttered against the slave-master here, who, in defiance of all laws of morality and justice, robs the slave of the sweat of his brow, and degrades a creature to the level of the brute by forcing him to live in that very socialism which the church denounces in Paris, but shuts its eyes on in Havana. The owners of these plantations, dwelling in Havana, Madrid, London, New York, and Paris, are Christians of the first water. Reverend fathers even are known to have an interest in human chattels. Owing to the bad treatment and hard work which the slaves undergo, they die usually at a much earlier age than the white population. Since the stoppage of the free importation of slaves from Africa, the difficulty in supplying the places of those who have died has been constantly felt on the estates, nor has the experiment of Chinese labor been altogether successful.* Its effects on the immigrants have been disastrous. About seventy-five per cent. of the coolies die during the eight years they are forced to labor by their contract. Very few of them can be persuaded to renew the contract, and the severest and most unjust laws are enacted in their regard to force them to work either for the benefit of a master or for the government.

In cases where they have succeeded in overcoming all obstacles and establishing themselves in business, they are exposed to the extortions of the police, who can ruin them at any moment. The condition of the coolie after he has fulfilled his contract is almost as bad as while he is on the plantation. He is treated as were the Jews in the Middle Ages. In many cases these coolie immigrants are very bad characters, and prove anything but a desirable acquisition on the estates. They are more malicious and infinitely less tractable than the negro, and considerable prejudice exists against them among the nigger-driving fraternity. In some cases the immigrants come voluntarily; but in the majority of cases they are decoyed and carried off, or induced to leave their country on false pretenses. An anonymous society in Havana, at the head of which is one of the richest planters on the island, has gone largely into the coolie business, which, under present conditions, is more remunerative than the old slave-trade used to be.

While at Havana I visited a Portuguese steamer which had just arrived from Macao, with a cargo of Celestials, some eight hundred and eighty-nine souls, all told. As I mounted the gangway, the shaven heads and round faces, with piercing eyes, of a crowd of Chinese were popped over the vessel's side, and they seemed as much amused with my appearance as I was with theirs. Everything on board the ship had been put into apple-

---

*While Spain outlawed the international slave trade in 1820, the importation of enslaved Africans increased significantly in the decades that followed (totaling 20,000–40,000 people annually). The shrinking market O'Kelly describes resulted from the abolition of slavery in the United States in 1865, which reduced American participation in the trade. See introduction, xxii.

pie order, and if it had not been for the threatening-looking iron *grille*, that cut off all approach from the coolie quarter of the ship to the quarter-deck, as well as the appearance of two small ship cannon, so placed as to sweep the decks in case of attack, one might have thought himself on board of one of those floating herring-boxes known as immigrant ships to the *habitués* of the port of New York. With the permission of the captain, I went through the ship until I found a Celestial who had the reputation among his fellows of speaking English. Unfortunately, his vocabulary was very limited, or I should have been able to get a pretty history from the cargo. His story; so far as he could tell it, was no doubt representative of many of the rest. He had been to California some years ago, and had returned to his native land with some money. Having settled down, he married, and, things going wrong with him, he accepted an offer of a situation in Macao, for which port he embarked; but, instead of being taken to Macao, he was put on board a coolie ship and carried to Havana. The poor fellow seemed to feel very much for the two juvenile Celestials and his wife, who were left without protectors or support by his absence.

In the case where this absolute bad faith is not exhibited, a deception scarcely less cruel is practiced. They are induced to engage themselves with the prospect of high wages, which to their eyes is fabulous, but which, in the different condition of society in which they find themselves on their arrival here, scarcely suffices for their support. The impossibility of communicating with the people by whom they are surrounded makes their position more hopeless even than that of the blacks. The Congo traders could allege, with some appearance of truth, that, however bad the position of the slave on the plantation, it was certainly better than it had been in his native land. There was a speciousness in this argument sufficient to smooth consciences not over-tender; but no such pretense can be put forth in defense of the coolie traffic. Here we have men of a high order of intelligence, citizens of a free nation, whose civilization was old while the remote ancestors of their masters were still savages as degraded as the Congo negroes enticed from their homes to be carried into servitude. It was only necessary to see the contrast between the new immigrants—full of strength and intelligence—and the wretched wrecks of humanity who survived the contract system, to understand the fatal result of the new slave-trade. The nine hundred Celestials crowded on the coolie ship in Havana could compare favorably, both physically and mentally, with a similar number of people taken at random from the population of any country. That they were not altogether willing immigrants was proved by several revolts which had to be repressed before the arrival of the ship in port. However, the profits of this infamous traffic are too great to allow any considerations of right or justice to weigh with those engaged in it.

According to the information furnished to me by the officers of the ship, there are regular agencies established in the Chinese ports, having ramifications in the interior, whose business it is to supply cargoes to the coolie ships. For each coolie shipped the agent receives fifty dollars; but he has no claim to his money until the "emigrant" is actually aboard. The cause of this clause is, that quite a number of the unfortunates, after being delivered to the boats, throw themselves into the water, preferring to be drowned, or to take the risk of drowning, to being carried into slavery. Once on board, there is little chance of escape, as the hatchways are guarded until the ship puts to sea. As the coolie represents a certain amount of cash, no unnecessary hardships are inflicted on him, unless there should be a revolt endangering the safety of the crew. In such circumstances death is dealt out unsparingly, until the captives are reduced to obedience by terror and have been taught how hopeless is a conflict of unarmed men with a well-armed and determined crew. It is very difficult to obtain reliable information of what passes on board during the voyage, as all the crew are compromised, and before entering port everything is put into apple-pie order. I was rather surprised to find the coolies well, and cleanly dressed in cheap suits of a strong cotton texture. Remarking this to one of the engineers, a sleek, oily Englishman, he informed me that each one was supplied with two suits, and that, by contract, the master who should purchase these coolies would be obliged to supply two suits annually to each man. The impression sought to be made on my mind by this oily person was that the Chinese were very well treated indeed, although he told me one of the passengers, who had been a professor in a Chinese college, was trying to get up a petition to government, complaining of the wrongs that been done to them. Poor fellow! He little knew what a misfortune it is to fall among Christians, and how little justice he could hope for in a so-called civilized community.

As I expressed some surprise at the *couleur-de-rose* picture the oily engineer had drawn from his interior consciousness, his assistant, who was a thorough John Bull, blurted out, "Yes, they looks well, and clean enough now, because they've been awashed and bathed, and got new clothes; but you ought to 'ave seen 'em a week ago. There warn't a whole shirt among 'em all." This outburst of candor on the part of the assistant quite shocked his oily superior, who looked deprecatingly at the assistant, remarking, at the same time, that while at sea it was very difficult to keep the coolies clean. I did not appear to attach any importance to what the assistant had unguardedly blurted out, as it might have got him into trouble, especially if it was afterwards discovered that the inquiring individual to whom he had so unguardedly expressed himself was a newspaper correspondent. Some of these immigrants I afterwards encountered on my way through the country, being conveyed, under guard, to the plantations of the men who had purchased them. There was no pretense on the part of any one to regard them in any other light than as slaves; the only difference being that, after a lapse of eight years, they would be entitled to their liberty, should they have the good or bad fortune to survive the hardships and cruelties to which, during that period, they were certain to be exposed. Kept at work for an average of fourteen hours a day, with the necessity of working for themselves on the holidays if they wished to have the means of procuring even the most ordinary luxuries in which the poor indulge; exposed to a trying climate, without proper food or proper care, it is not to be wondered at that within the time of contract seventy-five per cent. of the immigrants perish, though, for the most part, they come into the country in the prime of manhood.

Such is the demand for labor, that the planters willingly give five hundred dollars for the use of an able-bodied Chinaman during eight years. The profits of the traffic can, therefore, easily be calculated. The nine hundred human beings brought to market in the ship I visited were worth some four hundred and fifty thousand dollars to the importers; and, as they had cost originally less than fifty thousand, the anonymous society had some four hundred thousand dollars as the result of the voyage to meet contingent expenses. Never in the palmiest days of the African slave-trade were such tremendous profits realized, and it is needless to say that, so long as the law permits this infamous traffic, it will flourish with the proverbial rankness of ill weeds.*

The abolition of slavery in Porto Rico caused the greatest consternation among the *Negreros* or slave-masters.† Every effort was made by the slaveocracy to prevent the Captain-General carrying out the instructions from Madrid. The slaveocracy in Cuba look on America as the chief cause

---

*Chinese contract laborers first arrived in Cuba in 1847. By 1874, around 125,000 Chinese laborers had entered Cuba. See Lisa Yun and Ricardo René Laremont, "Chinese Coolies and African Slaves in Cuba, 1847–74," *Journal of Asian American Studies*, 4.2 (2001): 99–122.

†Since slavery was abolished in Puerto Rico on 22 March 1873, O'Kelly added this commentary when revising his original dispatches to the *Herald*. See *New York Herald*, 25 March 1873, 8.

of all their misfortunes. They allege that from jealousy of their prosperity the Americans desire to force the immediate liberation of the slaves. They pretend to be willing to abolish slavery at some future day, if they are only allowed time. Some think they would be ready in ten years, others claim that twenty years should be allowed for the gradual extinction of slavery.

The granting of immediate liberty would, according to the slave-masters, result in anarchy; but it is not certain that ten years hence the slaves will be any better fitted for liberty than they are now. If there was any honesty in the pretended desire to abolish slavery, steps would have been taken looking towards gradual emancipation. But the fact is, the ardor of the *Negreros* in favor of gradual abolition is simply a skillful move to postpone indefinitely the settlement of the question, and, unless some strong power interferes, slavery will be maintained in Cuba to the day of judgment, at least so far as the will of the slave-masters is concerned. Their cry about the "opportunity" of the abolition movement is only an effort to gain more time, and would be repeated with the same insistence ten or twenty years hence. If the *Negreros* are so anxious that the field should be cultivated at any cost of human suffering, let them cultivate themselves. For myself, I do not see why the blacks should not have a turn at driving as well as the whites; and, since the planters are so anxious for the interest of sugar-eating humanity, it ought to be a labor of love for them to cultivate the cane. When it has been watered with the sweat of their brows, it will taste to them sweeter than ever. Such a proposition will make them very indignant, for when they preach the necessity of industry, they mean that others should toil and sweat while they enjoy the fruits of the labor. Just now the position of the slave-owners is full of anxiety and uncertainty. The sentiment among the native population is very much in favor of the abolition of slavery, but the Spanish immigrants feel that it would weaken their hold on the island, and are to a man opposed to the proposed change. It is almost impossible to arrive at the opinion of the colored population. For the most part they are sunk in the deepest ignorance, but many among them are people of refinement and education.

4 On the Confines of Cuba Libre

THE VISIT to the sugar plantation cured me of any desire to pry further into the secrets of the slave system. My whole attention was therefore directed to pushing on to Puerto Principe overland, but to my astonishment this was not feasible. No guides would venture to accompany me even so far as Santo Espiritu.* It was stated that though no very considerable force of insurgents remained in the district, small parties were still frequently encountered. The dangerous region began at the outskirts of the town, and no one would venture a mile into the country without an armed escort. It was useless to offer the most tempting bribes; no one could be induced to face what was esteemed certain death in venturing into the mysterious region of Cuba Libre. The mirage-like frontier advanced and receded like phantom lakes in the desert. But though the frontier might be a phantom, the dread inspired by the spirits who wandered free within the mystic confines was proof that they were not "such stuff as dreams are made of," but solid bone and muscle. Under these circumstances it became necessary to abandon the idea of reaching the Eastern Department through Camarguey.† My object was to see Cespedes if alive; and if dead, his successor; and bring back as much information about the state and prospect of the insurrection as could be gathered in a hurried passage through the Cuban lines. In my interview with Madame Cespedes, before leaving New York, that lady indicated clearly that Cespedes's headquarters would be found east of the Cauto, in the mountainous regions lying between Cabo Cruz and Santiago de Cuba. This was my objective point; but, as it was improbable I would have an opportunity of acquainting myself with the state of the Spanish portion of the island after my return from Cuba Libre, I resolved to visit Santo Espiritu, in the hope of finding the military operations carried out on a large scale, before proceeding to Santiago de Cuba. The Villa Clara Railway joins the Cienfuegos line at Las Cruces. The railroad passes through a wild and uninteresting country to Cienfuegos, a new and prosperous town,

---

*"Santo Espiritu" should read "Sancti Spíritus," a city in central Cuba, west of the *trocha*.
†"Camarguey" should read "Camagüey," a city in central Cuba, east of the *trocha*.

laid out with great regularity. It possesses a magnificent harbor, and the inhabitants are remarkable for their energy and industry. Here I embarked on the South Coast steamer for Las Tunas, which is about two days' sail to the east. The scenery along the coast, especially in the neighborhood of Trinidad, was singularly impressive, and appealed to the imagination in all the majesty of utter desolation. Before the war the lower hills and the valleys near the coast were highly cultivated, but during the struggle all the estates have been abandoned or destroyed. So far as the eye can reach nothing is now visible but dark masses of forest clad hills, whose awful stillness is unbroken by any sign of habitation. Until a late period the almost inaccessible mountains and forests in this region gave shelter to important bands of insurgents; but the construction of the *trocha* southward had the effect of causing the majority of the bands to abandon the district, from fear of being cut off from their friends in the Central and Eastern Departments, where from the outset the chief strength of the insurrection has lain.* This abandonment of the Cinco Villas was one of the causes of dispute among the Cubans which led to the deposition of Cespedes by the Cuban Congress in November, 1873.

Although the Cuban sympathizers with whom I had come in contact admitted the actual state of affairs with a certain amount of frankness, I was unwilling to accept anything on mere hearsay, and therefore persisted in my intention of going to Santo Espiritu. A fog detained us some twelve hours beyond our time, but at last we arrived at Las Tunas, an embryo town, situated on a tongue of land. It is the seaport of Santo Espiritu. As only one train a day runs each way, I was obliged to put up at one of the *tiendas* for the night. The tienda was a large wooden frame house, built in the American style. It was hotel, grocery, and general store combined. There were several rooms which appeared chiefly to be used to stow away old lumber when not occupied by the guests, and one of these was divided into several compartments by thin wooden partitions, some seven or eight feet high. One of these boxes was offered to me; but as the house was likely to be crowded by rather rough-looking passengers who had arrived by the same steamer, I declined the offer, and requested a room to myself. This was puzzling; but as I was prepared to pay, it was arranged that a hall, or communication between the tienda and the

---

*Around fifty miles long and 200 yards wide, the *trocha* was a defensive line extending from Morón in the north to Júcaro in the south. Designed as a barrier to prevent insurgents from crossing into western Cuba, the *trocha* was fortified with militarized blockhouses, trenches, barbed wire, and land mines.

sleeping apartment, should be fitted up for my accommodation. Scarcely had this arrangement been made when the other travelers began to pour in. Everyone was curious to know my business, as my care about being alone immediately created the impression that I had a large sum of money, and was apprehensive of being robbed. At night I could hear my fellow-travelers discussing me and my probable wealth. It was agreed a person so careful of himself must have plenty of money about him; but as the doors of my room fastened with bolts on the inside, these speculations gave me no uneasiness.

Next morning I found the hour of starting depended on the amount of freight to be embarked, and the more or less industrious frame of mind of the colored men whose business it was to load the wagons. About two o'clock in the afternoon we steamed out of the station, which is about a quarter of a mile distant from the town, in the midst of a salt swamp.

Here a guard of soldiers came on board, and disposed themselves about so as to command a good view of the country—that is to say, of the woods and bushes, that, after a few miles of sand and swamp had been passed, extended for leagues on all sides during three-fourths of our journey. As we approached Santo Espiritu the country became more open, and signs of cultivation appeared. On the way, I managed to get into conversation with one of the guard, who seemed to me a likely subject to know something about the war; he was just the sort of fellow to drive a martinet to desperation. Untidy, and with a suspicion of the picturesqueness of dirt about him, but with a devil-may-care look in the eye, and a certain hard expression about the mouth, which was drawn at the corners. He had been inspecting me rather attentively, and I was expecting every minute a request to exhibit my papers—a formality which I confess to disliking heartily. A lucky stopping of the train in a deep cutting to take up wood for the engine, furnished me with a pretext to inquire the cause of the delay, and once the ice was broken the soldier and I got on very well together. He informed me that he had been over three years in active operations, and that it was pretty tiresome work. Like most of the Spanish soldiers, he entertained a supreme contempt for an enemy that never fired except from an ambuscade. He had been engaged with the insurgents any number of times, but had very seldom seen any of them. "They lie in wait," he said, deprecatingly, "in the forest, and fire just one volley, when they run away, and, as they know all the paths in the forest, they generally make good their escape. Most of the white men have been killed, or have surrendered themselves, and there are only the negroes remaining in the wood now. It is very difficult to find them, for they might be lying at twenty yards' distance in the forest where we pass by without our discovering them. In the interior of the forest the brushwood is so thick that we are obliged to cut our way through with our machetes. We have now got bloodhounds, however," he said, with animation, "and we can follow them into their hiding-places." In answer to an inquiry as to what they did with their prisoners, the soldier simply said, "Nearly all the white men have presented themselves, and we do not take many black prisoners; they are generally killed if found with arms; but if they present themselves, they are sent back to their masters. When the blacks catch a white man they kill him."

According to this man's computation, the refugees in the woods of the Santo Espiritu district did not number more than one hundred, and these, he said, were divided up into small bands, that never attacked any party of armed men, but cut off travelers and stragglers without mercy. Even when cornered, as sometimes happened, or surprised by parties of troops sent out in their pursuit, these negroes did not offer any very desperate resistance, but seemed to endeavor to escape to their hiding-places until the danger was passed. The soldier made this statement frankly, and without any clue to my character, which might have induced him to color the picture.

As we approached Santo Espiritu, we met a few large Cuban villages, in each of which are stationed a party of troops occupying a kind of blockhouse. Seen from the railway, there was nothing particularly noticeable in these places; but I was afterwards informed that a large part of the inhabitants were in a state of destitution bordering on starvation. This misery is attributable to the severe orders of the Spaniards, compelling the concentration of the people in the small towns and villages, where they have been decimated by famine and disease.

In the town of Santo Espiritu there is also great suffering, caused principally by the war. Strings of poverty-stricken women were to be met going from house to house to beg a little rice to keep soul and body together. In the faces of many of these could be read tales of sorrow; and the brow of many a one among them was darkened by the impending shadow of the angel of death. The same difficulty of procuring horses and a guide willing to accompany me by the land route forced me to abandon the idea of entering Camarguey. None of the Spanish party would venture alone with me into the neighborhood of the insurgents, who seemed to be everywhere and nowhere; and no Cuban would expose himself to the suspicion of the authorities by accompanying me. Nothing, therefore, remained but to return to Las Tunas and take the steamer to Santiago de Cuba.

5 Campaigning with the Dons

THE EVENING, or rather the night, of my arrival at Santiago de Cuba, Mr. Ramsden, the British Consul, presented me to the Governor of the town, Brigadier-General Morales, on the public square, as an Irish gentleman traveling through the island.* The general was already aware that I was the representative of the New York *Herald,* and as it was difficult to talk freely among the crowd of promenaders, General Morales invited me to the palace. He expressed himself desirous to be of service, and enable me to see the exact state of the island for myself. I thanked him for his kindness, and assured him that it would give me great pleasure to avail myself of whatever facilities he might be pleased to afford me.

Without any solicitation on my part, he offered to allow me to accompany a column which would leave in the morning on an expedition that was expected to last for ten days. Ample opportunity would thus be afforded me to observe the operations of the campaign. Most willingly would I accept the offer, I told the brigadier, but, unfortunately, having arrived only the same morning, I was not provided with horses for myself or servant, nor with the means of transport for the necessary provisions. The brigadier at once informed me that the column would give me a horse, and the officers be most happy to receive me as their guest during the expedition. He then introduced me to Lieutenant-Colonel Sostrada, the commander of the column.† This gentleman expressed himself well pleased at having the representative of an impartial journal to accompany the Spanish troops, and give a fair account of the war. The troops, he informed me, were ordered to march at half-past six in the morning, and it would be necessary to be at the railway station at that hour. He also advised me to provide myself with a hammock and blanket—no easy matter at half-past ten o'clock at night. As it was necessary to make some hurried preparations, I took leave of Brigadier Morales and Colonel

---

*O'Kelly refers here to Adolfo Morales de los Ríos, then the interim governor and commander general of Santiago de Cuba.
†The *Herald* reports Colonel Sostrada's death in a battle with insurgents near Manzanillo in an article published 24 June 1873.

Sostrada, to go in pursuit of the hammock and blanket, which, thanks to the good services of a friend, I secured.

It was still dark when I started from the hotel in the morning, under the guidance of one of the servants. In his anxiety to have me up in time, the proprietor roused me some hours before it was necessary. Arrived at the station, I found it already occupied by troops belonging to the mounted contra-guerrillas. All was stir and bustle. The embarking of the horses was proceeding rapidly and without confusion. The men who were not engaged in this service were gathered around a vender of coffee and cognac, who had improvised a restaurant on a rough deal table. I watched the proceedings with considerable interest, and found commendable order and organization to exist. These irregular troops were the scouts of the army, being in large part recruited from the native population and surrendered insurgents. They render invaluable service to the Spaniards on account of their knowledge of the mode of warfare carried on by the Cubans, as well as their acquaintance with the country. For the most part they are armed with Remington rifles, and all of them carry the formidable machete. The uniform worn by the troops on campaign consists of coarse linen trousers and blue cotton jacket, with a broad-brimmed straw hat, sometimes covered with white calico, and ornamented with a red or green band. As the contra-guerrillas moved out of the station, the regular infantry arrived, and took their seats in the train. They appeared to me to have seen much service, but in the dim light of the morning it was not possible to examine them very closely; besides, I was resolved to form my judgment of them more by their actions than their looks. A few moments later, I encountered Colonel Sostrada, who recognized me, and ordered one of the soldiers to take charge of my very slim baggage. As soon as everything was ready, the colonel invited me to take a seat by his side. The other officers of the battalion occupied seats in the same carriage, but no introduction was tendered to them, a circumstance which at first surprised me, but the explanation was soon forthcoming. The officers were in fighting trim, offering rather a strange spectacle to one only accustomed to the pomp and splendor of the parade-ground. All the little adornments of the person in which gallant *militaires* delight had been laid aside; even of the insignia of rank there was only retained the absolutely necessary. There was scarcely any pretense of uniform; even the showy sword had been exchanged for the more useful machete. A few wore the regulation cap, but by far the greater number selected for headgear straw hats, which were more useful than ornamental. From these signs I had hopes that serious work was intended, and that if fortune favored me I was going to be present at that somewhat intangible thing called a Cuban battle. After a toilsome ascent to Christo, the train stopped to take on board the remaining companies of the regular battalion.* As this would occasion some delay, we got off the train. Here the colonel called the officers of the battalion together, and formally introduced me as the representative of the New York *Herald,* specially recommended to them by Brigadier Morales to be looked upon as *un nuevo compañero.* The officers, who appeared to be a good set, bowed to their new comrade, and afterwards I was free of the corporation. This ceremony through, we embarked again for San Luis, the termination of the line.

The voyage over the railway from Santiago de Cuba to San Luis is one of the most interesting that can be made. The grade is so steep that for the greater part of the way it is with difficulty the engine can drag its freight up the incline. The track lies along the side of steep mountains, crossing deep valleys on wooden trelliswork, where the slightest accident would hurl train and passengers to inevitable destruction. The scenery is very beautiful, the wild grandeur of the mountains being relieved and softened by the cultivated *llanos,* or bottomlands, where the sugarcane and cornstalk give evidence of human interest. For the most part the mountains are clothed to their tops with the palm, the seiba, and the mango, which rise, file above file, until they seem lost in the clouds. The chief characteristic of this district is savage grandeur, and it is to me exceedingly strange that the insurgents do not take measures to destroy a line which it would take thousands of troops to defend from a bold and enterprising enemy. It is true that the Spaniards have the line strongly occupied, but it has so many weak points that if it were vigorously attacked it must be crippled. I expressed these views to the Spanish officers, and they were of my opinion. They adduced the fact as a proof of the inability of the Cubans to meet the Spaniards in anything like an open fight. All the points of vantage along the line are occupied by little wooden forts, garrisoned by from ten to fifty men, which, at a distance, resemble huge pigeon-boxes. In some instances they are surrounded by a shallow ditch, and at others a weak and totally ineffective *chevaux-de-frise* of bamboo had been constructed. Small openings are made in the wooden planks to enable the soldiers to fire through, and on the top of each is a square frame with shutters, capable of being raised or lowered at will by the sentinel, who from this elevated point keeps watch and ward over the country. The first impression made on my mind by one of these structures was tinged with a sense

---

*"Christo" should read "El Cristo," a town north of Santiago de Cuba.

of the ridiculous, for it strongly suggested a living Jack-in-the-box. As a matter of experience, however, they have been found to answer admirably the purpose for which they had been constructed. Every Spanish officer to whom I spoke on the matter assured me that in no instance had one of these towers been captured by the enemy when defended by the troops. This statement, however, is not literally true. Many of them have been surprised by the insurgents, but as they would not repay the trouble and loss of storming, the insurgents wisely avoid them. They are very unprofitable subjects for attack by men destitute of artillery, and, as they contain little else than a few days' provisions for the garrison, the insurgents think *le jeu ne vaut pas la chandelle.*

By the time we arrived at San Luis the morning was far advanced, and the sun shone out with tropical intensity. Under these circumstances, the colonel ordered the noonday halt, in order that the men should be able to breakfast and repose during the great heat of the day. There was now ample opportunity to observe the appearance and condition of the men. For the most part they were bronzed and weather-beaten, but still strong and vigorous. The effects of the climate and the constant fatigues to which they were exposed were visible in a great number of faces, whose expression showed clearly that the constitution was already undermined. For the most part, these men had suffered from the fevers of the climate, brought on by exposure to the weather, sleeping in the damp woods without any other protection than a blanket afforded, as the troops are wholly unprovided with tents or a sufficient supply of healthy food. Although we were within two hours' ride by rail of Santiago de Cuba, the troops were obliged to eat biscuit—a circumstance that reflects very little credit on the administration of the Spanish army. In connection with this subject, inquiries since made show that, bad as the commissariat department is at present, it is an immense improvement on what it was some time ago. In all countries the commissariat department is the favorite refuge of rogues, but it is open to doubt whether the soldiers of any other army would continue to support the great fatigues to which these Spaniards are exposed on such poor food. The fault is not with the regimental officers, for they sympathize with the men, whose sufferings they are often obliged to share, but with the higher officials, who grow rich at the expense of the poor fellows who are daily exposing their lives in defense of the honor and integrity of Spain. It has always appeared to me a strange contradiction that while the private soldier who, prompted by hunger, steals, is severely punished, the well-paid official who robs the troops not only escapes hanging, but is received as an honored and worthy member of society.

Many credible persons have assured me that more than one commissary-general has returned rich to Spain after a sufficiently short term of office; yet no inquiry has been instituted as to how he managed to acquire a fortune while living in a style that must have absorbed the income to which he was honestly entitled. Matters had reached that stage where a change becomes a necessity, when General Riquelme took command of the Eastern Department.* Convinced that unless the soldiers were fed they would die, he introduced considerable reforms, which, although they leave much to be desired, are yet an immense improvement on the old supply department.

On leaving the train, the men stacked arms and rested in the shadow of the houses until their simple meal was cooked. There was no hurry; and the officers informed me that, except in case of extreme necessity, they always allowed the men to repose during the noonday hours—a precaution which tends to alleviate the effects of the climate. Colonel Sostrada, having some matters to attend to in relation to his command, left me in charge of the doctor of the battalion, Patricio de la Corte y Baez, who proved to be an agreeable and intelligent companion. With him an opportunity was afforded me of seeing the sick. Some few men were suffering from fever, and had to be left in the hospital; others were suffering from old wounds or accidents. In all cases the men seemed to receive careful attention and humane consideration. What struck me most was the absence from the *visite* of the *carrotier* class, or those feigning sickness. Nearly every man who appeared bore in his face the confirmation of his story, and there were many men even in the ranks who, judging from their appearance, ought not to have been taken into the field. As soon as the colonel had given the necessary orders, he returned and requested me to accompany him in a visit to the colonel commanding in San Luis, who desired to be introduced to me. At breakfast the place of honor was given to me, and on that and all subsequent occasions I was treated with an attention and courtesy that will remain engraved on my heart forever.

Towards two o'clock in the afternoon the troops were ordered to fall in, and some minutes later were defiling before me. The colonel placed at my disposal his horses, and, having selected one, I took my place with him at the head of the column. We were accompanied by Lieutenant-Colonel Lopez, the adjutant, Captain Valderrama, and the doctor, Patricio de la Corte y Baez, who made up our party, or mess, during my short stay with

---

*O'Kelly refers to José Luis Riquelme y Gómez (1813–1888), who was chief of staff of the Spanish Army in Cuba from 1873 to 1874.

the Spanish forces. We were now really in campaign, and at night would reach the edge of the territory where Spanish power claims to rule without dispute. From the moment we left San Luis, we marched with all the precautions of war, and two negroes carrying stretchers reminded one that disagreeable accidents might happen at any moment. These negroes had been captured during the war, and had attached themselves to the battalion, refusing to leave even when offered their liberty. One of them had been decorated for courage on the field in succoring the wounded under fire. The country through which we passed was cultivated at intervals, but some of the estates were abandoned. The cane continued, however, to grow, though the careful husbandman was no longer present to care for or to reap it, and the rich harvest, waiting vainly for the reaper, seemed to reproach proud and insensate man for his violence and senseless ambition. As we moved into the interior the country became wilder, and we passed through large districts of wooded country.

Our first halt was made at the Ciudad, an estate of medium extent, in full operation. It was guarded by soldiers, as all the estates in this district are, to prevent the insurgents from destroying them. Here the process of sugar-making in all its details was carefully and minutely explained to me. Leaving this estate, we directed our march to Santa Anna, the last estate in this district now in operation. It is situated to the northeast, at the apex of the triangle formed by the range of mountains known as Dos Bocas and the prolongation of the range to which the Gran Piedra belongs. Here we were to halt for the night, and in the morning plunge into the mysterious land of unknown dangers known as Los Montes, or, contemptuously, La Manigua, or Cuba Libre, but which I prefer to designate the Mambi-Land. Mountain and plain are covered by dense forests, where the insurgents, or patriots, as they are variously styled, according to the sympathies of the speaker, defy the power of Spain. From the patches of wooded country through which we passed, I was able to comprehend the enormous difficulties that lay in the way of the pacification of the island by force. Many of the points on the march, if properly taken advantage of and well defended, could only have been forced by superior numbers at a great sacrifice of life. Fortunately, nothing occurred during the march to spoil the picturesqueness of the scene by introducing the horrible.

The long line of soldiers on either side of the road, that now dipped into valleys through which flowed shallow streams, now wound with serpentine course over the low hills, marched along silently and patiently, their blue jackets and white pantaloons dotting the valley's sides, producing a very animated and pleasing effect. More than once I turned in my saddle to enjoy the scene so full of life and color. No painter could transfer it to canvas; for its subtle pleasure lay in the constant change of color and grouping occurring every instant, presenting to the eye new combinations. Quite a number of these transverse valleys cut the road, and, had we been burdened with artillery or wagons, would have offered considerable difficulties to our march. On the road I learned that the battalion with which I had the honor to march was known as the San Quentin, and was one of the first to leave Havana for the war. It had continued in campaign during the four years of the insurrection. During that period it had been engaged, more or less seriously, with the enemy in more than ninety engagements. In some of these the battalion had suffered heavily, but, according to the Spanish account, had always managed to repay, with interest, the attentions of the enemy. The San Quentin was a representative corps, well fitted to sustain the honor of the Spanish arms.

We reached Santa Anna about five o'clock in the afternoon. Colonel Sostrada, the director of the estate, and myself visited the Quaninica River, which is remarkable as the haunt of an immense number of alligators. On the opposite bank we could see the dark mass of buildings belonging to an estate that had been destroyed by the rebels. It belongs to one of the leaders of the insurrection. The crop on this estate is burned down regularly every year to prevent the Spanish authorities deriving any benefit from it. Before the war there were on the Santa Anna plantation some four hundred slaves, but the insurgents carried off the greater part. Many of these were either recaptured, or, having no stomach for fighting, returned voluntarily, so that the estate could muster at the time of my visit some eighty hands. While I was making the round of the buildings with the director, the preparations for dinner were completed, and on my return the mess was waiting for me. During dinner the officers paid me the most delicate attention, nothing being neglected to make me feel completely at my ease. Our dinner was quite a *recherché* affair, and by far the best I had eaten from the time of my arrival in the island, and it had the advantage of being seasoned with the spice of good-fellowship. After the cloth had been removed most of the officers of the battalion assembled around the table to while away the time, chatting and recounting stories of accidents by flood and field. We would have had songs also, but the only guitar of which the battalion boasted had come to grief. Before the evening was over I was on the best footing with all the officers. The subject of my mission and its fulfillment was discussed, not with the company, but at intervals with some of the officers with whom I had established more intimate relations. All professed themselves anxious that a fair and impartial statement of the status of the insurrection should be given to the world. They were especially desirous that the impression which had gone abroad about the Spanish army should be corrected. At the same time there was not the slightest apparent desire to interfere with the independence of my judgment or the free expression of my opinions. The statement that the Spanish troops killed all their prisoners was strenuously denied. It was claimed that all prisoners taken are given up to the higher authorities, who, of course, dispose of them as they think fit. This, however, amounts to much the same thing, as the prisoners who escape death by the machete in the woods are in nearly every case shot by sentence of court-martial, to strike terror into the *laborantes* in the towns.

In the first years of the insurrection, not alone were the prisoners taken in arms executed with very little ceremony, but citizens simply suspected of connection with the insurrection were taken from their houses, and shot after the form of trial had been gone through before a drum-head court-martial. So many instances of cold-blooded butcheries have been cited to me, both by respectable foreigners and Cubans, that this charge must be held to be proved against the Spanish authorities. The opinions of the officers of the battalion San Quentin reflect credit on them, but they are by no means shared by all the officers of the army. On the contrary, it is by no means an unusual thing to hear the opinion openly expressed, even at hotel tables, that until the shooting of the civilians is recommenced the country will never be pacified. On one occasion an officer, dining at the same table with me, went so far as to suggest that the families of all men known to be in the field should be exterminated. I remarked to him that such a course would, no doubt, be effective, but that the civilized world would scarcely permit its adoption. From this it will be seen that there exists considerable difference of opinion as to the measures that should be taken to stamp out the insurrection. While the Spanish supporters point to the men who have been pardoned, the Cubans recount the long list of the men slain in cold blood. The executions of the past have unquestionably cowed the Cuban population; but they have also deepened the hate and detestation with which the Spanish government is regarded, and if by any chance the Cubans could get the upper hand, they would probably exterminate the Spanish population. The officers of the San Quentin battalion were particularly desirous of impressing me with the opinion that the people of the island were in favor of the Spaniards. With this view they named a number of gentlemen serving in the army, who they assured me belonged to the *crème de la crème* of Cuban society. My own experience, however, contradicts this, for nearly all the young men of intelligence with whom I have come in contact hate the Spaniards with inconceivable bitterness.

But much as they hate the Peninsulars and Catalans, they fear them more. The Spanish immigrants, rude and energetic as they chiefly are, do not conceal the contempt they feel for the more intelligent but effeminate Cubans, and so every day deepens the hatred and distrust between them. On the Spanish side there enters into this question a sentiment of patriotic pride that, however mistaken, is still respectable. Sometimes this feeling leads to the commission of acts which, when the hour of passion and excitement has passed, even the ultra Spaniards regret; but whatever wrong is done by the Spanish soldiers, they at least expose themselves bodily to the consequences. This, of course, is not a justification; but it shows an earnestness and a belief in the justice of their cause that we may look upon as political fanaticism, but cannot despise.

In my conversations with the Spanish officers, the points on which they principally laid weight were, that the insurgents possessed neither lands nor towns, and were totally unable to offer effective resistance to the march of even one Spanish battalion. Like all regular troops, they complain bitterly that the insurgents would never show themselves in the open field, but fired from ambuscades, and then retreated. It never seemed to strike them that an enemy has a right to choose whatever tactics he pleases, and that there is no law, moral or international, to compel a soldier to stand just in the position his enemy wishes in order to allow himself to be shot down with greater facility.

Each Spanish soldier is supplied with one hundred and twenty rounds of ammunition, besides having a reserve supply on the mules, while there are moments when there are not a thousand rounds of ammunition in a Cuban battalion. This fact has much to do with the tactics of the Cuban troops. Even the Spanish officers admit this, as the following anecdote related to me by one of them will show: A volunteer in the direction of Cerredero suddenly found himself confronted by four Cubans, who presented their rifles, ordering him to surrender; not relishing the idea, he refused, and prepared to defend himself with his machete. The position at once became complicated, for the Cubans had not a single cartridge between them, and were obliged to cut the volunteer down with their machetes. The appearance of a party of troops prevented them finishing the work, and the plucky volunteer escaped with a severe wound on his lower jaw. Little incidents of this kind enable one to form a pretty accurate estimate of the condition of things in Cuba Libre. If the insurgents could be completely cut off from communication with the outer world their position would indeed be desperate, but the arrival from time to time of even small supplies will enable them to hold out indefinitely. In order to note how these expeditions were regarded by the Spanish army, I informed a number of officers at dinner of the safe arrival of Colonel Agüero, with a considerable supply of munitions of war; the effect was electrical.* The officers had been chatting and joking in quite a merry mood, but the news acted like an extinguisher on their good spirits; there was not much said, but pretty decided opinions were expressed as to the value and activity of the navy. One officer stated his firm conviction that if he lived he would see the twentieth year of the independence of the Cuban republic, as he had seen the fifth. The Spaniards constantly assert that the insurrection is contemptible so far as its means of resistance or power of aggression is concerned; but when asked why they do not suppress it, they point to the difficulty of the country and the impossibility of crushing an enemy that only fights when he pleases. In this lies the greatest danger to the dominion of Spain, for it is impossible to conquer an enemy who can accept or refuse combat at will. It is now pretty generally felt that in attempting to reconquer St. Domingo Spain has brought upon herself a severe punishment. It was that campaign which taught the Cubans how they could free themselves from the sovereignty of the Peninsula. From whatever point of view this struggle is regarded, there seems to be no escape from a disastrous ending for the Spanish arms. If the question were to be settled by an open war, the Cuban republic would soon be counted among the things of the past; but it must be decided by the power of endurance of the hostile parties. The position is this: The Cubans possess a small army in the field, but behind that army are hundreds of thousands of sympathizers, from whom the losses by disease and death are constantly repaired. As the natives do not suffer much from the diseases that prove so fatal to Europeans, the principal gaps in the ranks are made by the bullets of the Spanish soldiers; but as these, according to their own account, never see the enemy, even when engaged with them, the losses from bullets cannot be very heavy, and are easily made good. On the other hand, the Spanish troops are constantly on the march, exposed to the inclemency of the climate and the special diseases of the country. How fatal these prove, aggravated by the fatigues undergone by the troops, may be judged

---

*O'Kelly refers to the arrival of the *Edgar Stuart,* commanded by Colonel Melchior Agüero, which brought men and supplies for the Cuban cause. For coverage of this filibustering expedition in the *Herald,* see "A Cuban Triumph," 14 Jan. 1873, 3, and "Insurgent Cuba," 16 Jan. 1873, 7.

from the statistics furnished me by the officers of the Staff. Since the outbreak of the rebellion, it appears from the official record that one hundred thousand men have been sent to Cuba. Of these, some twenty or thirty thousand, at a very liberal calculation, remain. Six thousand officers have fallen victims to disease and bullets in the same period; these are not the statistics of Cuban sympathizers, but have been furnished to me by officers of the army, the most determined in their resolution to suppress the insurrection. From this it will be seen that if the number of the insurgents in the field has diminished, the means at the disposal of the government for their suppression have diminished to a still greater extent.

There is another reason, also, why the chances of putting down the insurrection are lessened by time. In the beginning the Cubans knew little about war, and, though numerous, were by no means formidable enemies. Now, however, the men in the field have acquired considerable skill in the use of their arms, and the habits of obedience and control so necessary in warfare. The troubles in Spain, it is felt, will eventually so paralyze the government as to prevent the dispatch of reinforcements to Cuba. In view of all these difficulties, it is no wonder that even among the Spanish officers there is growing up a feeling that the war will be interminable—that is, if Spain can find the men and money to continue the struggle. It is a strange commentary on human intelligence, that under the specious plea of patriotism a people can be induced to make so great and so appalling sacrifices, in order that some few hundred men may continue to enjoy their ill-gotten wealth; for there is no escaping from the fact that these thousands of Spanish lives, and the wasted millions wrung from a people sunk in poverty and wretchedness, have been wasted in defense of a few hundred slave-owners. The Spanish nation derives no profit from the connection with Cuba: at most a few government employés become rich by stealing from the government they are supposed to serve. These people are very loud in professions of patriotism, and all the time they are crippling their country by putting a no inconsiderable portion of the revenue into their own pockets. This is a fact so notorious that even the gentry in question will scarcely attempt to deny it.

My authorities for the statement are almost every man I met who had had any dealings with the government employés. On the question of their rapaciousness there is no second opinion. Merchants have told me of transactions in which they were themselves engaged which would have appeared to me incredible, but that the information came from sources beyond suspicion. Testimony as to the general dishonesty of officials is borne by men of all parties and all conditions.

The discussion of my mission and the state of the island was carried on by the officers of the San Quentin battalion in the best humor and with marked delicacy. There was evident a strong desire to present the Spanish side of the question in as favorable a light as possible. The points presented were, however, nearly always the same. On the side of Spain were to be found all the valor and humanity, while the insurgents, as at present constituted, were principally ignorant and ferocious blacks, who waged not a war for freedom, but a war of extermination against the whites. In so far as this touched my own safety, I was assured that should any of the bands of negro marauders encounter me, my character as a neutral correspondent would avail me little. These assurances caused me considerable uneasiness, for even the *laborantes,* or Cuban sympathizers, told me the same thing, and I began to look on my mission as a rather unpleasant enterprise. However, the very blackness of the pictures drawn aroused my suspicion as to their correctness. Cuba appeared to me a land of *Croque-Mitaines,* where every danger was magnified a hundred-fold by the fears of the inhabitants, who live in a state of mental darkness. The slightest occurrence assumes awful proportions, because there is no means of throwing light on the shady places. The government, even when it tells the truth, is never believed, not even by its supporters. This is the natural result of the efforts constantly made to present a *couleur-de-rose* view of the situation. The presence, therefore, among the soldiers of a representative of the New York *Herald,* which was felt not alone to be free to express its opinions on all that passed, but also to be tinged with sympathy with the Cuban cause, excited no little interest. The officers from the first expressed themselves pleased that I should accompany them on what they hoped would be a long and interesting expedition, and there was a universal wish that the enemy would show himself, in order that the world might receive an impartial account of a Cuban battle. Full of hope that the morning would see us on our way to those mysterious woods where the insurrection has its strongholds, we all turned in, but were destined to disappointment, for during the night Colonel Sostrada received orders to return in the direction of San Luis, and to await further orders. This news threw a damper on all our enthusiasm; but as it was looked on only as a change of direction, the circumstance was not much thought about. The halt was made at the Caridad estate, where the column was to remain until further orders. Colonel Sostrada, accompanied by the adjutant, rode to San Luis to communicate with Brigadier Morales by telegraph, and returned in a few hours with news that the battalion would remain stationary until further orders. Colonel Sostrada told me that I was at liberty to remain or to return to Santiago de Cuba. This surprised me, as I had not spoken a word about leaving. I told him that I had come out to make the expedition with the battalion, and was inclined to remain until it was ended, if my presence was not inconvenient. He replied that the officers of the battalion would be delighted to have me remain. There was no definite reason given for the sudden abandonment of the expedition, and, as the subject was a delicate one, I did not make any pressing inquiries. It afterwards became known, however, that as soon as the battalion marched north a portion of the insurgents marched south, and others appeared threatening the plantations. In view of these movements, the battalion was ordered back to protect the harvest. A letter had been sent by Colonel Sostrada, about me, to Brigadier Morales, but no reply was received to it. The general opinion being that the column would remain stationary for some time, there was no object to serve in delaying my return to Santiago de Cuba, and so I resolved to say adieu to my new friends. On taking leave, Colonel Sostrada expressed the regret of himself and the other officers that I should be obliged to go away so soon. He seemed very anxious lest the impression should go abroad that the column retrograded from fear of the enemy, or that there was any force in front capable of barring the passage of the battalion. When assured that no such opinion was entertained by me, he replied, "I know you are too polite to express such an opinion; but I fear that such has been the impression made on your mind by the sudden return of the troops." He evidently felt only half satisfied, and was as much annoyed as I was at the unexpected termination of the expedition.

During my stay with the Spanish troops, I had been the object of unceasing attention. Nothing that could add to my comfort was neglected, and I was treated more like a spoiled child than the special correspondent of a paper which is assumed to be hostile to Spanish rule in the Antilles. Commander Lopez, one of the most distinguished officers of the battalion, accompanied me to Santiago de Cuba. We rode from the encampment at Caridad to the station of Christo—a distance of five long leagues—without any guard. This surprised me not a little, as the district is very wild and mountainous, and at times we rode through the bush for miles without meeting any living thing. We passed many a point where one cool fellow with an old shotgun and a taste for hedge-shooting could have disposed of both of us before we could have pulled rein; but fortunately we arrived at the station of Christo without encountering any enterprising Mambi. From this point we traveled by the railroad on a handcar, worked by two negroes, to Santiago de Cuba. The work was not difficult, for after the first few hundred yards we were on an inclined plane, and our only trouble was to keep the drag on so that the car would not rush down with dangerous velocity. The evening of my arrival I presented myself at the palacio. Brigadier Morales was absent, but the chief of staff expressed regret at the termination of the expedition, promising that notice should be given me as soon as the next column left for the insurgent district.

6 Preparing to Run the Gauntlet

THE TURNING back of the Spanish column has always been a puzzle to me, and there lurks in my mind a suspicion that the real cause was my presence, which, no doubt, was distasteful to the higher authorities. Short as was my stay with the Spanish troops, it created a new difficulty to the fulfillment of my mission. Nothing could well have been more awkward for me than the invitation to accompany the troops, and yet it was impossible to refuse without giving some ground for the suspicion that my mission was intended to be one-sided and partial. The apparent friendliness of the authorities at Santiago de Cuba prevented the Cuban sympathizers communicating to me any useful information. With a Machiavelism quite worthy of masters in the black art, the Spanish party carefully spread rumors that however neutral my professions were, I was in reality trying to serve the interests of Spain. Matters were not at all minced, and it was confidentially whispered about on authority that the Spanish government had won me by purchase. To have resented this cunning slander would have been worse than useless, it would have been folly, for either it had been invented in order to provoke a personal altercation, when I would have been handed over to some practiced sword, or it was intended to betray me into a public denial, which would have had the effect of confirming belief in its truth. So long as no one made the assertion in my presence, in an unfriendly spirit, it was clearly the wiser course on my part wholly to ignore it. This treatment proved thoroughly successful, and in a few weeks the slander, if not forgotten, ceased to circulate actively.

During my stay at Santiago de Cuba my whole attention was directed to gaining, if it were possible, the confidence of the Cuban population, without appearing to interest myself in their affairs, or mingling much in their society. Not very many Cubans were anxious for my acquaintance, and those who offered themselves most freely were just the class of men who could be of no possible service to me. As an indication of the state of terror in which the Cuban people live, the following experience will not be without value. A few days after my arrival in Santiago de Cuba I was introduced to a gentleman named Bell. He is the grandson of the person mentioned in the romantic narrative known as "Tom Cringle's Log."* The readers of that book will remember Ricardo Campaña, who is introduced as a thrifty and successful Scotch planter (in the books the Scotch always puff themselves as thrifty, cunning, and successful); but as it happened that Ricardo Campaña was a thrifty and successful Irish planter, his grandson, Ricardo Bell, received me as a countryman of his grandfather with much cordiality. This gentleman's acquaintance promised to be of real utility to me, as his plantation of *Esperanza* was one of the extreme outposts of the Spanish lines. It would, therefore, afford me a magnificent basis of operations, if only I could obtain an excuse for going there. The gentleman who introduced me to Mr. Bell did not inform him that I was the New York *Herald* correspondent, but only that I was an Irish gentleman traveling in the island. That was title enough to Mr. Bell's hospitality, and, on my expressing a desire to visit Ti-Arriba, a town close to the Esperanza plantation, a warm request was made that I should remain at Esperanza during my stay in the neighborhood. This offer was accepted by me, as it would enable me to make myself acquainted with the country without suspicion. I was already congratulating myself on my good fortune, when, next day, Mr. Bell called to request me not to avail myself of the invitation, as it might compromise him in the eyes of the authorities. The invitation, he assured me, was given in ignorance of the fact that I was the correspondent of the New York *Herald,* and this I knew to be a fact. Mr. Bell expected me to feel annoyed; but the matter did not surprise me in the least. It only showed how deeply terrorism had penetrated Cuban society. Mr. Bell was well known to be a loyal man; his brothers were officers in the army and navy, and his family lived in Spain; yet all this did not free him from apprehension in case he should be suspected of friendly communication with a *Herald* correspondent.

**Tom Cringle's Log* is a novel by Scottish author Michael Scott, set in 1820s Jamaica. Scott published the novel anonymously in Edinburgh's *Blackwood's Magazine,* starting in 1829.

Not content with making this explanation to me, Mr. Bell thought it due to his own safety to purge himself of suspicion, and went directly to the governor, Morales de los Rios, and related to him the story of the invitation and its withdrawal. Morales was wise enough to see that Mr. Bell's ultra-loyalty had led him to disclose the terrorism underlying the surface of an apparently peaceable and contented society. The executions on very slight suspicion of treason had been so cruelly and vigorously carried out that the people were completely cowed, and trembled at the mere idea of incurring the displeasure of the authorities.

Some experience of war had prepared me for the difficulties of passing through the Spanish outposts, but the peculiar nature of the struggle in Cuba was so distinct from all I had witnessed that my calculations proved to be completely at fault. My expectation was to have found the combatants occupying tracts of inhabited country more or less well defined, and that a rush through some carelessly guarded point in the Spanish line would enable me with certainty to reach the Cuban outposts; or that the insurgents were enabled constantly to communicate with their friends in the Spanish lines by means of *Arrieros* and travelers passing from one town to another. Under either condition it would not have been very difficult to make a junction with some of the Cuban forces, but a little acquaintance with the country and the disposition of the troops soon convinced me of my mistake. Owing to the forced concentration of the rural population around the forts, the Spanish lines occupied all the cultivated country, and they were guarded with as much care as their extent would admit of; beyond the outposts all was silent, mysterious, and unknown. Districts formerly inhabited had been reduced to howling deserts; both parties vying in the savage relentless destruction, until whatever would afford shelter or food to man had disappeared. No one was admitted to pass the outposts, except along certain lines of communication accompanied by a military guard. In the debatable land lying beyond, every man found was an enemy, and subject by severe military law to immediate execution. Strong Spanish columns marched and countermarched through the desolate regions, burning whatever miserable leaf-covered shanties they encountered, wreaking vengeance on the wounded, the sick, and the weakly, whose infirmities shut them off from escape, and hunting like bloodhounds the ill-armed and wretchedly-supplied soldiers of the Cuban republic.

The latter, unable for the most part to deliver battle to their pursuers from want of ammunition and arms, as well as from numerical inferiority, were constantly moving from point to point through the wild and uncultivated regions of the interior, so that it was impossible to know in what point the Cuban forces could with certainty be met. It had been stated in New York, by persons who ought to have been better informed, that the Cuban campfires were visible from Santiago de Cuba. In the beginning of the insurrection this was true, but it was no longer so, though Cuban encampments could still be reached in a day's march from Santiago de Cuba, if one were at liberty to pass through the Spanish lines. However, this information was only gained after a great deal of trouble and many fruitless search expeditions. All the lines of communication with the interior were carefully guarded by troops, and without considerable acquaintance with the topography of the country it would be very difficult to pass safely through the lines. The country round Santiago de Cuba is, in all directions, exceedingly mountainous, and hill and vale are covered by dense woods, except where clearings have been made for plantations. A few tracks have been opened through the woods, and have been dignified by the name of roads, but for the most part they are mere mule-paths. These roads in all cases lead through the posts and camps of the Spanish troops. On either side dark, impenetrable woods extend; through these pass trails only known to the skilled guides, and so slightly are they marked that even when following them it is difficult to distinguish the path. Only those who have seen a tropical forest can form an idea of these dark woods, with their giant trees, thorny bushes, cactus plants, and trailing lianas, gracefully pendent, swinging from branch to branch, and wound round trunk and limb of trees in most wonderful tracery, beautiful to the view, but well-nigh impossible to pass through. On foot a man armed with the useful machete could succeed in making his way in, but with infinite labor and sore trouble; whether or not a man unskilled in woodcraft would ever make his way out is more than doubtful. My impression is, that anything like a serious plunge into these awful woods without a guide would end in death from starvation, after hopeless efforts on the part of the rash adventurer to extricate himself. At least such was the conclusion forced on me as I surveyed from the summit of the mountains lying between Ramon las Yeguas and San Luis the magnificent panorama of mountains, valley, and plain, forest-clad in all primeval grandeur far as the eye could reach, a solitude scarcely broken save by chirp of grasshopper and monotonous whirr of winged insects, and the infinite noises that in the tropics make morn and eve hideous.*

In the depths of these woods fugitive families and disabled patriots

---

*"Ramon las Yeguas" should read "Ramón de las Yaguas."

have opened little clearings; but as every effort is made to conceal these homes of misfortune, it is next to impossible to discover them even by the aid of most skillful guides. Hid away in the most silent solitudes of those gloomy forests, little colonies of freemen, accepting rather suffering, want, danger, and death than submission to slave-masters, toil and watch and suffer, waiting for the terrible night of agony and sorrow to pass by. These are the disabled or the unarmed, the guides, the prefects, the toilers, who sow and reap that the soldiers of liberty, in the hour of disaster and defeat and bodily pain, may have bread to eat to restore shattered strength, and cheer in the hour of darkened hope. The wounded, the cancerous, the fever-stricken, are here conveyed and lovingly tended until the sharp pang of the wound has ceased and the delirium of the terrible fever has fled, thanks to bark decoctions made with unfair but most loving hands. Often the fierce Catalan, with bloodhound scent, finds his way through the tangled path, and bursts wrathfully on the startled dwellers. Woe to the wounded wretch disabled from flight! Small will be the measure of mercy shown to his helplessness. Happy is he if the eager, ruthless soldier cleave the unprotected head with life-crushing stroke; worse may be his fate should life continue when the slaying fierceness has abated with assured victory, and the cruel savage glee sets in: then the victim dies the lingering death a thousand-fold more terrible than the short pang of the swift battle-stroke. While this knowledge was forcing itself on my mind, there still lingered hope, growing hourly fainter, that a friendly hand would be outstretched from the misty and dark uncertainty in which I wandered to conduct me to the sinuous path that led to Cuba Libre. Anxious that none should suffer through me, I sought no confidences, content to accept whatever risks were incidental to my mission. Without asking to know who were *laborantes,* or who were not, I simply whispered in ears that seemed friendly my surprise that no sign was made by the patriots, no word of advice or anonymous hint sent me that would place me on the right road; as there could be no risk in some of the guides, or messengers, who were constantly passing between the town and insurgent camp, meeting me on the lonely roads where daily I rode unaccompanied.

At last came a vague hint that in the direction of Ti-Arriba it might be possible to open communications with some of the Cuban forces. In this hope I at once set out alone, as was my custom. No notice was given to the authorities of my departure, in order to test the amount of freedom to travel which could be counted on. My previous voyages of exploration, combined with the frequent use of my pocket-compass, enabled me to find my way with a certain amount of facility. The utter loneliness of the road, and, at times, the awful grandeur of the solitude, produced in the soul a feeling of awe not unmixed with terror.

7   In Search of the Mambi-Land

Leaving Santiago de Cuba and following the Guantanamo road, the little town of Caney is the first and only village of any consequence encountered between Santiago and Ti-Arriba. Before the war it was a pretty and prosperous town, as it is here called, but war has left its traces in a most unmistakable manner on the place, and it looks as deserted and silent as a ruined city in a desert. Not but that there are still some inhabitants, but they do not seem to belong to the place, but only to be camped in it, or wandering ghost-like about their houses, which are mostly shut up, bolted, and barred. The market-shed, in the center of the town, was occupied when I passed through by a company of soldiers, who were engaged burnishing their arms, brushing their coats, arranging their packs, evidently getting ready to parade, but their bustle seemed no part of the life of Caney, but something foreign and contrasting with it. Then there were some thirty sleepy, lazy-looking men with guns, very dirty, very ragged, with large straw hats having broad red or green ribbons around them, upon which was stamped a printed announcement to let the whole world know that these were the volunteers of Caney, the heroic sons of the soil who, for the consideration of twenty cents a day, were willing to forget that they were Cubans and fight for the flag of Castile. Their affection, however, for Castile never got so far as the soap: probably it was never pushed quite so far, lest it should be washed away. Be that as it may, the heroes were very dirty and rather ragged, and looked like shreds of the original population of Caney saved from the war deluge. Leaving the soldiers out of the picture, everything was desolate and ruinous in that waste of half-deserted houses. The very atmosphere of the place was depressing in spite of the mountain air and sunshine, and, as I passed, the streets moaned audibly under my horse's hoof-strokes. The road immediately begins to ascend the Sierra Maestra, and for leagues winds along the sides of precipitous hills, with fertile valleys a thousand feet below, and little huts of squatters perched above where apparently only winged things could arrive. The view at many points along the road is of a grandeur wholly indescribable by pen or brush, embracing the fertile valley of Santiago de Cuba, with the town seen in the distance, and the sea, with a stretch of beach running eastwards, foam-crowned, while the dark-green sea beyond lies in the deepest repose, fading away in the infinite distance until lost in the very skies. The road was almost abandoned, but now and then, during the first stage, a convoy of pack-mules, coffee laden, accompanied by an armed escort, was encountered, or an old soldier, or messenger, traveling from the military posts and *ingenios,* to Cuba.* In all cases these people were colored men, and armed. At first this puzzled me very much, as they were ragged-looking and dirty enough to be denizens of the Manigua. They were evidently surprised to see a white man alone, and on all occasions they held their guns ready to fire on the least show of hostility. I paid no attention to these warlike demonstrations, but rode on demurely. My peaceful air saved me from interruption or annoyance for a long while, though most of the fellows evidently did not trust me much, for they always spurred their horses as they passed, so as to avoid any possible treachery.

Gradually, however, the region of plantations was left behind, and I traveled hour after hour without meeting evidence of the existence of a human being, passing through gullies, sliding down the beds of mountain streams almost dried up, fording others uncomfortably deep, and plunging through stretches of morass, going at hap-hazard, with no other guide than my compass, and yet somehow stumbling into the right track. It was not a very pleasant ride; the silence was oppressive, and some portions of the road presented so wild an appearance that one might very well be excused for wishing himself some miles away. As I passed through a stretch of forest where the Spaniards had felled the trees for a considerable distance on either side of the road, a flock of auras—the vulture of the country—absolutely pursued me for miles. They evidently looked on me as almost as good as done for, so they flocked to the feast that was good natured enough to come to them. From time to time the flock would settle down on the tree-branches some fifty yards ahead of me, and wait for my approach, evidently thinking that I had gone far enough, and that it was unfair to keep them waiting; but as I passed they would rise with a hoarse, croaking noise, and proceed to head me, having, to all appearance, made up their minds to try how I tasted. Now this funeral cortege was by no

---

*In this context, "ingenio" means "sugar mill."

means to my liking, as I had not the remotest idea of being eaten if it could be at all avoided, so I resolved to try if a shot would not rid me of my persecutors. Unfortunately, my gun had been left in Santiago, or I should have lessened the flock considerably. When they settled again in front of me, I took out my revolver and rode up slowly to where they were waiting, and stopped my horse. Not one of the auras stirred, so I could take as good aim as the uneasiness of my horse would allow. It was not easy to cover my object, but at last I thought I had one fellow pretty well sighted, so I fired; the flock rose immediately, but the bird I had aimed at did not. He was not killed, however, but he was badly hit, and the blood stained his black plumage. The lesson was not lost on the flock, for though they circled about, croaking and screaming, they gradually disappeared, and I was certainly very glad to be rid of them.

On emerging from this pass, a small military post, placed on a commanding eminence, compelled me to give an account of myself. This was the first time any Spanish soldier interfered with my free movement. The soldiers were easily satisfied, and gave me some valuable directions about the road to be pursued.

It was late in the afternoon when the sentinel posted in the blockhouse that defends the southern side of Ti-Arriba halted me peremptorily, with a demand to know my business, and why I was alive. Having satisfied him on these important points, I was permitted to ride into the main street of the *pueblo*. Ti-Arriba is one of the extreme advanced posts of the Spanish lines. It consists of a number of *bohios*, a few frame houses, and two considerable blockhouses. The place looks frowsy and wretched, and it scarcely surprised me when, in reply to a request for lodging and entertainment at the principal tienda, I was told to try elsewhere. There was only one other place that appeared likely to act as temporary hotel, so I went there. It was the tienda of the Capitan de Partido, or mayor of the village. He consented to give me shelter and potluck. But before I could make final arrangements to get stowed away in a kind of lumber-room communicating with a bakery, where dough was nightly kneaded and roasted into indigestible bread, it was necessary to produce my *cedula*, to show that I was a person authorized to travel. My arrival had created quite a sensation, and all kinds of speculations were indulged in as to what my business might be. No traveler had ventured for years to ride to Ti-Arriba, and the sudden apparition of a foreigner, coming from no one knew where, caused considerable uneasiness. My riding-boots, revolver, and heavy machete gave me a military look which drew on me the suspicions of the community. The military commandant, a consumptive lieutenant-colonel, and his second in command came down on purpose to inspect me; and, as I had no permission to carry arms, the commandant was about to offer me accommodation in the blockhouse, when a messenger, riding in hot haste, arrived from Santiago de Cuba. He placed a letter from Morales de los Rios in the hands of the commandant, which quite softened that functionary in my regard. It was very decent of Morales, who would have acted like a reasonable man had it not been for the idiots in Havana.

The letter of Brigadier Morales made me a person of importance in the eyes of the hybrid inhabitants of the pueblo, and I was shown to my quarters with many excuses for their unsuitableness to so distinguished a señor as myself. In truth, some apology was needed. My quarters consisted of a miserable little lumber-room, off a bakery, where a settle bed had been arranged for me. The walls were hung round with pieces of harness and a most curious collection of odds and ends. Through crevices in the walls the air circulated freely, and chinks in the roof allowed me to count the stars at night. However, this is rather an advantage, and affords distraction as soon as one becomes used to it. The bare earth formed the floor, and at night I went to bed by the light of a miserable candle stuck in a stone bottle, which did service as candlestick. Ti-Arriban hotel accommodation is idyllic in its simplicity.

The population of Ti-Arriba was almost wholly composed of colored volunteers and some few Catalan shopkeepers. The volunteers were not very formidable. They were nearly all men who had been insurgents, but had surrendered from various causes, and now were in arms against their ancient comrades. It is true they did not do very much active damage to the Cubans, although from time to time they issued out on formidable scouts in the direction opposite to that in which they knew the enemy to be. Sometimes they even burned the encampments of the insurgents; but it was when the latter had gone away. When not engaged in their warlike toils, they managed to live in idleness on their scanty pay, eating sweet potatoes and drinking cane rum at about ten cents a gallon, so that it cost them only about five cents to make half a dozen drunk. So as their days passed in loafing, and their nights in dancing and drinking, it may well be imagined that the gallant fellows would not put an end to the war for any consideration. Hence patriotic devotion displays itself from time to time in furnishing the insurgents with food and ammunition, in order that the war may last forever. In this they only imitate their betters; for what would the generals and the commissaries do if the extraordinary expenses, which mostly go into their pockets, should suddenly be stopped? The

Spaniards know very well that they could not trust these volunteers if they should for a moment be unable to bribe them, and nothing is more likely than that someday the whole volunteer tribe will cut their officers' throats and join the insurgents. Already thousands of them have done so, and there is little reason to doubt that thousands more will follow. If that should happen, Spanish rule will be at an end, for, though they do not often put themselves to any great trouble about fighting, yet they act as guides, leading the Spaniards to points they could never reach without their assistance, for these men have the same wonderful instinct, or power, of finding their way about in a forest that novelists have endowed the American Indian with—a power rivaling the sense of scent in animals. As it was my intention to make this place the basis of my immediate operations, it was necessary to get on good terms with the people. The shortest and most expeditious way to do this appeared to me to be the giving a ball and free whisky. So, having asked and obtained permission of the military commander, and got the civil authority to undertake the arrangement, cards were issued to all the colored ladies and gentlemen, as well as to the mere white men and civil and military authorities, requesting the pleasure of their company at the HERALD BALL. I rode out to the Esperanza plantation to invite the military commandant, whose friendship I was anxious to cultivate, and some of the directors, whose acquaintance I had made, to give me the favor of their company.

It was a huge joke; but I kept a solemn face all through, and had the delightful pleasure of seeing the ball-room crowded with the *élite* of Ti-Arriba, the military and civil authorities of the town and district, and all the pretty girls within reach. Music was supplied by a fine organ, specially manufactured to play dance-music; and, as the rum was plentiful, and a drop of wine for the ladies to the fore, the fun was soon fast and furious. That night will not soon be forgotten in Ti-Arriba—the *Herald* ball was an event; and when the hour arrived at which, according to law, the fun should cease, the commandant did not have the heart to refuse an extension into the wee hours of the morning. How that dance ended I know not, for I retired to my lumber-room about midnight, and was lulled to sleep by the hum of human voices mingled with the shuffling of feet and the loud barbaric grinding of the organ. There was a general headache in Ti-Arriba next morning, and I was declared to have merited well of the community, which, from a strictly moral point of view, was somewhat doubtful. As I had expected, the ball enabled me to gather information that, were it not for unforeseen circumstances, might have proved extremely useful. For the next few days my time was occupied riding about the country and paying one or two visits to the Esperanza plantation, in order to study a very peculiar phase of Cuban life under the existing condition of things. For now, in Cuba, the plantation is turned into a kind of fortress, of which a feudal baron of the good, or rather bad, old days might have been pardonably proud. It is rather difficult to convey by a mere pen-and-ink description the imposing and formidable appearance presented by the fortified buildings of a Cuban plantation; but, in order that some slight idea may be formed of an object which plays such an important part in the insurrectionary struggle, the accompanying sketch is given.

These improvised forts serve exactly the same purpose, in the scheme of conquest and government in Cuba to-day, that the feudal castle played in Europe in the Middle Ages, or the blockhouses in the conquest and colonization of North America. They are the centers of organization and supply to the Spaniards, as well as places of refuge in case of defeat, although not counted among the military forces at the disposition of the government: they are, in fact, military colonies. When they occupy an exposed position they are, in all cases, supplied with a contingent of regular soldiers, often under the command of officers. In addition, each planter supplies a private corps of auxiliaries, sometimes reaching to the respectable figure of a hundred men, exclusive of overseers and machinists, who are all armed, as are the most trusted of the slaves, though with inferior weapons. So that these *ingenios,* for the most part, are defended by a really respectable force, although the number of regular soldiers may be exceedingly small. In many instances considerable engineering skill has been shown in the construction and planning of the defensive works, so much so as to render an attack by a force unprovided with artillery a very hazardous enterprise, and one that could only be brought to a successful conclusion by a great sacrifice of life on the part of the attacking party. Small towers are constructed at some distance from the main works, in positions that enable the lookouts to survey a wide stretch of country, so that no force can approach unseen. These towers are constructed in a very solid manner, the upper portion of a hard wood, difficult to set on fire, while the base, or support, on which they are placed, is built of stonework. The garrison can see perfectly from very small loopholes, while they are completely sheltered by their bullet-proof tower from the missiles of their assailants. The most dexterous rifleman might shoot at the loopholes for a day without injuring any one inside, while an attacking party, having to cross ground carefully cleared in every direction, would be exposed to a murderous fire.

These detached towers form the salient angles of the work, and are usually occupied by the regular soldiers, as being the points most exposed to attack, and requiring most coolness and decision in defense. At night, the spaces between the towers are brilliantly illuminated by means of *fariolas,* or large kerosene-lamps, furnished with reflectors, which throw, from nightfall to dawn, a flood of light on all the approaches, through which a mouse could not creep unperceived. The main body of the work is generally formed by the mill-shed, where all the machinery is placed. This is naturally a point of great strength. The foundations are constructed of solid brickwork, around which heavy logs and huge pieces of machinery are piled up to form a breastwork, while the entrance is defended by a rude tambour of the same solid construction. Where the house of the planter is of solid construction, it is loop-holed and barricaded in the same fashion, so as to furnish an effective flank defense. The towers and retrenched mill-shed, as well as the houses, naturally protect each other, so that an enemy, even after penetrating into the body of the work, would be exposed to a murderous fire from the isolated defenses; and, as the defenders are armed with the best modern weapons and plenty of ammunition, the work of capturing one of these *ingenios* is by no means so simple as might be thought. In fact, many of these fortified structures might stand a siege, and, in the hands of brave men, could only be reduced by artillery, or captured by a superior force, after immense loss of life. Now, these works are a great obstacle in the way of the Cuban insurgents, who, from want of artillery, are unable to capture them, especially as, owing to the poverty of their hospital arrangements, and the impediment caused by a large number of wounded, they dare not risk taking them by assault. There is, however, one dangerous feature to the Spanish government in these fortified mills and their armed garrisons. The immense majority of the men are Cubans and people of color, who, at bottom, have more sympathy with the insurgents than with the Spaniards, but who were so thoroughly frightened by the defeats and sufferings during the first disasters of the insurrection, that they are afraid to take part with the men in the field, although in many instances an active correspondence is maintained between these posts and the insurgents. The turn in the tide of Cuban opinion has already set in, and in Camarguey, Holguin, and Bayamo has brought an extraordinary accession of strength to the insurrection. Should this movement continue, the Cuban leaders will soon find themselves at the head of a numerous and well-armed force, which would enable them to continue the struggle for twenty years, if need should be, against the greatest forces that Spain could possibly maintain. And as the Cuban volunteers have to suffer all the dangers and inconveniences of the campaign, and are not very well treated by the government, they are becoming profoundly discontented. They see that Spain cannot put down the insurrection, and the *laborantes* are constantly instilling into their minds that it would be better for them to throw themselves into the insurgent ranks, and so, by destroying the existing balance of power, lead to the speedy triumph of the Cuban cause. That this preaching has not been without its effects is proved by the number of volunteers who have deserted to the insurgents lately. Between three and four hundred armed men, with their families, passed over to the Cubans while I was with Cespedes, and during my imprisonment at Manzanillo other camps revolted and went over to the insurgents. The same thing has occurred in Camarguey, where the insurrection has spread alarmingly since the heroic death of Agramonte, which appears to have reawakened the patriotic ardor of the Camargueans, and given new life to the struggle the Spaniards hoped it would bring to an end.* It may be that the mean and cowardly vengeance of the Spanish authorities in burning Agramonte's body, so that no trace of him should remain, kindled in the Cuban youth the holy flame of patriotism. Tyrants are always stupid, and in this case they imagined that the noble lesson of the Cuban hero's life would be destroyed; and when the frail tenement of his grand soul was reduced to ashes and scattered to the winds of heaven, little did they dream that the gases given out by his cinders would infest the air with the very spirit that in life he breathed into those who formed round him in the thundering charges when he swept like a whirlwind down on his country's foes, and that every atom scattered to the wind would spring into new life an armed and implacable avenger.

8 Captured by the Spaniards

DURING MY stay at Ti-Arriba I received information that the woody mountains in the vicinity of Filipinas were held by a band of insurgent negroes. Their leader, Guillermon, an escaped slave, a man of gigantic

---

*See note above on p. 21.

stature and terrible aspect, was represented to be as ferocious in disposition as terrible in aspect.* No quarter was said to be given by this band, and all white men who fell into their hands were, according to popular belief, disposed of in the most summary manner. In addition to his other amiable qualities, Guillermon was fond of the ladies, and kept a stock of wives on hand. There was a story current that one of the ladies of the harem, a white woman, had attempted to poison her lord from jealousy, but Guillermon discovered the treachery, and cut her head off. A similar fate was supposed to have befallen other ladies who had excited his jealousy or suspicion. My experience of these stories had made me skeptical, so I resolved to visit the district and see if there was any truth in the description of this redoubtable chief. The distance from Ti-Arriba to Ramon Las Yeguas is about five short leagues. The road runs through a wild and almost completely abandoned country, very mountainous, and thickly wooded. At intervals the ruins of coffee plantations and sugar-mills furnish sad proof of the destructive nature of the war. A small fort on the summit of the mountain which separates the villages commands a pass of Alpine grandeur. It was passed without difficulty, and I entered the embryo town of Yeguas without more trouble than answering the sentinel's challenge. The *Capitan de Partido*, who is the highest civil functionary, received me kindly, and in answer to a request to dispatch a telegram, informed me that the operator was at breakfast in the village. On descending I found the telegraphist, who undertook to send on my telegram, but as breakfast was about to be served, it was necessary to wait some time. As soon as the repast was over, the operator went to his post, promising to send me down the reply when it came to hand. Several officers of the garrison had come in, attracted by the unusual appearance of a stranger, alone, and armed, in so out-of-the-way a place as Ramon Las Yeguas. They were, however, very polite, and insisted on my joining them in a bottle of ale. My new acquaintances were very much interested in me, and asked a good many questions. They evidently looked on me with suspicion, and were trying to worm out of me information about myself and my business. In this they had but little success. Before long one of the mounted police came to request my presence in the house of the Capitan de Partido.

Not feeling inclined to walk up-hill in the sun, I sent that official my

---

*O'Kelly refers to Afro-Cuban general, and later folk hero, Guillermo Moncada (1841–1895), called Guillermón for his exceptional size. Moncada would fight in all three Cuban wars for independence.

cedula, thinking it would satisfy him. In a few moments, however, he appeared in person to request that I would accompany him to the *capitaneria*. At the same time he asked the captain of the guard, who was drinking with us, to go to his post, which I soon discovered was close to the dwelling of the Capitan de Partido. In fact, I was a prisoner. With many polite expressions, the functionary informed me that a telegram would have to be sent to General Morales de los Rios, to inquire into my character, and whether I had a right to travel and carry arms.

The captain was a small, energetic person, slightly pock marked. He had keen features, and small, dark eyes, and was a very Dogberry in disposition. He informed me that a slight irregularity existed in my passport, and that until an answer was received from General Morales, I would not be at liberty to proceed. He, however, ordered up some refreshments, and proposed to drink my health. This compliment I declined, but proposed to substitute the toast of "liberty." My two jailers were too polite to decline, but they drank the toast with an expression of face decidedly comical. While the captain of the guard, who was a feeble young man, with a grievance, engaged me in conversation, Dogberry undertook to draw a portrait of me, after the manner of the police reports. Without appearing to do so, I kept my eye on him, and at last caught him in *flagrante delicto*. He was rather disconcerted when I told him that he ought to hang out a shingle with the notice "Portraits Taken Here." As soon as the picture was finished, the captain of the guard asked me in a most polished manner if a visit to the tower would not give me pleasure. Not to be outdone in politeness, I said it would, and that tower-visiting was very much to my mind. Dogberry suggested that it would be convenient to leave my machete and revolver in his care. This I firmly declined to do, not liking the idea of being disarmed; and he, like a true Dogberry, did not insist. In order to give my imprisonment as much as possible the air of a visit, the captain of the guard conducted me to the sentinel post, where we enjoyed for some time a really beautiful prospect. Afterwards we descended to the officers' quarters, a little rookery formed on the first floor of the tower by a rude partition. Here I remained until Dogberry arrived, and requested me to go down to his house. As he was decidedly vulgar, and not a little pretentious, though he tried to be polite according to his lights, I asked to be left with the officers, alleging the coolness of the tower. It was, however, useless. Dogberry had had a qualm of conscience, and he said it pained him to see a gentleman like me in the tower, so I was forced to go along with him. The secret of this change of tone was the Cura of Ti-Arriba had arrived at Ramon Las Yeguas, and told him who

I was. He left me soon after under the supervision of some officers, and rode to a fort called Santa Maria, where the regiment of Alcantara was posted, to inform the colonel, the Marquis of Villa Etre, of my presence. This gentleman sent some of his officers to invite me to pass the night with the regiment; but as Dogberry, in order to clear himself, had told me that it was the officers who were drinking with me in the morning who caused my arrest, I declined the invitation, but accepted a guide to the *Cafetale* of Santa Isabel, the property of an Irish gentleman, some two leagues distant, where I was certain of a friendly reception.

It was already dark when the telegraphic dispatch ordering my release came from Brigadier Morales de los Rios, and therefore impossible for me to continue my journey towards Filipinas. In the mean time the arrival of a military convoy and many officers from the fort served as a distraction; and, had it not been for my indignation at the unworthy conduct of the officers who in the early part of the day had caused my arrest while I was to a certain extent their guest, I might have passed an agreeable night in the fort to which the Marquis had kindly invited me. However, a little scrap of news picked up in the general conversation decided me on changing my basis of operations. One of the new arrivals, with that want of caution which is a marked feature among Spanish military men, told his comrades, in my hearing, that Cespedes was known to be at Cambute with Jesus Perez and many other prominent Cuban chiefs, and that a forward movement would be made by the troops in a few days.* This was the first scrap of useful news I had picked up during my sojourn on the island. All other information had been of the vaguest kind; but now, at last, there was a definite point, which, could it be reached, the chief difficulty of my mission would have been overcome. How to find out the exact position of Cambute was not, however, so simple an affair as at first it seemed. Now was the time when the help of the *laborante* would have been invaluable if it could have been obtained. A plan of the roads, with directions what paths to take, what points to avoid, how to recognize the right from the wrong road, would have been beyond price. I at once resolved to return to Santiago de Cuba without a moment's delay, as it was evidently the quickest way to obtain the needed information; but, in order not to excite any suspicion, it was necessary to proceed cautiously. Excusing myself to the officer who brought me the invitation from the Marquis of Villa Etra on the ground of a previous engagement, I requested that a guide should

---

*Colonel Jesús Pérez commanded two regiments at Cobre under the command of Máximo Gómez.

be furnished to accompany me to the *Cafetale* of Santa Isabel, some miles away. Our road lay over mountain-roads bordered on either side by dense woods, or abandoned plantations, where groups of fugitives still sought a precarious subsistence by raiding into the corn-fields and among the coffee-shrubs in the silence and darkness of the night, in search of scanty supplies of those provisions which their insecure and fugitive life in the woods prevented them from cultivating. My guide, who was a reformed rebel, black as the ace of spades, told me, confidentially, that two companies of volunteers were in ambush in the hope of surprising a party that had been making somewhat too free of late among the canes. Under other circumstances it would have been very pleasant to chat with this sable militaire; but both were anxious to get over the road as soon as possible; and the rate we rode over that broken and jagged road, except where it was so bad as to compel us to break into a walk on pain of broken necks, would have astonished an owl-sighted on-looker. The ride over the same road in the morning had been delightful, when the eye swept over the majestic forms of the dark mountains, whose sides at long intervals were adorned with green patches of verdure that in the distance looked like the nests of some monstrous race of birds rather than habitations of man; but now all that was hidden in the dense night-gloom that wrapped hill and valley, and the only signs of life were the vigilant *fariolas* keeping their sleepless watch away up in the black mass which we knew to be a mountain. Not having overmuch confidence in my guide, I kept my eye pretty steadily on him; and, in order to be ready for any treachery on his part, having loosened my machete in its scabbard, I drew my revolver quietly, resolved not to be taken off my guard, whatever might turn up. For an instant on the way these preparations of mine seemed about to be justified: the guide, swinging suddenly to the right, drew his machete, and proceeded to lop off the branch of a tree. This maneuver rather surprised me; and having heard much of the wonderful dexterity of these people in cutting heads off at a single, sudden stroke with Arab-like dexterity, I reined in my horse so as to keep out of reach. The poor fellow's intentions were, however, of the most peaceful kind, as it was simply a question of cutting an improvised riding-whip to urge his Rosinante to better speed, for my more powerful animal was pressing him hard.

At last the *Cafetale* was reached; and our approach being announced by a loud barking of dogs, the garrison of six men got under arms in the little tower which acted as citadel, while the fluttering lights told the tale of a household startled by the somewhat untimely visit. A long time had passed since any visitor had ventured to make a call after dark, and so, for a moment, we were taken for enemies, and the stern voice of the sentinel proclaimed war as he brought down his rifle with that short, sharp slap, accompanied rather than followed by the click of a mainspring, which, to the initiated, means shooting on sight. My sable companion evidently knew this, and felt there was no time to be lost in answering the challenge, which, to his credit, he did lustily, and with such promptness and clearness that even a deaf sentinel must have been immediately satisfied.

Notwithstanding the scare created by my unlooked-for arrival, I was soon installed in the best quarters, and pressed to make a prolonged stay; but the necessity for reaching Santiago de Cuba in time forced me to refuse this hospitable offer. It was not, however, without much difficulty that I succeeded in pursuing my way next day, as all kinds of reasonings and persuasions were exhausted in kind efforts to retain me.

After a day wasted in Santiago de Cuba, endeavoring to obtain trustworthy information as to the best way of reaching Cambute, I was obliged to set out and to grope my way as best I could.

9 On the Trail of Cespedes

CAMBUTE WAS simply a camp in the mountains beyond Cobre, somewhere. None but the soldiers knew exactly where, and it would not do to ask them. How I swore deeply, but not loudly, at Cuban laborantism; but as this would not mend matters, it was necessary to trust to luck, or lose the only chance for a rush that had as yet offered; especially as there was no knowing to what corner of the mysterious land Cespedes might retreat before the threatened advance of the Spaniards. Finding news as to the whereabouts of Cambute unattainable in Santiago, I resolved to proceed to Cobre, and endeavor to elicit some information on this delicate point from the director of the English mines, who had lived for some years in the district, and therefore, one would suppose, knew something about the locality. But this gentleman had only the vaguest notions of the existence of such a place as Cambute; his reception, however, was kind, if not very cordial, and had my aim been to obtain information as to the state of the mines, there can be little doubt it would have been furnished with blunt good sense. While still engaged in the fruitless task of cross-questioning my Englishman, a Spanish military doctor appeared on the ground. Whether his coming was accidental, or he had been sent to look after me, is of course unknown to me, but he had scarcely seated himself when he began to talk on the very subject upon which I desired information. After a good deal of reflection on the subject, I had settled in my own mind that Cambute lay southwest of the road to Palma Sorianna, and, if this military doctor had not appeared on the ground, would have taken the roads running in that direction; but the doctor assured me he had been several times at Cambute with operating columns, and the Cuban position was southeast.* As it would have been dangerous to follow the question too far, the conversation was turned into other channels. Soon after the Spaniard rose and took his leave, having, by his stupidity or his cunning, rendered good service to the state. An hour later saw me on my way out of Cobre. Scarcely had the town been lost to view, when suddenly a company of soldiers, under the command of an officer, appeared at a turning in the road, and owing to my somewhat warlike appearance seemed inclined to halt me. Indeed, the word was given, although I rode straight up to them, but at the last moment the officer changed his mind, and with a wave of his hand, and that exclamation, so full of meaning in the mouth of a Spaniard, "*Nada*," allowed me to proceed in peace.

For a few miles the broad road swept through a bleak, bare, mountainous country, steeped in lethal silence, and were it not for the distant watchtowers perched on the summits of the hills, all evidence of human life would have been wanting. In the noontide this awful silence is singularly oppressive, because it consorts so badly with the sentiment of joy and fullness of life that we feel within us when the Day-God beams down on us his warm, life-giving smiles. The repellant aspect of the unwooded hills was in part compensated for by security from surprise. Here there was no danger that the crouching negro would spring from his hiding-place to deal with lightning suddenness the terrible machete-stroke to the unwary traveler, so that it was possible to enjoy the wild grandeur of the mountains, drinking in satisfaction in a half-conscious, dreamy state, while ambling along the white sunlit road, that wound, with many a curious turn, like a broad golden stream, around the base of gigantic brown-baked mountains. The amplitude of the way, and the wide-embracing view, as, at intervals, extensive valleys on either hand opened to the sight, only served to lift into stronger relief the unnatural loneliness and wide-

---

*"Palma Sorianna" should read "Palma Soriano."

extending desolation, until a feeling of sadness stole imperceptibly over the heart as it dwelt on the folly and wickedness of horrible war, that made a desert of the fairest and most fertile spots of God's earth.

That day, however, there was little time for dreaming or philosophizing. After an hour's ride, the road bifurcated, and it was necessary to decide whether it was better to be guided by my own deductions, or by the dogmatic assertion of the Spaniard. There was no apparent reason for the latter misinforming me, as he could not have the remotest idea that I was on my way to the Cuban lines. Undecided what course to pursue, I had made up my mind to be guided by the nature of the country in the selection of my route. It was now, however, necessary to make a choice: away before me stretched the broad *Camino Real,* and in the distance loomed up a huge stone-built church, perched on the summit of a hill commanding the road that wound by it.* My instinct told me that it was garrisoned; if I followed that road would I not be again arrested? Then it was most unlikely that the king's highway should lead to the insurgent camp. On the other hand the road plunged into the mountains, and looked as lonely and desolate as if ages had swept by since the highway had been used by man. My pocket-compass showed that its general direction, so far as it could be made out, agreed with what the Spanish doctor had told me. This at once decided me, and, turning my horse's head eastward, I plunged into a country so picturesque, that under ordinary conditions the ride would have been the source of a thousand pleasurable sensations to anyone who loves the beauties of nature.

After passing over low hills for some time, the road followed the course of an extensive valley, and on either hand were seen in the abandoned cane-fields, and roofless, silent *ingenios,* the sad traces of war. During hours I rode without finding any traces of life, and it was almost with enthusiasm I beheld, shining in the middle of the road, a brass Remington cartridge. It appeared to me evidence that I was on the right road, for whether the cartridge belonged to the Spanish or to the Mambi, it appeared to me certain that I must be approaching the frontiers of Cuba Libre. What in the beginning had been a broad and well-defined road, soon merged into a mere bridle-path, wandering capriciously by wood and meadow through the long Guinea grass, and sometimes following the bed of shallow, leaf-embowered streams until it seemed lost definitely, then reappearing in a scarcely perceptible break in the bushes beyond. At

---

*The "Camino Real" ("royal road" or "King's Highway") connected the southeastern coastal town of Siboney to Santiago de Cuba.

length the country opened out, and in the distance I was startled to see evidences of extensive cultivation, but even by the aid of my glasses it was impossible to discover whether the cane-fields now suddenly visible were abandoned like those already met with. The extent and apparent richness of the crop seemed to argue against this assumption, and it became necessary to proceed with caution.

Only once during the day had I been tempted to diverge from the road by the appearance of a slight trail leading through a deserted plantation, but my pocket-compass saved me from a mistake that might have led to serious consequences. This path, strangely enough, was the one I afterwards followed on my way to the Cuban lines, but in the direction opposite to that I was first tempted to enter it. Had some little local information been furnished me by the *laborantes,* I could from this point have ridden to the Cuban outposts in a few hours, but want of information about the topography of the country left me to wander on, groping my way as best I could, in the hope of falling in with some Cuban scouts or outposts. This time it was not to be, and so following the direct path I came to an elevation which enabled me to command a view of the distant *ingenio,* and satisfy myself it was inhabited, and, of course, garrisoned. To venture near the plantation would ensure my arrest and detention, involving the loss of the one opportunity upon which I had set my heart. To avoid this I resolved to try a plunge into the woods, trusting to my pocket-compass to bring me out at some point beyond the *ingenio,* out of reach of the garrison. For some time my progress was satisfactory, if somewhat slow, and there seemed good reason to hope for a successful issue to my first wood adventure. In this, as in so many other hopes, disappointment was lying in wait to dispel all the brilliant promises. As the ground became broken, and the underwood more formidably tangled, my horse became restive, and at last refused point-blank to proceed. In vain spurs were brought into requisition; the animal only became more doggedly obstinate, and after several narrow escapes from the fate of King David's rebel son, I was regretfully compelled to abandon the attempt to pierce through the tangled forest. It was all the more annoying, having worked hard with my machete to open the road, to be forced to abandon the attempt when more than half accomplished. My object was to get by the *ingenio* unnoticed, lest the mounted patrols should follow and arrest me. It was no longer possible to avoid being seen, but I made up my mind that if the Spaniards were to capture me again that at least they would have a run for it.

Abandoning the wood, as the passage was no longer practicable, it was necessary to cross a country affording scarcely any shelter, and it soon became evident that it was impossible to pass round the *ingenio* without approaching within rifle-shot of the buildings, because they stood close to the point where the valley bifurcated, and the mountains at this point were too steep to be crossed by a stranger to Cuban travel. Indeed, at the moment it did not seem to me possible to ride over so steep a mountain, but later experience has shown me that this was an error. The appearance of a strange horseman making a circuit to avoid the *ingenio* naturally attracted notice, and created quite an excitement about the building. Without paying any heed to what was passing in the *ingenio,* I rode so as to keep well out of range until the few moments necessary to pass into a narrow gorge, which offered me the only means of escape. It was evident from the movement in the *ingenio* that I was at first mistaken for a hostile scout, and in all probability the garrison and workpeople saw me depart with as much real pleasure as I enjoyed in having for the moment escaped detention.

The trail now ran through a narrow valley, with steep, densely timbered hills rising on either side, dark and threatening in aspect. The savage loneliness of the place irresistibly suggested throat-cutting, and instinctively my gun was thrown across the saddlebow, so as to be ready for instant use in case of any sudden aggression. It is certainly not a very comfortable feeling to be peering into tangled forest-undergrowth in momentary expectation of hearing a bullet whistling in close proximity at one's ear, or, more terrible still, to be startled by the apparition of some squad of half-savage fugitives, or *Maja* (Cubans not regularly enrolled in the army, but living in the woods), thirsting for vengeance and excited by hope of plunder.

Well-to-do, easy-going people, who have always lived under the shadow of a policeman's club, will no doubt find this picture of the impressions of Cuban travel very shocking, and be inclined to think the poor *Maja* a very wretched creature indeed, but if the public would not condemn him too rashly, there will be found much to be said in justification of this much-suffering being. No doubt it is very wrong, and very brutal, even, for outlaws and patriots carrying on a war where no quarter is given on either side, to shoot down an inoffensive foreigner, but it must be remembered that had I been met and fired on by a party of Cubans, it would have been simply an error. They would have shot me as a Spaniard, not an inoffensive foreigner. Unfortunately, in the class of war carried on in Cuba, it is not usual among any people to bother much about challenging;

in fact, the rule is to shoot first and challenge afterwards. If any mistake occurs, it is very unfortunate for the victim, but then the strict letter of the law is fulfilled.

After a few miles the valley opened out gradually, and ever-changing scenery distracted the mind from the rather gloomy reflections and apprehensions which would force themselves into prominence while passing through the mysterious half-gloom of the sad woods, where one felt cut off from the rest of the world, and driven into communication with one's own thoughts, which were pretty sure to be none of the liveliest. At the end of a couple of hours' ride the trail suddenly entered a patch of canefield, but for some time it was impossible to know whether or not it was part of some abandoned plantation like those already encountered. In the distance there was the remains of what had once been a large *ingenio,* but it had evidently been destroyed by fire, as the charred rafters looked black and skeleton-like against the sky. It was with something like satisfaction that I made these observations, when suddenly I stumbled on a group of blacks working among the canes which had concealed them from my view. They were evidently startled and even considerably frightened by my appearance, and some of the men who were a little distant at once retired on the main group as if for protection; but seeing that I was alone, and evidently not hostile in my intentions, they awaited my approach. It was too late for me to retreat, so inquiring the name of the *ingenio,* and making some civil remarks, I turned my horse's head towards the buildings, where a group of soldiers were already watching my approach. The marks of fire were everywhere visible, but energetic efforts were being made to restore at least in part the works. The detachment of soldiers being small, there was the usual slackness of discipline in the post, and so I escaped any very close interrogatory; besides, when I perceived that the planter was a Frenchman my Gallic tongue was at once put into requisition, for experience had taught me that this was the quickest and most effective way to obtain the help of Frenchmen; nor in this instance did the maneuver fail: before half a dozen words were exchanged the planter insisted on my dismounting and taking some refreshment while chatting about "La Belle France." The offer was of a kind not to be refused, especially as it might be possible to obtain such information about the roads as would enable me to reach Cambute. The subject, however, was a delicate one, in view of the natural irritation of the planter-class against the insurgents, who burn down the plantations in order to deprive the Spanish government of all revenue from Cuban sources. But a few stories of the Franco-German war, and the assurance that on more than one occasion I had helped to carry the tri-color to victory, so opened the patriotic Frenchman's heart that he quite forgot that the Cubans had burned down his plantation three times, thereby reducing him from a position of wealth and independence to comparative poverty.* There was a shade of comic sorrow on his face as he pointed out the danger which unconsciously I had passed through while making my way to his plantation, as he assured me that the deeply-wooded hills which enclosed the narrow valley were infested by a gang of desperate robbers, who, had they seen me, would undoubtedly have brought my search expedition to a prompt and eminently unsatisfactory termination. As I had distinctly heard human voices in rather uproarious merriment, and had actually stopped in the hope of seeing someone, this news quite consoled me for the disappointment. Only a few days before, my informant asserted, this band had seized nine mules and their loads, which they carried off in triumph to their fastness in the hills. Sometime after, when relating this adventure to some of the Cuban outposts, they laughed heartily, and assured me that they were the parties guilty of appropriating the mules, which they declared were in excellent condition and remarkably tender. In fact, the camp had had several days' feasting at the Frenchman's expense. Under these circumstances the newspaper correspondent endeavoring to go into the insurgent camp would have been received with little more than the merest civility, but, *sacré bleu*, a stranger who had been fighting for France quite altered the case! So after chatting for a long time of battles, reverses, and the inevitable *revanche*, we gradually settled down to the Cuban question, and my mission in particular. Half confidences would have been worse than useless, so the question how to get to Cambute the quickest way possible was put to the planter. To my infinite annoyance he informed me that on two different occasions my selections of paths had been faulty, and that the Cambute trail would have met my view had I persevered in piercing through the wood, and in two hours I would have been close to the Cuban outposts. But it was now getting late; besides, to return along the track would ensure my arrest by the soldiers in the *ingenio* which was situated at the junction of the roads. There was also another difficulty which more than anything else deterred me from returning: the road to Cambute was said to go over the steepest part of the mountains, where it was impossible to

---

*O'Kelly joined the French Foreign Legion in 1863 when he was eighteen years old. He served as a volunteer soldier in Algeria, French occupied Mexico, and the Franco-Prussian War. For more on O'Kelly's biography, see Peter Hulme's foreword to this edition.

go on horseback. It would therefore be necessary to abandon my horse, and as I was most unwilling to do this, it appeared better to continue to Palma Sorianna, from whence a level road led into the Cuban camp. This was quite true; and on the way to join General Garcia's headquarters I traveled along this route, which passes within about two miles of Palma Sorianna, communicating with that post by a cross-trail.

My hospitable entertainer sent a young negro with me as guide through a few miles of very difficult country. Towards evening Palma Sorianna was reached, and my advent created a sensation that well-nigh degenerated into a panic before the night passed. My first care was to seek the military commander, and report my presence. He had heard of my arrival, and was about to take measures for my immediate arrest; an intention my frank presentation caused him to abandon, or rather to modify, for it was soon evident that a close and jealous *espionage* had been established over me. As no one alluded to this, it was my policy to appear ignorant of it. At the same time it was impossible to avoid wondering how it would all end. It was very annoying, because it took away my chance of reaching Cambute before Cespedes would have left. If I did not "swear a prayer or two" for the *laborantes*, and the Spanish medico who had set me astray, in actual words, there is reason to fear that mentally both parties were fervently consigned to a *purgatorio* where they might have time to reflect.

The commander of Palma Sorianna turned out to be a Major O'Ryan, one of the Hispano-Irish officers. My name and country recommended me at once to his attention, and it is only justice to say that, while keeping me under close observation as a possible enemy, he treated me with much consideration and kindness. He was evidently quite proud of introducing his *paisano*, as he insisted on calling me, to all the officers of the command, and conversed at length with me about the country of his forefathers, and the intimate relations maintained among their descendants in Spain. From the number of officers that visited the unpretentious *tienda* where I had been compelled, from the absence of any better place, to take up my residence, it was evident my arrival had created quite a lively sensation, and that for the moment at least all eyes were fixed on the strange guest. In the existing state of the country, this curiosity about a stranger appeared to me natural enough; therefore, though it was unquestionably inconvenient, there was no particular reason to feel angry or annoyed about it. The matter of most immediate interest to me was the direction of the road to Cambute, but it was evident that it would be unwise to make any inquiries in the town, which might increase suspicion. Several times I made efforts to move in the direction of the outposts of this fortified village, but was on every occasion caught up in the most vexatiously polite manner by someone connected with the "autoridad," so that there was nothing left but to give up gracefully and await the chapter of accidents. Fortune before many hours forgot to frown, as by a singular accident all the information that could be desired was given to me by Major O'Ryan in person, while taking an evening stroll with a number of the officers of the garrison. Away in the distance, behind the hills, he pointed out to me the position of Cambute, giving me details as to who lived there, and how they lived, which my own experience afterwards showed me, in the main, to be correct. O'Ryan was a keen and intelligent soldier, as polished and as sharp as his own sword-blade, a nice fellow to talk to, but an extremely ugly customer to fight with. He had organized a system of espionage so cleverly, by aid of recreant Cubans and fugitive slaves, that he was almost as well informed of what passed in the neighboring Cuban camp as were the Cuban chiefs themselves. When he learned that my object was to reach Cambute, he said that if General Morales de los Rios gave me permission to go, he would place me in communication with Jesus Perez within forty-eight hours. The same offer was made to me on a former occasion by the commander of a mounted contra-guerrilla, whose acquaintance I made while with poor Sostrada and the San Quentin battalion; both have since perished in battle at the hands of those invisible and impalpable enemies they despised so much. At the time, it struck me as rather strange that the Spaniards who pretended they never knew where to find the Cubans to fight, could find them without any difficulty to parley with. This, however, was not in fact such a contradiction as it seemed, but it was a *Cosa de Cuba,* which it requires intimate knowledge of the country and the people to fully understand.

Although well disposed towards me, Major O'Ryan, as a soldier, was responsible for the complete isolation of the enemy in his district; he was therefore somewhat puzzled how to deal with my case. Not caring either to take the responsibility of stopping me, still less of allowing me to communicate with the enemy, the mode of solving the difficulty that seemed most agreeable to himself personally was to refer the matter to the higher authorities, and so throw the onus of whatever was decided on other shoulders than his own.

Up to the hour of bidding him good night no reply had come to his telegram. He therefore used a good many little artifices to persuade me not to leave in the morning; but, as time was now invaluable, it was impossible to accede to his rather anxious invitation to remain till the following day. My *cedula* was not, however, returned to me, and it would therefore have been impossible for me to have left, even if nothing had transpired before morning. Sleep had for some time closed my weary eyes when a loud knocking at my bedroom door caused me to start bolt upright, without being quite awake, and only half-conscious that there was an awful row being made in the house. However, a repetition of the thundering on the door-panels that might well have shook the very fragile shanty in which I was housed, brought me quickly to my senses; and asking, in no very gentle voice, who was thumping at my door and what he wanted, was answered that the noise-maker was the bearer of a message from Major O'Ryan. Unlocking the door, an officer informed me that by order of the government my departure from Palma Sorianna, until further orders, was forbidden. Politely expressing regret for disturbing my slumbers, the officer withdrew to place an additional sentinel on the house, in order to defeat any endeavor to escape. He might have saved himself the trouble; for, taking the matter very coolly, I went to bed and slept soundly, after unburdening my mind of a few hearty wishes for the salvation of all the *autoridads,* civil and military, in the "Ever-Faithful Isle." In the morning, on attempting to leave the house, a sentinel informed me that, without permission from the major, I could not do so. As this occurred in the presence of a crowd of soldiers and townspeople, it rather nettled me, and at once I dispatched the servant with a telegram to the English consul, informing him that the authorities held me a close prisoner. This being shown to O'Ryan, without whose approval it could not be forwarded, he at once sent word that it was a mistake on the part of the guard, informing me that the prohibition only meant that I should not leave the town, explaining at the same time that it applied equally to all others, and was simply a military precaution in view of some important movements of the troops. Being simple enough to believe in the "important movement," I at once telegraphed for leave to accompany one of the columns, to which request even the scant courtesy of a reply was refused. In the evening, however, arrived the famous "advertencia," in which the Spanish authorities threw aside the hypocritical mask they had long been wearing, and showed clearly that they were resolved to make war on light at all hazards. This "advertencia" put an end to the possibility of my reaching Cambute from Palma. O'Ryan explained frankly and clearly that, in view of the ban of outlawry which the "advertencia" proclaimed, he would be obliged to give stringent orders to the outposts and scouts to shoot me in case I was found in the direction of the Cuban lines; besides that, he did not consider himself at liberty to allow me to travel in any direction, unless under the escort of Spanish troops. This, in fact, amounted to making me a prisoner guarded at sight. It would have been as useless as impolitic to show any bad temper in the affair; and as for running the gauntlet, even if the outposts could have been passed, I would have been captured, and shot like a dog by the scouts, who knew every path, and, indeed, every tree, for miles round. Affecting not to see that the advice given by the major was in reality a command which must be obeyed, if unpleasant consequences were to be avoided, my feelings of annoyance were packed into the smallest possible compass and hid out of sight.

It was agreed, therefore, that I should return with a convoy to San Luis, where I could get the train for Santiago de Cuba. The convoy was expected to arrive at midday; but, owing to some cause, it was delayed on the road. This excited a good deal of uneasiness; and a slight panic occurred among the volunteers when, at two o'clock, a soldier rode in from the outposts, announcing that heavy firing was going on in the direction from which the column was coming. The bugles sounded the alarm, and troops and volunteers assembled under arms. The regular troops marched out in the quiet, orderly way which I before noticed with the Spanish soldier; but the volunteers, made up of a hybrid collection of all colors and conditions, conducted themselves in a disorderly and disgraceful manner. If the enemy had really attacked the town, I verily believe that the soldiers would have been in as much danger from these undisciplined rascals as they would have been from the Mambis. A few mounted contra-guerrillas and some companies of the marine infantry moved out to succor the convoy, and by the permission of the colonel commanding I accompanied. After a short ride of a league and a half we met the head of the convoy, and learned that all the trouble had been occasioned by some soldiers firing at two suspicious persons whom they saw in the woods. This news, of course, put an end to our sortie, and we returned to town, where the Cuban volunteers celebrated the grand victory by an impromptu ball in my hotel. As I rode by these gentry on my way home, they made quite a hostile demonstration against me. I did not mention the fact to O'Ryan, or to anyone else, because I did not want to create trouble; but I remark it as the only instance of anything of the kind occurring. Next day I accompanied a convoy to San Luis, and the only incident worthy of notice was the discovery of the traces of a band, estimated by the guides from the track to number about one hundred men. On arriving at Santiago de Cuba, my first care was to telegraph to the *Herald* notice of the threat to shoot me made by the authorities. The use of the word "arrested" in relation to my detention at Ramon caused the authorities to stop my telegram.

General Morales sent for me to go to his house immediately. When I arrived he was at dinner with his aid-de-camp and the Attorney-General. The general requested me to be seated, and, having ordered some sherry, said, "You desire to telegraph that you were arrested in Ramon and Palma. You were not arrested, but detained, as a natural precaution, by the authorities, who, seeing a man going about alone and armed, desired to know something about him."

"Still, I was arrested and prevented from continuing my journey. When I am stopped I am arrested. You find fault with the word 'arrested'; but in my country, when the authorities deprive a man of the right to move about freely, we say he is 'arrested.'"

"The physical explanation you give of this word is correct, but in Spain we only arrest where there is a crime. In your case there was none, and you were only detained in order that your identity could be ascertained."

"I was held a prisoner for eight hours, and part of the time I spent in the tower. It is true I was treated with attention and civility, but still I was a prisoner."

"I did not know this; but you must see that the authorities only exercised necessary vigilance and caution in detaining you until they consulted me. As soon as I received the telegram I ordered your release, and that you should be permitted to go where you pleased."

"Permit me to thank you for your kindness, and to assure you that I should regret very much if one of these days you should be obliged to shoot me."

General Morales turned to the gentleman in black (the Attorney-General) with a half-amused, half-inquiring, look on his face. After a moment's pause he said, "I would regret it very much also; but if you are found in the insurgent lines, or coming from them, you will be treated as a spy or as one of the insurgents."

"Then all the prisoners who are taken are shot?"

"That depends: those taken in arms are handed over to the tribunals; others who have surrendered themselves are allowed to live in perfect freedom, if they have been guilty of no crime. Indeed, there are plenty of them even holding high positions among us who ought to have been executed. No; if you present yourself and ask pardon you will be treated with the same generosity as the other insurgents, but if you leave the Spanish lines you will expose yourself to the danger of being treated as an enemy, should the Spanish troops fall in with you."

"Well, it is to prevent this that I have requested the authorities to give me a military pass."

"The Captain-General alone can give you such a pass. Why do you not endeavor to obtain one?"

"In the interview which I had with General Ceballos he expressed a desire to aid me, but, owing to the clamor which had been raised by certain factionists, he was unwilling to commit himself so as to give cause for further agitation on this subject. He told me, however, that I was at liberty to proceed at my own risk without interference to any part of the island I pleased. Not wishing to embarrass the Captain-General, I have preferred to run the additional risk rather than expose him to any trouble or censure for his kindness to me."

At this point the new Archbishop, who has been appointed by Amadeus *à la* Harry the Eighth, entered the audience chamber, and General Morales left me with the gentleman in black.* The Attorney-General assured me that there "would be a certain regret felt if I should be killed—not a very deep sorrow, for, after all, I was of no particular account or interest to the inhabitants of Cuba." Still, my death seemed in some mysterious way to foreshadow trouble. "If in an engagement with the troops a bullet should kill you by accident, or even by design—for I do not conceal from myself that if the Spanish soldiers should see you among the insurgents they would say, 'There is that American; let us bring him down,' and they would shoot at you rather than at the Mambis—if you should happen to be killed in one of these encounters, the insurgents would carry off your body and accuse the Spaniards of having assassinated you, and the American press would make an outcry against our supposed brutality."

"No; it is well understood that a war correspondent is exposed to all these dangers; there were many correspondents killed during the Franco-Prussian War."

"Here it is, however, different."

"I am aware of this; but there are positions in which we must only think of our duty without taking into account the danger. Like soldiers, we journalists must execute our orders at whatever cost."

"If you were to go as correspondent to St. Domingo, for instance, with the army of Baez, and one of the opposing generals should capture

---

*O'Kelly refers to Amadeo I, king of Spain from 1870 to 1873, when his abdication led to the declaration of the First Spanish Republic (1873–74). There was much speculation as to whether a newly republican Spain would hasten the end of slavery in Cuba. For Calixto García's and Carlos Manuel de Céspedes's commentary on the new Spanish republic's implications for Cuba, see pp. 227–28 and 145–46.

you, do you think that your character as newspaper correspondent would protect you?"*

"Possibly not; but I suppose Spain does not wish to be regarded as occupying the same place in the pale of civilization as St. Domingo."

The Attorney-General perceived he had made a mistake in what he had intended to be a crushing illustration of the right of the authorities to shoot me. He turned the conversation at once into a complimentary vein, and, as I was myself the object, I had to admit myself routed after the first discharge. Seeing there was nothing to be gained by remaining, I saluted the man in black, and made my bow to General Morales. The general was deeply engaged with the Archbishop, but he rose politely and advanced to dismiss me with the friendly courtesy that he manifested towards me on all occasions.

I asked him if my telegram could go, by altering the word "arrested" to "detained." He replied "that it could"; and, drawing the paper from his pocket, handed it to me, assuring me at the same time that I might always count upon his friendship, which struck me as very polite from a gentleman who had just informed me that he would be obliged to shoot me under circumstances likely to occur.

10 Menacing Attitude of the Authorities

THE SPANISH authorities had at last shown the cloven foot. It was now placed on record in the most striking manner that they were resolved to keep the world ignorant of the events passing in Cuba, and that, to preserve the mysterious veil they had thrown over the insurrectionary struggle, they were even prepared to commit a crime which would involve

---

*The attorney general refers to the five-term president of Santo Domingo (now the Dominican Republic), Buenaventura Báez (1812–1884). In 1869, Báez negotiated with President Ulysses S. Grant for the annexation of Santo Domingo, but the US Senate voted against the treaty in 1870.

the killing of the rash adventurer who should dare to present himself as a witness of the light. Whether or not the resolution of the authorities, in their jealousy and fear of the truth, was a wise or a just one, will be better judged when the facts of the case are better known to the reader. There was, however, one advantage in the decided enunciation of the real views of the men in power. It is by no means an easy matter for a person not very well acquainted with Spanish character to weigh the exact value of what may be said or promised by Spanish officials, because they have at least the merit, if it be a merit, of performing unpleasant and obnoxious duties with an outward politeness which, in the minds of people less accustomed to polished forms in public functionaries, would be likely to beget very erroneous ideas. Although I had had some previous experience among the Spanish race, there existed in my mind a doubt as to the probable action of the authorities, so well had they feigned indifference to my mission in Santiago de Cuba. On the occasion of my setting out for Ti-Arriba, it is quite true that proof was given me how closely and jealously the authorities were watching my movements, but even that supervision only went to prove a certain benevolence of intention on the part of General Morales de los Rios, as was shown by his hurried dispatch, which just arrived in time to save me from arrest, and his action afterwards in ordering my liberation at Ramon las Yeguas. For a moment the authorities had persuaded me that they were really indifferent, and would offer no real opposition to my crossing their lines, though they would not aid me in any way. If this were really so, the great obstacle would have been removed from my path, but all these illusions were rudely dissipated by the exceedingly savage *advertencia,* which enabled the world to see the exact nature of the government in Cuba. In fact, for the reflective mind there was much instruction in the few telegraphic lines that brought me up at Palma, much as a rider might suddenly stop his horse riding at full speed to the edge of a precipice. The benevolence shown to me was, in fact, all humbug: it was thought that horrible stories would prevent my venturing across the lines, just as if I were an overgrown baby; and so long as my wanderings were confined to the wild and mountainous districts, which, from their strategic position, could not be occupied permanently by the Cuban forces, the fullest liberty was allowed me, only a certain watch being kept on my movements. It was impossible, however, for the authorities to keep me constantly in sight, as most of the time I rode through lonely roads, where no one could follow me without being seen, and where very few Spaniards would care to ride alone, because, though the whole district is fenced round at the outlets by Spanish posts, small parties of insurgents were constantly passing through the mountains, and if, by accident, they should fall in with a single Spaniard, bullet and machete would soon relieve him from all worldly cares. The moment, however, I moved in the direction where the authorities knew the insurgents could be met with, they made up their minds to stop me at whatever cost. Perhaps the chief cause of this resolution was an unwillingness to let it be known that Cespedes could be met within an easy day's march of Santiago de Cuba at the moment when the Spanish government pretended they thought him dead, and that the chief cause why the rebellion continued was their inability to find the insurgent bands. It is rather instructive to remember that while these statements were being deliberately made, Cespedes was lying with a comparatively small force at Cambute, at some hours' march from the Spanish outposts, and within an easy day's march of the general's headquarters at Santiago de Cuba. The mere publication of the fact was calculated to damage exceedingly the prestige of the government, by laying bare the falseness of the pretenses urged in explanation of the continuation of the Cuban insurrection, and also to show how very little reliance could be placed either on the official, or officious, statements of the pro-Spanish party. From this point of view, the *advertencia* was a victory gained in the cause of truth, because it has placed the real character of the authorities on record in a way that leaves no room for any possible misapprehension, and will remain as a historical testimony of the temper of the Spanish party, after the first fit of passionate violence which deluged Cuba with innocent blood had passed, and a cold and deliberate policy of repression had replaced it. It is to the last phase of the insurrectionary movement, as less known than the sanguinary acts that have affrighted and horrified the civilized world, that most attention will be paid in this narrative.

If the difficulties in the way of meeting with Cespedes were great and apparently insurmountable so long as the authorities preserved the appearance of an indifferent neutrality, now that the veto was spoken, with its accompanying threat, the project seemed to all my friends too dangerous to be undertaken. "You surely will not attempt to go to the insurgent camp after the warning?" was the constantly repeated question to which I was hourly subjected, accompanied by long exhortations about the folly and madness of attempting to defy such a terrible power as the omnipotent *autoridad*. It was no longer safe to talk even to friends, and a number of harmless answers had to be invented which gave no information of my real intentions, and yet did not bind me to any course of action. There was only one chance left, and if it failed there was an end to my mission. It is natural to a man in my position not to like to fail, and so much had the conduct of the government annoyed me that I was more than ever resolved to reach the Cuban lines at whatever cost. It was certainly a desperate game, for the espionage to which I was subjected was of the closest kind. Everyone interested in defeating me had become so well acquainted with my appearance that all chance of disguise was done away with. Besides, during my comings and goings to Santiago I had made acquaintance with officers belonging to almost all the regiments, so that there was not a post probably where I should not have been immediately recognized. This compelled me to start from Santiago de Cuba, so that it would be necessary to run the gauntlet of all the Spanish posts. This was anything but a pleasant prospect, as it was quite possible that, if caught, the threatened shooting might be carried out to the letter. This source of uneasiness was increased by the knowledge that orders had already been given to the outposts to keep a sharp lookout for me, and many of the Spanish officers whose acquaintance I had made, with a want of delicacy probably the result of being engaged for a long while in a brutal warfare, said they supposed that an objection to be shot would prevent me visiting the insurgents. As it was desirable to encourage this opinion, I told them that, in all probability, I would content myself with visiting as much of the insurgent camp as might be seen from Santiago de Cuba, at which they smiled patronizingly, as to say they thought so, and that pensmen naturally objected to lead except in the form of type.

My whole attention was now directed to inducing the *laborantes* to come to my aid. This was especially difficult on account of the jealous watch kept over me, for not alone the many volunteers, but even the army officers, did not think it, in many cases, beneath their dignity to establish a surveillance over my movements. With a view to eventualities my visits to the country were continued, though more irregularly than before the *advertencia*. These unaccountable outgoings and incomings were a source of great annoyance to a number of officers who lived in the hotel, and on one occasion some rather inquisitive remarks very nearly brought about an open rupture at table, as I was beginning to get somewhat savage at my continued ill luck and their continued impertinence. However, the difficulty was smoothed over, and, though the private speculations as to what brought me into the country alone were carried on as usual, they only came to me at second hand.

The unpleasant turn in affairs with the authorities proved in the end very fortunate, for the *laborantes* began to look more favorably on me, and the suspicion created by the ugly report put into circulation by the

Spanish party began to disappear. In my excursions I had made numerous attempts to sound persons who scarcely attempted to conceal their disaffection to the Spaniards, but without the slightest success. The terrible severity of the Spanish government made the people shrink from placing the slightest trust in a stranger, and though thousands must have been in sympathy with the insurrection, and though many persons spoke to me in a way to leave no doubt on my mind as to their being rebels, yet they were too much cowed to pass from mere words to actions. The fear of involving their families in suspicion, or exposing them to vengeance, caused these persons to refuse me all practical aid. Everywhere the marks of a reign of terror were visible, however much concealed under the forms of law, or rather the phraseology of law. In fact, the state of apprehension in which Cubans live is something passing belief, and the cruelties that have been committed in order to reduce a people, naturally talkative and boastful, to a state of abject, dumb subjection, must have been as horrible as the enemies of Spain represent them. If anyone imagines that, because the Cubans make no complaint, they are satisfied or content, he falls into a vulgar error. It has been my lot in life to mix a good deal with discontented people—rebels, revolutionists, reformers, and, in fact, all categories of men who look on themselves as oppressed: Poles, whose families were shivering in Siberian wastes; Frenchmen, whose kith and kin had been sent to a better world by the blood-stained mountebank who dissipated Lamartine's poetic republic with artillery volleys; and many others of the same genus—but, until I listened to Cubans giving vent to their hate of Spain, I never had any conception with what diabolical hatred one nation can look upon another. There is no use attempting to paint the feelings of the Cubans still under the power of Spain for the race from which they have sprung, because all painting would be a weak and ineffective representation of the reality. In all probability, if the present disturbed state of affairs continues in Spain, the pent-up rage of this much-oppressed people will find vent in a new Sicilian vespers; and, if it were not for the fear of exposing their families to a renewal of the insults and outrages to which they were subjected after the first reverses in the revolution, the attempt would long since have been made.

11 News from the Mambis

MATTERS WERE in this state, when, on returning from a long ride in the wildest part of the mountains near Santiago, I found a letter in a strange hand lying on the floor of my room. It had evidently been slipped, or shot, in through the latticed door, as the servants were very careful to place all letters left for me on the table, so that I could not fail to see them the moment I entered. The letter was written in Spanish, in a bold hand, and bore no signature. It stated that if Mr. O'Kelly wished to put himself in communication with the Cuban forces, he would proceed on the morrow, alone, and without having notified any one of his intention, to a point indicated, which was in the very direction from which I had just ridden. The roads and paths to be followed were clearly marked out, and such signs given as would enable me, with a little attention, to find my way, although there were a good many turnings and twistings before the trysting-place could be reached. The only difficulty was the hour appointed; it would be dark by the time I arrived, and the slightest error would compromise success. Then came the doubt, is this a trap? Impossible to make the slightest inquiry; for, if the letter were in good faith, the merest breath of suspicion aroused might lead to my own destruction, as well as the death of the men who were risking their lives to serve me. Still, the doubt of the genuineness of the letter would return; the danger of just such an ambush as this had been foreseen by those kind friends who were always comforting me with the prospect of having my throat cut. There was a general impression that I was very rich, and also that I always carried a large quantity of gold; indeed, the latter fact was known to the servants of the hotel through one of them accidentally finding my money-belt, whose weight and generally prosperous appearance would have endangered the lives of a dozen men. It may have been rash to have put a premium on my death; but it would have been infinitely more foolish to have found myself in a difficulty for want of "all-conquering gold." To the knowledge of this danger was added that of a still greater one, that the letter might have been concocted by some patriotic volunteers anxious to serve their country and increase their fortunes at the same time. If it should turn out so, I was lost, and I knew it; but, if it were merely a plundering scheme, I thought it might be possible to make a bargain with the thieves to bring me to the insurgent outposts, for which service I would willingly have given them a thousand dollars. It consoled me somewhat to think that they would prefer this arrangement to having to take my money and my life, an operation which I had made up my mind should cost pretty dearly to anyone who should attempt it. It was a source of grief to me that circumstances would prevent me taking my double-barreled shot-gun, as my faith in heavy duck-shot as an argument was very great; but, after reviewing the whole question as dispassionately as its nature would admit, I resolved to venture, trusting to good fortune to come out all right. However, this resolution was not taken without a good deal of perturbation of spirit; for, though this life is certainly not much worth having, somehow even the prospect of a chance of being sent suddenly out of it, "with all one's sins upon one's head," causes in most people an unaccountable and very illogical weakness about the knees, to say nothing of a slight squeamishness about such an unpoetic organ as the stomach. I remember very well that the mysterious letter quite spoiled my appetite, although I had just returned from a mountain-ride, feeling as ravenous as a bear just awakened from his winter's nap. However, it was necessary to avoid arousing the suspicions of any of the numerous officials in the hotel; and the dinner-bell having rung some time before, after a hasty toilet I strode into the dining-room, trying to look as innocent as possible, but feeling that every particular guest in the room could see that my careless air was all a sham, and that I was going over to the rebels on the morrow. It was necessary to show them that there was no foundation whatever for their suspicions; so, after dinner, I strolled about the plaza, and, as there was no music, went to the club to gamble. One cannot well live in Cuba without gambling; but let the virtuous be comforted, for I do not approve of gambling, and only dipped in on the strength of the old saw about heretics in Rome kissing the Pope's toe. When my eyes opened next day it was rather late, which was an immense advantage, as it would not be advisable to leave before the afternoon; so I occupied myself with making some necessary preparations, by writing some letters and generally making ready for a voyage which might be eternal. Most people, it is to be supposed, make preparations of this sort at least once in their lives; but others, more lucky, or less so, eventually get so used to it that the last time comes quite as a surprise to them. My horse was brought round to the little side-door at the appointed hour; and, as the people had become accustomed to see me go out as if for a campaign, the careful equipment of my horse attracted no notice. It was only my customary promenade, so they thought, and that day I was more than usually exacting as to the brightness of my spurs and the burnish of my machete. In addition to the latter formidable weapon, I carried two revolvers, one being a small Smith & Wesson seven-shooter. In my own opinion, I was pretty well able to take care of myself, and, unless shot down treacherously by a concealed foe, it struck me that, in case of any foul play, whoever should get my money-belt would have earned it. Still, my reflections were not very gay, and I do remember that my lips stuck pretty close together all the rest of that day.

At first the road was familiar, and I rode along wondering how the adventure would end; were the persons who sent the mysterious note robbers, and if so, how many were they? It may be well to remark that only a few days before, just in this same neighborhood, two residents of Santiago de Cuba had been macheted to death, that is to say, chopped up until they were scarcely recognizable. One of them was a Frenchman, the other a free negro in his employ. It was supposed that in looking after the cattle belonging to the Frenchman they had been surprised, and killed either for plunder or for vengeance. The day before I had in my road to the mountains passed close to the spot where they had fallen, and now I found myself in the same region—what if I were going to meet the same band? All around was lonely, and I had already passed many ruined habitations where the war-demon had passed, but there was no longer any sign of life. In my anxiety not to miss the trysting-place I had left Santiago de Cuba some hours earlier than was necessary, and had ridden pretty hard until the neighborhood of the town and forts was left some distance behind. Although the directions were very clearly set down, in my very eagerness to be right I lost my road, but after a little delay found it again, and much to my delight came upon the trysting-place. It was a frightfully lonely spot, but had at least one advantage—if I got there first it would be difficult to surprise me, and almost impossible to take me unawares. In the middle of what had once been a large *potrero* stood a single gigantic tree, a lonely ceiba, blasted by lightning, with its huge, bare arms shot out most fantastically.* The tree itself, like a giant ghoul, seemed to watch over the field threateningly. In its withered grandeur it looked a fitter representative of death and terror than any grinning skull of human manikin, while the parasite plants perched on the stately boughs seemed to mock at the decay of so much grandeur. No one who has not seen a tropical forest can form an idea of the striking, majestic appearance of these lords of the forest, which grow to the height of a hundred feet, and whose boughs

---

*O'Kelly later translates "potrero" as "cattle farm."

would shame the pretensions of our trees to any prominent place among the aristocracy of the forest.

There were still well-nigh two mortal hours to wait before the night would fall, and it was dangerous to remain near the place of appointment, so, with a view to eventualities, I reconnoitered the ground thoroughly and then rode away to let the hours slip by more rapidly. Probably they went by in the usual jogtrot, but it seemed to me that never would the night come; there were clouds but no night, and the sun seemed to linger on purpose just because I wanted him to be gone. If "old Harry," my horse, could have talked, I fear he would have protested against my whole proceedings, for during those two hours twenty times I changed direction, and conducted myself in a way which no well-bred animal like old Harry could be expected to submit to quietly. But in the end old Sol, in obedience to an immemorial custom, dipped behind the hills, and the welcome shadows came trooping quickly over the sky, rubbing the gilding off nature which the artist Sun had left on tree and rock as a memento of his passage. It was now time to return in order to be first at the tryst. Loosening my machete so that it would come out of its peaceful sheath like a lightning-flash if need should be, and pulling round my revolver so that it also was ready for instant use, I rode slowly back with the shadows. When I arrived a gray twilight had settled over the *potrero,* and the dark, menacing form of the ceiba rose up more gaunt and fantastic than in the day. Around the base the gloom of night had gathered, but the outreaching, giant arms seemed to grope for victims high up in the semi-gloom. Then came to my mind the remembrance of the superstitious dread entertained by the negroes for this tree, which they can with difficulty be compelled to cut down, as they believe that one out of the number who cut down a ceiba will surely die before a year has expired. Probably the belief is as well founded as many of the superstitions of more intelligent races. A ride round the tree convinced me that I was first on the ground, so, dismounting, I resolved to wait patiently for the *dénouement.* The night swept on apace, and ink-black clouds shut out the light of moon and stars, so that before the hour appointed the darkness had become so great that at the distance of a dozen feet it was impossible to distinguish anything. This was a contingency upon which I had not counted, and certainly it gave me little satisfaction. My horse fortunately remained perfectly still as I leaned on his neck, listening with painfully strained attention for the noise of footsteps, but the minutes lengthened into hours, and ages seemed not to move. Old Harry from time to time turned towards me inquiringly, as if he was anxious to know whether or not I was in my right mind, but as

I patted him on the neck the intelligent animal, flattered at the attention, decided that I knew what I was about. Nearly three-quarters of an hour had elapsed in this, painful, anxious state, when the stillness was broken by the noise of stealthy footsteps coming near. Old Harry arched his neck and became suddenly attentive. Although I peered eagerly into the gloom it was impossible to make out who was approaching, so drawing my revolver and arming it noiselessly, I awaited. In about half a minute I heard a low "hist." I at once gave the Cuban challenge, "Quien va?" and was answered by the welcome countersign, "Cuba Libre." A man then approached, but he was so black that even after he had taken my hand, which I held out as the voice approached me, I could scarcely make him out, so much did he appear a part of the general gloom. In an instant we mutually convinced each other that we were the right persons. So far as I was concerned, there remained no doubt on my mind that this man was the representative of the people who sent the mysterious letter, but who they were was still to be settled. It was so dark the man's features were not visible, but as he gave the right answers according to the letter, he was evidently one of the men I came to see. He told me he had four more men with him at some distance, and asked me if I was prepared to follow him. Having assured him that I was, and slipped my revolver, which, during our interview, I held ready for use in my left hand, quietly into the holster, I mounted, and followed my strange guide.

When I say I followed the mysterious guide, the impression conveyed to the reader is somewhat incorrect. The man walked, or rather glided, over the ground so rapidly, and the darkness was so great, that the atmosphere seemed palpably thick, rendering it very difficult for me to keep in view the shadowy form that appeared ready at every instant to evaporate in the night-mists.* More than once in that strange march the gliding figure vanished completely from view, though I was leaning eagerly over my horse's neck peering after my strange companion; at other times only the wonderful instinct of the horse prevented me from trampling on the silent form that marched through the jet-black night, as though it were a spirit of darkness before which all material difficulties disappeared. After some time we reached a small wooded ravine, where the guide halted and warned me not to speak, then began again his silent, gliding march.

---

*In describing his escort as gliding over the ground, O'Kelly contributes to a long tradition of depicting black people as naturally equipped for maroon life. For more on the conflation of blackness with marronage, see M. Allewaert's "Swamp Sublime: Ecologies of Resistance in the American Plantation Zone," *PMLA,* 123.2 (2008): 340–57.

From the rolling of the small stones under the horse's feet it was clear we were following the dry bottom of what, in the rainy season, would be turned into a mountain stream. It was necessary to lie along the horse's neck in order to avoid being swept out of the saddle by the tree-branches that frequently formed a leafy arcade above my head. Soon after emerging from this covered way the woods became more open, and from the heavy, black clouds large raindrops fell at intervals. Our further march was here stopped by the *Camino Real,* or King's Highway. Here the guide whispered I should remain until he went in search of his companions, who were hid in the wood close by; there were four men, he informed me, one of them being a white man. For the first time I noticed that my guide was a strong, athletic fellow, and was armed with a gun. Without waiting for a reply he left me, and plunged into the woods at the farther side of the road, where, soon after, a series of low whistlings were heard, which I conjectured were signals. The rain had begun to fall pretty heavily, so I dismounted and put on my waterproof cape, and, again taking out my revolver, prepared to meet my new acquaintances. All around me was waste and desolate, the stillness of the black night being only broken at intervals by the low whistle that from time to time resounded in the woods without apparently meeting a response. This circumstance appeared to me very suspicious, and I peered round anxiously, trying to discover any approaching form in the darkness, and listening eagerly for some step to break the dreadful stillness. I remained like a statue, leaning over the horse's neck, certainly not quite at ease, but watchful, and prepared for anything that might happen. If there was any intention to attack me it would have to be done in front, as my horse formed a kind of rampart which rendered a sudden assault from behind impossible. In spite of all these precautions my heart beat quicker as the moments glided away and no answer came to the low whistle, which I could hear repeated at intervals by the guide. This furnished a new source of disquietude. Were they really Cuban patriots, and had they been surprised? This was by no means impossible, for the spot where we stood was in the very center of Spanish posts extending for leagues in every direction. My fears on this point were almost immediately set at rest by a responsive whistle, repeated several times, in imitation of some of the numerous night-birds of this region, and a few minutes after a rustling of the bushes was followed by the appearance of two men on the road. One of them was the guide, and the other, a white man, informed me that he was a lieutenant in the Cuban army, and that he had been sent specially to escort me to the patriot lines. I thanked him very briefly, and informed him that I was ready to follow him. While we were speaking three other human forms glided out of the bushes, and each one approached and saluted me. They, like the guide, were colored men, and the stealthy, rapid way they moved about in the darkness, as well as the raggedness of their scanty clothing and the wildness of the spot, were little calculated to tranquillize my apprehensions; and even then I was far from sure that my new acquaintances were respectable parties. When the guide left me to go in search of his companions he had deposited under my charge a bag, which, in the darkness of the night, I had not before perceived. This bag was now opened and provisions drawn out for the men, who, the lieutenant told me, had eaten nothing all day, as they were obliged to remain concealed in the wood to avoid discovery. To see the ravenous way the poor fellows pounced on some cold rice seasoned with *bacallao* was really painful, and I was almost glad that the darkness prevented me from seeing distinctly their faces. With that hospitable feeling and politeness so ingrained in Spanish-speaking races, one of the men invited me to partake of their scanty meal; and though the dish, which was the man's cap, and its contents were detestable, I thought it better to swallow some of the stuff, excusing myself from any large indulgence on the pretense of having recently dined. As the rain was falling pretty heavily, and the men were shivering from lying in the damp grass, I offered them my brandy-flask, which was partaken of, but very slightly, by all. It had, however, an excellent effect on the men, for, when the orders to start were given, they pressed round to hold my horse while I mounted, and to fix my foot in the stirrup—little attentions which showed they felt grateful that I sympathized with them.

After distributing the provisions, and, as I afterwards learned, the correspondence, brought from the town by the guide, the party began the march. Crossing the *Camino Real* we plunged into the woods, where the darkness became again so great that I was obliged to depend almost wholly on the instinct of my horse to follow the trail. Fortunately, he had been well broken to this sort of travel, having at one time belonged to a Spanish colonel, otherwise it would have been next to impossible to have kept long in company with those men, who, in spite of the weight of their arms and provisions, seemed to glide over the ground without effort and without noise. In fact, the only notice of their passage was the breaking from time to time of some dry branch or twig, with a short, snappish sound, when all around became silent and ghostlike as before. Not a word was spoken, not even a whisper was heard, as we wound in most tortuous way through woods, gullies, and briery paths, sometimes emerging into cultivated fields and skirting cane-fields, advancing without pause in the most wonderful manner through those tangled ways, though so dark was the night that, putting up one's hand, it was difficult to distinguish it. How those phantom men, who seemed ready every minute to melt from my view, found their way so unerringly is a puzzle. Some say it is instinct; it may be so; but, if so, then to my mind instinct very often leaves poor, boasted human intelligence behind. Some of the passages were so tangled that I was obliged to cut my way through the branches and trailing plants that were constantly entangling and threatening to hang me up much as a spider hangs up a fly. On these occasions my machete proved invaluable, though the brier and cactus families played the very deuce with my face, neck, and hands, so that by morning I presented the appearance of a hero that had come badly mauled out of an encounter with a legion of cats. Indeed, it is almost a miracle that the toll of an eye was not exacted for my passage through brier-land by the envious thorns that at every step took hold of flesh and clothing as if anxious to retard our progress. It would be difficult in the extreme to convey anything like a correct idea of the tortuous windings of our way, even had the night been clear enough to allow me to distinguish the features of the country. At first, owing to my acquaintance with the formation of the ground, I was able to form a vague notion of the route we were following, but, after crossing some hills, passing along the crests of others, dipping down into the depths of valleys, and again emerging on comparatively level ground, all my topographical ideas became so confused that speculation had to be abandoned as useless. All my attention was directed to an effort to save one eye at least for use in Cuba Libre. In this, fortunately, success to an unlooked-for degree attended my efforts, for though my eyes were in constant danger, and had very many narrow escapes, they came out of the trial whole. Our first halt was made, after about three hours' rapid and most fatiguing marching, under a huge tree. The perfect discipline of the men, their uncomplaining support of fatigue that would have tired the strongest and best-cared-for troops, had, to a great extent, dissipated any latent feelings of suspicion which had remained after the white lieutenant's explanation of his mission; and as the poor fellows, exposed in their thin, scanty clothing to the pelting rain, excited my sympathy, my brandy was freely distributed among them—an impulsive generosity which afterwards proved a source of considerable inconvenience to myself; but whoever, under the circumstances, could weigh the possible results to himself of his liberality would be a person of very privileged organization. In order to avoid awakening any suspicion, or appearing to entertain the slightest want of confidence in my guides, I carefully avoided asking them where we were going or what route we were pursuing. As we soon established good relations, however, under the influence of the brandy-flask, I ventured to inquire if they were certain that my horse could cross the mountains, to which they replied in the affirmative. This was a most important piece of information for me, and gave me real pleasure, as the condition of my health would render a long and painful journey very trying; my equipments also were unfitted for traveling on foot, and the loss of my horse would place me in as sorry and painful a condition as a dismounted *cuirassier,* a fate which, unfortunately, the gods had in store for me.

As we left Santiago de Cuba behind us our march became freer, and from time to time we availed ourselves of the *Camino Real,* taking the precaution of sending a scout ahead. At last we reached the base of the mountains at the foot of the Puerto de Bayamo, and began the ascent. The rainfall had ceased, and the ink-black clouds dispersed. The moon was beginning to force her way through opposing darkness, and we could see the city of Santiago de Cuba lying at our feet like an illuminated fairy palace, while the patch of utter blackness lying beside it we knew to be the harbor. Looking down from the great height of the mountains over the dark space that intervened, the city seemed to be drawn under our very feet, although it was leagues away, and it required but small effort of the imagination to people the familiar Plaza with the gay crowds that were at that moment promenading under the rows of brilliant lamps, which, seen in bird's-eye view, were infinitely more lovely and full of charm than when seen under ordinary circumstances. It is not quite certain that I did not expect my sable guide of the owl-like instinct to lift up, Asmodeus-like, the roofs of the houses and show me what was passing within; but certainly I did think that there is more real beauty and marvelous scenes in nature than the richest Eastern fairy-tale has ever painted, if we would only consent to see them. More than once I stopped my horse and turned regretfully to the fairy-land vision that would soon be lost to my sight forever, and if only a few of the delightful impressions of the moment, and the crowd of suggestive fleeting beauties called up in my imagination in those few moments could be painted in words, so that others could feel them as I felt them, my readers would owe me at least one charming chapter. But, unfortunately, these impressions are fleeting, and are blotted and blurred, when not completely wiped out, by newer impressions that succeed, also to perish in their turn.

Before we had half climbed the mountain's side it became necessary to dismount and abandon my horse, to be led by one of the men, owing to the steepness of the ascent. Imagine a *caballero,* with heavy riding-boots, spurred, a long machete, which insisted on getting between his legs, hanging at his side, with other *impedimenta,* climbing a hill so steep that most of the time one moved almost on all-fours, and at moments progress being only possible by gymnastics. My companions seemed to mount the almost perpendicular slope of the mountain's side as if they were, indeed, creatures of upper air instead of the place where their color would more naturally, according to our prejudices, assign them.

How my horse managed to climb up this hill was a puzzle to me, and as the ground grew at every step more steep, my faith in his crossing the mountains soon began to waver. To add to the difficulties of the ascent, the rain had loosened the clayey soil, which crumbled under the foot, and more than once I narrowly escaped coming to grief through these miniature landslips. The moment of anguish at length arrived: in endeavoring to pass a steep curve in the path, the earth gave way, and poor old Harry was precipitated some twenty feet—not a direct fall, for that was impossible, owing to the trees and undergrowth, but very nearly so. In his fall he tore up trees and bushes by the roots; and when at last he stopped, caught up by creeping plants, and jammed against the trunk of a large tree, he was almost buried in *débris* and fallen timber. It seemed to me that he was killed; but the guides, with their machetes, soon cut through the trailers and branches that prevented him from rising, and when some logs that had also rolled over him were removed, much to my surprise old Harry got on his feet again; but all his fine trappings had been swept away in that awful tumble, and some of my havings were never seen again. However, all the more necessary part of my equipment was taken by the guides with the best will, and carried during our long and fatiguing marches. Not that old Harry was then abandoned; one of the men stayed with him, and for nearly an hour the horse could be heard plunging his way up the hill-side; but, after several very heavy falls similar in character to the one described, old Harry positively refused to go an inch farther, and, after a few preliminary kicks, started down the mountain-side in such brilliant style that the astonished guides were never tired telling their friends of the loss of the *bello caballo,* as they admiringly named him. Not being able to render any assistance in conducting the horse, having quite enough to do to keep myself from sliding back to the starting-point, I had made my way to the summit of the mountain, where the Cuban lieutenant, Señor de la Torre, had arrived before me.* How I ever got there is a mystery to

---

*O'Kelly may be referring to José Loreto de la Torre. See CubaGenWeb's "Database of Officers of the Ten Years War 1868–1878," http://www.cubagenweb.org/mil/grande/.

me. Certainly, in getting over some of the rocks which barred my passage, I presented more the appearance of a huge lizard than anything else. It was now long past midnight; and, though the rain had ceased and the moon had risen, the damp air chilled to the very marrow. My brandy-flask had been emptied preliminary to the ascent; so I sat down, shivering and chattering in the cold night air, while the struggle to bring up my horse was being fought out gallantly by the guides. At length the direful news was brought me that old Harry had gone to Santiago on his own hook, and that it would therefore be necessary to continue the march on foot. The production at this moment of a small jar of cane-brandy—a cheap, strong, burning liquor of the worst class, but which tasted just then like nectar—consoled me somewhat for the loss of my horse, and, as there was no remedy, we started on to continue our journey as jollily as possible. We were now entering a less dangerous district, where my guides were not afraid to march openly in the day. The spot where we had rested on the summit of the mountain was quite close to a Spanish fort, so close that we could hear the voice of the sentinel crying the *alerta*, or that all was well, which we were very glad to learn on such good authority.

With the morning light, I began to have a better opinion, as well as better knowledge, of the men in whose company I had traveled all night; they improved with acquaintance, which is a good feature in new friends. Three of them were black, the guide who had come to meet me especially so, and Pio, a broad-shouldered fellow, who attached himself to me from the first, and continued with me till I reached the camp of Modesto Diaz, in the quality of sable esquire and valet.* All the men were armed with rifles, except the lieutenant, who contented himself with a knife, which gave his equipment at once an air of simplicity and usefulness. Though the men, in addition to their arms, were laden with the equipments of my horse, as well as my personal effects and provisions for the journey, they marched at a surprisingly rapid rate. The night's work had told on me, but I was unwilling to acknowledge fatigue; so we pushed on at a swinging pace down the mountains. My equipments, as well as the state of my health, put me at a terrible disadvantage, in spite of the men being more heavily weighted. The flannel shirt and heavy riding-boots, in this up-hill-down-hollow work, played the very deuce with me; but still I resolved not to be left behind. To aggravate my trouble, the soft Cuban

---

*Modesto Díaz (1826–1892) was a Dominican major general in the Cuban army. He fought for the Spanish in Santo Domingo before moving to Cuba. He joined the Cuban forces at the beginning of the Ten Years' War.

sole-leather of my boots slipped on the wet clay and stones, so that I was constantly sliding backwards at the imminent risk of falling. The work was killing and disheartening, but there was nothing for it but to go on. It was all very well in the cool of the morning; but when the sun came out and showered down tons of heat on our unfortunate heads, every minute became an hour, and every mile ten. Had it been a decently-level road, I could have got along well enough; but the up-hill struggle was too much for my lungs when not a breath of air was stirring. About nine o'clock we halted in a cane-field, and, as I was terribly fatigued, it was proposed to get me some coffee; but the people on whom we counted could not be found, and so it was necessary to content myself with a drink of water and some sugar-cane, a rather novel breakfast.

Here we rested for nearly an hour, as in the next stretch we would have to march for hours unceasingly in an open country, passing within sight of two Spanish forts. This was agreeable news for me, as I felt perfectly certain that in the event of a pursuit I could scarcely get away, and I was by no means certain that my companions would have bothered much about me. In justice to these men I must now say that better acquaintance has convinced me that they would not have deserted without making all the efforts to save and help me that honor would demand, but I did not then know that. Besides, we were only six men, with one breech-loading rifle and three muzzle-loaders. We could not, therefore, hope to fight any detachment of Spanish troops, for only strong detachments move about in the country. It would, therefore, be a question of running, and as I was completely out of training, there was no doubt on my mind what would be the result in case any pursuit should take place. With a view to eventualities I got possession of the single Remington, so that I felt if it was possible to get away I would. However, no enemy crossed our path, and we had only to contend against the awful heat and fatigue. About three o'clock in the afternoon we had almost reached the top of the hill known as *el Purgatorio*. If the truth must be told, I was completely beaten up, and was more dead than alive. From the point we had reached two Spanish forts were visible in the valley below, and they must have seen us plainly during the hours we passed over open ground. We might be pursued, and if so, I at least would be done for, for I could not go any farther; it was absolutely impossible. I was willing to try, but my legs were not. They bent about in all sorts of curious ways, and at last would absolutely go no farther; so I told the Cubans to go on and I would follow the trail as well as I could when able to walk, but to their credit they refused to leave. One man went in search of sugarcane in a field close by, and we sat down in Guinea-grass in full sight of the fort below, but in as sheltered a situation as the open hillside afforded. There was a wood five hundred yards farther on, but I could not reach it. It was very stupid to sit down in the grass where we might be seen; I knew it, and would have liked to go on, but I could not. All my strength, energy, and resolution had been absolutely exhausted in the awful, pauseless march through the occupied region, and there was nothing left but to lie down till nature could recuperate. Never in my life was I so overwhelmed with shame. I would have given anything to purchase physical strength enough to get to the top of the hill. The men insisted on taking off my heavy riding-boots and flannel, which were killing me with heat. Half an hour's rest and some sugarcane, however, restored me sufficiently to enable me to continue the march, but much more lightly equipped, and by the time we reached the outlying encampment which placed me in the territory of Cuba Libre, my strength had somewhat returned.

12   In Cuba Libre at Last

WE HAD been marching on the second day for some time over comparatively level ground, when suddenly we came on a number of tracks in the woods running in different directions. We were near a halting-place, which to me was exceedingly welcome news. A turn in the path brought us face to face with a young girl who, though evidently glad to see the *convoyeros,* looked on me with very little confidence. My garb was too suggestive of a Spanish officer to be pleasing, and my appearance created quite a sensation in the hamlet, where a number of families were assembled. It was not, however, of a pleasurable kind, and was very nearly having an unpleasant result. Treachery has unfortunately not been unknown in the Cuban struggle, and my unannounced appearance at the heels of the guides frightened some women, who thought I might be followed by Spanish soldiers. The panic was about to spread, some of the women having already snatched up whatever was readiest and most valuable, to flee into the woods for safety, and a convalescent soldier had seized his gun to fire at me when he fortunately recognized his brother, who was one of the guides, and, laying aside his gun, calmed the women about him with the assurance that I must be a friend. This incident passed so rapidly that it escaped my notice at the time, as my attention was naturally distracted, wandering over the novel scenes of life in Cuba Libre, where I was at last arrived. There were not more than half a dozen leaf-covered huts visible; but at a short distance there was another group of similar structures occupied by families. A leaf shelter, open at all sides, was at once prepared for my reception, a bed of laths, or rather twigs, was constructed, and while these preparations were being completed, the women presented me with delightful coffee; at least I found it more delicious than ever the best Mocha had tasted to me in civilized life.

After all the stories told me about savage negroes, ignorant as ferocious, wandering naked in the woods, respecting no laws, human or divine, and merely stopping short of cannibalism, it was some relief to me to be able to look around and find myself surrounded by persons of gentle, and even polished, manners. It is true that clothing was rather scanty, but there was enough for decency, and in this favored clime little more is needed. The women were all adequately clothed, and in many instances were even able to exhibit a certain amount of coquetry in their dress, which no true woman having an opportunity to do would be likely to let slip. Without being at all intrusive, the few men in the settlement came to welcome me and make a polite offer of service. Indeed, considering that very many of these people had been slaves—all of them except de la Torre were colored—their conduct contrasted very favorably with what I have since observed among the white Catalans and Castilians, who contemptuously look upon them as barbarians and *negros sueltos,* or to translate the idea, "runaway niggers." Before I was half an hour among them I was perfectly at my ease, and feeling as safe from all insult or aggression as though seated in an aristocratic quarter of a European capital. This little nameless hamlet belongs to a numerous class of settlements scattered over Cuba Libre. For the most part the inhabitants were peaceable people, anxious to be let alone, but quite resolved never to submit to Spanish authority. There was the inevitable prefect, whose duty it was to look after such wounded or helpless persons as might be left in his district, and furnish skilled guides to the operating forces. Beyond this the inhabitants have little to do with the warlike operations, and would fain be allowed to work in peace. The settlement occupied a small clearing in the forest, not much larger than was absolutely necessary to allow the erection of houses; and when any new erections are found necessary, the needed space is opened under the direction of the prefect. It was to me extremely interesting to watch this germ of a new society, and endeavor to go back mentally through numberless ages to the time when little communities like this were formed in the primeval forests, to grow with time into great nations; and, just as the seed cast into the ground to-day comes out into air and light, and absorbs nourishment, to grow into a stately tree, just as other trees did in the millions of ages that have left only geological traces of their existence, so this human seed, I thought, represents the growth of society, even as it grew in the primeval times, in all matters essential. The analogy may appear forced, but take away a few iron machetes and the guns, and what do these people possess which, after the first few ages of existence, the primitive man might not possess? Nothing, absolutely nothing. The state of society in which they live prevents them working metals, even had they the necessary skill or knowledge, and the trees furnish all instruments of household or field use, and they are of the simplest—a sharp stick to root up the sweet potatoes, an improvised mill to crush the sugar-cane, whose honey-juice is collected in a gourd cut in half, or some contrivance equally primitive. Their manufactures are confined to the chief necessaries of life, and here bounteous nature supplies them with all needful materials, only having to stretch out their hands to take the gifts a rich and tender motherland offers to her children. The cotton-tree gives pods that are skillfully spun into thread; the majagua, twine, from which hammocks, sandals, shoes even, are made, as well as those most useful huge sacks in which the patriot often carries a crop he has reaped, though he had not sown it; and many kinds of grasses are woven into sombreros to shelter patriot heads from the fierce ardor of the sun.

These manufactures are carried on by women, as is right they should be, while the men hunt the wood-rat, or dig for the sweet root, or gather the luscious orange, or cut the succulent sugar-cane, each one contributing something in some way to the general prosperity. Not for this, however, is there any approach to common property, or socialism; each one is absolute master of what he gathers, and distributes as seems good to him the result of his labor. Mostly, for convenience, the people live in small groups, but each member of the group has his or her worldly goods apart, be they gold-pieces, or guns, or gowns, or whatever else. Nothing more surprised me than this feature of respect for property, little to be looked for under the circumstances in which these people have lived for nearly five years.

These Mambi settlements are the special object of hatred to the Spanish authorities, and hence no effort is spared to destroy and root them out. For this reason the habitations are separated from the fields whence the means of subsistence are derived, and hid away in the most secret part of the woods, far from the path of the Spanish columns. Much indignation is given vent to by Spanish officials and their foreign nigger-whipping, sugar-worshiping sympathizers, noble Saxons, free Americans, and other worthy representatives of civilized communities, because the Cuban patriots burn down plantations which furnish the principal revenue to their Spanish enemies, and which are turned into actual forts, garrisoned by Spanish soldiers, but it never for a moment enters the minds of these defenders of property and its sacred rights that it is also a crime against civilization and humanity to burn down the leaf-thatched hut of the Cuban, and his sugar-cane, and cut down his banana-tree, at the imminent risk of causing him and his young family—for young families are numerous in Cuba Libre—to die of starvation. More than once have I listened with loathing and disgust to noble hidalgos and "illustrious swords" recounting with glee how their troops had fallen suddenly on some little settlement in the night, and how the trembling women fled to the woods with the children and what little they could save, but thankful that they had not the evil fortune to fall into Spanish hands. On such occasions the property of the poor people is carried off or destroyed, and their miserable homes consigned to the flames, while the conquerors of helpless women and children march proudly back to civilization, and loudly proclaim the capture of another rebel encampment. Sometimes it happens that a crippled or wounded Cuban is found unable to escape. If he is fortunate he is at once killed; if not, he dies more slowly. The prisoners that are brought in sometimes from these most glorious expeditions are, for the most part, women, worn out from sickness and fatigue, who present themselves to the troops in order to be allowed to return to the towns; and, as they are paraded as captives, and shown to foreigners as a proof of the nobleness and generosity with which the Spanish party make war, they are sometimes taken to the towns and allowed to dwell in peace. But for those captured in fight, or after a surprise, quite a different fate is reserved. Indeed, these histories are far too shocking to find a place here; and, unfortunately for humanity, they are not only of frequent occurrence, but men who would be offended if it were hinted that they were not gentlemen witness these acts of outrage and barbarity, and yet think it no dishonor to wear a sword in a service where nameless crimes are not alone suffered, but applauded and rewarded.

It is seldom that the poor people go far from the scene of their misfortunes, but remain hidden in the recesses of the forests in fear and trembling, suffering hunger and thirst, to which is often added excruciating mental torture, in the fear that some loved one has perished. When it is hoped that the civilizers have departed, some venturesome explorer moves out to reconnoiter the spot where humble homes had been, and if he brings back the joyful news that the storm has passed, and that the Spaniard has departed, those wretched people steal back like ghosts of their former selves, and dwell in fear and trembling until the memory of that day of sorrow has been forgotten in the glorious sunshine of this unhappy land, where nature hastens to cover up every scar inflicted on her fair face by the brutal hand of thoughtless, passionful man. If the life of this people has not more analogy with that of the generations in the past, whose strength was justice, I am much mistaken. Certainly there appears to me no reason to draw any distinction between the rifle-armed columns that march under the flag of Castile and the not more brutal band of the hunting age pouncing on some weaker tribe, slaying the valiant and carrying into slavery such as preferred a dishonored life to death. In each case the aim and the excuse are similar, and it cannot much alter the nature of the act that one band slays with rifle-bullets while the other killed with clubs, or other rude contrivance. It is at once creditable to the constancy and nobility of these people that five years of such life has failed to make them in reality as savage and as barbarous as their persecutors represent them. That it has altered the natural docility of character is unquestionable, and men who, in the beginning, were mild and harmless, have acquired a severity which, under great excitement, would possibly become akin to ferocity. Indeed, the Cubans, black and white, would be the most contemptible of God's kind if they were not severe, to the uttermost edge of the law, after the barbarous wrongs they have suffered. It is not good that nations any more than individuals should be allowed to commit crimes with impunity, and the arm that smites murderously merits to be cut off mercilessly. Sitting among these gentle-natured and good-hearted people, I could not refrain from wondering how boldly men can lie, how cruelly the character of a people can be blackened, and the crimes committed against them be turned into virtues by the serpent tongue that defames cunningly and has the ear of mankind. Here were men who for months had been represented to me as ferocious savages, without respect for God or man, owning no laws but force, steeped in brutality, and employing their days and nights in wild revelry, only thinking of satisfying the lowest and most bestial passions; in a word, beings whom it was a duty to slay, enemies of God and of humanity: and here, face to face with this terrible race, I find them peaceful, respectful, good-hearted, gentle, and hospitable. Such is the result of human passion and malignity.

At the moment of our arrival a good number of the dwellers in this settlement had gone in various directions to search for food, and, as the evening began to close in, quite a long train of young children of both sexes arrived in the hamlet, bearing loads of cane-stalks, sweet potatoes, oranges, and other fruits which they had gathered in the abandoned plantations, which were numerous in the neighborhood of the settlement, and furnished the principal means of support to the inhabitants. The file of children moved in gravely and demurely, looking just like a swarm of ants. The oldest among them could scarcely have passed twelve or thirteen years of age. Being too young to take arms, these little ones were gradually being formed to habits of order and industry. It was said, and my own observation confirmed the correctness of the judgment, that the young children growing up in this semi-wild state were infinitely more industrious and enterprising than the grown people who had been reared as slaves on the plantations. These little men and women were certainly untiring, and during my stay they brought sufficient provisions into the settlement to support the grown-up people for a week, at least it appeared so to me. After-experience taught me that as the young Mambis were harder-working they were infinitely harder-fighting than the older men. Now the flower of the Cuban army is composed of those who were little more than children when the cry of Yara went up and invoked the God of freedom to aid in making Cuba a nation.*

The evening was fast closing in when the little ones filed past, and though I had partaken of at least a dozen cups of coffee and sundry sweet potatoes, cakes of cassava plant, and many other Mambi luxuries, I was expected to eat at least two dinners, for everyone was desirous that the stranger should partake of something from his particular store, and it was rather fortunate that the number of families was limited, or I might have been killed with kindness. But even dining must have an end, and, in order that the time should not lie too heavily on my hands, it was determined to get up a ball in my honor. There was, however, a great difficulty: neither music nor musician was at hand; but, when people have made up their minds to dance, such trifles are never suffered to stand in the way, so an improvised tamtam of the most barbarous kind was put into requisition, and the ball began by the children dancing. Then the ladies in their finery appeared, and the native *danza* was kept up until the stars came out and warned the revelers to be gone.

The amusement was certainly rude, and the whole scene tinged with something of the grotesque, as the dusky forms of the dancers moved

*For more on the "Grito de Yara," see introduction, xxi.

about in the narrow space, lighted up by the glare of torches, to the monotonous beat of the tamtam. But an incident that occurred in the midst of the somewhat boisterous gayety of my new acquaintances has impressed that night on my memory as one of the sweetest and most instructive in my life. The fun was at its height when a charming little colored girl about four years old came up and stood before me, looking full into my face, her large, full eyes turned upon me with a gentle appealing expression. The posture of the child, too, was striking: her hands were crossed upon her breast, and the sweet, smiling face reminded me of the tender, heavenly Madonnas of poetic Murillo. At first the idea came to me that the child wished me to give her some present, as a civilized child would have expected one; but, fearful of giving any cause of offense, and seeing that other children were presenting themselves in similar postures to the various lookers-on, I turned to the lieutenant, who was seated beside me, and asked him what the children were doing.

"Oh," was the reply, "they are asking the evening blessing from all the grown-up people; it is their custom to do so every night before retiring to rest."

As I turned round, the infant was still standing in the Madonna-like posture, with the same sweet smile, waiting for my blessing; and as I placed my hand on her head, and wished that God would always protect such innocence, I think a tear rolled down my cheek, at least I hope one did; for, though not a religious man in any sense of the word, the sweetness and beauty of this custom, so much in contrast with the wildness of Mambi life, and so foreign to the scenes of slaughter and outrage which make up the daily history of this suffering people, deeply impressed me, and I felt my heart soften and turn to the Almighty Being who holds our microcosm in the hollow of his hand, and smiles pityingly at our sorrows and passionate struggles.

13 Life in Cuba Libre

AT BREAK of dawn everyone in this leafy village was astir, and as I looked out of my shelter I could see that a general activity prevailed. The improvised sugar-mills were in full activity, and it was surprising to see how effectively and rapidly they performed the work for which they were intended. The Mambi-mill—*ingenio-mambi* as the patriots call it—is the very acme of simplicity. A tree is cut down and a kind of ledge cut on the trunk, and through a hole made in the trunk, about six inches above the ledge, a long pole, three or four inches in diameter, is fastened, which is used as a lever to crush the cane placed on the ledge. A piece of copper or tin is fastened to act as a shoot in conveying the juice to the vessels placed to receive it. This juice is afterwards boiled and made into sugar, or used in the manufacture of chocolate, which is carried on quite extensively, though at present for home consumption merely. These matters were full of interest to me as being exceedingly novel, but I was chiefly anxious to reach Cambute, which was distant some six or seven leagues. Tempü, a considerable encampment, under the command of Colonel Matias Vega, was only two leagues away, and as word had been sent of my arrival, orders were hourly expected. In the mean time, the question of the moment was to supply the loss of my horse. It was agreed on all hands that the matter was difficult, as all four-legged animals in that region had long since been turned into steaks, and more or less savory stews, by hungry patriots. However, there was one animal known to be in existence somewhere, and scouts were sent out to bring it in, by coaxing, or bullying, or fighting, if necessary; so, with these wide-reaching orders, parties went out in search of a horse, and I was promising myself a remount, when a messenger arrived with the joyful intelligence that two horses were outside the hamlet. The prospect of getting astride anything in the shape of a horse roused me up to something approaching enthusiasm, but when I arrived where the horses were my feelings experienced a shock. A poor, foundered beast, with unbendable legs, scraggy neck, dull, leaden eyes, and a frightful sore shoulder, was presented to me as my Rosinante, but, shade of Quixote, what an insult to thy charger! Had I consented for an instant to get on the poor animal's back, I should have lived in eternal dread of the just vengeance of Bergh. The other horse, small but strong, young and active as a cat, belonged to a black soldier who was conducting him to the camp of his chief, where the poor animal was going to be eaten. Every effort was made to induce the soldier to sell the horse, but he would not. His duty to his chief was above all considerations, and though I could not help admiring the sterling honesty of the man, I had to admit that virtue is sometimes most inconvenient. If the chief had been present the horse would have been given at once, but the sable Spartan only knew that it was his duty to bring the horse to the Monte del Toro, and to the mountain he brought him, leaving me to admire his sense of discipline and bewail my own ill luck. As nothing could induce me to have anything to do with the animated skeleton of a horse, an enterprising person, with an eye to business, purchased and killed him. At first I thought he was about to be distributed for the benefit of every one, but soon discovered that the laws of *meum* and *tuum* were much more rigidly observed than I had had any notion of, and that the dwellers in the hamlet would no more take a slice of horse-flesh without giving an equivalent, than would a citizen of Paris think of appropriating the contents of a stall in the Halles.

Towards evening a colored officer arrived with a guard of thirty men to escort me to Tempü. It was rather a surprise to find that they were all colored, and not by any means a pleasant one; not that I have any objection to colored people, but there came a chill over me lest the reports which had been constantly dinned into my ears that all the white men, except some half-dozen, had been killed, or were dead from sickness and disease, should prove well founded. Had this been true, the chance of success of the Cuban revolution would have been at an end, because ignorant men, however brave, cannot hope successfully to maintain a struggle which requires delicate combinations and great forethought to render success possible. The men, however, conducted themselves admirably, and such of them as had the means invested in old horse, while those who had nothing grinned, and hoped for better times, but made no attempt to appropriate even a bone. This moderation quite astonished me, as it certainly would not be exhibited by European rebels under similar circumstances. That property in effects should be recognized as sacred was not to be so much wondered at, but that one man of a patriotic army should have food, and another go hungry because he had no money to buy food, was carrying respect for vested rights to an extreme. If these men be robbers and vagabonds, then there must be very few honest people in the world. That evening was one of feasting and rejoicing, as it is not every day that these folk fall on the framework of a horse. My own dinner, however, suffered from what I had seen. For the first time in my life I had knowingly eaten horseflesh, and as my grinders closed on a specially savory morsel reserved for me, the specter of the animated framework appeared, with those sad, leaden eyes, and both my conscience and my stomach reproached me for my bad taste. Never again shall I eat horse-flesh without thinking of this poor victim of carnivorous man.

Next morning my bronze and ebony guard paraded at an early hour; so, after much hand-shaking and the exchange of mutual good wishes, I took leave of my hospitable entertainers, and, taking up the position assigned to me in the center of the line, set out in good earnest in search of Cespedes and his republican government. My hopes of meeting him at Cambute were dashed by the news, brought by the brown colonel, that he had already left that encampment to join Calisto Garcia Iniguez; so there was a prospect of a long hunt before he could be come up with.* However, as I was now beyond question on the right road, and found that the most complete order and organization, in all essential points possible under existing conditions, were maintained, I felt quite satisfied that the success of my mission was secured, and this being so, the delay of a week or a month was to me a matter of merely secondary importance. A few steps from the leaf-thatched huts brought us into the virgin forest with its wealth of creeping plants, lianas, vines, and wonderful parasite growth that swayed in festoons far above our heads in lofty independence; graceful trailing vines; dangling, cord-suspended pods; delicate, leaf-tipped branches, swaying gently in the morning breeze, diamond-dew laden; while through the fretwork of the leafy arch overhead struggled the roseate beams of the newly-risen sun, tinting tree-trunk, stem, and leaf, and dew-drop with colors of the emerald, agate, ruby, and all other precious stones, and changing the tall, graceful stems that shot up among the delicate fretwork into gold and silver pillars, until the whole forest seemed changed into some most wonderful fairy palace, wrought with such skill as never human mind conceived nor clumsy-handed man created. How pale the richest colors of Gothic windows compared with the living, liquid hues of the crystal-decked foliage, transparent in the roseate light that shone through the cunning tracery of the foliate arches, reflected in our path, lighting up the dim, shadowed nave, where we poor earthworms crawled, only half conscious of the wondrous beauty surrounding us on every side! Wherever the eye turned it rested on the same intricate, delicate tangle, that began nowhere and ended nowhere. Vegetable threads, like silk cords, and vines, that in the distance looked like ship's cables, hung gracefully over boughs in countless festoons, or climbed up into trees, and winding, snake-like, through their branches, stretched out into other trees beyond, like huge serpents, and lost themselves amidst the foliage in the air-world beyond our vision.

For nearly two hours we wound along the narrow, sinuous track which led to Tempü, and though the sun was scorching in the open stretches, beneath the canopy of the forest the air was cool, and even chill. A broad, clear stream blocked our farther passage, but, skirting the riverbanks

---

*The Cuban general's name should read "Calixto García Íñiguez." General Calixto García (1839–1898) fought in all three Cuban wars for independence.

for some hundred yards, we came to a shallow ford, into which the men plunged at once. One of the soldiers immediately offered to carry me across, but the temptation of a pleasant footbath was irresistible, and, taking off my boots and gaiters, I waded across. Arrived on the opposite bank, the character of the country underwent a change; the trees disappeared to the horizon, or became very sparse, and large stretches of pasture and cane-field were presented to the view. In the distance rose the chimney of the *ingenio* of Tempü, which before the war must have been one of the largest and most prosperous in Cuba, but was now little more than a mass of ruins, though the cane-fields, waving with richest verdure, extended gracefully and peacefully over large tracts of country.

As we approached the *ingenio,* a group of officers was seen on a slight eminence evidently awaiting our approach. They proved to be Colonel Matias Vega and a number of white officers, waiting to receive me and conduct me to their encampment. The sight of a crowd of white faces was certainly a pleasure, and it was a great relief to me to see that Cuba Libre was not made up wholly of *negros sueltos.*

After about half an hour's march through tall, rank, Guinea-grass, and the still more stifling cane-fields, we entered the encampment of Tempü, where some hundreds of human beings were working like bees, and everything gave evidence of even better order and discipline than existed in the little outside resting settlement. Here was a regularly organized Cuban encampment, where everyone was completely under the orders of the chief. Some were hut building, and the buildings were more solid and more pretentious than in the outpost settlement. Sugar-making was being carried on very extensively, and some of the numerous Mambi-mills were imposing in size and worked by a number of men. Large pans had been taken from the *ingenio,* and were now fixed in the camp, and the process of sugar-boiling was being carried on with evident skill. The women and children, and most of the men, crowded round to see the new arrival from the outside world, from which they had been so long cut off; but, as I was conducted directly to the neat hut of Colonel Vega, I was saved from all inconvenience on the score of curiosity. It is due to these people to say that they exhibited a delicacy in this, as in many other matters, that would put to shame a more pretentious society. After a little rest and partaking of some coffee, it was proposed to me to inspect the camp.

The camp of Tempü was situated in a large, circular clearing, at the base of wooded hills which closed round in a semicircle, and on the side of the plain was screened from view by a wide belt of timber, which effectually cut the camp off from all observation. Inside, the ground was disposed with as much order and regularity as its somewhat broken nature would admit of; the houses were constructed on parallel lines, and this regulation was rigorously enforced, to prevent the place becoming a jumble. Perfect order seemed to be maintained, and no loafing permitted. Everyone was occupied in some way, and the whole air of the place was redolent of industry and labor. From time to time groups emerged from the belt of wood carrying cane cut in the fields we had passed through; others brought bushels of fagots to feed the fires; and of those in camp, such as were not engaged in sugar-boiling or hut-building were occupied in some useful way. This society, rude and primitive as it certainly was, made on me the impression that it possessed as much organization as could be expected to exist under the difficult circumstances in which it was placed. It was rather surprising to find a Cuban town so close to the Spanish outposts, apparently not apprehensive of any danger. It must be remembered that this spot could not be more than nine or ten miles from the town of Cobre, strongly occupied by Spanish troops on the one side, and a less distance from Palma Sorianna on the other. My wonder was increased when Colonel Vega informed me that, since the outbreak of the insurrection, he had never been more than a few miles distant from the spot he now occupied, although he had been attacked and had his encampment burned by the enemy several times. "You see," said Colonel Vega to me, "the Spaniards think they can conquer us by burning our camps; but it is a great error; we do not defend the camp, because, if we did, we might be surrounded by the enemy; but, as soon as they approach, we retire to the woods, and, while they are exposed burning the huts, we shoot them down. If they are too strong, we retire into the woods until they are gone, when we return to the camp, and in a few days it is built up again, just as if nothing ever had happened. Sometimes the Spaniards pay very dearly for these burnings. You remember the hill I pointed out to you coming to the camp? Well, a year ago a Spanish column attacked a camp we had about a mile from this place, and burned it down. They thought we had run away; but we were waiting for them in ambush in the forest when they returned, and, just as they reached the center of the open glade, we poured in volley after volley on them, causing awful slaughter. That day they lost over one hundred and fifty men, while our loss was quite insignificant. Since then they have not troubled me much. We change our camps about from time to time, according to the facility of obtaining provisions. We have only come here about ten days ago, in order to be near the cane-fields, as we are now gathering our sugar harvest; but during the whole insurrection my command has never been many miles distant from this point, and if the

Spanish soldiers want to find me they know very well where I am." The colonel gave me many other interesting details of the struggle; but, as they belong rather to the province of history than to a narrative of personal experience, they are not reproduced here.

A chat with Colonel Vega soon convinced me that it would be waste of time to go to Cambute. Jesus Perez, the general commanding the district, had left for the coast on some important business, and could not return before a couple of weeks. It was therefore better to join Calisto Garcia Iñiguez, who would have opportunities of sending me to the presidential residence. There was no horse in camp, but an offer was made to send scouts to hunt one up, or capture one; but, as they might not return for some days, I thought better to decline. It was certainly annoying, but, as Calisto Garcia's camp was only three days' march over a fairly level country, it appeared to me much better to undertake the march than to wait, and, perhaps, in the end have to walk. My resolution was communicated to Colonel Vega, who approved of it, and immediately gave orders for thirty of the best-armed men to be ready to accompany me.

14 In Search of Cespedes

THE ESCORT paraded about seven o'clock next morning, and ammunition was distributed to the men. Major Vega, the colonel's brother, took the command; we were also to be accompanied by some half-dozen white subaltern officers, an arrangement that gave me a good deal of satisfaction, as it would enable me to become acquainted with the views and character of the Cubans in the field. As it turned out afterwards, all those young men proved most agreeable and thoughtful companions. Though none of them were what could be called well educated, or informed in matters scholastic, they possessed a fund of information of a different kind, much more useful to them than any vain appendage of classic lore. Without being learned, they had knowledge, some of it of a most surprising kind. Every tree and flower and grass had a use or virtue with which they seemed acquainted, and the histories told about them were exceedingly novel and interesting. It is true, implicit reliance could not be placed on all that was told me, but for this the stories did not cease to be interesting. In the five years' struggle very many points had acquired an historic interest as the scene of an adventure, a lucky escape, a battle, or a massacre, and as my companions took infinite pains to point out all these spots, and recount, with Oriental picturesqueness, the surprise, the flight, or the battle, the hours glided quickly enough away.*

The first day we passed close to Palma Sorianna, so close that it was easy to recognize the patch of wood through which ran the road it was my intention to have followed had the Spaniards permitted me to continue my journey to the Cuban lines, and now this turning-back point was passed with a certain grim satisfaction. It was refreshing to think how much annoyed the wonderful *autoridad* would be when that awful fogy should learn that, in spite of all precautions and warning, the *Herald* correspondent had succeeded in entering Cuba Libre. It must have been about noon when we passed, and, doubtless, the Spaniards were tranquilly enjoying their *siesta;* however, in order to be prepared for eventualities, our party closed up, keeping a pretty sharp lookout. Fortunately, no enemy was encountered, and we again plunged into the forest, where we were comparatively safe. About an hour later we emerged on the *Camino Real,* where the party cut the telegraph-wires before proceeding on our way. This was the first military operation witnessed by me, and it reminded me that we were now actually on the warpath, and that, should we fall in with a large force of Spanish troops, the result might be very unpleasant for me. The danger of a *rencontre* arose from the smallness of our force, which, although a very respectable bodyguard, could have had no chance against the large Spanish columns, seldom numbering less than five hundred men, that moved about the country. A better understanding of the nature of the war would have lessened my apprehensions on this score, for the danger was more apparent than real. Whatever Spanish force we might encounter, we could easily escape from it, as the Spaniards would not dare to follow us for any distance into the recesses of the woods. The confidence of my companions appeared to me overweening, as they seemed perfectly indifferent to the meeting of a superior force. Indeed, their openly proclaimed contempt for the Spanish troops produced rather an unfavorable impression on my mind, as it appeared to me *fanfaronade*. This impression, however, wore off with time, when I became more

---

*Earlier O'Kelly counts "six years of war" (28). *The Mambi-Land* contains both real-time and retrospective narration, as O'Kelly edited and added to his original *Herald* dispatches (1872–1873).

acquainted with the habits of thought and inflated mode of expression of this people, to which the richness and sonorousness of their language so much induces. It seems natural to the Cubans to declaim poetically. The cold dignity of the Spaniard has thawed in this genial clime, and the magniloquent forms of his language have felt the influence of the fertilizing and enriching tropic clime; hence we can scarcely accept literally what the ordinary Cuban may say. Unconsciously he exaggerates, even when talking in the best faith. Perhaps one of the most amusing features in his character is the objection he has to admit defeat. If you listen to him he has always been individually successful. It may be that he has been driven from his position, and even pursued pretty vigorously, but this, in his eyes, does not constitute defeat; and one may hear him giving his version of the fight with a most amusing indifference to its general results. The Cuban army may be dispersed, but the soldier, in his own estimation, is never beaten; and this feeling is perhaps one of the great sources of the indomitable resolution of the men in the Manigua.

An amusing instance of this weakness was furnished by Major Vega, who could not resist the temptation of giving me an account of one of the first battles of the war, as we passed over the ground where it was fought. The different incidents of the battle were descanted on with a certain amount of correctness, the attack, feints, mistakes, and repulses were painted with a vividness really remarkable, in which the wonderful courage and devotion of the Cubans were awarded no faint need of praise. Fortunately, the other side of the story was familiar to me, as Commandante Lopez of the San Quentin battalion had been a prominent actor in the fight, and had given me more than once the Spanish version, no doubt as much colored by prejudice as the more poetical description of the Creole, which, therefore, afforded me considerable amusement, as I wickedly took a pleasure in encouraging the Cuban major in his exaggerations just to see how far his Oriental imagination would carry him.

Towards evening we halted in a barranca where some pools of clear rainwater enabled us to cook. The track we had followed ran through our camping-place, but it was thought that our safety would be sufficiently secured by placing a guard on each side, as we were surrounded by the impenetrable forest. Fires were soon lighted, and the odor of the welcome coffee was sniffed with real pleasure. Pio, my sable squire, having suspended my hammock between two trees, went off to aid in the culinary operations, at which he was quite *au fait*. The scene presented in a few moments was certainly remarkably picturesque—the groups of men in their strange and varied attire, their packs and arms carefully placed where they could be seized at a moment's notice, while the rapidly deepening gloom settling overhead was strangely lighted up by the flames of the little fires which had been kindled by the various groups. Salvator Rosa would have been delighted with such a scene; the, dark, waving trees illuminated by the flames, the many-hued faces of the men, moving about or resting, and the general abandon of their postures, gave us very much the appearance of ferocious bandits. As the men were not by any means encumbered with provisions, and we should be obliged next day to halt in a forest where nothing could be procured, a detachment was sent out to cut cane in a field close by, and try if fortune would not direct them to a good boniato plot. The sugarcane was plenty, but unfortunately the sweet potatoes proved to be rather scarce, so provisions for the next day's march were somewhat scanty; but as the Mambi have become accustomed to the frowns of fortune, this little disappointment did not cause any particular lowness of spirits. Long before the sun had risen we had resumed our march, and plunged into a wilderness of trees, twisted, tangled, and festooned with the ever-present parasites, whose seeds seem to flourish everywhere.

At intervals in the forest we came upon ruined huts, whose blackened timbers told too plainly the history of their desolation. These ruins had once been the homes of Cuban families who, at the beginning of the war, took refuge in these almost untrodden woods in hopes to escape the terrible scourge of war. For a time they had dwelt in peace, forgotten even by their compatriots, until the hour of reverses came, and Valmaseda's bloodhounds, in their thirst for blood and plunder, unearthed the unfortunates, and gave their homes to the flames, and, too often, their persons to outrage and slaughter.* It was impossible not to feel a chill on passing by these silent remains where once were peace, and love, and life, where now all is desolation and loneliness. Even the humble graves in the little clearing by the trail, marked by a rude cross which points out the last resting-place of the Cuban victims of war or of disease, whose ashes have been piously placed in a Mambi grave, are not so sadly suggestive of havoc and butchery as these charred timbers, piled confusedly one above another in utter shapelessness and ruin, while the tall grasses and the creeping plants hasten to cover up and hide from mortal eye the traces of man's violence and ruthlessness. Still plodding on through the endless, changeless woods,

---

*By "Valmaseda's bloodhounds," O'Kelly makes a slightly confused reference to Blas Villate y de la Herra (1824–1882), count of Valmaceda, known for merciless treatment of insurgents during his governorship of Cuba (1870–1872).

with ever the same foliage swaying overhead, and on either hand the countless stems, and vines, and trunks of tall trees aspiring ambitiously to reach up and beyond the leafy fields that almost shut out the deep blue skies that seemed so far away in the endless, boundless space that spread away, vast as an eternity. Wonders enough, truly, were here in the leaves, and strange flowers, and giant trees, to have furnished food for a life of busy speculation; but the unceasing tramp, tramp, tramp of the escort left no time to botanize, and the leaves, and trees, and flowers passed as in a panorama or a dream, just awakening curiosity, or wonder, or pleasure, and then disappearing as if moved away by some invisible hand. There was only time to go onwards, and so the mind abandoned these fugitive beauties, and turned to the contemplation of the more melancholy incidents which the monotony of the way and the sad landmarks did not fail to call up. While in this humor my attention was suddenly called by one of the officers to a polished, grinning skull of unnatural whiteness that lay with some other bones of a human skeleton in our path. They were the sad remains of some Spanish soldier left unburied, a prey to the beasts of the forest, as a mark of the unquenchable hate of the people whom he came to subjugate. Poor fool—the plaything of others' ambition, who, for the vain names of glory and country, had quit his weeping mother to die miserably in a foreign land, that a few conscienceless rich men might coin gold from the tears and blood of their fellow-man.

Continuing our march ever through the woods, we came upon a spot, comparatively open, near the bed of a river, which, at this season, was almost dried up. Here we found a hut which had evidently been quite recently occupied, as the fire was still smoldering, but trace of human being there was none. Our guide, however, soon brought us to another hut, where we found two women. This was the dwelling of that important functionary known as the prefect, who, we learned, had gone away the day before to guide a patriot battalion through the woods, but might be expected back at any minute. In answer to the question if it were possible to obtain any food, the women assured us with some concern that none was to be had; evidently fearful lest we should eat up the scanty provision upon which they depended for existence. Had we been one or two, probably all hospitality would have been shown, but thirty or forty, we were looked on with much the kind of apprehension with which an Eastern would regard a swarm of locusts. However, we were by no means so hungry as the poor women imagined; there was enough for supper, and we should be able to go through the form of breakfasting in the morning. No one would have taken any notice of the shortness of the commissariat stores if it had not been for my presence, as they could never get it into their heads that, on a push, a newspaper correspondent could rough it as well as they could. My chief grief was due to the coffee having given out after the first day, and we had to fall back on chocolate, which by no means replaced my favorite campaigning beverage. But this was, after all, a very small matter, as next morning we hoped to arrive at the headquarters of Calisto Garcia Iñiguez.

The spot where we were halted was a favorite camping-ground of the Cuban force; and among the trees were numbers of rude couches, constructed out of slender sticks, which such as are careful of their health go to the trouble of making in order to avoid lying on the damp, cold ground. When come upon suddenly these skeleton beds are too suggestive of coffins and biers to be pleasant to look upon. It may have been merely a personal fancy, but they always produced on me the effect of having stumbled on a necropolis in the wilderness. Their appearance is certainly very curious, and were it not for their long, coffin-like shape, being just made wide enough to accommodate comfortably one person, they might be taken for huge *grils*. Indeed, they are often used both as bed and gridiron, as the Mambi, when fortunate enough to secure a large supply of meat, cuts it in long strips, which he lays along one of these open-work couches, and, having lighted a fire underneath, he is enabled to smoke dry his meat so that it will keep for many days; the greenness of the sticks protects them from the flames.

We had not been long in camp when an incident illustrative of the trials and sorrows of the Mambi life occurred most unexpectedly. Immediately on arrival, as was the usual custom, guards were placed on all the roads leading to the camp, and soon after one of the soldiers appeared conducting a young child by the hand who seemed half dead from terror, and wept as though his little heart would break. The soldier informed the major that soon after one of the sentries had taken his post his attention was aroused by a rustling in the woods, and that almost immediately he caught sight of this child, who, as soon as he perceived the sentry, endeavored to escape, but was captured after a little chase. It appeared, from what could be gathered from the little fellow, that he had been traveling in the forest with his mother, but somehow had lost her and could not find his way. When asked if he knew where anyone lived in the forest, the child, thinking we were Spaniards, stoutly denied that he did. Poor child! He was in mortal dread that he had fallen into the hands of Spaniards, an idea that my presence seemed to strengthen. Efforts to tranquillize him were of no avail, and though he accepted such small hospitality as we could offer him, he sat down in utter misery, refusing to be comforted. What a commentary the terror of this child, at the idea of having fallen into the hands of the Spaniards, furnished on the life of the non-combatants in Cuba Libre, and how much constancy do not these people make proof of in their battle for freedom! Some hours later the child's mother arrived in anguished search of the little lost one, and her joy at finding him safe and somewhat more resigned can be left to the imagination of the reader. Next day mother and child accompanied us to the camp of Calisto Garcia, marching, without apparent concern, some seven or eight pretty long leagues.

Before setting out we made an attempt to procure something to eat by fowling, as our morning meal threatened to be reduced to a little more than a small cup of unsweetened chocolate and one or two sweet potatoes. As there was no shot, however, and the birds were almost invisible away up among the thickly-clustering leaves of giant trees, our chances of success were somewhat doubtful. One man was known to have his rifle loaded with rude slugs, and, as this was the nearest approach to shot, and our solitary chance of success, the rifle was handed over to an officer who had the reputation of being an excellent hunter. After some searching a pretty large bird good to eat was discovered, but far away up in the trees; the officer fired, but, to my infinite disgust, the bird rose up and swept lazily away. There was only the desperate chance of shooting with a bullet left, and as it was against the laws for the soldiers to waste ammunition bird-shooting, I was allowed to try, and had also the great satisfaction of missing.

We were now rapidly approaching the region of the Cauto, and the country became quite level. After marching some leagues we struck a broad straight road through the forest, which had been at one time a *Camino Real,* but was now overgrown with grass and weeds. It led directly into the camp of Calisto Garcia, which we entered without any trouble or ceremony. There was a guard outside the camp, at least there was a sentinel placed in the middle of the road, who stood still as a statue while we passed, gazing down the long vista of the road, and looking like nothing so much as a huge heron perched motionless on one leg in the midst of sedgy grass. There may have been a guard somewhere, but it did not turn out as it ought to have done. This did not much surprise me, for the outpost service appeared to me to be performed by the Cuban army in a very lax manner. Having heard a good deal about surprises on both sides, my attention was naturally attracted to this important question. It seemed to me that the over-confidence of the Cuban officers in their security is a source of constant danger to the Cuban cause. On more than one occasion the Spanish troops, themselves exceedingly careless, have succeeded in surprising Cuban forces in a country where all the advantages were against them, and where the most ordinary precautions should have rendered surprise impossible. On one occasion, permission to visit the outposts to see how the service was performed was given to me, but the visit was postponed for a few hours, and when the rounds were made it was clear to me that the outposts had been organized in the interval, in order to conceal the negligent way in which this most important duty is performed. Many of the men I recognized as having been on parade a short time before my visit to the outposts, and the same men were back in camp not long after. This proved to me beyond doubt that an effort had been made to impose on me. However, in these matters it is not so easy to deceive an old soldier. This absence of proper vigilance is full of danger, and if one day the Cuban cause receives a crushing blow, it will be due, in all probability, to the want of proper precautions against surprise.

15 On the War Path

THE CAMP of Calisto Garcia, at Dos Bocas, occupied a rectangular opening in the woods. It consisted of a number of leaf-thatched huts, forming regular streets, and scrupulously aligned. In the center there were open spaces in which banana-trees were cultivated. Altogether, there was evidence of effort after order, and a camp-marshal saw that cleanliness was maintained, at least within the camp. So much cannot be said for the outskirts, which were in a state of filth impossible to describe, from the habit of throwing offal and garbage among the bushes, where it became rapidly decomposed, and filled the air with poisonous effluvia which must have been very injurious to health. If a large number of troops had been kept in this camp for any length of time, sickness would undoubtedly have made its appearance. Fortunately, at the time of my arrival, not more than a few hundred men were encamped; and, as the forces came in very rapidly, it was not necessary to delay long in this festering place.

General Garcia was not in camp when I arrived; he did not expect me, as some days before he dispatched an escort of twenty *rifleros,* or men armed with breech-loaders, to Cambute, to convey me to headquarters. In the mean time, however, I had left the encampment of Tempü, accompanied by Commandante Vega and some thirty of his battalion, and, having taken a different route, missed the *rifleros*. General Maximo Gomez and General Calvar were at the headquarters when I arrived, and received me in the absence of the general commanding the troops, who soon after rode in from a reconnoissance.* He expressed satisfaction at my safe arrival in the Cuban lines, where, for some time, my coming had been looked for. General Calisto Garcia Iñiguez is a young man, rather tall, and very slightly built. He is thirty-three years of age, and, though his hair is prematurely tinged with gray, scarcely appears so old. In his manner he is affable, and not wanting in grace and even a certain distinguished air. He speaks rapidly, and at times imperatively. In character, he is nervous, energetic, and astute, and evidently possesses the properties of mind necessary for a leader in the peculiar class of war waged by the Cubans. Like the majority of the Cuban officers, he has not had the advantage of a military education, and knows little about the science of war, except what he has learned from experience during the six years' struggle for independence. The fundamental principles of guerrilla warfare are well understood by the Cuban officers, thanks to the instruction of two Dominicans, Generals Gomez and Diaz.†

General Gomez, who now commands in the Central Department, is a war-worn soldier, brave, energetic, and of a character of iron. He is, however, wanting in the higher education of an officer, and he has apparently received a general education less broad than his pupil, Calisto Garcia. He has, however, the advantage of a very long experience of war, and a thorough practical knowledge of irregular warfare. In great part the successful resistance of the Cubans during the first years of the war was due to the constancy and unwavering resolution of Diaz and Gomez, and whatever may be the final issue of the struggle, these two men must occupy a prominent position in the history of Cuba. The news of the establishment of the republic in Spain, which was brought by me, created a good deal of interest, and was the chief topic of discussion during the day. There seemed to be a very general agreement of opinion that it would

---

*O'Kelly refers to Major General Manuel de Jesús Calvar Odoardo (1832–1895), who served as president of the Cuban Republic from 16 March to 28 May 1878.

†By "two Dominicans," O'Kelly refers to Modesto Díaz and Máximo Gómez (1836–1905), the latter a major general in the Ten Years' War and Cuba's military commander in the Cuban War of Independence (1895–1898).

be of short duration, and would share the fate of most other Spanish governments, after a more or less prolonged struggle. As I was anxious to know how the change of form of government was likely to affect the conduct of the insurgent leaders, I asked General Garcia whether, in the event of the definite establishment of the republic in Spain, the insurgents would be content to allow Cuba to remain an integral portion of the Spanish dominions. To this the general replied, "The well-known instability of Spanish governments gives us no guarantee that the republic, even if definitely established, would exist for any length of time. The same insubordinate spirit that has overthrown the government of Amadeus today may upset the republic next month. We might accept the republic today; but who will say that before many weeks we might not be called upon to recognize Alfonso, or the reactionary Don Carlos, or the representative of some other form of monarchical government? If we remain a part of the Spanish dominions, we must accept every revolutionary change, however reactionary it may be; must be subject to constant variations of policy, and the general want of confidence which results from them. We do not wish this. We are too far separated from Spain by distance and by interests to submit to be dragged after her in the ever-recurring conspiracies and revolutions by which her government is marked. We desire to be independent, but, if this is impossible, we wish to attach ourselves to some strong government that will be able to guarantee to us liberty and order, so that we may develop in peace the resources of our country. But, above all things, we desire first to achieve independence; and I believe I express the opinion of the immense majority of the Cubans who have arms in their hands when I say that all reconciliation with Spain is impossible, except on the basis of independence. The only terms we have to offer are, that the Spaniards shall go away and leave Cuba to take care of its own future. It appears to me that there exists a large party in favor of annexation to the United States. In the Central Department the annexationists have always been very strong, but in the Eastern Department the main idea has been independence. In the beginning of the war the English sympathized with us a good deal, and even afforded us some slight aid. They suggested the formation of a confederation of the Antilles, and were strongly opposed to the idea of annexation. Indeed, they warned us strongly against thinking of it, and hopes were held out that England would abandon Jamaica, as she had abandoned the Ionian Islands, in order to facilitate the formation of the confederation of the Antilles.

"In the Eastern Department this project has been received with most favor, especially on account of the manner in which the United States has acted toward us during our struggle for independence. Many of the strongest annexationists have become disgusted. However, we are all pretty well agreed that before adopting any project for the future it is necessary to achieve our independence."

These views were accepted with slight modifications by those present, and, though I conversed with all the prominent and a large number of the subordinate officers, not one man was willing to accept a reconciliation with Spain on the condition of Cuba remaining an integral part of the Spanish dominion. Rather than do so, it seemed to be generally resolved to continue the war until the Cubans or the Spaniards were exterminated.

General Garcia informed me that he was about to undertake some operations of importance, and as there was reason to fear that President Cespedes had set out on a projected visit to another district, it was agreed that a special messenger should be sent to him, advising him of my safe arrival, and requesting that he would indicate a point where I would be certain to meet him.

At the time of my arrival at the headquarters of General Garcia, who had lately been raised to the rank of major-general commanding the Eastern Department, there were not more than two hundred armed men in camp. But the troops were concentrating, and within a few days detachments were expected to arrive from the forces of Holguin, Santiago de Cuba, and Jiguani, which with Guantanamo constitute the command of Calisto Garcia Iñiguez. Among the more distinguished Cuban officers at the camp of General Garcia were Ignacio Mora, ex-secretary of state, Colonel Bartolomé Maso, ex-secretary of war, Brigadier-General Felix Figueredo, chief of the medical staff, Brigadier-General Manuel Calvar (Holguin), Colonel Leonardo del Marmol (Guantanamo), Major Pedro Martinez Freire, Colonel Manuel Sanguilly, a member of the Cuban Congress and brother to the celebrated cavalry general of Camarguey, Major Rios, a native of Porto Rico, attached to General Garcia's staff, Lieutenant-Colonel Guerra, a Mexican officer, Lieutenant-Colonel Saladriguez (Jiguani), Lieutenant-Colonel Limbano Sanchez, and General Maximo Gomez, who succeeded to the command of the Central Department after the death of Agramonte.

On the 1st of March the last detachment of troops arrived, under the command of Colonel Peralta, a brother of General Peralta, who perished in one of the ill-fated Cuban expeditions. The colonel had been wounded on the road, and was obliged to be carried in an improvised hammock. His battalion consisted of over two hundred men, more than half of whom, in addition to the *convoyeros,* were unarmed. In the evening a general review of the troops was held, when over four hundred men appeared on parade. About one-third of the whole number were armed with breech-loading rifles, the others with Springfield and Enfield muzzle-loading rifles. Some of the battalions looked tolerably decent, while others were in a frightfully ragged condition. Falstaff's army of ragamuffins presented a respectable appearance in comparison, at least so far as the clothes were concerned. Measured by the standard of my expectations, the force was well clothed and equipped; for the Spanish officers had told me so many stories of the wretched condition of the Cubans that I expected to find soldiers and officers in uniforms closely resembling that of our first parents on leaving Paradise. This was far from being true; all the officers were well dressed, and some even tastefully. There was no attempt at uniformity, but nearly all were scrupulously clean. The doubtful exceptions being among the colored officers. In the ranks there was more diversity, and many of the soldiers were not alone ragged, but very nearly naked. One strapping brown man struck my imagination as the impersonation of heroic patriotism. His costume consisted of the rim of a straw hat, through which appeared the crown of a woolly head, and something resembling a ragged and scanty dishcloth was bound around his loins. A rifle and a *cartouchière* completed this patriot's equipment. To the eye accustomed to the neatness and order of regular troops it would have been impossible to present a more ridiculous sight than that varied line of armed men. It was with difficulty I repressed a smile as I walked down the line; but though to the eye the scene was grotesque, to the imagination and to the intellect it was sublime. Shoeless, blanketless, in many cases without coats, often with a piece of ragged linen doing service as a uniform, these men support the hardships and fatigues of an unequal struggle with a patience and courage that have seldom been equaled and never excelled. If we would respect the Cuban character we must see it here in the camps. Between the men in the field and the effeminate race of the towns there is a separation so wide and so distinct that it is difficult to believe they are of the same blood. Yet they assured me that the change has been made in the war. About one-third of the fighting men are white, and the majority of the other two-thirds are of color other than black, all shades of brown predominating. There were some half-dozen Chinamen, one of whom acted as aid surgeon. The most perfect equality exists between the white and colored races, the officers taking precedence by rank, and although the majority of the officers are white, a very large proportion are colored.

In order to avoid repetitions, many phases of life in Cuba Libre, common to all camps, are simply treated as incidents occurring at particular places where they assumed most importance. One of the most striking features of the Cuban character, whether seen under the shadow of Spanish rule, repressed and sullen, or abandoned to the wildest impulse in Mambi-Land, is the passion for dancing. The *baile* appears to be the one absorbing passion of the Cuban soul. Sufferings, fatigues, dangers, are all forgotten. The dormant energy of the Creole is aroused, and both sexes seem absorbed in a passionate joy while moving to the dreary, sensuous measures of the native *danza,* that resembles in some sort the craze of the opium-eater. Wherever the encampment is established for even a few days this passion must be satisfied. The families scattered about in the woods seem to know by instinct when a long halt is to be made, and crowd in to meet parents, husbands, and lovers. The commander of the forces immediately organizes the *baile,* and while the troops remain dancing takes place nightly, and is kept up with spirit until the warning *silencio* is sounded through the camp, when, as if by magic, the music and the hum of voices cease, and the pattering steps of the revelers can be heard with painful distinctness making their way to their quarters. Perhaps nothing is more remarkable than the absolute obedience with which men and women, who have worked themselves into something like a dancing frenzy, cease from this amusement as soon as the *silencio* sounds, and disperse as quietly as if a fire-engine had begun to play on them. In all the fixed camps this custom is observed, but in Calisto Garcia's camp, on account of its extent, and the possession of a brass-band, the *baile* was peculiarly imposing. The brass instruments had been captured from the Spaniards, and therefore both the general and soldiers took pride and delight in dancing to a music that constantly reminded them of victory.

As these *bailes* take place at night by the glare of tapers, and the costumes of the assistants are very varied, if not very brilliant, the scene presented is full of picturesque effect, which is heightened by the barbaric character of the music. Although the soldiers are allowed to be present, they are not permitted to dance in the same *baile* with the officers. In some camps different nights are set apart. There is, however, no distinction of color made, all officers being at liberty to dance. Owing doubtless to the extent of the camp, the arrangements at Dos Bocas were somewhat different, officers and soldiers dancing at the same time, but separated. The ball rooms consisted simply of level pieces of ground, round which some rude seats had been constructed, and outside these the on-lookers were grouped, while the band blew away lustily, and dancers whirled merrily about in the half-gloom, their faces from time to time lighted up by the red flare of beeswax tapers, supported by grinning, human candlesticks.

Not very far from where the officers were assembled, another group of dancers challenged my attention. If the officers were picturesque, these latter were weird and well-nigh savage. It required an effort, looking on the sight, to convince one's self that the spot where he stood was in America, and not in the African jungle. A group of black men were gathered around some dancers, who moved about with strange, uncouth motions to the monotonous chant of musicians, who seconded their vocal efforts with loud clapping of hands; and as the dancers moved steadily about to the savage chant the enthusiasm of the spectators seemed to grow uncontrollable, until they gave vent to their feelings in loud yah, yahs! and clapping of hands, and uncouth laughter, as if the ceremony or dance called up some remembrance of intense pleasure. This was the Voudou dance, a religious ceremony, kept up by the African blacks, but whose import none could explain to me. The assistants were all as black as the ace of spades, and while looking at them one could easily imagine the Evil One broke loose and enjoying himself in an infernal orgie. Most of the colored people turned up their noses at this ceremonial dance, and pretty freely characterized the people who took part in it as savages—*barbaros;* but, except for its uncouthness, there was nothing offensive or repulsive, if we omit its utter stupidity.

On the 3rd of March General Garcia broke camp, and marched in a westerly direction through a wild and deserted country, more level than usual, and presenting at intervals savannas of considerable extent. The heat passing through the tall Guinea-grass was suffocating, and was aggravated by the absence of drinkable water. With the exception of one small stream, we had to depend for our supply on a few wells, the quality of the water being detestable, having in some cases been poisoned by the Spaniards. In one the half-decomposed body of a man was visible.

In the afternoon we halted at a wooded hill called Cañadon, about four miles from Jiguani, a town of some importance, where we took up a position and prepared to give battle. In front of this hill there is a large open space, or glade, surrounded on all sides by woods, through which the road from Jiguani to Dos Bocas passes. The forces under General Garcia occupied the Hill of Cañadon, with the flanks resting in the woods on either side commanding the road. In order to strengthen the position the timber on the face of a considerable portion of the hill was felled, and a slight parapet erected at the head of the clearing. I was informed by General Garcia that the motive for this preparation was his intention to provoke the Spanish forces to battle, in the hope that they would attack him in this advantageous position. When we left the encampment of Dos Bocas in the morning the force mustered five hundred and twenty armed men. We were afterwards joined by three companies of the forces of General Calvar, which numbered about one hundred men. I do not know if there were other troops; but it appeared to me there were some seven hundred armed men on the ground, in addition to some four or five hundred *convoyeros,* who were unarmed. As it was expected the Spanish troops would attack the position, the officers of the staff were anxious to put down the fighting strength of the Cuban forces to its lowest figure, and they admitted there were present over six hundred men. In the night a force of about one hundred and thirty men was sent on a reconnoissance to Jiguani, with orders to fire on the soldiers, in order to induce them to pursue the party. When the Cuban detachment arrived everything was as still as death in the town. A scout was sent forward twice, and he reported the houses abandoned as far as the *trinchera,* or fortifications. Although this circumstance was very suspicious, the detachment commanded by Lieutenant-Colonel Saladriguez entered the town in three divisions, and arrived close to the barricades occupied by the Spaniards. As the Cuban troops entered, the Spanish soldiers were crying the *alerta,* and nothing transpired to indicate that they were aware of the presence of the Cubans until the sentinels on the barricade challenged the advancing parties. Not receiving a satisfactory reply, the guards fired with deadly effect, especially on one division that, disobeying orders, had advanced too close to the barricade. The Cubans replied with a volley, and retreated rapidly, carrying off their dead and wounded. When the divisions reunited, it was found that two men had been killed and eight wounded, two of the latter mortally. The only compensation for this severe loss was a few articles of clothing found in the deserted houses. This check seemed in no way to dampen the spirits of the troops, and the hope was constantly expressed that the garrison would be encouraged by their success to pursue the party. In this the Cubans were fated to be disappointed, as, owing either to the smallness of the garrison, or a knowledge of the design of the Cuban generals, the Spaniards contented themselves with sending out a small reconnoitering party, that did not venture to approach the position, but, having noticed the trail, returned to the town. Next day a detachment was sent to kill cattle in a *potrero,* or cattle-farm, close to the town, a service they accomplished without interruption. It was evident from this circumstance that the Spaniards would not come out to attack the position of Cañadon; so a force of some three hundred armed men and about one hundred and fifty *convoyeros* and servants were sent to complete the destruction of the cattle-farm, with instructions to carry off as many of the cattle as they could catch, and in any case to kill as many as possible of the animals, so as to deprive the town of its chief means of support. These orders were faithfully carried out by Colonel Sanchez and the troops under his command. By half-past eight the *potrero* was in flames for a distance of a league, and the cattle either dead or driven into the woods. The soldiers and the unarmed men were laden with the meat, and orders were given to form a line of march to return to the encampment. At the entrance of the *potrero* the road is slightly depressed, and a wood extending in the direction of the town forms a semicircle commanding completely the outlet. The Cuban forces had reached this point when their bugles sounded silence. Scarcely had the sound died away when a volley was delivered from a Spanish ambuscade distributed in three divisions. By a miracle no one was touched, and the colonel, dismounting, ordered the men to advance. In a moment the sacks of meat fell to the ground, and a rapid and well-sustained fire was opened on the Spanish ambuscade. It was the soldiers' turn now to be surprised, for the Cubans possessed plenty of ammunition, and were confident in their numbers. The Spanish forces did not number over one hundred and fifty, and by a strange freak of fortune their three buglers had been shot, one after another, as soon as they sounded an order. Notwithstanding the disparity of the forces, the Spaniards fought with valor and tenacity, as they always fight, but were obliged to give way before superior numbers. A movement of retreat in the face of a Cuban force is disastrous. The moment the Cubans perceived that the Spaniards were retreating, they advanced with a rush, and the defeat was turned into a rout. Then the horrors of the situation were developed. The Spanish soldiers, lost in the darkness, fell an easy prey to their enemies. So dark was the night that it was necessary to inquire whether the person encountered was an enemy or a friend before striking. This did not last long; for what remained of the Spanish troops were in full flight for the town, which, fortunately for them, was close at hand. The most terrible and inhuman feature of this awful warfare was, fortunately, hidden by the dark cloak of night. The wounded Spaniards crawled into the woods to save themselves from the vengeance of their foes. Here the Cubans followed them, groping in the dark, and listening for the sigh or groan of the wretched men to direct them to where the helpless wounded lay. In most cases the unfortunate were discovered, and the deadly machete finished the work of the rifle.

"Ave Maria, me van Matar!" exclaimed one poor fellow as the heavy machete cut his cord of life, and the appeals for mercy of the helpless were the more heart-rending that they were made to ears that were deaf and to hearts steeled by the bloody memories of five years of war to the death.

The material results of the victory consisted in three bugles, seventeen rifles, the boots, clothes, and other effects of the slain, and the sentiment that the men who had fallen a few nights before were amply avenged. The loss of the Spaniards in dead was estimated at twenty-five killed on the spot, and thirty wounded in the retreat, who had not been discovered in the darkness of the night, or, owing to the proximity of the town, had escaped. The Cuban loss was one officer killed, two wounded, and six soldiers wounded.

The night was black, with the damp chill that heavy rain just ceased leaves in the atmosphere, when a sudden commotion close to my hammock aroused me. General Garcia was swung up a few feet from where my cot was suspended, and as my eyes opened I became conscious that someone was speaking to him excitedly. "Tres cornetas" were the first words I heard consciously. They were sufficient to wake me thoroughly. The man whose conversation had disturbed my slumbers was a messenger from Colonel Sanchez, informing the general of his victory over the contra-guerrilla of Bailen, that had long been a scourge to the patriots of Jiguani. Being anxious to hear for myself this man's report, I did not move until he ceased talking, when I sat up and asked General Garcia what had happened. He repeated what the soldier had reported to him. At this moment the bugles of the returning force were heard, ringing through the night notes of defiance and victory. The news of the victory had already began to spread through the camp, and the bugles brought everyone to his feet to welcome the victors. Lights began to flit through the trees, until the wood became perfectly illuminated, and the men passing about through the trees with lighted tapers looked like a swarm of huge glow-worms. Dressing quickly, I descended the slippery hill to see how the men looked after the fight, and discover from personal observation the number of the wounded.

The scene presented below was most impressive, and full of a martial grandeur no mere words can convey. As the troops arrived they filed away at once to where their companions were stationed, and they could be seen moving off surrounded by groups of comrades eagerly listening to the story of the fight, of which every particular soldier, in his own estimation, was the hero. My attention, however, was attracted by a sadder sight. The train of wounded men were beginning to ascend the hill to the hospital, which was placed in rear of the position. A few were able to walk, and one black officer, wounded in the thigh, was mounted on the only horse that returned from the fight. The poor fellow looked awfully pale, but uttered no word of complaint. The figure, however, that impressed itself on my mind most deeply, and excited my admiration by a character of Roman fortitude, was young Pedro Vasquez, captain and adjutant in one of the battalions. Poor fellow! He was little more than a boy in years, though in service a veteran, and now he was carried by me lying on a rude litter borne by four stalwart soldiers, struck down, it was feared fatally, with the third wound received in the struggle for freedom. The pain he suffered must have been intense, for he was shot in the thigh so close to the bone that it was feared the bone was shattered; but though the face was rigid with pain he uttered no word, but half sat up on the litter, leaning on his elbow, and looking quietly and composedly on the scene. No Roman warrior borne from battle on his shield ever showed a nobler or more truly heroic courage than this Cuban boy, who smiled at the cheering words of comfort spoken softly to him by men who feared to trust too much their voices. Only seven or eight men were so seriously wounded as to be considered *hors de combat*, though several had wonderfully narrow escapes of being sent out of this world, and yet the actual wounds received were so slight as not to be thought worthy of treatment.

The convoy of wounded moved up the slippery hill, winding in and out through the trees in search of the nearest and smoothest path, directed by the waving torch-lights and the shouts of the guides, presenting a scene full of gloomy grandeur well in keeping with the glorious, sad occasion. The night, black and gloomy as the fight against fearful odds; the flashing torchlights, like the gleams of victory that cheer the patriot in a seemingly hopeless struggle. One by one the lights were extinguished among the trees, and the victors weary of their toils sunk to rest, and the glory and the triumph were forgotten; not so the pain, for high up on the reverse slope of the hill the fevered wounded tossed in agony, or, stunned by their hurt, lay in half-conscious pain until returning life should give them knowledge of their misfortune. With such means as they possessed, the doctors tried to soothe the pain of sufferers; but, unfortunately, there was wanting many a necessary drug to dull the mangled nerve, and induce unwilling sleep to the anguished brow. The sight of the wounded and the slain after a battle has ever been to me a hideous and repulsive sight, and I have never entered a military hospital, where freshly wounded men were stationed, without feeling sick and faint. Nothing but an absolute sense of duty would induce me to visit one of these charnel-houses. It was therefore with much reluctance I went as soon as there was light to see how the poor fellows who had been wounded were situated. One splendid-looking black man, whose arm had been shattered near the shoulder, had succumbed, and some of the others were so seriously wounded that but little hope was entertained for their recovery. These had sunk into a lethargic state from which they might never wake up. Others, whose hurts were not so severe, gave vent to their agony in suppressed groans. Fortunately, the sufferers were not many, and nothing that could be done to assuage their pain was neglected by the medical officers, a band of gentlemen whose noble devotion to the cause of humanity has never been excelled. Unfortunately, the medical staff is not nearly so numerous as it ought to be, a fact which reflects infinite discredit on the numerous Cuban doctors who are content with giving lip-sympathy to their heroic countrymen. Owing also to the scarcity of medical stores, the doctors are obliged to economize even the most necessary drugs, thereby causing increased suffering of the wounded. If ever there was a case when the red cross should come to the aid of suffering humanity, such a case exists in Cuba.

Preparations were being made to transfer the wounded to a place of safety when I visited the temporary hospital; the way in which this is done is simple and effective: the wounded are placed in a hammock which is suspended from a long pole, and four men are detailed in two reliefs to carry each man, the bearers relieving each other at intervals. In addition to the bearers a guard accompanies the convoy to the hospital, and opens the way so that the wounded can pass without difficulty. For motives of safety the hospitals are placed in the very deepest recesses of the forest, the paths being known only to the most devoted guides. It is astonishing with what rapidity the wounded are removed, considering the very primitive means available for this service; but even in the hours of defeat and untiring pursuit, there is scarcely an instance on record in which a wounded man once in the hands of the carriers has been taken by the enemy.

Indeed, in nothing do the Cubans differ more widely from their opponents than in the care given to their wounded and the efforts they make to prevent a disabled man falling into the hands of the Spaniards. No matter how hard pressed the Mambis may be, the moment a man falls he is seized by his comrades, and removed to the rear; and so certain is this that the Cuban soldier is absolutely convinced that while he breathes he will never be abandoned by his comrades. It is owing to this system that even when defeated no wounded prisoners fall into the enemy's hands, though the dead are abandoned without much compunction when matters are looking very serious, but the soldiers must be fully convinced that their comrade is beyond earthly help before they consent to abandon him. It sometimes happens that the pursuit is carried on with terrible earnestness, and that the pursuers and pursued are scarcely separated by fifty yards of wood, often even less. The unfortunate who is so badly hit under these circumstances as to be unable to continue the retreat suffers terribly, but even then is not abandoned. The two nearest comrades seize him, one by each arm, and, having first secured his rifle, drag him "*arrestranlo*" along the ground at a rush, through bush and brier, until he is removed beyond range, where he is handed over to the *convoyeros*, or carriers, and receives such hurried care as the nature of the case will admit. Under this rude treatment it often happens that the unfortunate succumbs, and, unless so fortunate as to be insensible, must in all cases suffer intensely; but it is a chance for life, and, though a rough kindness, still, it is a kindness, and often preserves life. It must be kept well in mind that in this war no quarter is given, however much hypocritical authorities may try to impose on the credulity of mankind by lying orders and assertions. Even where orders to extend quarter to prisoners are given they are never carried out, nor is it intended that they should be, but only that these living lies can be used as offering proof of humane intentions that never had any existence. The wounded found on the field or in the hospital are butchered without mercy. This is a fact that not all the lying documents in the archives can alter, or efface; it is written too deeply in blood-stains that cannot be washed out. Neither will the honest, straightforward soldiers deny it, but only the lying, sneaking *autoridades,* who make profession of humanity and generosity in public, but who urge in secret the most inflexible severity. "Kill and say nothing about it" is their maxim, and they carefully abstain from inquiring too closely whether the conditions of their hypocritical proclamations have been put in force. This is why the disabled Cuban prefers to be dragged through the brambles, and over the rough ground full of thorns and protruding stumps of rotted trees, with mangled limb and cracking bone, to being left in the power of an implacable enemy. Oftentimes in these fearful courses, these rushes for life, the arms are wrenched from the sockets, or the bones snap unheeded, in the fierce hurry of flight, and when at last the line of fire is passed, and the men bend down to care more tenderly for their wounded comrade, he responds not to their call; the body is saved but the soul has fled. Strong constitutions, however, resist even this rough treatment. One of Calisto Garcia's officers, a splendid-looking man, showed me where he had been dragged from out a line of fire when the Spaniards were so close that they could almost touch him with their bayonets. But his men would not desert him, and in their terrible haste they broke both his arms above the elbow dragging him to a place of safety. And, though he had already received a severe wound in the thigh, with good care and strong constitution he recovered, and was fighting away again as sound as a bell when I made his acquaintance.

The Spaniards, on the other hand, notwithstanding their immensely superior resources, constantly abandon their wounded. So long as they are successful, provision, more or less adequate, is made for them; but in the moment of defeat they are shamefully left to the machete of their foes, who show them scant mercy. One would imagine that the "illustrious swords" of the Spanish nation would display at least as much heroism and devotion to their comrades as those despised *negros sueltos,* or "runaway niggers," as they politely call the inhabitants of the Manigua, and would, like them, risk life and limb to save the wounded.

But no! These chivalrous caballeros the moment they find themselves in danger think only of saving their worthless selves, and abandon wounded friends and comrades to the mercy of Providence. Unfortunately, those good-natured old gods who used to succor distressed heroes have been ousted by more intellectual and selfish successors, who content themselves with roasting in the next world such unhappy mortals as have not conducted themselves according to their strait-laced and somewhat gloomy notions in this. For want of the favoring cloud, or ready ægide, the Mambi machete cleaves through upraised, imploring hand, merciless as fate, and pours out Castilian life-streams to fertilize the wasted Cuban fields. The heavy comparative loss of the Spaniards in dead in the Cuban struggle is mainly owing to the cowardly abandonment of the wounded. Everyone who is at all acquainted with military matters knows that the proportion of wounded to killed in battle is very large, even where artillery causes large losses. In Cuba the proportion of wounded is larger than in European battles, owing to the bodies of the men being generally covered by trees, and injuries from artillery almost unknown. As the Cubans carry off, in nearly every case, as one can see by even the Spanish reports, their wounded, though sometimes adopting the rude mode already described, their loss consists only of the men actually killed from the chances of battle—and a percentage of wounded somewhat larger than would occur if they possessed better hospital facilities, and, above all, better and more plentiful medical stores. The Spaniards being nearly always the attacking party have more men hit, and, as wounds are very fatal to foreigners in Cuba, their losses in dead are out of all proportion to the number of wounded. Add to this the slaughter of their disabled men when defeated, and the Spanish loss in dead will probably exceed anything known in modern war in proportion to the number of troops engaged. Crime brings its own punishment. The selfishness and cynicism of the Spanish commanders in abandoning their wounded when hard pressed reacts on the Spanish soldier, who, awed by the silent forest, whose tangled recesses fill him with apprehension, fears to plunge into the maze after an invisible enemy, lest he be lost, or find himself suddenly in the power of a concealed foe from whom he can expect no mercy. Usually, therefore, they huddle in the open spaces, where they become a target for a foe they feel but never see, so that at last they come to entertain an instinctive dread of the woods, and if checked in their advance are subject to panic. Once the danger of defeat becomes evident, the knowledge that if wounded they will be abandoned to their fate makes everyone anxious to get away as quickly as possible, and the result is that a check becomes a defeat, a rout, and a massacre, unless the way happens to be very clear, or refuge close at hand. Both at Jiguani, and in fights near Manzanillo, while I was a prisoner, the Spanish forces engaged fled from the scene of conflict in disgraceful disorder. All discipline was forgotten, and had it not been for the proximity of fortified towns which afforded refuge, they would have perished to a man, cut up in detail, as they did in the battle of Palo Seco, where the Cubans killed two hundred men, with a loss to themselves of some twenty to thirty killed and wounded.

The Cubans are fully aware of the importance of maintaining the confidence of their soldiers in their absolute security from falling into the hands of the Spaniards. In order to make duty more binding, they have established among the fighting men, under the title of "*El Silencio,*" a secret society, or brotherhood, in fact, a kind of masonry, in which the initiated promise never to abandon a comrade, and to carry off the wounded, even should they fall amid the opposing ranks. This brotherhood has its rites and ceremonies, which, no doubt, are not without their effect on the rude, credulous minds of the soldiers. At least so far the effect of this association has been very favorable, not alone in giving greater courage and sense of security to individuals, but also in strengthening the bonds between the patriots, and rendering possible a more rigorous discipline. During my stay among the Mambi, an instance of the value of the brotherhood occurred. In a skirmish between a small party of Modesto Diaz's forces and a strong party of Spaniards, the captain of the Cubans, who was a black man, rashly exposed himself, and was shot through the head, falling well-nigh among the advancing Spaniard. It was almost certain death to attempt to succor him, but nevertheless his brothers of the *Silencio* would not leave him. Three men rushed out under fire, recovered the body and rifle, and carried both off. The officer was dead, but the body was carried some distance and hid in the bushes, as the pursuit was being hotly pushed. Instances of devotion similar to this, and even more striking, are so frequent among the Cuban soldiers that they almost pass unnoticed, and if a tithe of the splendid actions performed by individuals during the obscure war were to be written down, there would be quite a Homeric story. The Mambis have maintained a struggle as glorious as the Suliote or Cretan wars against the Turk, and in all history there are no more gallant struggles than these, but modern society is such a sham that it can see nothing great in the struggle of a weak people holding out against fearful odds; sacrificing fortune, family, and life; perishing by sabre-stroke, and bullet, and fell disease; seeing their wives and children hunted like beasts of the forest, sinking with fatigue and hunger, dying miserably in the savage woods; and amid all their suffering and desolation remaining unshaken in their resolve to conquer or to die. Yet all human history cannot furnish a greater example of heroic purpose. Thermopylæ was but the passing effort of an hour, whereas the heroism of the Cubans has been constant, and displayed in a hundred fields.

16 With Cespedes

THE MORNING after the battle of Jiguani the Cubans quitted their encampment according to custom, so that when the Spanish columns should concentrate to avenge their comrades they would find no one. While we were preparing to march, a messenger arrived from President Cespedes bearing letters in which he expressed satisfaction at the arrival of the *Herald* commissioner, and indicating a point where he could be met with, as fortunately he had not set out on his intended journey. Under these circumstances I took leave of General Garcia and the officers of his staff, and set out in search of the President, escorted by a battalion of infantry. Our first day's march lay through a level country, studded with Spanish camps, and at night we halted in a wood, about two miles from Baire. In our bivouac we could distinctly hear the bugle-calls of the Spanish garrison. Next day we had crossed the points considered most dangerous, and the battalion returned to join the forces of Calisto Garcia, leaving me in charge of Lieutenant-Colonel Benjamin Ramirez and an escort of fifteen men.

Our route now lay through a frightfully gloomy country, the road passing through dense forests and over precipitous mountains. So dense were the woods that it was impossible to travel on horseback, and it was with the greatest difficulty and only by the constant use of the machete that a passage could be made for my horse. It is to me a marvel how the horse succeeded in passing here, for the road at times lay through heaped-up boulders of limestone formation, over which I climbed with difficulty and not without suffering. The edges of the rocks were sharp as the points of *chevaux-de-frise,* and seemed to be placed by nature as an obstacle to advance in this silent and awful region, where the stillness was only broken by the dull chop of the machete or the monotonous note of some lonely bird. We had penetrated the mountain regions of Jiguani, and the sense of loneliness was absolutely oppressive. In the heart of these awful solitudes the government of Cuba Libre had chosen its temporary abode, for reasons of policy and safety. After passing through a succession of mountain-passes, sometimes presenting a continuous ascent for miles over frightful rocks, bleached and creviced by time, we arrived on the banks of the Rio Azul, through whose crystal waters can be counted the pebbles on the sand beneath. Rock and wood blend delightfully in the composition of a scene which combines the picturesquely savage with the softer sylvan beauties. At intervals the placid current of the transparent stream is broken by huge boulders rising out of the bed of the river, forming irregular barriers, that seem to meditate stopping the flow of the water; but a few yards farther the river moves on in peaceful grandeur, reflecting on its unruffled surface the majestic trees and banks.

Continuing our journey, we passed through a forest wet, sad, and gloomy, strewn with dead and dying leaves, that produced a sentiment of depression and sadness on the mind, recalling too forcibly the withered hopes and shattered fortunes of the many thousands of gallant hearts that answered to the cry of freedom sent up at Yara. Like these leaves have perished thousands, and suffering and disease have already stamped with the seal of death hearts that were the light and hope of happy homes. These reflections were fortunately brought to a sudden close by the harsh challenge of a negro sentinel posted at some distance in the wood. He declined to take the word of the advance-guard as a sufficient assurance that they were Cubans and good patriots, and ordered the commander to advance. Colonel Ramirez was at once recognized, and, with the commissioner of the *Herald,* allowed to proceed to the camp where President Cespedes and members of his Cabinet had their headquarters.

The appearance of the residence of the government was certainly far from impressive for the strictly material mind. A narrow path through the forest led to a small clearing in the woods, in which were situated some twenty huts, constructed of *pencas de manaca*. The ground was encumbered with stumps of trees, and two tall, bare-looking trees, with scattered boughs and scant foliage, rising on either side of a very small rivulet which ran through the center of the encampment, increased the melancholy look of the place. On the farther side of the little rivulet a group of young officers were waiting to receive me, among them the son of the President, Colonel Cespedes.* As soon as the presentation of these gentlemen was over, I was informed they were sent to conduct me to the presence of the President. I followed them some distance to a hut a little larger and somewhat more commodious than its neighbors, but the difference could not excite discontent in the most envious mind.

On entering, a small, well-built man, rather stout of body and below the middle height, rose to receive me. One of the officers said, "This is the President," and at the same time President Cespedes, advancing with hand extended, said very distinctly, in English—

"I am very glad to see you."

I was frightfully tempted to try a little stage effect and leave a *mot* for posterity. In fact, like other people in similar circumstances, I had arranged in my own mind, while toiling over those sharp, pointed rocks, a very magnificent phrase; but at the last moment either my moral courage failed or my national modesty overcame me. I said nothing worthy of posterity, but simply expressed my satisfaction at seeing President Cespedes well, and thanked him for the cordial reception he was pleased to extend me.

President Cespedes was a small man with a good deal of iron in his composition, stood remarkably erect, and was nervous in action and in temperament. His features were small, with a claim to regularity. The forehead high and well formed; the face oval and a little worn by time and care; his eyes, gray with a tinge of brown, were bright and penetrating. His mouth and the lower part of his face being concealed by a moustache and beard of iron-gray, with a few black hairs interspersed. When he smiled he showed his teeth, which were extremely white, and with one exception remarkably well preserved.

As soon as the first exchange of courtesies was concluded the President introduced me to Señor Miguel Bravo, Secretario de Guerra, and afterwards to the members of his staff. President Cespedes then requested me to be seated, pointing to a fixed stool made of rudely planed laths, close to the table, on which were placed some pamphlets relative to the Cuban

---

*Céspedes's son, Carlos Manuel de Céspedes y Céspedes (1840–1915).

question, and a few copies of the *Herald*. A few books and bundles of papers were arranged in an orderly manner about the hut, which contained no furniture but a hammock, a table rudely constructed of sticks bound together by the *majajua*, a vegetable cord which abounds in the woods. A few valises were placed against the side of the hut, containing the presidential wardrobe. A revolver suspended from a belt of golden texture and a sixteen-shooting Winchester rifle completed the very simple furniture of the residence of the President of the Cuban republic.

The first questions were about my entering into the Cuban lines, and whether the Spaniards had permitted me to pass freely. On learning the threat of General Morales de los Rios to shoot me in case I should be captured, President Cespedes offered to send me to Jamaica in one of the Cuban boats that constantly make the passage. This offer I declined, as I had made up my mind to return through the Spanish lines unless something very unexpected happened to make me alter my resolution. I then expressed a wish to be allowed to pass through the Cuban lines to the Camarguey district, in order that I should be made acquainted with the state of the whole insurrection. President Cespedes at once replied, "Every facility shall be placed at your disposal to see and examine into the state of our forces, and whatever information or papers you may require relative to the civil or military organization shall be freely placed at your disposal." Referring then to my letter on slavery in Cuba, he said, "We were pleased with this letter, because it showed a desire to present the case of Cuba fully and truly. . . . There are many points in it, however, about which I shall speak to you at a future time. . . . A hut has been placed at your disposal, and as you must be fatigued and may desire to rest, I will not detain you longer now, but expect you will do me the favor of breakfasting with me."

Having accepted this kind invitation, I withdrew to my shelter of leaves to change my travel-stained garments. When the hour of breakfast arrived, an aid-de-camp presented himself to conduct me to the house of the President. Breakfast was waiting, and as there was no other guest, I immediately sat down opposite the President. The table was not over twenty inches wide, and about two feet and a half long. Owing to the irregularities of the surface of the smoothened sticks, the few plates were rather unsteady, and it required attention in order to avoid upsetting some of the presidential plate. Everything was in keeping with the modest exterior of the hut. The plates were mostly of tin, polished, and scrupulously clean. Breakfast consisted of a little broiled steak, some minced meat, sweet potatoes, a little boiled corn, with cassava bread, and a kind of

Indian corn paste. Our beverage was water, and in place of coffee we had to console ourselves with *agua mona,* or hot water sweetened with wild honey and flavored with a little ginger. But though the fare was frugal in the extreme, it was served with all the formality to be looked for in the White House. If the occasion was not marked by the pomp and splendor which attend the hospitalities of more prosperous rulers, *en revanche* it possessed a moral grandeur which in my eyes more than compensated for the absence of worldly pomps.

When we had discussed the very frugal meal before us, I asked the President his opinion of the Spanish republic. He immediately asked me if its existence had been officially announced; and I answered him that General Morales de los Rios had officially announced the abdication of Amadeus and the establishment of the republic to the consuls the day preceding my departure from Santiago de Cuba. The President then actually proceeded to interview me relative to my opinions on the subject; but I reminded him that I came to interview him, not to be interviewed. A compromise being effected, he spoke, in effect, as follows, about the republic in Spain: "Spain is not a republican country, and the military aristocracy will never consent to the permanent establishment of a republican form of government. The present government may last a little while; but before four months you will see a struggle inaugurated between the monarchists and the republicans. It is impossible to say how the republic may affect the cause of Cuba; but it can make no difference to the men in arms, for they will accept no condition from Spain except independence. Many of the prominent republicans have advocated a right to freedom; but there is a great difference between theory and practice. Now that they are, as you assure me, really in possession of power, we shall see how they will act."

"Castelar, I believe, is opposed to the abandonment of Cuba?"*

"Yes, Castelar has falsified his republican principles. It is some time since he declared that he was a better Spaniard than republican, so that we can look for very little from him."

"But if Spain should finally adopt a republican form of government, would not Cuba be disposed to become reconciled to her?"

"I cannot say what the sentiment or feelings of the people in the towns may be; but the Cubans in arms will accept no reconciliation or peace with Spain except on the condition of independence. We are separated from Spain by an ocean of water, and have interests different to hers; but

---

*Emilio Castelar y Ripoll (1832–1899) was the minister of foreign affairs of the First Spanish Republic, later becoming president in September 1873.

we are also separated by an ocean of blood, and by the remembrance of cruelty unnecessarily used by the Spanish government in their efforts to subdue us. The blood of our fathers and our brothers, and of helpless, defenseless families, slaughtered in cold blood, forbids our ever accepting any conditions from the Spaniards. They must go away and leave us in peace, or continue the war until we are all dead or they have been exterminated."

"What would become of the Spanish population in case of the abandonment of the island by Spain?"

"At present we look upon all Spaniards as enemies, and treat them so; but if the independence of Cuba were conceded, and a treaty of peace made with Spain, those Spaniards who might select to remain would receive the same protection as other citizens; and, as the Cubans are a very orderly and law-abiding people, if it were only shown that the Spaniards were permitted by law to remain, they could do so without any fear of interference or injury."

"A proposition that a certain sum of money, guaranteed by America, should be paid to Spain, as the price of abandoning her claim to Cuba, has been put in circulation by some parties. Would the Cubans accept such a solution of this difficulty?"

"No authoritative proposition of this nature was ever made; but if such a solution would be accepted by Spain, and the sum required were not unreasonable, the Cubans, in my opinion, would be willing to accept such terms, in order to put an end to the war so barbarously waged by Spain. We desire peace, that we may return to the reconstruction of our homes and the well-being of the country; but before everything we want our independence. If Spain will continue the war, we will fight until the country is a desert, so that Spain shall receive no benefits from the blood she is shedding uselessly.

"But I believe that the public opinion of the world will not long delay in coming to our aid. The prospect for Cuba is very favorable; the Spaniards are everywhere abandoning the towns and encampments in the interior, because they have no longer the strength to defend all the country. It is my opinion that they intend retiring to the seacoast and trying to maintain themselves; but as soon as we can procure cannon, and organize thoroughly our army, we shall attack them in the towns. There was a moment, about a year ago, when we were reduced to terrible extremities, and we wanted everything—clothes, ammunition, arms; but to-day we have all things, and in great part taken from the enemy. If the war should continue, we hope to profit by the experience of the past, and to continue our system of attacking the enemy, which has produced such good results. In fact, we are now living on the enemy. We take from them clothes and food, and whatever else we may need. In the beginning we acted with too much generosity, setting at liberty the Spanish prisoners, even after the proclamation of the Spanish government announcing that all taken in arms would be shot, and that even the women captured in the insurgent districts would be subject to ten years' imprisonment or deportation to Fernando Po.* Several times I have made efforts to induce the Spanish government to carry on the war in a civilized manner, but without results. The Spaniards have resorted to the most barbarous expedients to subdue us. Six different commissions have left Havana with the intention of assassinating me. Three returned, having abandoned the enterprise, and two of the others are supposed to have perished. The third was a man who presented himself to enlist in the bodyguard of General Quesada.† Something suspicious about him caused his arrest, and concealed on his person was found a knife. Being questioned, he confessed that he had been sent from Havana with the mission to assassinate me. Of course he was at once hanged; but these circumstances show you to what lengths the Spanish authorities are capable of proceeding. It is pleasant to record that during the four years of the insurrection no attempts have been made on my life, although I live, as you see, without guards and without precautions. Everyone is at liberty to come in here. Only at night there is a single sentinel on duty before my door."

I then asked what might be the number of the armed Cubans in the field. He replied, "That is somewhat difficult to answer correctly. Owing to the condition of disorganization to which we were reduced a year ago, a good deal of disorder crept in, and the difficulty of communicating with the generals, as well as the absolute want of paper and ink with which to make reports, rendered it impossible for the generals to furnish the proper returns. At one time we did not have a piece of paper as big as this envelope on which to write a communication, and were obliged to write on the leaves of the trees; but, speaking generally, I think we must have

---

*Fernando Po is a Spanish controlled island in the Bight of Biafra, off the West African coast. In the final decades of the nineteenth century, Spain used the island as a penal colony for Cuban political prisoners.

†O'Kelly refers to Manuel de Quesada y Loynaz (1830–1884). Quesada was made chief of the armed forces of the Cuban army in 1869, and later represented the Cuban Republic abroad. For remarks on Quesada's address to the president of the United States (1873), see introduction, xxxviii.

from ten to twelve thousand armed men in the field, with about an equal number of *convoyeros* and servants, who perform service in the army. The strength of our forces is also liable to great fluctuations. In the moments of defeat large numbers disperse, or desert, and when any success has been gained the army is suddenly augmented to an extraordinary extent. We have lately been receiving large accessions from the Spanish ranks, principally from the Cuban volunteers, many of whom come over to us with their arms and ammunition. In the district of Bayamo I am informed, in a letter lately received, that nearly four hundred volunteers have presented themselves, mostly white men, and a large proportion of these have brought with them their arms. The same thing happened in Mayari after our attack. I believe that in time all the Cuban volunteers will take sides with us against Spain. Should this happen our triumph will be assured."

Cespedes was hurrying off in the direction of Manzanillo when the news of my arrival reached him. After my interview preparations were immediately made to continue his march. Cespedes was desirous that I should go to the coast with a guard, and embark at once for Jamaica, because he was anxious that what I had seen should be made known as soon as possible; besides, it was considered the shortest and safest way out. However, my mind was made up to continue with Cespedes, and leave the insurgent lines at a point remote from Santiago de Cuba, in order to render it impossible for the Spanish authorities to deny that I had visited the Cuban camp. As there had been already some misrepresentation on the part of correspondents, I could not afford to have even the Spaniards doubt the truth of what I should write. It appeared to me better to accept all the risks of my mission and so place my testimony beyond question. After some difficulty I convinced Cespedes that from my point of view I was right, though of course so far as Cuban interests were concerned Cespedes was justified in hurrying me away, expecting to derive advantage from my testimony as to the reality of the existence of Cuba Libre.

But not being in any sense a Cuban agent or official, I naturally adopted the course most to the advantage of the *Herald* and my own.

During our short stay in the little camp at Rio Azul, the only incident of any interest that occurred was a scare caused by me in the following stupid manner. There are plenty of snakes, scorpions, and chameleons in Cuba, but, with the exception of the latter animal, none are poisonous.

The bite of a large green chameleon is said to cause madness, and even death. Having a constitutional dread and hatred to the venomous tribe, I never let slip an opportunity of destroying such specimens as happen to come in my way. Now a pretty large chameleon had taken it into his head to sun himself on a tree near my hut. Objecting to the presence of such a neighbor, I took my revolver, and, totally forgetting that I was in a military camp, fired at the chameleon. The effect was electric on more than the poor chameleon, whose nose was cut off by the bullet, making him a most hideous sight. In all directions men issued from the huts; tumbled out of hammocks; rushed to saddle horses; looked to the priming of guns; and, generally speaking, there was the deuce to pay all through the camp. The long beard of the President appeared at the door of his hut. He was anxious to know what had caused the firing. I stood looking very foolish, and not quite certain whether it was my own nose or the chameleon's I had shot off. Colonel Cespedes, however, soon came to my relief, and after a little trouble, quiet was restored, and I went to make my excuses to the President. He took the affair very good-naturedly, simply saying it had given a means of testing the troops who were new to him. It was very much to the credit of the men that in an instant, almost before the echo of the shot died away, all the fighting men in the camp were under arms, and assembled in the direction of the firing.

Next morning we broke up camp and began our long and weary marches through the mountains. So far as I was concerned, the beginning was certainly inauspicious. Before we had marched five hundred yards in the new direction we had forded the Rio Azul two or three times, and on one of those occasions the horse which had been procured for me slipped into a hole, and though I got off his back in time to avoid being crushed, I found that standing in a river icy cold, up to one's waist, was a very disagreeable performance. There was no opportunity to change my nether garments, and I was consoled with the information that there were numerous other rivers to be crossed; and as the chances of being ducked again before night had to be taken into consideration, I rode on feeling decidedly chilly, and wishing there was a little brandy among the party; but there was none. Of course no pity was extended to me; quite the contrary, which rendered it all the more agreeable. Before the day was passed, however, we had two or three magnificent thundershowers, which pretty well damped the fun of my companions.

We halted in the woods about five in the evening, and the men sat to work to construct temporary shelter-huts. Rough frames made of lopped branches, bound together by the natural twine, or majajua, and covered by leaves of the palm-tree, or layers of tall Guinea-grass, were run up with wonderful promptitude, but it was too late. The awful downpours had washed through our waterproofs just as though they were so much brown paper, and rain was rushing down our pantaloons as though they were water-pipes. However, as soon as the shelter-huts were constructed, and we were thoroughly soaked, the rain stopped for a few hours, and gave us the chance to dry our clothes at the fires. Historic characters might be seen sitting somewhat disconsolately on their hammocks, holding their nether garments over the little fires, lighted expressly for their convenience. This was certainly not encouraging to begin with, though it was quite picturesque to be swung up in a hammock between two trees, with a shed of leaves and grasses, supported on a rude frame-work, just managing to keep off the body of the rain, but leaving the wind-gusts and rain-spray to sweep refreshingly over the occupant. The poetry of the situation can, however, be best admired from a distance, for nothing can well be drearier than to be obliged to gather one's self up in order to offer the smallest mark for the rain, that somehow would make its way to the hammock, and render everything cold, clammy, and death-like. Conversation or amusement under these circumstances is impossible, as each one camps alone, swung up on his own hook.

It rained so hard that the forest was converted into a regular swamp, and the roads became impassable even for the Cubans. This procured for us the pleasure of a day's halt in this delightful locality, and so there was nothing for it but to remain suspended, and drink *agua-mona gengibre*, which is only ginger and hot water, in the wakeful intervals of the day. Poor Cespedes was down with the chills and fever, and if the ground had not been so muddy I should have paid him a visit of condolence, but in view of the state of the weather I thought a message by his son would do as well. Fortunately, towards evening the drizzle ceased, and next morning we were enabled to pursue our journey.

During some weeks I traveled with Cespedes through the wildest and strangest scenes it has ever been my lot to witness, and so impressed was I with the self-sacrifice and devotion of the President and the band of men by whom he is surrounded, that had I been unfavorable to the Cuban cause, their patient endurance of hardship, and even want, would have converted and made me a friend. Not that my own position was a very enviable or pleasant one, for though whatever luxuries were at hand were reserved for my use, the unwonted fatigues, and the strange and, to me, unpalatable food, subjected me to great sufferings, though I endeavored to conceal the fact as much as possible. After the first few days the marches became dreadfully monotonous, ever through endless woods, up steep hills, down through precipitous valleys, scrambling, slipping, fording, momentarily in danger of breaking one's neck through a false step of the horse. These things, however, would have been bearable enough only for the bad state of my health. Low fever and a disordered stomach are capable of destroying all the pleasures of life, and certainly they were sufficiently potent to render me, if not insensible, at least indifferent, to the many scenes of marvelous grandeur encountered during our march.

The presidential party consisted of eight members of the staff, including Señor Miguel Bravo y Senties, who discharged the duties of Minister of War. These gentlemen were mounted on excellent horses, which—with the exception of two mules captured from the Spaniards, were the only quadrupeds in the party. The better part of the way a man on foot could certainly make his way more rapidly and more safely than on horseback; but there were occasions in crossing the savannas when the use of mounted scouts would have been of great value to the party in insuring it from ambush or surprise. Miguel Bravo, the Minister of War, is by profession a doctor, and, like most of the wealthy Cubans, was educated in Europe. At the outbreak of the insurrection he was arrested and deported to Fernando Po, but after a few years made his escape, and returned to Cuba in one of the patriotic expeditions. He is a gentleman of refined manners, and has a mind well cultivated. Colonel C. M. Cespedes, son of the President, was educated in the United States, and speaks English with fluency. Major Fernando Figueredo, a relative of Figueredo, the former Minister of War, executed by the Spaniards, was also educated in the United States, and speaks English with remarkable fluency and correctness. The other members of the party were Captain José Ignacio Queseda, brother-in-law of Cespedes, Major Francisco Estrada, his nephew, and Major Rafael Caymari.*

These gentlemen not only perform the duties of the staff, but form the President's guard of honor. In order to prevent any attempt on the life of the President they keep nightly watch. Whether in camp or on the march, after nightfall one of these gentlemen remains constantly in the hut of the President. Each one watches for two hours; a light is kept burning, which enables them to read and to notice the approach of any unauthorized person. In addition, a single sentry paces outside the hut; this simple guard secured Cespedes from any attempt against his life during the whole period of his presidency. The mode of life of the presidential party was anything but attractive, and the sufferings and hardships it involved must have taxed to the utmost the devotion and patriotism of the gentlemen

---

*O'Kelly likely refers rather to Colonel Francisco Estrada Céspedes, member of Carlos Manuel de Céspedes's personal guard.

who composed it. The constant fatigues were such as to try the rudest constitution. Unceasing activity, mental and physical, was demanded from them, and submitted to with the best humor, so that in spite of sufferings and hardships they were always gay and light-hearted. If the necessaries of life were moderately plentiful they were glad, if food were absolutely wanting they were thankful that things were no worse, and consoled themselves with the reflection that a day of plenty was not far off.

Towards the end of 1871–2, in common with all the Cuban forces, the President and his staff were reduced to extreme misery. They were wanting in nearly all the necessaries of life. Even the President was in tatters, and most of his staff in rags. The military operations of the Spaniards were carried out with great vigor in the hope of completely crushing the insurrection. The insurgents, without arms or ammunition, could offer no effective resistance to the columns which swept through the island in all directions. Flight only was possible, and the increasing vigor of the pursuit left no time for repose or rest. On one occasion a Spanish column pursued the presidential party so closely, that in order to avoid capture they were obliged to take refuge in the wildest regions of Cuba Libre. For six days they marched through the wood, their sole means of subsistence being sour oranges. It appears incredible that men should voluntarily undergo so much hardship, but it proves beyond question the constancy and valor of the people. The age of chivalry has not passed away.

In 1871 the Cubans were reduced to the greatest misery, and for some time it appeared as if all the sacrifices that had been made were to prove unproductive. During three months the insurgents wandered about in the wildest recesses of the mountains, living on wood-rats and roots, flying before an enemy who pursued with the fierce ardor of the bloodhound. In this terrible period the Cubans were wholly without ammunition, and the Spaniards, perceiving their opportunity, used it to the utmost. Column after column attacked the insurgents, and considerable numbers fell under the volleys of their enemies without having the power of defending themselves.

But they would not surrender, nor abandon their cause; hunted like wolves, they fled to the wildest districts, and sought refuge in the savage woods, but even here the Spanish soldiers followed them. Fearful as was the scourge of war and the fierce anger of men, a more terrible enemy still appeared. Cholera attacked the insurgents. There were no hospitals, and but little medicine available. The enemy pressed his attacks, and the sick and dying had to ford rivers and struggle through the thick brushwood, and clamber over mountains, in order to avoid Spanish vengeance.

Human nature could not resist the strain, and the track of the retreating Cubans was marked with heaps of dead. Then came the horrid pestilence that swept away friend and foe alike. The Cuban camps were encumbered with the dead. Men arrived with dispatches for the President, and dropped dead as they delivered them. Staff officers let fall their pens in the middle of an unfinished dispatch, and died without a word. The sentries fell dead at their posts, and it was no unusual sight to see a number of corpses lying scattered about the President's hut.

It would be impossible to estimate with anything like accuracy the losses of the Cubans during those days of horror. But in the midst of this pestilence and death, there was still no thought of surrender. At first the Spaniards swept through the infected encampment, but the pestilence broke out with such fearful violence among the troops that all military operations had to be abandoned, but not before thousands of Spanish soldiers sunk down among their plague-stricken enemy.

During this period whole families were swept away, and battalions melted as if the angel of death had breathed on them. When at last the pestilence had worn itself out, Cuba Libre was well-nigh reduced to a desert; the famished and disease-stricken inhabitants wandered about like ghosts of their former selves, and the prospects of the patriots looked black and hopeless indeed. Despair led to the adoption of new tactics, and as they had neither clothing nor ammunition they resolved to supply themselves from the stores of their enemies. The attack on Jibara and Holguin proved eminently successful.* Money, clothing, and ammunition, as well as arms, fell into the hands of the Cubans. For the first time the leaders clearly perceived the mistake they had made in carrying on a strictly defensive war, and the new tactics were put into vigorous operation. No town in the Central or Eastern Departments can now consider itself secure from attack. It has therefore been necessary to garrison every village, and as a result the Spaniards are unable to put a really effective army into the field. The Cubans, comparatively well supplied with arms, clothing, munitions, have acquired new confidence in themselves, and are proving more than a match for the unwilling soldiers sent against them by Spain. When Holguin was attacked and plundered, the Spanish authorities would only admit that the enemy had penetrated into the town and burned some half-dozen *bohios,* or Cuban huts. Yet the resources captured at Holguin and Jibara, among them the military chest, gave new life to the Cuban insurrection. Such is the value of Spanish official information.

*"Jibara" should read "Gibara," a coastal town in the eastern province of Holguín.

The road taken by Cespedes on leaving Rio Azul lay through the wildest part of the mountain districts of Jiguani, Bayamo, and Manzanillo. It was not the one usually made use of by the Cuban forces, though there were certain points of contact. It would be tiresome to relate each day's march, for, with few exceptions, they resembled each other closely, only fortunately the days were not all wet, though in the mountains we scarcely ever escaped a shower or two in the day. We were in some measure compensated, however, by the comparative coolness of this higher region, and the shelter of the woods which constantly surrounded us. We did not continue all the time among the mountains, but descended to the *llanos,* or plains, whenever we thought well to do so, either for convenience of travel or in search of food. The troops guarding the presidential party are generally hard up, as they cannot venture to forage so extensively as other troops, on account of the presence of Cespedes. However, several raids were made in the course of the journey, notably one at Bueycito, a village that has distinguished itself from the beginning by its bitter hostility to the Cuban cause. All the inhabitants are volunteers, and wage unceasing war on their countrymen. It was, therefore, with hearty good will that the Mambi soldiers obeyed the order to move out and sack the farms in the immediate neighborhood of the village, which is fortified. The men were tired, after a long and very fatiguing march, and, to my mind, wanted rest. They preferred, however, something to eat, although they had to march about ten miles to get the raw material, and ten back before they could cook it. It would make in all about fifty miles, which, considering the state of the roads, and number of days the men had been marching previously, I thought very hard work, especially as the rations were particularly short. The expedition was most successfully carried out, and the men returned towards morning absolutely laden with provisions and an enormous quantity of green tobacco. Had it not been for the stupidity of one of the guards firing at a cow, and so creating alarm, the whole tobacco crop of Bueycito would have been confiscated to the use of the Mambis. As it was, they had cigarettes for quite a long while. The green tobacco is dried over the fire, and so the Mambis are enabled to use it in their cigarettes. It is, of course, very unwholesome in this state, but the Cubans are so very much attached to smoking that they cannot do without some kind of weed. Almost as soon as the foragers returned orders were given to march, and the poor fellows had to pack up again. The march, however, was a very short one, and was undertaken rather as a military precaution than for the purpose of covering ground.

It may be well to explain a little how the Cuban commissariat department is carried on; for in this, as in most other matters, the arrangements are unique. No rations are issued to either troops or officers, nor is there any such thing as transportation or pay. The soldier not only fights, but he must feed himself. If he should be hungry he has no one to blame but himself, as he is his own commissary-general. After a march he starts out to the nearest plantation, and digs for boniatos, cassava-roots, yams, and many other succulent roots, or he eats sugarcane, and lays in his store. If cattle are killed, the meat is distributed to the men; this is the only approach to issuing rations known in Cuba. As the officers cannot provide themselves with food, they are supplied with a number of servants, in proportion to their rank, whose business it is to collect food and perform all menial duties for their chiefs. These men are called *ayudantes*, or assistants. They are taken from the *convoyero* class, and are unarmed. The services rendered to the Cuban cause by these men are very great, as without their aid the white officers would scarcely be able to resist the fatigues of the campaign. They are principally drawn from the slave class, and are capable of undergoing an enormous amount of fatigue, but are usually very bad soldiers. It has been found of more benefit, in carrying on the war, not to arm the most ignorant of the slaves, as they are so broken in spirit by the flogging system that they have no self-respect, and are therefore very unreliable as fighting material. There are, however, a great many exceptions, for quite a considerable number of the slaves have displayed marked courage and risen to high command. They were, however, in nearly all cases, Creole negroes, or, as they are now more politely called, *Morenos*.

Although the camp was not always well provided with food, my supply was constant. In fact, quite undevourable quantities of food were sent to me, to the great joy of my esquire, Pio, whose appetite was a wonder in itself. Whatever came was welcome, and if I could not dispose of it Pio could. It was a sacrifice of self he made on my behalf, and, like most good actions, had its reward, for when I took leave of him to go to Manzanillo, he was looking so fat and prosperous that his friends must have found some difficulty in recognizing him. He was very much attached to me, but could not resist taking the one bottle of brandy which I procured in Cuba Libre. However, he more than repaired that little failing by the present of numerous cocoanuts, and many other luxuries he sought out for me. He could go up a cocoa-tree like a monkey, and it was a real pleasure to see how he would toss down the milky treasure to the thirsty folks below. During my stay with President Cespedes I was supplied from his kitchen, but was by no means confined to his rather humble fare. His son furnished me with coffee, which was the great solace of my days, and when other officers fell on any luxury my share was always reserved. But, except beef, which could not always be had, and coffee, neither the food nor the luxuries agreed with me.

17 How the Insurgents Live

THE WONDERFUL endurance of the soldiers and *convoyeros* astonished me: these men seemed absolutely fatigue-proof. In the morning they rose before daylight and prepared for the march. If they had been lucky the day before, they partook of some cold jutia meat and roasted boniato, or bread made from cassava-root, before setting out; if not, they were animated with the hope of finding something edible at night. The more careful were laden down with several days' provisions as a precautionary measure; but every man's strength did not permit him to become an ambulating provision-store.

The boniato, or sweet potato, the plantain, the calabash, cassava-root, sugarcane, and sometimes Indian corn, were the principal vegetable food of the Mambi. In seasons of great distress the pulpy top of the palm-tree was also used as food; and the number of these trees felled in the forest which we encountered on our march bore evidence to the frequency with which the soldiers of the Cuban republic were forced to have recourse to this class of food. The Mambi kitchen is not very varied, the chief dish among all classes being a kind of stew made of boniatos, calabash, and plantain, seasoned with the flesh of the jutia, or with beef when within reach. In order to secure a change, the ingredients were generally served roasted separately, and to my palate were much more agreeable than in the stew. Indian corn, rudely broken between stones, and made into a kind of paste, which tried severely the masticating power, was among the luxuries not often within reach. The beverages peculiar to Cuba Libre were agua mona and gengibre. The former consisted merely of hot water sweetened with wild honey; the latter was the Mambi punch, and made by the addition of ginger-root to the agua mona. It acted as a stimulant, and was considered good for the stomach, taken in small quantities. After long marches on wet days I found it a very refreshing beverage, and not a bad substitute for whisky-punch. It had, however, no intoxicating effect, but acted as a stimulant. Coffee and chocolate were also to be had in limited quantities. Wild honey supplies the place of sugar in the mountain districts. Most of these elements of subsistence are to be found in restricted quantities all over Cuba Libre. Owing to the wonderful fertility of the soil, the abandoned plantations do not cease to produce because man no longer labors in the fields. Many classes of root-food grow wild in the forests, and the boniato continues producing for years. The root grows at the end of a *bejuco,* or kind of trailer, and many of these trailers belong to one plant. In fact, the boniato may be said to grow by families, as the one plant will have sometimes half a dozen roots in different stages of development. Only the well-grown root is plucked, and the trailer allowed to fall on the ground becomes again fruitful, and after a few months produces a new root. As the Spaniards cannot either burn or root up this vegetable, it is not possible ever to reduce the Cubans to submission by starvation. The jutia and the boniato alone would enable them to continue the war indefinitely. But the plantain, the sugarcane, and the numberless wild fruit-trees also bear their harvests without the aid of man; so that, though the insurgents may suffer from want in certain wild districts, anything like a general failure of food is well-nigh impossible. In order to diminish the hardships of the patriots, orders have been given for the establishment of *fincas* in the large uncultivated districts, and the sowing of various classes of vegetables in all the Cuban camps. This system will place the insurgents in a position to continue the war indefinitely, and render the failure of supplies impossible. Many classes of beans are fit for food thirty days after they are planted, such is the wonderful fertility of the soil.

Colonel Cespedes was fortunately supplied with quite a respectable bag of coffee, and every morning and evening a cup of the delightful beverage was brought to me by one of the *ayudantes.*

As soon as the roll had been called we took up the line of march. The President and staff, with whom I rode, occupied the center of the line, and our party was preceded by two lusty *macheteros,* who lopped down inconvenient branches, and cleared a way through the brush for our horses. We marched for three or four hours without making a halt, and almost without pause. It must have been killing work for the men, but they bore it wonderfully well. Two objects were served by this custom. In case troops were advancing in the hope of surprising the party, they were left far behind in a short time, and so the danger of pursuit was lessened, and the men were enabled to get over a good deal of the way in the cool hours of the morning. About half an hour was given to rest, and those who had anything to eat made their breakfast. We always were pretty well supplied, and the little *al fresco* repasts in the shadow of the trees were really enjoyable. Stories of adventures, more or less ridiculous, were never wanting, and we laughed and joked while disposing of our humble fare with a hearty good will seldom found at more pretentious *déjeûners*. For the nonce we were children of nature, and twittered as merrily as the little song-birds among the trees. Whenever we encountered abandoned plantations, a short halt was made to allow the soldiers to collect provisions. The scenery was such as would have delighted the heart of a painter or a poet, and every mile passed over presented new subjects for admiration. Trees, fruits, and flowers unknown to our northern clime, the wide-extending savanna, and the forest with its rank richness of life, its tender saplings, and kingly forest-trees, offered endless subjects for reflection and speculation.

Wonder is excited by the number of hidden resources which the skilled woodsman finds in these Cuban forests. Where the stranger would perish amid a wilderness of timber, of creepers, lianas, vines, and the thousand strange and beautiful parasite-plants, that wonderful creature, *el hombre del campo,* who seems to have surprised all nature's secrets, finds in these awful solitudes root-food, and honey, and purest distilled water to restore the wearied traveler. Among all these wonders, to my mind the bejuco, or hanging-fountain, is at once most beautiful and most useful. Imagine a huge vine, thick as a man's arm, falling in graceful festoons from tree to tree, whose roots are lost somewhere in the infinite tangle, and whose head has hid itself away amid the leafy roof of the forest, where, exactly, none can tell, but away somewhere, lazzarone-like, basking in the sun. At first one is inclined to think that this huge flexible vine is a ship's cable that somehow has found its way into the forest, but the moment you touch it the hempen idea vanishes, and you find out that it is unmistakably a fibrous wood, and apparently nothing more. One's first impulse is to be angry, because the apparently useless festoons have a knack of falling across the path in a most inconvenient and obstructive manner. If your guide wishes to initiate you into the wonders about you, and he happens to be thirsty, which is very probable, he will draw his machete and begin lopping at the vine, as you will imagine, simply to get it out of the way. When he has cut it through as far up as he can reach, he will cut it low down, so that the piece that he holds in his hand will be some four feet long. Then you will be astonished to see him hold up above his head this piece of vine, and allow a stream of crystal water to pour down his parched throat. You naturally try it also, and, not being skilled in this mode of drinking, pour a quantity of very cool water down the collar of your shirt—if you have a collar; but finally you gauge more correctly, and the grateful liquid tiny stream pours down your throat, and you think never have you drunk such pure, delightful water as from this hanging-fountain—this air-stream placed by nature in the depths of the trackless forest, that those who love her, and learn her secrets, may never parch, even in her wildest recesses.

The most curious tree, or plant, in the forest is a parasite known as the Cupey. Its appearance is very picturesque, but not alone is it useless itself, but it possesses an assassin-like instinct of destruction. Hence I christened it "the Thug of the Forest"; for like that human reptile its great pleasure in life is to strangle such unfortunates as fall within its grasp. In the beginning it is humble enough: its seeds are borne by the wind and deposited on other trees. Having found shelter on the bough of some unsuspicious tree, it sends down a fine root like a silken twine that with time reaches the ground and takes root. In the mean time other cords have been dropped tentatively, until the unfortunate that thoughtlessly gave shelter to this parasite finds itself surrounded on every side by fibrous, rope-like roots growing daily stronger and more taut, until its trunk resembles the mast of a ship surrounded by tight-drawn ropes. At this stage the villainous character of the tree is no longer concealed, and, as the victim is securely in the Thug's grasp, a stout twine is cast around the original tree, and day by day the grasp tightens until the victim dies choked and rots to decay. In the English-speaking West Indies the Cupey is known as the "Scotch Attorney," a rather doubtful compliment to that canny class. Like the attorney, the Thug of the Forest grows fat and strong on the ruin of its victim, and as the strangled tree is crushed more ruthlessly in the fierce grip until life is crushed out, the parasite grows into a great tree, whose trunk springs from the seed that sent down the wonderful transparent, silk-like cords now grown into strong fibrous roots, rising often fifty feet into the air, and supporting at that height the massive trunk of the Cupey, that upstart-like pushes its way with effrontery among the grandest and noblest inhabitants of the woods, fated too soon to become the prey of the treacherous intruder. Sometimes the struggle for life is desperate, but from the Thug-folds there is no escape, unless by the aid of friendly man. It often happens that the victim succumbing drags down its enemy, and they lie side by side, branches entwined in deadliest struggle, as though in life they had known the passionate throbbing of love and hate, and, irreconcilable enemies, had died in a fierce embrace that not even death could loosen.

But though hateful to the woodman, this tree, with the single exception of the ceiba, is the most picturesque of all the varied tree-family of the Antilles. Seen in the moonlight it is of exquisite beauty, and the long, slender roots, from between which the original tree has rotted, look like silver ladders leading up to some enchanted palace hanging in mid-air. No artist would consent to the extirpation of this wood-scourge; as well might one propose to do away with picturesque, ragged urchins and crazy, tumble-down rookeries, bringing the world to the mediocre dead level of respectability. No one, however, need fear their hasty extinction; for, like most evil things in this sad world of ours, they thrive apace. Since the war no friendly hand is extended to rid the peaceful dweller in the woods of its savage foe; the machete is too much occupied cutting short the threads of men's lives to have time to devote to saving trees. So this monstrous ghoul-like parasite rejoices, and grows fat and strong feeding on its defenseless neighbors.

Long before entering Cuba Libre the name of the curious little animal upon which it was said the Cubans principally depended for their meat-supply was familiar to me. In some localities the reported scarcity of meat in the Cuban camp is quite true, but it is by no means well founded when made to apply to the whole of Cuba Libre. On the contrary, great scarcity of meat only exists in the mountain regions of Santiago de Cuba, Jiguani, and, possibly, though this is not certain, towards the Guantanamo district. Even so close to Santiago as Bayamo meat is more plentiful among the Mambis than with the Spanish troops; nor can it well be otherwise, as, although the immense potreros which formed the chief wealth of the country lying between the Sierra Maestra and the Cauto, and spreading thence towards Holguin and Camarguey, are destroyed, and the owners wandering shoeless and mayhap shirtless among the patriot bands, the animal wealth of the country continues immense. The cattle abandoned by their owners wander in the woods and the *llanos* wild as buffalo herds; but the natives have the knack of hunting them with the lasso, so that, though commons may be short from time to time, there is no constant dearth of meat in the wide territory of Cuba Libre, but only in some districts. In Cuba and Jiguani, the wildest and most uncultivated portions of the island, the horse, the mule, but principally the jutia, are the sources whence is derived the meat supply. As both enemy and friend had talked so much about the latter animal, my curiosity to catch a glimpse of him in his native state was excited, but it was by no means so easy as it would seem to satisfy it. From what has already been stated, it may be inferred that the seeing of anything amid the cloud of leaves in the forest is extremely difficult. Indeed, it requires some practice to be able to distinguish birds even of brilliant plumage in a forest where the process of growth and decay goes on at the same moment. For here we are in a world where seasons seem unknown, and while one tree blossoms with the freshness of early spring, the rich autumn-tinted leaves of its neighbor tells that for it the winter is approaching. So closely are life and death associated that even in the same tree it is by no means unusual to find one bough mourning in winter garb, full of sadness and decay, while the fresh sprouts, that in less favored climes are children of spring, peep out laughingly from the same trunk as if conscious of new-born life. Vegetable life seems long since to have established the republic here, and every plant, in accordance with its free and sovereign will untrammeled by the despotism of seasons, has chosen its own winter and summer time, while the more turbulent have thrown away all obedience or respect for such fogy notions, and grow when and where they list.

It was not, therefore, until long after my meeting with President Cespedes that a good chance offered to see the jutia in his native element. Dead, there was no scarcity, for the soldiers showed something like instinct in the pursuit of this animal. Owing to the constant raids on the jutia colonies, by troops passing along the trails, even the foolish jutia has perceived the necessity of removing more into the interior. Hence, unless one is prepared to plunge into the woods and undergo a considerable amount of fatigue, for which, after a long ride, one feels by no means enthusiastic, an opportunity to study the habits of this tree-dwelling animal may not easily be found. However, by waiting long enough, curiosity is certain to be satisfied. We had just reached the outskirts of a delightful nook, where the camp was to be made, when a soldier brought the welcome news that great numbers of jutia were in the trees about the camp. Major Figueredo, of the President's staff, rode up to say that a hunt was in progress, and recommended me to at once dismount.

It was not necessary to repeat the notice, so, throwing our bridles to some soldiers, we made our way into the woods, where a grand hunt was in progress. A number of soldiers and officers' servants were assembled, watching a boy essaying to climb a very large tree in which a jutia was ensconced. To my uneducated eye nothing in the shape of an animal was visible, though the adepts assured me that in the fork of the tree a jutia was lying concealed. Half-way up the trunk a huge parasite of the cactus family had grown, blocking farther advance. It formed a kind of *cheveaux-de-frise,* which the boy vainly endeavored to remove, and which he could not surmount, so he was obliged to give up the chase, to my infinite disgust, as there appeared some danger of losing the sight;

but a Jew would sooner let slip a good percentage than a Mambi allow a jutia to escape. As soon as it was evident that the boy had abandoned the enterprise, a strong, athletic fellow sprang on a neighboring tree, climbing into the branches with an agility a monkey might envy. The object of this manœuvre was soon explained, as the man running along a bough dropped into the tree where the jutia was supposed to be, above the obstruction that had defeated the boy. This movement, though masterly, was full of danger, for had he missed his hold he would have fallen at least fifty feet among piled-up logs of decaying timber. The somewhat sudden apparition of the man startled the poor little animal, that had been wisely lying hid in the fork of the tree, and instinctively it took refuge among the high branches, where nothing larger than a monkey could safely have followed, for the slender bough swayed under the animal's weight. It appeared to me impossible that a man could follow, and so it was; but now the hunting trick based on the well-known habits of the animal was brought into play. When the soldier had mounted as high as he could safely go, and the tree-top bent most threateningly under his weight, he was still far from being able to reach his wily antagonist, who retreated so as to be completely out of reach, and there faced the pursuer.

At this juncture the man seized the bough in both hands and shook it violently, so much so that the animal found it difficult to maintain its position, which became at every instant more insecure. Although a gluttonous and very sedentary animal, the jutia is by no means wanting in courage, and seeing that it was no longer possible to avoid being thrown off the branch if the soldier were not driven away, the animal advanced resolutely to the attack; the soldier immediately let go the bough and steadied himself, ready to strike with the machete. As soon as the jutia found a secure footing it rushed at the soldier with astonishing courage, and had he not dealt it a heavy blow, knocking it to the ground, he would unquestionably have felt the animal's claws and teeth.

Sometimes on the banks of rivers the jutia burrows, or rather takes advantage of the crevices in the rocks and roots of decayed trees to make its home. Under these circumstances the hunt is still more lively, as the animal roused by fear from its usual inactive state gives proof of surprising agility. On one occasion we smoked out a fine fat fellow, and though he ran the gauntlet of some eight or ten persons, there was so much eagerness to strike the animal that everyone put himself in everybody else's way, so that to have hit the jutia it would have been necessary to cut some one's head off; and, as we were not hungry enough to do so, the jutia escaped, leaving us looking rather foolish, especially one gentleman, who was intently watching the chief crevice, machete in hand, when the very animal he was looking for jumped on his head and skedaddled back into his burrow before the astonished hunter could find out what was the matter, he being fairly scared lest a rock or a tree were coming down on him. The presence of the jutia in the tree is discovered by teeth-marks upon the leaves fallen to the ground; the initiated are able to tell by the gnawing on the leaves whether the animal is likely to be in the tree or not.

Not far from Guisa we encountered a detachment of the forces of General Diaz, under the command of Lieutenant-Colonel Emilio Noguera, a small, hardy, determined-looking man. His troops were so placed as to protect the march of the President; and, as soon as the junction was effected, both detachments marched to join the main body, under the command of General Diaz, at the camp of Guá. Colonel Noguera had had several successful skirmishes with the Spanish guerrillas, and, luckily, had captured a small convoy, so that the camp was well supplied with such luxuries as chocolate Menier, boxes of sardines, and real Havana cigarettes, as well as the latest numbers of the *Diario de la Marina*. From this delightful organ of the Spanish authorities I learned some startling facts about the attack on Jiguani led by Lieutenant-Colonel Saladriguez the night before the battle already described. According to the Spanish version, the forces of General Garcia had made an attack on the town, and had been vigorously repulsed by the gallant defenders. No one was injured on the Spanish side—according to official reports no one ever is. Two dead bodies of supposed insurgents were reported to have been found at some distance from the town, abandoned by the enemy. This circumstance was true enough, only the officials forgot that one of the dead bodies was that of a Spanish volunteer killed in the streets by the fire of his own friends, and carried away by the Cubans, in the hurry of retreat, by mistake. They brought his rifle and *cartouchière* back to the camp. There was also an amusing account of the capture of the convoy by Noguera in a local Manzanillo sheet. Somehow they turned the affair round, so as to make the convoy be captured from the insurgents, forgetting that the Mambis are supposed not to have any convoys, and to live on wood-rats, yams, and cassava-roots.

We halted for the night in a historic spot—an old barn on the top of a hill, where the Spanish prisoners made at Bayamo in the beginning of the war were for a long time confined. Colonel Noguera had made several prisoners in the combats with the Spanish guerrillas, and held them to await the order of the President. There were some half-dozen, all of them Cubans, and men who in the beginning of the insurrection had been rebels. On surrendering, the Spaniards forced them to enter the guerrillas, where they had fought against their countrymen until captured. The insurgents adopted a very wise policy in dealing with these men: instead of treating them as traitors, and punishing them with death, they were simply disarmed, and allowed to choose between entering the Cuban army or returning to the Spanish camp. This policy at first sight seems weak, but its wisdom has been proved by experience. The offer to let the men return to the Spanish lines appeared to me to be a mere matter of form, and understood in this light by both parties. My surprise was considerable when one of the prisoners replied to President Cespedes, "I am a good Cuban, and would like to remain with my countrymen; but my family is in the hands of the Spaniards, and therefore I wish to return." He was followed by another man who spoke in the same strain. The other prisoners, being young, unmarried men, decided on remaining with the Cubans. Several women, also, who had been surprised and made prisoners, were informed that they would be allowed to depart in peace in the morning as soon as the troops began their march. These acts of clemency encourage the Cuban volunteers in the Spanish service to return without fear to the patriot ranks. The released prisoners and their families nearly always maintain friendly relations with the Mambis, and supply them with information and ammunition. An active propagandism is carried on among the Cuban volunteers in the Spanish service, and its results are seen in the desertion by hundreds of armed and disciplined men to the insurgents.

As we had arrived somewhat earlier than usual, and everyone was in good spirits, it was resolved to get up a concert to while away the long evening. It was chiefly to afford me an opportunity of hearing the chants with which the insurgents encouraged hope, or recorded some brilliant exploit of the war. Many of the songs were written by the men who sang them, like Fornaris y Cespedes and Major Figueredo. They were wild and bold, with a tinge of melancholy. It was soon bruited that the force of Noguera had also an *artiste,* and as the soldiers of Bayamo did not wish to have all the laurels of the evening carried off by the President's staff, a man was sent to hunt the genius up. He was a colored man, and a mixture of a minstrel and comedian. He gave sketches of life in Cuba Libre, supplying the plot and the words himself. As he enjoyed great local fame, President Cespedes, who had been lying in his hammock during the concert, got up and came into the outer room of the barn, which had been arranged for the representation. The soldier soon appeared, and made his bow to the President and the audience. He then began a series of comic sketches of the various classes of Mambis, which were so true to nature, but with a subtle touch of exaggeration, that everyone present was kept in a roar of laughter. The satirist did not spare the failings or defects of his audience, and one of his most successful sketches showed a *convoyero* in search of food near the Spanish outposts. The nervous excitement of the man, due to his sense of danger, and his terror when suddenly challenged by a concealed Spaniard; his precipitate flight and abandonment of his provision-sack, were most masterly, and would have made a genuine success on any stage. On inquiring, I found the actor had at one time been a clown. Desiring to mark my appreciation of the man's genius and good nature, I sent him a present of a five-dollar gold-piece by my servant Pio. At first he wished to refuse the money, but owing to Pio's insistence he accepted it. In a few minutes, however, the comedian approached me, and said that while he thanked me very much, he could only accept my present on one condition—"that I would take the money back with me to New York and give it for the benefit of some poor Cubans who might be in want." This action on the part of a poor fellow to whom a five-dollar gold-piece was a small fortune appeared to me very noble, and it showed that colored men were quite as capable of elevated thought as their paler-skinned comrades.

In the course of our journeying we crossed the Cauto several times, the Contra-maestre, the Guananoa, the Mogote, Guama, the Grusa, and the Bayamo Rivers; nothing of interest occurred after the raid on Bueycito until we reached the Bayamo. Here the ford was very deep, and, owing to the steepness of the bank in front of the ford, it was necessary to ride in the river, hugging the land for a short distance. The water reached the saddle-girths, and to avoid being wetted we had to quit the stirrups and gather up well our feet. A very narrow gap in the bank, almost perpendicular, rose directly from the water, and furnished the only issue from the ford. All the mounted party passed before me successfully, but their passage had made the ground quite slippery, and they were grouped somewhat inconveniently at the top of the gap, owing to an obstruction in the woods. My horse was a small, active animal, wonderfully plucky, but not very strong. Seeing the top of the gap blocked, I had made up my mind to wait for a moment until the party should move forward and give me room to effect safely a landing on the ground above, so I pulled on the rein; but the animal, while crossing the river, had taken the bit between his teeth, and, without heeding the pull, mounted the gap. To have checked him would have brought him back into the deep water, where both of us might have been swept away, so there was nothing for it but to let him go. Just at this moment a servant of Cespedes took it into his head to dart into the gap instead of mounting the banks like the other men through the tangled bush, and as my horse was about to trample the man down I touched the reins to draw him to one side. The animal was straining at his best, and my touch, light as it was, caused him to rear, lose his balance on the almost perpendicular slope, and fall over with a plash into the river. The incident occurred in a moment, and created considerable alarm. Everyone thought I was killed. But my usual good fortune had not deserted me. Recognizing the danger of my position, I had thrown myself from the horse, and slid down the bank with my arms crossed before my face; a precaution which saved me from serious injury, as the horse, in falling over, kicked out and struck me with his hind feet on both arms. Fortunately, he was not shod, and I escaped with a couple of slight bruises and a very severe fright.

18   In the Camp of Modesto Diaz

THE CAMP of Guá is situated on the summit of a high mountain which overlooks the plains of Yara and Manzanillo. It is the favorite resting-place of General Modesto Diaz. From the *Vigia,* or outlook, steamers entering and leaving the harbor of Manzanillo are distinctly visible, and also the Spanish encampments dotting the plain. At night the huge watch-lights of the towers mark the position of the Spanish camps, while the vast plain black as pitch extends on every side. Seen from the mountain all detail was lost, even on comparatively clear nights, so that the sense of loneliness was only broken by the watch-lights that looked like monstrous fireflies in the night gloom. Zarzal, Vegitas, Yara, were distinctly visible, and a white speck on the horizon marked the locality of Demajagua, where Cespedes first sent up the cry of independence on the 10th of October, 1868.

The arrival of the presidential party created quite a stir in camp, and the soldiers were turned out under arms to receive the chief magistrate of the republic. There were not more than a few hundred men present, as General Xavier Cespedes, the brother of the President, was absent on a military expedition, and several small detachments were also operating. Owing to the steepness of the hill, I had been obliged to dismount and scramble up as best I could to the top of the mountain where General Diaz was perched. My horse did not much like the work of climbing, and broke away from the soldier into whose care I had given him, so that when the summit was reached I was obliged to make my way on foot to the headquarters, where the President and his party, who had been more lucky than myself, were assembled. President Cespedes presented me to General Diaz, who received me very cordially, offering me his hospitality during my stay.

Modesto Diaz is by birth a Dominican, and in the war of St. Domingo took sides with the Spaniards against his own countrymen. At the time of the outbreak of the Cuban insurrection he was living in the neighborhood of Manzanillo, on a small pension granted to him by the Spaniards, but feeling himself neglected and slighted by the government for which he had abandoned his own country, he took up arms for Cuban independence, and rendered service of great importance at the outbreak of the insurrection. He is between fifty and sixty years of age, but enjoys excellent health; he is a man of great physical strength, though not much above the medium height; his shoulders are as massive as those of Hercules; his limbs are light, and cleanly-shaped, with remarkably small feet. His whole build indicates immense strength, joined with activity. And in fact, though now an old man, Modesto Diaz is one of the most agile men in the Cuban forces. His horsemanship is proverbial; anywhere a horse can go Modesto Diaz will ride him. He never dismounts, no matter how steep and perilous the road; he rides on as though he was a centaur. This peculiarity came more than once under my observation during my subsequent journeyings with him. He has no pretensions to education, but possesses a native shrewdness and quickness of device much more valuable than any amount of book-learning. All kinds of wood-knowledge he possesses, and with his machete, without map or compass, will lead men through forests where all the savants, military and civil, of Europe would lose themselves and perish. In addition, he is courageous and indomitable; he knows exactly what he wants to do, and what he can do. He is a true *guerrillero,* and though he will sustain the war as long as he lives, should it be necessary, he will never strike any decisive blow. It is against his principle to risk too much on a single engagement. But, though he possesses no qualities that would entitle him to be regarded as a great soldier, his place in the history of Cuba will ever be a prominent one. Next to Cespedes, Cuba will owe to him her independence. It is not too much to say that only for Modesto Diaz the insurrection would have been crushed in its infancy. When the insurgents attacked Bayamo, a Spanish column advanced to the relief of the garrison that defended the barracks. Had this column entered Bayamo the insurrection would have at once succumbed. In this critical moment Modesto Diaz, with a handful of men, advanced to dispute the passage of the relieving column. Collecting a few hundred slaves, armed with machetes, and some twenty men armed with guns and rifles, Diaz placed himself before a Spanish column of several hundred men. None of the insurgents had ever seen a shot fired, and many, frightened by the unequal nature of the combat, deserted. In this supreme moment Diaz, with about a dozen men, took his place behind a huge tree commanding a ford, and having instructed the men not to fire, but only to load and hand him the guns, coolly waited the approach of the Spanish advance-guard. As soon as they came within range Diaz opened fire, and a regular battle began between one man and the skirmishers of the advancing column. They, of course, never imagined that it was the one man who sustained the rapid fire. But, so well was the fire directed, that no Spanish soldier could pass the ford. They were astonished at the tenacity of the resistance, and imagined that the whole Cuban army was posted in support. The officer in command showed criminal indecision, and the sudden appearance of a couple of hundred slaves, armed with machetes, on one of the flanks, persuaded the officer that he was in front of the Cuban army, which was making a movement to cut him off. Under this impression, a retreat was ordered, and next day Bayamo surrendered. This is one of the most remarkable instances in military history of what can be accomplished by the valor and decision of one man. Had the column advanced, Bayamo would have been relieved and the Cuban insurrection suppressed, but one man blocked the way.

Among the gentlemen whom I met in the camp of Modesto Diaz, Señor Don Tomas Estrada deserves especial mention. He is a member of the Cuban Congress, and owns the land of Guá and the country surrounding it for many square miles; yet his wardrobe was restricted to one suit of clothes, a few changes of linen, while his boots were very much worn and exhibited several yawning crevices. He was a young man, quiet and gentle in disposition, well-read, and of a thoughtful, practical mind. He had been educated in France, and was well posted in the revolutionary literature of that cradle of liberal aspirations. At the outbreak of the war he was living with his widowed mother on his estate. The attachment between them was unusually tender, and the old lady, though far advanced in years, insisted on accompanying her son to the Cuban camp. A small detached residence was built for her accommodation in a secluded part of the forest, and here she was surprised and captured by a Spanish detachment.

The old lady stoutly refused to accompany her captors, but was dragged away by main force. The captors soon got tired of their prisoner, and, after dragging her for some miles through the forest, abandoned her in a senseless condition in the midst of the woods. Next morning the Cubans pursued the trail and found where the old lady had been abandoned, but she was nowhere to be found. In vain all parts of the wood were searched for several days; but at last the old lady was found under a chestnut tree, dying from starvation, having subsisted for several days on the few nuts and wild fruits she could gather. Though every attention was paid to her, she died in a few days from the effects of the cruel treatment to which she had been subjected. This sad incident had thrown a shadow over the life of Estrada which no sunshine will ever completely clear away.*

The officer charged with keeping up communications with Manzanillo was absent with his squad when we arrived at Guá. Every week he was dispatched regularly for letters, medicine, and ammunition, all of which were supplied in small quantities by sympathizers in the town. No definite course could be decided on until his return; but most of the officers considered it would be extremely dangerous to venture into Manzanillo. The question was constantly discussed, and efforts were made by several officers with whom I had formed a special intimacy to induce me to reconsider my determination of going into the Spanish lines. As the camp at Guá could not furnish sufficient resources for the largely increased garrison, it was necessary to organize expeditions against the Spanish settlements in order to secure food. Two forays of this nature were successfully carried out under my eyes. For, from the outlook on the mountains, the Cuban forces engaged on the expedition could be seen moving across the plain, disappearing into the woods, and issuing out into the savannas like a huge black serpent. We could follow them with the naked eye into the cultivated fields of Zarzal. On one occasion shots were exchanged and some wounds inflicted; but the insurgents carried off the needed supplies and returned to camp to enjoy them. This is what they call "living on the enemy." The effect of these tactics has told wonderfully against the Spaniards; for the Cuban volunteers, who mainly occupy these settlements, find themselves plundered both by the Mambis and the Spaniards. It is impossible to protect the crops; for, whenever these raids are made, the Spanish garrison, too weak to face the Cubans in the field, are obliged to retire to their fortifications, while the Mambis carry off the harvest. Our

---

*Tomás Estrada Palma (1835–1908) became president of the Cuban Republic in Arms in 1876, as well as the first president of Cuba in 1902, reelected in 1905.

life in camp was exceedingly jolly. After coffee in the morning we read books captured from the Spaniards or discussed the military operations, the defects of the present system of tactics, the advisability of carrying the war vigorously into the Cinco Villas and Western Department. The men cleaned their arms or mended their garments, or wove new provision-sacks or hammocks from the twine of *majajua*, or loafed about in the sun, enjoying grateful repose after the fatigues of their forays. In the night we repaired to a beautiful platform, embowered in trees, arranged near the lookout on the highest point of the mountain as a ballroom. Exposed to every breeze, it was delightfully cool, and at night, when crowded with the picturesque inhabitants of the Mambi-Land, it presented a scene of great beauty.

The day on which the expedition returned laden with provisions, a messenger arrived in camp from Lieutenant-Colonel Antonio Bello, commanding a detachment at the encampment of *El Macho*, bearing most important tidings. An attack had been made on the camp by a Spanish column of four hundred men, and had been repulsed after a prolonged skirmish, in which some ten or twelve men had been wounded on the Cuban side. This was, however, nothing to the announcement that the Spanish garrisons of Congo and Punta Piedra had deserted to the Cubans, taking with them their horses, arms, ammunition, and families, as well as their commander, a Spanish major. Orders were at once given for a strong detachment of the troops to prepare to march on the morrow, and it was decided that I should accompany them, so as to see with my own eyes the men who had passed over to the Mambi flag. Next morning, as arranged, the men paraded under the command of Modesto Diaz, and I took leave, not without regret, of President Cespedes and his staff. When the moment of parting arrived, I extended my hand to bid the President farewell, but he insisted on embracing me in the Cuban fashion, assuring me that he looked on me not alone as an ambassador from the outer world, but that he would ever esteem me as a personal friend. In token of that esteem and friendship he embraced me before the assembled troops. Before setting out the President presented me a lieutenant's commission in favor of the black guide who met me under the ceiba-tree, as a recognition of the dangerous and important service he had rendered in guiding me safely through the Spanish lines.*

Descending from the mountains, we marched in a southerly direc-

---

*Later in 1873, the Cuban Assembly will depose Céspedes, replacing him with Salvador Cisneros. Céspedes will be killed in a sudden attack by a patrol of Spanish troops on 27 February 1874.

tion through the woods and savannas that lie at their base. The country through which we passed was remarkably beautiful, and at many points in the woods resembled those fairy bowers with which artists delight the public in pantomimes.

When we arrived at *El Macho* we found the veteran Mambi and late Spanish volunteers drawn up in line facing each other. The veterans did not number over eighty men, and were generally very rusty and even ragged-looking. Over two hundred deserters were drawn up in front of them, well armed, well dressed, and looking very much more prosperous than their new comrades. Their late commander, the Spanish major, was also present; he was allowed to go about at pleasure, but not to leave the camp. His wife, who was a Cuban, and his child were also in camp. He was presented to General Diaz, who treated him civilly but very coldly. It was sad to see the efforts he made to ingratiate himself with his captors, who exhibited no enthusiasm in his regard. As no one else seemed inclined to listen to him, he opened his heart to me, explained the hardship of his position, and declared his readiness to join the Cuban army if only his life would be spared. It was impossible not to pity the poor fellow and his young wife. He urged me to speak in his behalf, and, though I had made my mind up not to interfere between the belligerents, I spoke to Tomas Estrada in favor of the major's life being spared. Notwithstanding his own griefs against the Spaniards, he used his influence to obtain mercy for the prisoner. One of the officers in my presence recalled to Estrada his mother's barbarous murder, when he made the noble reply, "My mother's memory is too sacred to be defiled by a thought of vengeance." It struck me as one of the noblest sentiments I ever heard, and made me esteem Tomas Estrada even more than I had esteemed him before. Next day, however, General Diaz took me aside, and explained many reasons why this man could not with safety be spared, and, in view of the gravity of the circumstances, I did not think myself justified in further interfering. My interference also was liable to misapprehension, as it was evident that being about to return to the Spanish lines I was interested in clemency being shown to the prisoner, lest in retaliation the Spaniards should shoot me.

The addition of some six hundred souls to the camp of *El Macho* made it necessary to organize expeditions to procure food. The newly-deserted volunteers seemed to fall naturally into the way of life of the veteran Mambis, and as they had brought with them some two hundred horses of various qualities, a hundred mounted men were dispatched to the deserted encampment of Punta Piedra, to carry off whatever provisions had been left behind. This was accomplished after a smart skirmish between the volunteers and the Spanish troops.

Two days passed before the officer in charge of the *commissionarios* came into camp, and he brought news that sealed the prisoner's fate. General Rubalcaba, who was captured in a temporary hospital, had been shot by the republican government, and it was resolved to retaliate on the Spanish major. Next morning a court-martial, composed of three officers, was assembled, and the prisoner was brought before it under guard. One of the Cuban officers defended him; and, after the rules of war condemning prisoners to death were read, he was allowed to speak in his own defense, and also produce any witnesses who could show reason why mercy should be extended to him. Like most court-martials, however, it was a mere matter of form. The accused was a Spanish soldier, had fought against the Cubans and been wounded in different engagements, and he was a prisoner of war; by Cuban law such crimes deserve death. As the anxiety of the prisoner was very painful, I left the shed where the court-martial was progressing, and, in company with the son of General Diaz, went down the river, which flowed near the encampment, to bathe. As the day was very sultry we enjoyed our swim very much, and had forgotten all about the poor prisoner. We were chatting, while dressing, with some other officers whom we met, also bathing, when a volley of musketry broke the stillness of the afternoon, and was followed by one or two dropping shots and the screams of terrified women. For a moment we thought the camp was surprised, and a soldier was dispatched to inquire into the cause of the firing. We hurriedly completed our dressing; but, as the firing was not renewed, we began to think that it must have been some of the troops discharging their arms to clean them. However, we returned quickly in the direction of the camp, and met the soldier, who informed us that it was only the Spanish major being executed—only a man shot. Such a trifle appeared of no moment to the man, but an involuntary shudder passed through me as I remembered that scarcely half an hour had passed since I left a human being in the full enjoyment of life, and that on my return I would find him a mangled heap of matter; but—it was only a man shot.

We hurried back to the camp, and when we arrived near the place of execution the Cuban battalions had just completed the march past the dead body, and were forming up to listen to an address from Fornaris y Cespedes, the Secretary of the Cuban Congress. It was a strange sight to watch the orator speaking in impassioned words to his soldier audience in presence of the dead Spaniard, who lay stiff and motionless in his torn and bloody garments, staring vacantly at the sky, while a group of women and boys who, in life, had feared him, gathered at a little distance, gazed half pityingly, and with something of terror in their looks, at the mangled corpse. At the conclusion of the address the soldiers sent up the patriotic cry, "Viva Cuba Libre, y muere España!" and then slowly marched off to their quarters, leaving the poor corpse to blister in the sun.

The execution had taken place on a cleared space on the top of a slight hill in the center of the camp. The victim had been placed against the stump of a tree, and, when the firing-party delivered their volley, had fallen backwards, and died without a struggle. The aim of the men had been true, and every bullet had struck the major. It was better so; his death must have been instantaneous, and, save a convulsive action of the hands, there was no evidence of pain. It was a sad sight, and I turned away with a shudder from the dead man, lying cold and pallid in the bright sunshine, to such quietness and solitude as the camp would afford me.

This incident was unpleasantly suggestive of what my own fate might be, and showed me very clearly that little humanity or forgiveness was to be expected from men hardened by such scenes to human suffering. Next day I was to leave the Cuban camp on my way to the Spanish lines, with the sentence of death, pronounced in advance, hanging over me. "IF YOU ARE TAKEN IN THE ENEMY'S CAMP, OR GOING TO IT, OR RETURNING FROM IT, YOU WILL BE SHOT AS A SPY." Such was the terrible *"advertencia"* of Brigadier Morales de los Rios. Would it be carried out? Would the Spaniards, when they learned the death of the major, shoot me in retaliation? These were some of the thoughts suggested by the sight of the dead soldier. Next morning would find me on my way to what most of the Cubans considered certain death. In the midst of these gloomy thoughts an officer came to tell me that in the evening there would be a grand *baile,* in commemoration of the desertion of the Congo volunteers and as a send-off for myself. In a few hours the execution was forgotten, and only the bloodstained ground and the bullet-scarred tree-trunk remained to mark the tragedy.

19 Return to the Spanish Lines

THE MOMENT at last arrived for taking leave of the Cuban patriots, who overwhelmed me with protestations of friendship and regard. It is wonderful in what a short time strong, hearty friendships grow up in the wild Mambi-Land, where the hollow conventionalities of civilized life are laid aside, and men abandon themselves to their natural impulses of love and hate with a fervor unknown to the dull, plodding life of civilization. It was not without sincere regret I parted from men whom I had learned to respect and admire. In my short stay among the Cuban patriots I formed many warm and lasting friendships. A guard of twenty men were selected to accompany me to a point close to the Spanish outposts. This dangerous service was intrusted to Captain Rodriguez, a young and dashing officer belonging to the staff of Modesto Diaz, and a great favorite with the general. General Diaz and his son, Fornaris y Cespedes, Tomas Estrada, and a number of Cuban officers rode with me for some miles from the camp, where we bade a final adieu to each other in a stirrup-cup which the general had procured for the occasion. Our parting took place in a wide road in the forest; the general and his friends rode back to camp, and, as they reached a point where the road turned at a sharp angle, they waved a last adieu.

The road taken by my escort lay through the woods which partially cover the level country lying between the mountains and the town of Manzanillo. Large tracts were quite bare of timber, and in crossing these we ran considerable danger of discovery by the guerrillas of the enemy. In order to avoid entering the cultivated zone before nightfall, we halted for a short time in an abandoned plantation, where we lunched. When about half-way to Manzanillo, a herd of wild cattle was discovered quietly grazing in a large savanna; the wind blowing towards us prevented the animals from noticing our presence. After a short consultation it was resolved to endeavor to capture some of the herd. It would not be safe to use our firearms, lest we should alarm some hostile party in the neighborhood. Myself and Captain Rodriguez were the only mounted men of the party. We surrendered our horses to two of the most skillful hunters of the party. Their preparations were soon made. Two lassos were forthcoming, and away the men rode in the shade of the trees, in order to get as close to the browsing animals as possible. Although they were fully two miles away, in the center of the savanna, the hunters were perfectly confident that they could catch one or more of them. The two men had not long disappeared in the woods when it became evident that their presence was noticed, and several of the older and more wary of the cattle moved in the direction of the woods. Very soon the herd scattered in every direction. This was the signal for the horsemen to break cover, and a most exciting chase began. The cattle ran with wonderful swiftness, and it began to be doubtful whether or not the hunters would succeed. After a chase of some five miles a young heifer was lassoed by the man who had my horse. The heifer was not more than three years old, and was in splendid condition. It was soon dispatched, and in a few minutes six or seven of the men were working away with the dexterity of accomplished butchers skinning the unfortunate victim. In less than a quarter of an hour the carcass was cut up conveniently, and divided among the escort, who marched along merrily, cheered by the prospect of a good supper.

Night had fallen before we reached the cultivated zone, and we were obliged to use torches marching through a stretch of wood where the trail was much encumbered by felled logs that lay rotting on the ground. The scene was remarkably picturesque as the glare of some seven or eight torches lighted up the gloom of the forest, and gave the trees and foliage a weird, fantastic effect. We were now quite close to the cultivated zone, and on either hand there were Spanish advanced posts behind us; but the escort marched on without the least hesitation, apparently feeling quite confident that whatever might happen they were well able to take care of themselves. I did not at all share their sense of security. The critical moment was fast approaching when my life would have to be placed in the power of men not accustomed to show much mercy. They had warned me fairly that if I visited the insurgent camp and returned, I should be shot as a spy. In defiance of that threat I had gone into the Mambi-Land, and now I was on my way back to place myself in the power of the Spaniards, and the question unceasingly suggested itself, What would they do with me? Would they shoot me, or let me go? It was a riddle no one could solve.

The first point reached was a small *finca,* or plantation, where we refreshed ourselves with sugarcane. There was a large quantity of tobacco hung up to dry, and the party supplied themselves freely. There was, however, no attempt to injure the shed, or to confiscate the stock, as the plantation belonged to a friend. It was situated outside the lines, and the owner and his workmen retired behind the pickets every night, so that there was not much fear of interruption.

Resuming our march, we reached about two o'clock in the morning a thick wood, into the center of which we made our way with a good deal of difficulty, care being taken to cover up our tracks as much as possible. With this object every man entered the wood at a different point, so as to leave no trail. We were now within a mile of the outlying Spanish pickets, and the least indiscretion might lead to the death of the whole party. A scout was sent to find out how the sentries were posted, and was fired on by some very wide-awake picket. He escaped, however, unhurt. It was not considered prudent to pursue further investigations that night. Much to my surprise the party lighted fires to roast meat and prepare coffee. When

I remarked on the danger of the proceeding, the officers simply said that even if the fires were seen the soldiers would take us for negro shepherds, or watchmen guarding the crops. This scarcely satisfied me; but, of course, it was not my place to make any further remark, so after supper I turned into my hammock, and was soon fast asleep. One man was supposed to keep watch over us to prevent surprise, but I am persuaded that he was snoring away like the rest of us, though we might be said to be sleeping at the very muzzle of Spanish guns. It was not thought advisable that I should go into Manzanillo, on account of the sentry having alarmed the post I would have to pass by; so next day was passed slung up in our hammocks, keeping as quiet as we could. We were all in want of the rest; and I improved the opportunity to get thoroughly instructed in all the windings of the road I would have to follow to reach Manzanillo, which was yet some ten miles away. All my property was distributed to friends according to their necessities. My machete which I carried during the expedition I sent as a present to General Calisto Garcia Iñiguez as a token of esteem and friendship.

It was astonishing to see the coolness of my escort. We were almost within hail of the Spanish pickets, and should we be discovered our destruction would be almost certain; but the men smoked their cigarettes, made out of the tobacco we had appropriated on the march, and conversed in a quiet way without appearing in the least bit nervous. For myself, I was too much occupied examining my own prospects to trouble much about our common safety. The remembrance of the court-martial on the Spanish major suggested unpleasant reflections, and somehow the picture of the dead officer lying cold and bloody, staring with meaningless eyes at the noonday sun, would come back vividly to my imagination. The prospect of being taken out and shot was certainly not cheering; but, as I had made up my mind to go through the Spanish lines at all hazards, it was necessary to brace one's self up to the sticking-point. More than once I was inclined to abandon the idea of returning to New York. It seemed so much safer to merely send on the letters by the *laborantes* and join the Cuban forces. Such a course would undoubtedly have been less dangerous than to surrender myself to the Spanish authorities, but as I had entered the Cuban lines as a neutral, after mature consideration I decided that it was more honorable to leave as a neutral, and accept the risk of surrendering to the Spaniards.

Long before daybreak the little party had bestirred themselves, and, as I turned out of my Mambi hammock for the last time, the welcome odor of coffee came to me on the morning air. It was still dark, but the first faint light-streaks announced approaching day. There was little time to spare, as it was necessary to approach close to the Spanish posts under favor of the twilight, and take the chances of passing unchallenged. The hope of doing so depended on approaching unperceived so close that when seen, as I inevitably would be, the sentries might mistake me for someone connected with the neighboring *ingenios* or posts. In order to have as little the look of a Mambi traveler as possible I had prepared a perfectly clean suit of white linen, which contrasted strangely enough with the discolored straw hat which was my only headgear. Having donned this suit, and partaken of coffee, I bade the members of the escort farewell, and set out on my journey to the Spanish lines. Captain Rodriguez and the officer of the *commissionarios* accompanied me to the edge of the wood, where I took leave of them. It was agreed that the escort would wait twenty-four hours until word reached them of my fate. In case I should be discovered by the pickets, it was my intention to resist capture and endeavor to rejoin the escort. These details having been agreed upon, the Cuban officers left me in charge of a *practico,* or soldier well acquainted with the country, who accompanied me to the road which led to the Spanish outposts, where he shook hands with me, and wished me God-speed, then returning to rejoin the escort.

Less than a mile away I could see two massive-looking buildings on either side of the road. They were *ingenios,* occupied by troops, and my road lay between them. It was at this time daylight, and the sun was rising rapidly in the east. Long before I could reach the outposts he would have risen far above the horizon. At first sight this appeared to be a disadvantage, but in fact it was not. The night-pickets had been withdrawn from the roads; the sentinels, tired out with their night watch, were drowsy and inattentive, and were distracted by the overseers and workingmen moving out to work on the different plantations. Still, my heart beat quickly as I moved into the road between the two posts, and groups of soldiers and workingmen stopped to look at me. Fortunately, they were some distance away, and the whiteness of my clothes and the assumed carelessness of my air cheated them into the belief that I was some overseer who had been looking after cattle or some other matter concerned with the plantation. When I found that no one stopped me, and that now I was actually within the Spanish lines, my breath came more freely, and hope dawned that in the end my attempt would be successful. At this point let me pause to take breath. If a man always understood the full danger of his acts, how much some lives would be changed! It is quite true that I had a vague feeling that if any of the patrols or outposts made me prisoner, I might be shot, but it was far from being a conviction. Some lurking faith in the chivalry of the Spanish nation unconsciously affected my resolution, and I half pooh-poohed the shooting idea under any circumstances. Trained in the liberal opinions of republican Europe, I have an almost indestructible faith in humanity, and it is well-nigh impossible for me to believe in wanton barbarity, or that men will slaughter for the pleasure of slaying. Notwithstanding this generous faith, it is satisfactory to me that the Spanish outposts took no notice of the strange-looking man that walked by them in the open day, endeavoring to appear as unconcerned as possible, but whose heart pumped so nervously that its beatings were distinctly audible.

At intervals along the road I encountered groups of men going to their labors. For the most part these people saluted me politely, though my appearance evidently struck them as strange. This was far from reassuring, and as soon as they were well out of sight I lengthened my pace, so as to get over the ground as quickly as possible without running. Several small detachments of troops scattered along the road caused me much uneasiness, but fortunately for me the posts were at some distance from the highway, so that no difficulty was experienced in passing them.

On one occasion, while walking through a hollow road that runs by one of these posts, I suddenly came against a soldier on sentry. This meeting was so unexpected as almost to make me lose my presence of mind. Instinctively my hand sought my revolver, while I felt the strongest mixture of fear and ferocity take possession of me. I was frightened; there is no doubt of that. The bitterness of failure, and the danger of being shot as a spy, flashed through my mind like lightning. My resolution was taken on the instant. If the soldier challenged I would shoot him, and make my way back to the escort. Fortunately, the soldier took no notice of me, and I pretended to take none of him; not even the customary salutation was exchanged between us. Evidently my face did not betray my feelings to the soldier, but when I had left him a hundred yards behind drops of cold sweat were standing out on my forehead. A cur dog next drew the attention of some mobilized Cuban volunteers on me, but one of them called off the dog, and I proceeded in peace. The town was now close at hand, and nothing further worthy of note occurred until the outskirts of Manzanillo were reached. Groups of worthless, two-legged curs loafing about the dram-shops, waiting for their "morning," were my next source of anxiety, and had I possessed a magician's wand I would have turned them into London cab-nags; but as this supernatural power was not mine I avoided them as much as possible, and after a series of zigzags reached the harbor, where the office of the British Vice-Consul was situated.

Groups of custom-house officials were engaged overseeing the discharges of the two or three melancholy-looking vessels moored at the long wharves; and, as I passed by, they looked at me in a lazy, sleepy kind of fashion, but without interfering with my progress or asking any questions. Not that they were very busy; for it appeared to me that there were more official superintendents than there were workers. A few minutes later the harbor of refuge was reached, and I read the words of salvation, "British Vice-Consulate," with more pleasure than I ever read any announcement of the kind before.

Mr. William Lauten, the representative of the power and majesty of Great Britain, was in his office, and, on my inquiring for the consul, a large, grave-looking man, somewhat resembling Kaiser William, informed me in English, but with a slight German accent, that he was that dignitary. Having explained to him that I was traveling with a British passport, and that I wanted my papers arranged to enable me to proceed to Havana, I handed him my passport, and also my *cedula,* informing him that I was the special correspondent of the New York *Herald,* and that I wished him to accompany me to the governor of the town, to whom it was my intention "to present myself." Mr. Lauten replied that he thought there would be no difficulty, saying that he would first present my papers, and that if the governor desired to see me, we would afterwards go to see him together.

With this understanding we separated, Mr. Lauten advising me to take up my quarters in the "Caballo Blanco" until noontime, when the Havana steamer would arrive.

As I had arrived from the Manigua without anything that could stand in the place of a wardrobe, and the clothes I wore bore patent evidence of my travels in Cuba Libre, my first care was to visit the various shops of the town in order to modify, as much as possible, my costume, so as to look as much like the rest of the inhabitants as possible. A shirt-collar at one place, a hat in another, and a few other trifles of this nature, combined with a barbering, succeeded in restoring me to the dead level of a mere civilized human being.

I was congratulating myself on the transformation when I came in sight of the famous "Caballo Blanco," which presented the appearance of one of those dirty dram-shops which one meets with in the poorest quarters of French towns. There was a small bar and a very large billiard-table, with a couple of greasy-looking marble tables occupying the space between. Although it was not much past seven o'clock A.M., a number of Spanish officers were deeply occupied in their usual intellectual exercise of making the little ivory balls strike against one another. To see the joy spread over the faces of these bearded men at a more than usually lucky stroke, one would naturally doubt that persons who pass whole days in such innocent amusement could be capable of committing deliberate crimes against humanity. Such sportive joy seemed inconsistent with a disregard for the rights of a stranger such as would not be shown by a savage tribe in Africa. Encouraged by these delusive appearances, I entered the "Caballo Blanco" with that confidence which is the sorrowful heritage of the ingenuous.

The effect of my appearance was electric. Every eye was turned on the intruder in a fiercely inquisitive manner. The signs of good nature and innocent contentment disappeared like magic, and I found myself the center of observation of various groups of scowling pandours. Even the loved billiard-balls were neglected for a moment, and I was inspected with unpleasant minuteness. The situation was a trying one. A person of more nerve than I lay claim to might well confess to a certain palpitation of the heart under the hostile gaze of those terrible Spaniards. It was impossible to retreat without exposing one's self to annihilation, so I advanced with what appearance of courage and indifference I could muster to a table which was unoccupied. Having knocked on the marble surface several times without eliciting any response, I turned in the direction of the bar to see why no one was attending to me. The waiters were in a state of suspended animation in view of the terrible aspect of the *señores officiales,* and were absolutely afraid to approach me.

It was evident that this would not do; so, mustering the small amount of courage left me, I knocked again on the table vigorously and whistled for the waiter. Indignation overcame my natural timidity, and I must have looked the impersonation of ferocity, for the waiter advanced in double-quick time to take my order. In the mean time I thought it would be well to do a little of the Bombastes Furioso.* Half turning in the direction of a group of officers, who were presided over by a small, black-looking man, with black beard and moustache cut after the fashion of the Spanish muleteer, I looked as fiercely as I could. This person appeared the very impersonation of "the terribly awful"; and I confess to a feeling of satisfaction that it was daylight and that I was the possessor of a revolver when I met

---

*O'Kelly tends to present his time in Spanish Cuba as burlesque comedy. *Bombastes Furioso*—written in 1810 by British writer William Barnes Rhodes, subtitled "A Burlesque Tragic Opera"—spoofs the Italian romantic epic *Orlando Furioso* by Ludovico Ariosto.

his withering glances. It is even now a matter of surprise that this terrible person did not cause my death from fright; but the fates would have it otherwise. As I looked at him steadily, and, I flatter myself, somewhat menacingly, this Don Whiskerandos turned white and green, and I know not how many other colors.* It was evident his ferocity was rising to the extinguishing point, and I was thinking of consulting my safety by flight when the portentous person of the Vice-Consul loomed in sight.

This diversion gave me a momentary relief, but it was of short duration. An invitation to take "the morning" was declined by the Consul, who informed me that the governor was particularly anxious to see me. Don Whiskerandos was known to the Consul, and joined the party without any invitation, accompanying us to the house of the governor, who was waiting to receive us. What a reception! Señor Don Aristides de Santalis, a lieutenant-colonel in the army and temporary governor of the town, is a person above the medium height, and not at all ferocious in aspect. On the contrary, being fair, with regular features, he might claim to be rather good-looking, if he were so inclined. On presenting myself to this official he looked at me with lofty severity.

"Your name is James J. O'Kelly, a newspaper correspondent," he said, in a tone of voice that left no doubt how the unfortunate O'K. was regarded by authority. Having confessed that I was guilty of the name of O'Kelly and newspaper correspondentism, I added for the governor's information that I had just arrived from the insurgent lines (*campo insurrecto*).

"Then you shall go to the fort," replied the Spanish Aristides, drawing himself up to his full height, and motioning with his hand in the direction of Gerona. The aspect of the governor at this moment recalled my boyish notions of Jupiter commanding the gods, and will always be associated in my mind with the idea of the "grandly awful." It is wonderful how much human nature can bear. The scene in the "Caballo Blanco" had almost used up the last shred of courage which I possessed, but this new outrage, instead of killing me off, as it ought in mercy to have done, only gave me courage to suffer more. Indignant with this Manzanillian Jove, I told him it "was well," which was one of the blackest lies I ever told in my life.

No motive was assigned for my arrest, and as I had heard so much about summary executions, the thought came to me that it would be well to secure my notebooks by handing them over to the Vice-Consul. The governor insisted that they should be given to him. This I declined, and

---

*O'Kelly names this menacing enforcer of Spanish authority after the character Don Ferolo Whiskerandos, from Richard Brinsley Sheridan's 1770 farce, *The Critic*.

told him that he would have to take them by force. He assured me that force would be resorted to, and dispatched Don Whiskerandos for assistance. Under these circumstances I gave up the notebooks, and all other papers I had with me, among them a letter of courtesy from Carlos Manuel de Cespedes to Mr. James Gordon Bennett, and another letter to the same gentleman from Señor Fornaris y Cespedes, one of the Secretaries of the Cuban Congress. On reflection, the governor said the British Vice-Consul could seal the papers, but that they would remain in the hands of the authorities.

Having descended to earth, the "grandly awful" proposed a drink, and, having no objection, both the Consul and myself consented smilingly. I requested the Vice-Consul to telegraph immediately to the British Consul-General the facts of my arrest, and the Governor promised that it should be sent immediately, a promise which he did not consider himself obliged to keep. As the Spanish officials do not pay the slightest heed to the representations of the consular agents, and only allow them to telegraph just what is agreeable to the Spanish government, a man in my position has just the amount of advice and help from the representatives of his government that the people in power choose to permit. Not a single telegram was allowed to pass during my detention except at the pleasure of the governor, so that it was impossible for me to inform my friends of my exact position and danger.

As soon as the formality of sealing up my papers had been gone through, and the drinks ordered by the governor had been disposed of, I was escorted by Don Whiskerandos and another officer of the army to Fort Gerona. On inquiry, I found that Don Whiskerandos was captain of the *plaza*, a kind of official combining the duties of policeman and aid-de-camp. After this person's conduct in the "Caballo Blanco," it is needless to say that there were no very fine compliments exchanged on the way.

There are never many people in the streets of a Cuban town, but the few scattered groups on the principal square through which we passed stared inquiringly at me, and the curiosity of the inhabitants on the line of march was evidently very much excited by the last Spanish capture. Most of the inhabitants of Cuban origin being connected with the insurgents by blood as well as by sympathy, naturally feel an interest in all prisoners, which they are very careful not to manifest too openly, for fear of rendering themselves suspected. It is, therefore, not to be wondered at that my person was scanned eagerly from many a window, and that everyone who encountered us did me the honor to stare at me as though I was a new specimen being conducted to a museum.

The fierce rays of the sun beat down on us as we walked up the steep hill which leads to the fort, and when we arrived at the top a mean-looking brick building confronted us. It had ominous loop-holed flanking defenses, and was surrounded by a ditch about twelve feet wide, crossed by a rude drawbridge, that is raised every night so that no enterprising Mambi can sneak in. Four cannon carrying twelve-pound shot are mounted on the ramparts. The fort is garrisoned by about fifty men, and is the chief depot for the arms and munitions of war stored in Manzanillo. It was originally a hospital, but on account of its commanding position it was turned into a fort at the outbreak of the insurrection. It contains a governor, who is an officer in the artillery corps, and some ten artillerymen as permanent garrison. This force is strengthened by a detachment of infantry, which is changed every day. In this country the fort is a place of importance, but some of our folks would be inclined to laugh at the idea of calling such a place as this a fort. On my arrival, I was handed over to the governor, and accommodated with a share of the *calabozo*.

When I had time to examine my new quarters, I found for companions another of the human species and several rabbits. The stench of the place was horrible. A sorrowful impression immediately took possession of my mind, that in case I escaped death from asphyxia I would certainly fall a victim to the yellow fever.

Turning my attention to my companion in captivity, I found that he was worth while studying. It would have been difficult at the first glance to decide his nationality or vocation. He was of the mongrel kind—a mixture of a navvy and an organ-grinder: the head Italian, the paunch decidedly British, and, taken all in all, not a bad specimen of the biped kind. When I fixed my attention on him he was seated on the wooden banquette before a kind of stool, which, with the exception of a settle-bed, was the only piece of furniture in the cell. While I was still trying to make out what manner of man he might be, and what the chances were of his cutting my throat during the night, if he were so advised, he suddenly began to telegraph in a most energetic style. My curiosity being aroused, I approached him, and asked him if he were learning to be a telegraphist. He replied that he was. The ice was now broken, and he showed me an ingenious telegraphing machine which he had constructed out of sundry pieces of zinc, brass, and wood. It worked admirably, and my fellow-prisoner took immense delight in displaying his dexterity as a telegraphist, as well as the effectiveness of his machine, of which he was naturally very proud. He was a soldier of the sanitary corps, and had been in prison more than six months on the charge of having committed a forgery.

No doubt, in the minds of intelligent Spanish officers, the companionship seemed quite appropriate. Indeed, it is not certain that they did not think a forger too good an associate for a newspaper correspondent.

These "illustrious swords," as Castelar ironically calls them, hate nothing so much as a newspaper, except the writers, and would willingly employ their "illustrious" blades in wiping the editorial class out of existence. The sense of newspaper power seems to aggravate them, for they feel that the wounds of a pen are incurable. These men, whose swords are for auction, hate correspondents and editors the more intensely because they know that "illustrious swords" are powerless against the force of an idea. Before I crossed the Spanish lines, and while they imagined that I did not understand the value of their "illustrious swords," these men protested a love and reverence for the press, and a desire for light on this Cuban question, which might have persuaded a person less incredulous than I am. But when I returned, and they knew that I had learned the secret history of the Cuban campaigns, about which we have heard so much exaggeration and bombast, they would willingly have quenched the light with my blood. There were exceptions, honorable exceptions; but the hatred of the light was pretty general. One fellow, who disgraced a soldier's uniform, told me that he thought I was much worse than an insurgent chief, and that I ought to be treated with corresponding severity.

It was very fortunate for me that there were other considerations to be taken into account as well as the wishes and passions of the "illustrious swords" and their jackals the volunteers. Shut off from all communication with my friends for the first four days, my position was far from reassuring. No notice was given me that the telegram of the Vice-Consul had been detained, and the failure to receive a reply from any quarter increased my anxiety as to the measures the authorities were prepared to take in my regard. Having ventured to defy public opinion by arresting me, there was no longer any security that they would not go further to justify their first step.

It would be difficult to convey to the minds of the people accustomed to the public administration of justice, and enjoying numberless safeguards against the abuse of power, even a faint idea of the mental suffering to which one who finds himself in the hands of men practically irresponsible may be exposed. All confidence in the loyalty and chivalry of Spanish officials was dissipated by my arrest and by the aspect of the men with whom I came into contact. Extreme precautions were taken by the authorities lest I should escape, which had the effect of convincing me that my case was serious. It would be difficult, if not impossible, to convey to those who are unacquainted with Cuba, and the manner in which a war of mutual vengeance is waged, the feeling of apprehension which oppressed me.

Life is no more considered than if it were a thing of no value, and, under the pretense of fulfilling the law, the most revolting severity is practiced by the belligerents. It is true that I was not in any way mixed up with the mutual slaughter that goes on unceasingly, but the same right which justified my arrest would easily excuse my assassination. Once a man is dead, it is easy to invent motives to justify his execution; and what I had seen of consular representation left me but little faith either in its efficacy or its disinterestedness. Had I been shot at the outposts, it is even possible that no one would have heard of my death, which would have been registered after the stereotyped fashion, "At such a point a man fit to bear arms was killed by the troops." That, in all probability, would have been my elegy. Knowing this, it is not surprising that the first days of my prison-life were days of suffering and terrible anxiety. It is a theory of mine that most men die bravely when death is inevitable, but the bravest man will shrink from an obscure and unhonored grave when no principle is involved in his dying. To fall a victim to the savage passions of brutal soldiers, with the certainty that one's death will pass unnoticed and unavenged, is the saddest fate that can present itself to the imagination of a human being. It may be thought that these fears were exaggerated. All that I can say is, that those who think so ought to visit Cuba and mix among all classes as I did; perhaps they would then find those fears very natural.

The second day of my imprisonment the governor of the fort came into my cell accompanied by a man who was introduced to me as a captain in the Spanish service. Like many others, he was a prisoner awaiting trial for some breach of discipline. His appearance did not impress me very favorably; he had a false, insincere face, which was rendered still more disagreeable by a squint in the left eye, and an unpleasant habit of looking at the person he was talking to with the squint-eye, while the honest, straight one was engaged taking surveys in a totally different direction. In order to establish a chord of sympathy, he told me that although originally belonging to the regular army, he had also been an editor, and had been sent to prison for some over-truthful statements about the governor of the town. The man was not calculated to win much sympathy. His lean figure, and somewhat melancholy face, joined with the squint-eye, suggested near relationship with the melancholy Knight of La Mancha, but his practical views of life showed that he was rather a disciple of the worthy squire Sancho Panza. After talking a good deal, and he talked well, about my position, the possible actions of the courts, and adroitly trying to worm some information out of me about the insurgents, he touched on the object of his visit. He commenced by saying he would give a good deal to be in my position, and that if he were he would soon be a rich man. Having put out this feeler, he remained silent for some time, and as I made no reply he repeated what he had said. My first impulse had been to order the fellow out of my cell, but a second's reflection showed me that such a course might cost me my life; so I resolved to wait developments. Time was what I wanted. No word had yet reached me from any quarter, and if I destroyed all hope of the government turning me to profit, my execution might be ordered immediately. It was necessary to have patience; time was life. These thoughts shot through my mind in the momentary pause of my visitor's conversation. We were alone, for the governor had seized some excuse almost as soon as the introduction had been gone through to retire. This was the first time any one was allowed to speak freely with me without the presence of my jailers. This man who came to tempt me was sharp, keen, and remarkably adroit; he was well informed too, and could talk well. Unlike all the others who had spoken to me, he endeavored to calm my fears as to my possible fate. If nothing further could be proved against me than having visited the insurgent lines as a newspaper correspondent, he said my restoration to liberty would no doubt be prompt; and then he expressed his private opinion that any other course would be an act of barbarism unworthy of the great Spanish nation. Now all these professions of liberality, spoken glibly, and with the manner and air of a man of the world, did not deceive me. If I had been weak enough to pay much attention to such palaver, that false squint-eye, looking at me with a dull, serpent-like regard, would have warned me to beware.

While the captain was speaking I was mentally resolving what course would be the best to pursue. He was angling cleverly, and to have nibbled the bait thrown out might have aroused his suspicions; so when he repeated the assertion about my becoming suddenly rich, I simply told him that I did not see the opportunity of which he spoke, at the same time allowing myself to make a naïve confession that it would not be at all displeasing to me to become rich. When I said this the dull squint-eye actually lighted up and flashed; the captain thought the bait had been swallowed, and was mentally congratulating himself on his victory. So was I, for it was evident the captain had fallen into his own trap, and was about to enable me to fight the authorities with their own weapons. At this moment the governor of the fort appeared and carried off my visitor, who requested me at parting to think seriously over what he had said to me. This was quite unnecessary, and I was glad when the pair were gone, so that I might lay plans for my future action. It was a dangerous game to play with the authorities, but it was of the utmost importance that I should be able to gain time, so as to communicate with Havana. To give the authorities hopes of gaining important information offered the very best means of restraining any precipitate action on their part, and I resolved that this captain, with all his cunning, should help me to gain the delay I wanted. Some bodies politic are wise enough to desire ardently the conversion of enemies into friends, but the military oligarchy that, unfortunately for themselves and for Spain, rule the destinies of Cuba, by their folly, force well-disposed neutrals into a position of hostility. The more that is seen of Spanish government the less one likes it. My experience disenchanted me of many absurd prepossessions in its favor. Under the pretense of fulfilling the law, I was mystified and terrorized while a prisoner in a way that, for the sake of common humanity, it is to be hoped would be impossible in any other country pretending to be civilized.

On my third day in prison there was an encounter with the insurgents somewhere in the neighborhood. This news was withheld from me by order, but it leaked out bit by bit. My first observation that something unusual had happened was founded on the temporary withdrawal of the regular soldiers from the fort, which was occupied for one day by the volunteers. These gentry did not fail to mark their little friendship for me in every way in which they dared to manifest their feelings. It was, therefore, with something like relief that I saw myself again under the guardianship of the regular soldiers, who, having buried their dead comrades, came back to town to await their turn to be slaughtered by the bullet or wasted by disease. It was impossible not to feel sympathy for the poor dupes, who bled and suffered for the exaggerated ambition of others. In the main, they were good-hearted, simple, and stupid, wonderfully obedient, and passably brave. It has always been a puzzle to me why so many men whom nature intended only for minding sheep should have the pretension to don a soldier's uniform, in which they appear as much out of place as would an ass in a lion's hide. But human nature is full of contradictions, and these people, for the most part, while liking the soldier's clothes, dislike infinitely the hardships and dangers of a soldier's life.

I had scarcely been reassured for my immediate safety by the return of the regular troops, when an incident occurred that threw me again into the greatest uncertainty as to my probable fate. On the evening of the fourth day of my incarceration I was preparing to seek forgetfulness of my troubles in sleep when the cell-door suddenly opened, and the corporal of the guard ordered me, in a peremptory tone, "to pass this way."

I was already *en déshabille*, but I obeyed the order of the corporal. On reaching the door, I perceived that there were a number of officers waiting outside, and not wishing to appear bare headed before such gentry, returned to my cell to seek my hat. The corporal conducted me into a small room adjacent to the one I occupied, where three officers, in full uniform, and a civilian were waiting to receive me. It was already dark, and the room was lighted by a small lamp placed on the table before one of the officers, who appeared to perform the duties of a secretary. There was something spectral in the uncertain glimmering of that lamp. The assistants were half in shadow, and the scene full of mystery and gloom. The effect on my imagination was terrific: all the stories of secret murders and assassinations that had been recounted to me from the moment of my arrival in Cuba rushed into my mind, and I saw myself a victim to the vengeance and hatred of the authorities. Military law and military justice had been recently exemplified in the shooting of the Spanish major, so that the prospect of being tried by court-martial called up the picture of the dead soldier lying by the tree-trunk at *El Macho*. It would be difficult, if not absolutely impossible, to give anything like an idea of the feelings of the first moments in which I found myself so suddenly and unexpectedly before a court-martial.

A small, wiry man, nervous in expression and movement, sharp in feature, and evidently possessing more than the average intelligence of Spanish officers, addressed me in Spanish, informing me that he was the fiscal appointed by the Captain-General to examine me as to the causes of my arrest, and that the other persons present were Lieutenant Manuel Lopez, the secretary, and the Comte de San Luis and Señor Miguel Caceres, appointed to assist me as interpreters. This was repeated, for form's sake, by one of the interpreters, in English. In the mean time I had leisure to examine the "court" with more attention. The fiscal wore the uniform of a major, and his quick, impatient action and manner of speaking, as well as his close-cropped, iron-gray hair, gave him more the appearance of a Frenchman than of a Spaniard. Neither of the interpreters spoke English very fluently, or understood it very profoundly, although the civilian, who was the Alcalde of Manzanillo, informed me that he had been seven years in the United States.

This person deserves more than a passing notice. Much above the ordinary size, he belongs to that class of giants who devote their immense physical strength to the manly employment of selling ribbons, pins, and matters of that nature. His whole person conveyed an idea of the nobility of soul naturally associated with his elevated pursuit. He had been prosperous in life—that was in evidence—and if things continue in the same road for many years, he may hope one day to rival the celebrated Daniel Lambert. Such is the advantage of a quiet, if not a very clear, conscience. Over a fat, round face of unusual pallor plays a constant angelic smile, typical of innocence and goodness of heart. Notwithstanding these personal advantages, this good man fell under the suspicion of the authorities as not having been able to resist the temptation to turn an honest penny by selling supplies to the insurgents at a good profit. His connections were suspicious, although Old Spain had the honor of giving birth to this prosperous and simpering alcalde. Somehow the suspicions never went to proof, and, as is usual in this changeable clime, the suspected rebel of one day became the devoted patriot of the next. It appeared to this worthy that my arrest offered an easy and safe way of exhibiting his devotion to the Spanish cause; and, during my various examinations before the fiscal, he on all occasions endeavored to give the most unfavorable interpretations to what I said, in order to prove his patriotism. As soon as this smiling personage had concluded speaking, I informed the fiscal that I refused to take any part in the proceedings until my Consul was present.

This objection seemed to take them somewhat by surprise; but it was admitted, the fiscal informing me that the presence of my Consul could not be claimed as a right, but that, in order to give me more confidence in the good faith of the tribunal, he would notify the Consul to be present in the morning. When the session came to an end I felt relieved. The impression made on my mind by the whole proceeding was most unfavorable.

All the guarantees that we are accustomed to look for in a court of law were absent. Confined in a fort, surrounded by soldiers, no witnesses allowed to be present, the refusal of liberty of speech, the semigloom of the room, and the secrecy of the proceedings, all tended to recall memories of the barbarous ages. It would have been easy to imagine one's self before the judges of the Inquisition—there was only need to introduce the rack, and to change the uniform of the soldier for the frock of the priest. Nor am I satisfied that there were not more guarantees for the life and liberty of an accused man in the courts of the Inquisition than are afforded by the military courts-martial of the nineteenth century.

Next morning the court assembled early, Mr. Lauten, the Vice-Consul, being present. After the form of opening the court, I was asked my name, country, age, and religion. To this series of questions I replied by asking who were the persons that made the inquiry. This information having been given, I asked whether the tribunal was military or civil in its character. The fiscal answered that it was military. I then, in the presence of the British Vice-Consul, refused, as the subject of an independent state, to acknowledge the jurisdiction of a military court. I was proceeding to offer further reasons, in a short speech which I had sketched out in the morning, when I was suddenly stopped by the fiscal, who informed me that I was to answer categorically his questions, and not to enter into any inconvenient discussions. He then read for me a portion of some regulations, in which he warned me that my conduct would be prejudicial in case I continued to deny the authority of the court.

Notwithstanding this warning I persisted in my refusal, and after a number of formalities the court adjourned, leaving me in doubt as to what course would be pursued in my regard. One advantage derived from these legal proceedings was the removal of absolute prohibition to communicate with the outer world. Permission was given to renew my wardrobe, which was sadly in need of renovation.

The night of my refusal to acknowledge the military court I was alarmed by the frightful noise made by the soldiers after I went to bed; truly the thought came to me that my last hour had arrived, and, in order to receive the expected notification of my execution with becoming dignity, I got up and dressed myself. The tramp of soldiers, the rattle of grounding arms, and the clanging of swords on the paved court continued for a long time, during which I suffered the most terrible suspense. No reply had come to my telegrams or letters, though five days had passed, and I felt assured that if the news of my arrest had been communicated to the British Consul-General, or the representative of the *Herald* in Havana, that I would not have been left without some word. It was only natural that my first fears should return with renewed force. The temptation to go to the door to learn the cause of the unusual movement was very great; but, unwilling to give to my jailers the satisfaction of witnessing my anxiety, I laid down on the bed to wait the result. There the idea of being shot, without being able to communicate with my friends, slaughtered like a sheep without the power or the means of resistance, caused me to pass hours of bitter anguish.

How I cursed my foolish confidence in the honor and faith of Spanish officials! I would have given all I possessed in the world to be a hundred yards from the Spanish outposts with a rifle in my hands.

One of the least pleasurable subjects for reflection is a military execution, when one has reason to fear that he may be the central figure in the picture that presents itself to the mind. Next to being shot, the least enjoyable thing that I know is to imagine that one may be a subject for target practice; but this is one of those truths that can only be known to a select few who have the distinction to pass through the experience and survive it. Still, when one finds himself exposed to this risk, although it is an unpleasant subject—or rather because it is so—the mind of the unfortunate obstinately centers in all the details of the scene, which is presented to the imagination with terrible distinctness.

In my case, this tendency was aggravated by the remembrance of the trial and execution of the Spanish major. The shock of that event had been severe. It was not the first death by bullets among the insurgents during my stay with them; but it was the one that made me feel most keenly the terrible state of society into which I had been thrown. All my previous ideas of the sanctity of life and the protection of the law were annihilated, and I had come to recognize that force was the only law which could impose respect for right or life in this island of Cuba. With these impressions fresh and vivid in my mind, it is not surprising that I fell asleep wondering why men who are shot fall forward, and if I should furnish an exception to this general rule.

Next morning, having somewhat recovered from the depression of spirits in which I had been for some days, I wrote a letter to the Vice-Consul, asking him to see the fiscal and request him to suspend further proceedings until a reply came to a telegram which I desired to be sent to Mr. Dunlop, the British Consul-General in Cuba, asking that functionary to obtain my removal to Havana for trial. The fiscal sent me back word that he would await the reply, and nothing was done till next day, when the court reassembled, although no reply had been received to my telegram. There is no certainty that this telegram was delivered, as no acknowledgment of its receipt ever reached me, either by telegraph or mail.

The court reassembled on the 6th of April, and I was surprised to find that Mr. Lauten, the British Vice-Consul, appeared as a witness in the case. I wished to protest, but was ordered to remain silent, and the fiscal further forbade any communication between me and the representative of my government. The Vice-Consul, under protest, then recognized the packet of papers which I had delivered to him as my property, and the fiscal, in a theatrical fashion, broke the cover, saying that if the English government protested, he, as judge, would assume the responsibility of his act. It was difficult to refrain from laughing at the figure cut by this official while, like a modern Ajax, he was defying the British thunder. In the packet were found three note-books, filled with information concerning the state of Cuba, a letter from Carlos Manuel de Cespedes, and one from Fornaris y Cespedes, one of the secretaries of the Cuban Camara, or Congress, addressed to Mr. Bennett, a list of women and children whom the insurgents alleged to have been killed by the Spaniards in cold blood, and some unimportant private papers. These made up the contents of the packet. As it was necessary to have the notes translated into Spanish, in order to prepare the charges against me, the court adjourned, and I was left in peace to ruminate over the beauties of Spanish justice.

Two or three days elapsed before the Spanish Mephistopheles returned to the charge. In the mean time I had arranged in my own mind a course of action which would enable me to gain time without committing myself to any definite policy with regard to the government. It consisted in expressing in general terms my absolutely neutral position between the belligerents, and my willingness to do anything consistent with honor to bring the struggle to a close. Beyond this I was resolved only to listen to what the agents of the government had to say, and endeavor to obtain written proofs of any dishonorable propositions that might be made to me. In the interval of the captain's visit the accused forger had been put back into my cell, and I was curious to know how he was to be disposed of in the event of any further propositions. The conduct of the governor would also furnish me with a clue as to whether or not the propositions were advanced on authority. When the moment came for the captain's visit the soldier was taken out of the cell, and sent to perform some duty outside. As he passed out, he looked at me intelligently, and muttered, "Don't trust him." The soldier's interest in me was due to certain sums of money which I gave him from a feeling of compassion, as the poor fellow was in a wretched state when I arrived.

As soon as my visitor was seated, he opened the business by asking me if I had thought on what he had said to me.

In reply I laughed, and told him that I had been puzzling my head how to become rich, but had not been able to solve the problem to my satisfaction.

This treatment of the subject rather nettled him, and he remarked that he thought I was too intelligent a man not to have perfectly understood him.

To this compliment I merely bowed, and reminded him that though I was able to follow his main argument, yet, not being very well acquainted with the Spanish language, that unless statements were put very clearly and very plainly, it was difficult for me to seize their exact meaning.

The captain fidgeted a little at this answer, and looked at me very attentively with the squint-eye, while the straight one was directed out of the window, but, after a little effort, came directly to the point. "The government," he said, "is most anxious to put an end to the war, and would be willing to make almost any sacrifice to this end. Now, you must be possessed of most valuable information; the insurgents have no doubt acquainted you with their plans, and, if you would consent to aid the government, there is no doubt but that you could render most important service." He then paused.

While he spoke I lay back in my chair, and looked at him straight in the face, making a strong effort to conceal all trace of the indignation I naturally felt at the treason proposed. But when a man is playing with his life as the stake it is wonderful how cool and self-contained he can be. The captain had not been as explicit as I wanted him to be, and, though the aim of his proposition was perfectly clear, it was my intention to understand nothing which was not stated in so many words. As my tempter paused for some reply, and showed no disposition to proceed, I simply remarked "that I was not unfriendly to the government, and, if there was anything which I could honorably do to bring the war to a close, I should be most happy to do it, but that I feared the government attached too much importance to my relations with the insurgents."

This parry threw the captain a little off his guard, and he hastened to assure me that whatever relations I might have held with the insurgents would be no obstacle, as the government was prepared to condone any infraction of the laws if "important services" were rendered by me.

I replied coldly, that "not having violated any laws, and not recognizing any right on the part of the Spanish government to punish me, there was nothing to condone, and no reason to purchase pardon. And that the first condition to opening any serious negotiations should be my restoration to liberty."

"Let us not discuss the question of the legality of your detention," was his reply; "in view of the serious propositions I am prepared to make to you, the question whether you have broken our laws or not is of secondary importance. You can, I am sure, render services of the utmost importance, services that the government would not hesitate to repay with a quarter, or even half a million of dollars. I do not conceal from you that I have a personal interest in the success of the scheme, and that I too hope to gain a large fortune if we are successful in what I am about to propose." As he spoke his haggard-looking face lighted up with enthusiasm, as in imagination he saw the golden treasure within his grasp. "Would you not like to gain two hundred and fifty thousand dollars, or perhaps half a million?"

"Yes, very much, if I could see the way to do so honorably," was my answer.

"You are a foreigner," he continued, "and therefore can have no feeling for either party, except what may spring from self-interest. It can make no difference to you who rules in Cuba. The expenses of the war are very great, and the government is willing to give a large reward to anyone who should aid in bringing the struggle to an end. The quickest way to do so would be by the capture or death of Cespedes, and such other of the prominent leaders as could be reached. The Spanish law does not allow a price to be set on even a rebel's head by the government, but the Casino Español of Havana has offered a reward of two hundred thousand dollars to be paid to whoever secures the capture or death of Cespedes. The government would add at least as much more if the capture of Cespedes could be effected."

Here was a chance to become rich, and infamous! The captain glowed with enthusiasm, and concluded by asking me, with nervous anxiety, what I thought of the proposition.

I told him it was magnificent. Half a million dollars was a prize worth working for, and after all it might not be so difficult to win as it appeared.

Mephistopheles, overjoyed at this answer, complimented me on my good sense, assured me that the prison-doors would soon fly open, and that both of us would leave Cuba rich. If the man could have read my heart he would not have liked much to trust himself, even for a moment, out of the Spanish dominions in my society. However, it was necessary to play so dangerous a rôle carefully, and I had therefore to seem to share something of the fellow's enthusiasm. "There was only needed now some act on my part to give the authorities in Havana confidence in the sincerity of my desire to help them," the captain said; "for instance, to point out the secret agents of the Cubans in Santiago de Cuba and Manzanillo. That of itself would be looked on as a most important service, and would be liberally rewarded."

This "illustrious sword" talked of selling men's blood as coolly as though it were an article of grocery to be weighed and measured, at so much an ounce. I contented myself with saying that the agents were unknown to me, but that if it were otherwise, I would not betray them; as my position in life rendered scoundrelism, on a small scale, unprofitable. The betrayal of Cespedes would of course be an act of treachery, but its importance, and the largeness of the reward, redeemed it from vulgarity, while the half-million would act as an efficient balm to my wounded conscience.

The captain was not pleased at this resolution. He was inwardly convinced that I knew very well who were *laborantes* and who were not; but was so blinded at the prospect of capturing Cespedes by my aid that he saw in my refusal to betray the men who had placed their lives in my hands, only a disinclination on my part to admit any compromising connection with the insurgents. It never seemed to strike him that there are men who hold their honor and good name above price, and that even millions of dollars would not tempt them to imbrue their hands traitorously in a fellow-being's blood. He informed me that he had already written to one of the chiefs of the Casino Español, who would inform the Captain-General of his project, and that no doubt the Captain-General would ratify the offer that he—the captain—had made on behalf of the government.

The fiscal had been obliged to leave his battalion in order to take charge of my case, and was very anxious to finish the affair up. In his mind my fate was sealed, and, as I had to be shot, in his opinion the sooner it was done the better. He told me that the affair would only last a few days, as the proofs against me were very clear. It was evident that unless the authorities at Havana interfered I should be shot, and as no word had reached me up to this time from any quarter, my position appeared to me very critical. In a few days, however, an incident occurred which showed that my plan for gaining time had been successful. The court martial was only waiting for the translation of my papers to proceed to try me for "*infidencia,*" or high treason, but owing to some cause the translators suddenly stopped work, so that, in fact, the proceedings were suspended. The Captain-General had ordered them to go slowly!

The first answer to any of my communications came from the consulate at Santiago de Cuba, where the news of my arrest had been received five days after the first telegram. This is a sample of the freedom of communication that was permitted me, and the ideas of justice and fair play entertained by the people in whose hands I so confidingly placed myself.

On the 8th of April I was again brought out of my cell at the command of authority, to take part in a most disgraceful farce. Up to this date I feared the vengeance of the authorities, but did not believe them capable of descending to contemptible means to excuse their action against me. When my cell-door opened I saw a number of civilians ranged in the court-way, and while I was puzzling my brain to imagine what these people had to do with me, the fiscal told me to take off my hat, and afterwards my coat. Although very much surprised and puzzled, I obeyed. A hat and coat belonging to another man were then handed me to put on. Then the fiscal ordered me to place myself among the civilians and await the result. I did so; and an instant after the door of the room next my cell was opened carefully, as if to allow the issue of a wild animal. Instead of a wild beast, a young colored girl came out, and was immediately requested by the fiscal to recognize the "Englishman whom she had seen with Cespedes in the camp of Panchulucas, in the district of Cuba." The whole import of the farce was at once evident. Never in the girl's life had she seen me with Cespedes, for I had neither been to Panchulucas, nor had I seen Cespedes in that district of Cuba. However, it was very easy to recognize me. For some days before my attention had been drawn to an unusual concourse of colored visitors in the fort, and even if this had no influence, it is very easy to pick out an Irishman from any number of Cuban civilians; besides, in their great hurry, I was placed in line with my slippers and blue flannel trowsers, which, taken together with the Cuban hat and a white coat, must have presented a costume capable of attracting the attention of even an ignorant negro. Three times the farce of changing portions of my costume was gone through, and, in order to make assurance doubly sure, one of the officials entered the room where the girl was confined each time that a slight change of costume was effected; not, of course, with the object of informing her of the change in case she should be sufficiently stupid not to know me again—a stupidity so great that it passes belief. I requested to be spared this farce, but the fiscal informed me that it was only a formality. This was not difficult to believe, because so much as I knew of Spanish legal proceedings were little more than the merest formalities.

This incident, however, had considerable influence in determining me to recognize the military court, in order to hasten the proceedings. The conviction was forced upon me that I was completely in the power of the authorities, because, if they could find a person willing to swear that I had been in a point where I never set my foot, it was evident they could find others willing to swear whatever they thought pleasing to the authorities. Under such a system no man's life could be considered safe, and I thought the best thing to be done was to have the matter settled before too many aspirants to the distinction of perjury could have time to present themselves. I, therefore, made a pretty general statement, admitting that, as the *Herald* correspondent, I had entered the insurgent lines, visited the camp of Calisto Garcia, Modesto Diaz, and other chiefs, as well as "the residence of the republic, and its occupant, Carlos Manuel de Cespedes."

While lying in Fort Gerona, at Manzanillo, I had some opportunity of judging for myself the truth about the charges of corruption and dishonesty among the official class in Cuba. The American Vice-Consul, poor Roca, was a Spaniard who had lived many years in America, but whose faith in the incorruptibility of mankind appears not to have been strengthened by his residence in the great republic. I had been in prison some time before Roca visited me, but when he did come he interested himself earnestly in my affairs. According to his notion, which he assured me was based on an intimate knowledge of the official character, my case had been sadly mismanaged. Telegraphing to consuls-general, in his estimation, was all humbug, and in this he was certainly right; the proper way was to approach delicately the people having charge of the case, and see if they could not be influenced, or, in plain English, bribed. Now, it was not my intention to buy myself out of the scrape, but as Roca insisted on the feasibility of the transaction, he was authorized from curiosity to make the approach. He did so, skillfully, and the person addressed attempted next day to borrow a hundred and seventy dollars from my agent; but as my mind was made up not to give a cent, the borrowing did not take place. Still, the negotiations were by no means broken off, and had it not been for the sad death of poor Roca within a few days, some very interesting insight into the administration of Spanish justice might have been obtained. The baited hook thrown was at once nibbled, and there is little doubt that if the angling had continued some large fish would have been landed. Unfortunately, poor Roca went out on the bay in a boat, which upset, and he was eaten by the sharks the moment he fell overboard, as well as another of his companions. This unfortunate accident interrupted the pending negotiations, which, for want of delicate and experienced hands to guide them, were not resumed.

From the leaf-covered huts of the Mambi-Land to the calaboose of Fort Gerona, what a change! Hard as was my life among the Mambis, it had one attraction which is never thoroughly appreciated until we have ceased to enjoy it—liberty. In the midst of the so-called bandits and escaped negroes my person and my profession were sacred, and I was as free as the circumstances would permit. Indeed, the only restraint of which I could complain was imposed by nature. On all sides the luxuriant forests tempted the enterprising spirit to wander amid tropical glories, but the amusement could only be enjoyed by those who had the benefit of a forest education. Although I had the feeling of liberty in its wildest sense, the physical obstacles kept me in some sort a prisoner during my stay in Cuba Libre; but at least the moral atmosphere which I breathed was redolent of freedom. All that was now changed: the blue skies and the ever-changing shadows among the trees, the soft forest twilights, and the gorgeous noon-day glories had vanished, and I had to content myself with gazing on four white walls, and console myself with an occasional glimpse of Heaven's vault caught through envious prison bars.

After a few days' absence my forger friend had been restored to me; and, in truth, there are doubts in my mind if he was not the honestest companion Fort Gerona could afford me. There were other rooms vacant where the accommodation was better, as well as the air, and during the first days there was evidence of a desire or intention on the part of the governor to place me in better quarters; but, as no proposition of a reciprocal nature was made on my part, nothing was done, and I remained mured up in the calaboose during my imprisonment at Manzanillo. My cell was an oblong room, twenty feet by twelve. The iron bars of the door and window gave it somewhat the appearance of the cage of a wild beast in a zoological garden. A writing-table, on which were placed a few bottles doing service as candlesticks, some books and a lot of writing-paper scattered about, with a few chairs, formed the principal furniture of the place. Two wooden benches, looking very old and very dirty, and two small, mean-looking boxes, and some clothes hanging from nails in the wall, completed the picture. The appearance of the room was exceedingly wretched and depressing, and it would have been absolutely intolerable only for a large window opening out on the country, through which glimpses of the trees and fields and sea were caught. The floor was full of holes—almost in the center the brick pavement was broken and the earth visible. Numbers of rats were in the habit of sallying out of these holes in search of food, and sometimes half a dozen might be seen running fearlessly about the room. Sometimes they became so enterprising as to attempt to carry off my dinner from before me; but it was necessary to draw the line somewhere, and I objected to too close a familiarity. My temper was somewhat ruffled by close confinement, subject to the most annoying kind of espionage. The sentinel at my door could see into the room, and he never absented himself for an instant, night or day. If I moved, his vigilance was aroused; and if I looked in his direction, two inquisitive and not over-friendly eyes were fixed on me. At night a light was kept constantly burning in my cell, and every half-hour the sentry was changed, so that my sleep was constantly broken; when the wind blew out the little lamp, the corporal of the guard was at once called to light it, and when for a moment I left the room, three men, with loaded muskets, followed at my heels. All this was very ridiculous, but it was not the less annoying. To judge from the way the authorities conducted themselves in my regard, one might have imagined me to be some famous warrior, upon whose safe custody depended the safety of Spain. And this burlesque was carried on with all the pompous gravity of the Spanish character.

The stage effect was heightened by the fact that the subordinate actors were entirely in earnest, for it was the firm conviction of the soldiers guarding me that I was to be disposed of by four bullets, homeopathically administered. The atmosphere created around me by this impression was rendered still more unpleasant and unsafe by the presence of the insurgents in the immediate neighborhood of the town. Their operations furnished constant distraction, and from time to time I experienced what the French call an emotion. The dullness of the days was frequently relieved by a sudden outburst of rifle-music, heard in the distance. This was only an exchange of compliments between the outposts, and for the most part had nothing serious in it. Still, as there was no knowing what might have been the gravity of the situation, anything like *ennui* was quite impossible. The enterprises of the insurgents in this district were by no means confined to bootless skirmishing. From my cell-window I saw the sky lighted up by the conflagration of four important estates, which were reduced to ashes, and the slaves and employés either scattered or carried off. Report stated that most of the armed volunteers joined the insurgents without any scruple. One night the largest estate in the immediate outskirts of the town was destroyed, as well as a smaller one a little farther off. The conflagration could be seen perfectly from my cell. Both estates were completely destroyed. The nearest was within cannon-shot of the fort, and the forms of the men passing before the fire were distinctly visible. Preparations were made in the fort to resist attack. The guns were hauled about in a way which led me to expect at every moment a discharge, but nothing was done. In town everyone was in a state of panic, as the advance of the enemy was momentarily expected. No efforts were made by the troops to save the property, or to punish the insurgents, who, having completed their work, retired tranquilly to their camps in the mountains. Only two important estates remained in the neighborhood of the town after these operations, and though they were strongly fortified, fears were entertained that they would not escape the fate of the others. Most of these *ingenios* had been burned down before and rebuilt; the loss was consequently very heavy. The wide-spread disaffection of the Cuban volunteers in this district was also a source of great difficulty to the authorities. In fact, they did not know whom to trust. The desertion of a part of the garrison of Congo, and the whole of the encampment of Punta Piedra, was followed by evidences of insubordination in several other encampments. Some weeks after my arrest, forty persons, men, women, and children, were brought to Manzanillo, prisoners from Yara. They were captured in the very act of going over to the insurgents. A Spanish officer told me that unpleasant symptoms of the same nature had appeared in other districts. Although some small reinforcements arrived during my detention, the garrison did not feel strong enough to take care of the town and at the same time send forces in pursuit of the enemy. The safety of the town is naturally considered of the greatest importance, and up to the present day the insurgents have maintained a pretty strict blockade, cutting off all communications on the land side with the town.

Well-nigh a month had elapsed, and still the proceeding against me dragged on. My evil genius was unceasing in his attentions and in his exhortations to betray the confidence that had been reposed in me. As I showed no disposition, however, to comply with the wishes of the authorities, they began to perceive that I had only been duping them. This suspicion aroused their ferocity, and my treatment in prison began to be marked by increasing severity and brutality. As they could not buy me, they were resolved to see if terror could not accomplish what money had failed to do. Every officer who mounted guard altered my *status* at his good pleasure. I was searched for files and arms; my food was detained by the guard under pretense of examining it, until it was cold, and the sentries were ordered to allow no one to approach me without the permission of the officer of the guard. One night a soldier mad drunk was thrown into my cell, as the captain of the guard said he was afraid he might kill some of the soldiers if kept in the guardhouse. The infuriate ruffian no sooner found himself in my cell than he grabbed at some heavy stone bottles, which he was about to throw, when my forger companion seized him, and called the guard to remove the madman. Mephistopheles had witnessed the outrage, and having more common sense than the captain of the guard, spoke to that worthy, and showed him he had made a mistake; so the soldier was removed and tied to a cannon, where he made night hideous with his blasphemies.

Two most important events happened about this time: a letter came from the Captain-General to Mephistopheles, approving of what he had done, and authorizing him to act as the agent of the government; and the British gunboat Plover had steamed into port to afford me the protection to which as a British subject I was entitled. The letter was signed by the chief of the staff of General Pieltain, the *republican* Captain-General, and was shown to me by this Spaniard, who urged me to embrace the opportunity of making my fortune.* The exhortation, however, failed to produce any enthusiasm, and I contented myself with repeating I would listen to

---

*Cándido Pieltan replaced Francisco Ceballos as captain general on 26 March 1873, following the declaration of the First Spanish Republic the month prior.

no propositions until set at liberty; that while quite willing to help them to put an end to the war, if I could do so honorably, it was necessary for the government to tell me clearly and explicitly what they wanted; but before everything it was necessary that I should be set at liberty, in order that there could be no possible misrepresentation as to my motives in carrying on these negotiations. I wrote a letter to Mr. Bennett, strictly private and confidential, in which the transaction was explained. That letter was sent by a special and trustworthy messenger from Manzanillo early in May, and arrived safely. Had it fallen into the hands of the authorities, it is probable I should have remained in the Ever-Faithful Isle until summoned away by the last trumpet. When the infamous letter of the chief of the staff arrived, Mephistopheles ceaselessly urged me to give ever such a little piece of information which would lead to the arrest of the agent in Manzanillo. To have obtained a clue that would enable the government to fix on a victim through whom to strike terror almost any conditions would have been granted, but, as I steadily insisted that I did not know the Manzanillian agent, even Mephistopheles began to understand that there were men who would not barter their honor for wealth, or even to save their lives. It was at this point that terrorism began to assume most dangerous proportions, and culminated by the placing of a soldier in my cell at night, with orders to bayonet me should I attempt to rise; this gave the soldier *carte blanche,* for if any ruffian should take into his head to assassinate me at night, he would have the excuse that I attempted to rise. The object of this conduct, however, viewed by the light of the secret history, becomes plain and obvious enough. As the authorities could not buy me, they thought to terrify me into betraying the men who had trusted me. Knowing the nature and object of this terrorism, my sufferings at this period can well be understood. It is not a pleasant matter to go nightly to sleep with the consciousness that one may wake up in another world, and what I had seen of my jailers gave me good reason to look on them as men capable of committing any crime. Assassination by bullet, knife, and poison have notoriously marked the progress of this struggle. My authorities on this point cannot be brought into question, for men among the Spaniards have confessed to me that poison was put in their presence in jars of wine which were to be abandoned to the insurgents, in the hope of killing off by this means Modesto Diaz; and I have seen the scars of terrible wounds inflicted on one officer when his brother and himself were left for dead, by the machetes of Spanish assassins; fortunately, the arrival of Commander Hippisly and the British gunboat Plover afforded me unlooked-for protection—the gallant commander's decided action convinced the authorities that it would be dangerous to go too far. Had he received the support and encouragement which he deserved from the unworthy representatives of the British Empire at Havana no doubt my troubles would have been brought to an end at this period; but the traders of Havana were looking after their own interest, and not after my safety or the dignity of their country. Crawford, if not a slave-owner himself, though possibly he is, has his interests so wound up with theirs that for all practical purposes he is one of the black band.* It was therefore natural that he should take upon himself to instruct Mr. Lauten, a German subject, to order the commander of a British war-vessel not to interfere with my business. Commander Hippisly naturally told this shopkeeper to go to the devil; and had this pretty specimen of an English Consul been within hail, he would have been treated to a bath that would have been more instructive than agreeable. At this juncture orders came for my removal to Santiago de Cuba, directed not so much in kindness or consideration for me as in fear of Commander Hippisly. Manzanillo is by no means a strong place, and the authorities were in constant dread lest the energetic commander should take me out by force; the danger of a conflict at Manzanillo was increased by the presence of the Cuban forces, who were so close that their firing could be heard on many occasions. It was feared that a conflict with the Plover would encourage the insurgents to assault the town, and probably lead to a revolt of the people within, ending in a complete massacre of the Spanish garrison.

20   Prison Experience

THE ILL treatment to which I was subjected at first was due to an impression which somehow had gone abroad that the British government would not interfere in my behalf. This idea was, however, soon dissipated by the timely arrival of the British gunboat "Plover." Commander Hippisly immediately demanded information as to the cause of my arrest, and protested energetically against my being detained in the

---

*For more on British Vice Consul John V. Crawford, see introduction, xxxvii–xxxviii.

calaboose, but was answered evasively. The tone of the people about me soon changed, however, when they saw the attention paid me by the officers of the Plover, and the really warm interest they took in my wellbeing. Indeed, over-confidence in their certain hold on me gave way to a panic fear that the Plover meant to take me out of Fort Gerona by force.

The immediate result was a closer surveillance than ever over my movements, which led to some unpleasant incidents. These inconveniences were, however, more than counterbalanced by the marked respect with which I was treated, and which contrasted so very strongly with the cavalier way in which my demands for better treatment had been received when I was looked on as a mere wanderer, without any strong government to protect me.

The rage of the Spanish officials was in part turned away from me to the Plover, which had appeared so inopportunely to interfere with their schemes. It had been more than once hinted to me that my claim to be removed from Manzanillo was inadmissible, and that the court-martial would proceed with the farce of trying me without paying any heed to my protests or my objections. It was never the intention or desire of the volunteer party to allow me a fair trial, but being a foreigner, it was necessary to preserve some appearance of legality in the measures adopted against me. Only the direct interference of the Captain-General, under orders from Señor Castelar, prevented my condemnation to death. The fiscal charged with the preparations of my *sumario* allowed himself to be carried away by his enthusiastic patriotism, and it was well known that the penalty of death had been demanded against me.

On the 6th of May, 1873, the fiscal, or military judge, Major Marangez, unexpectedly visited me in my cell at Manzanillo. He informed me that orders had been given by the general at Santiago de Cuba for my translation to that town. The notice, though abrupt, was most welcome, for I longed to leave the stink and fanaticism of Manzanillo behind me. As the officers of the Plover had been very kind to me, I requested permission to inform them, and also the Vice-Consul, of the voyage I was about to take; but the fiscal interrupted me with a negative wave of his hand, informing me at the same time that I was *incomunicado,* and could communicate with no one—absolutely no one. At the same time the legal major pledged his word of honor that I should be conducted safely to Santiago de Cuba; the reason of this promise being a doubt which he suspected to exist in my mind lest the soldiers should play what is known in Cuba as "the foraging trick," by which inconvenient people are cleared off the track. However, the word of the major reassured me very little, for my experience of Spanish promises was not such as would allow me to place any very implicit faith in the most solemn vow, even of an archbishop. A request to write letters to be delivered after my departure was likewise refused, but this piece of official impertinence made me resolve to test the fiscal's right in the matter. I wrote letters to the Vice-Consul and Commander Hippisly, intrusting them to the governor of the fort, who promised to deliver them in the morning. Between ten and eleven o'clock at night the fiscal came again, and I was roused out of a sound sleep to go on board the steamer for Cuba. At this point I was informed that, as a matter of precaution, it was thought necessary to pinion me. Knowing the chivalrous character of the people with whom I had to do, I submitted to this outrage, simply informing the major that, being his prisoner, he could dispose of me as he thought fit. A sergeant then advanced with a long rope, with which he bound my arms tightly above the elbows, drawing them back with force. The rope was wound round my arms many times, and so tightly that for many days my arms bore the marks of the bruises. As soon as the tying up was completed, I set out, surrounded by some sixteen soldiers, who were ordered to load their arms, and three "illustrious swords," a powerful soldier holding on to the end of the rope in order to make assurance doubly sure.

In this order we left Fort Gerona, and directed our footsteps towards the town, which lay at our feet, bathed in a flood of silver light, the square, flat-roofed houses looking like checkered patches of light and shadow in the calm moonbeams. Whether the pleasure of quitting my prison affected my judgment I cannot say, but the night seemed to me one of the most beautiful I had ever witnessed. It was owing to this fact, no doubt, that many groups still loitered in the streets and on the doorsteps, although the hour of midnight was fast approaching, when, under ordinary circumstances, a Cuban town is as silent and deserted as a graveyard. The party on reaching the town carefully avoided the more populous streets, and marched zigzag through the blocks, so as to reach the steamer, which was moored at the farthest outlying wharf from the center of the town. Our passage had created a subdued sensation among such of the inhabitants as had not retired to rest. They looked on me, no doubt, as "one more unfortunate" going to his doom; and in truth there were moments when I doubted whether or not my destination was the one announced. However, all disquietude on this point was soon set at rest by our debouching at the head of the wharf, and our arrival, a few minutes later, on board one of the South Coast steamers. Here I had the honor of being stared at by some hundreds of passengers, idlers, and porters, who evidently had something of the feeling of curiosity in my regard that a cockney out for a holiday at the Zoo experiences at the sight of a caged wild animal. It is well that umbrellas are scarce in these regions, or I am certain that some inquiring genius would have poked me in the ribs to see if I would not growl or show my teeth. After about ten minutes of this open-mouthed examination, which was indulged in with just as little delicacy as though I were a wild animal rather than a man, the fiscal conducted me to a cabin, and informed me that I might go to bed if I liked; but this was sarcastic, as, even if I had liked, the manner in which I was pinioned precluded the possibility of my doing so. Under these circumstances, I inquired when my guardians intended to take the cords off, as it was impossible to go to bed under existing conditions. The fiscal replied that the steamer would not leave for some hours, and that the twenty armed men who were guarding me did not think it safe to loosen my hands until we had left the harbor. With this pleasing prospect before me, I sat down to await the good will and pleasure of my amiable guardians, consoling myself with reflecting on the honor, the generosity, and chivalric valor of the Spanish nation. After a short time the fiscal became ashamed of himself, and orders were given to take off the rope, so that I might go to bed, with orders, however, to leave the door open, so that the sentry could keep me in view all night.

The following afternoon we arrived in the bay of Santiago de Cuba, where the steamer was overhauled by a police-boat with the object of carrying me to the Castillo del Morro, which is situated on a bold headland at the mouth of the harbor, a most romantic-looking old edifice, that in old times must have been a formidable defense, but nowadays, like most Spanish glory, is a subject for the antiquary. A quarter of an hour's rowing from the point where I was taken off the steamer brought us to a small cove lying between the Morro and the battery of the Estrella. We were allowed to approach without being challenged, and it was only when the noise of the boat grating on the beach called the attention of the colored sentinel to our presence that any notice was taken of us, and even then not much. Full twenty minutes were occupied in toiling up the winding path that leads to the citadel that crowns the works. After crossing a heavy-looking drawbridge, about which other groups of lazy, dirty-looking colored troops were lounging, who straightened themselves up as well as they could to salute his mightiness, the major who had me in charge, I found myself passing through a series of arched passages, dim and low-vaulted, into a dingy-looking courtyard, and, climbing flights of time-eaten stone steps, which seemed to crumble beneath the tread of the venturesome passenger, at last I found myself ushered into a lofty casemate, completely empty, but which differed from the rest of the fortress in looking clean, if somewhat cheerless. Everything about the Morro would have delighted an artist's eye, and a wandering member of that peculiar tribe might have enjoyed, in all its fullness, "the poetry of dirt" and the sentiment of decay. The swarthy faces of the soldiers, their almost fantastic raggedness, the sheen of arms, and the clanging of chains as some unfortunate convict hobbled across the courtyard, would have supplied inexhaustible food for brush and pencil, if one were at liberty and could enjoy these sights from a strictly artistic point of view; but seen through a grated hole, some nine inches square, in one's cell-door, the most romantic scenes quite lose their interest.

While I was discussing in my own mind how I should dispose of myself, the door of my cell opened to allow the entrance of a canteen-keeper, who wished to know if I desired to eat something, expressing his regret at the same time that there was nothing to be had but some bread and preserved mutton, seasoned with canteen wine. The prospect was not very inviting, but it was necessary to eat, so I told him to furnish the luxurious repast, at the same time requesting that he would send me a chair and table until such time as I could procure furniture from Santiago de Cuba. Notwithstanding a long fast and excellent good will, the preserved mutton was too much for me, and I was obliged to content myself with a cup of coffee and dry bread until morning. While I was still discussing this humble fare some convicts arrived from Santiago de Cuba with chairs, a table, and a bed, sent to me by the military administrators, by order of General Burriel, who afterward became notorious through the *Virginius* massacre, so that I found myself in comparatively comfortable quarters.* Here, in addition to being free from the obsession of my evil spirit, Mephistopheles, I had the advantage of better air and better accommodations. As the garrison was permanent, I was freed from the capricious imprisonment from which I had suffered a good deal of annoyance. My window at Napoles, which is the title of the battery where my casemate was built, commanded a beautiful view of the bay of Santiago, and the mountains beyond, so that I could amuse myself trying to trace the course of my night march over these mountains some months previously. When I had been about a fortnight in the Morro, permission was given to me to promenade for two hours daily, with the right of descending to Santa Barbara, from which the view of sea and land is one of the most magnificent in the world. It was just such a spot as one would choose to dream his life away in, if

---

*See introduction, note 35.

its beauty and charm were not destroyed by the consciousness of the loss of freedom, without which the loveliest scenes are deserts to the heart.

During my stay in this fort more consideration was shown to me than at any other point. This was chiefly due to the warm interest taken in my welfare by the American, English, and French Consuls, supported by the presence of the Plover, whose commander had put to sea as soon as he had heard of my abduction from Gerona. The mystery attending my removal was due to fears entertained by the authorities lest the commander of the Plover should attempt to release me by force. On this account they did not hesitate to slight the British commander in a most marked manner; indeed, the indifference of the Spaniards to the representations and protests of England in this affair has been most marked, at times bordering closely on contempt. An instance of this occurred at Santiago de Cuba, where Commander Hippisly paid the authorities two visits, neither of which was returned until the commander telegraphed the fact to the commodore at Jamaica, when the governor sent one of his aids-de-camp to go through the form of acknowledging the visit. On another occasion, in obedience to instructions received from Jamaica, Commander Hippisly asked to be informed of the date of my trial and the constitution of the court. After some days he received a reply from the governor stating that he would find the required information in the newspapers. This piece of impertinence had to be submitted to, as the England of Gladstone & Co. was believed incapable of any effort in defense of the national honor.

On the 21st of May I was put on board the steamer for Havana, without any further explanation than that it was done by order of the Captain-General. That awful name was enough for me; besides, my friends assured me that to a certainty I should be immediately released on my arrival at Havana. This idea was encouraged by the considerate treatment I received during the voyage from Major Fernandez, in whose charge I was placed. On my arrival in Havana all illusions of this kind were somewhat rudely dissipated by the news of the arrest of the resident *Herald* correspondent, and the order for my confinement in the Cabañas fortress, where I was conducted by the special order of the republican Captain-General. Here, at least, I expected to be treated with consideration, but was fated to the rudest kind of disappointment. No one could tell me why Mr. Price had been arrested, and even the Consul-General had been refused permission to see him unless under conditions which it was not in keeping with his dignity as the representative of the United States to accept. The question of the right of the Spanish government to seize upon citizens of a free country, cast them into prison, and deprive them of all communication, not alone with their friends, but also with the representatives of their nation, is one that is justly open to question. Under our laws no such outrage could be perpetrated on a Spanish citizen, and this is a point on which reciprocity is of more importance than in questions of selling pins or patent medicines.

As I was being led to my quarters in the calaboose of the Cabañas, from which a robber was removed to make way for me, I passed the *boveda* where Mr. Price was confined. The captain of the guard called my attention to the other "Englishman," not being aware that we were old acquaintances. At the moment of passing he stopped to say a few words to the *Herald* correspondent, which gave me the opportunity of seeing Mr. Price without his having the most remote idea that out of the gloom of the night a friendly face was peering anxiously at him in the hope of being recognized. The captain had warned me not to speak, so I was obliged to remain a mute spectator. For five days Mr. Price had been cut off from all intercourse with his family and friends, having even been refused the aid of a doctor, unless he wished to accept the services of a Spanish *Sangrado*. Not caring to trust himself with that class of gentlemen, Mr. Price was compelled to do without medical help. When I saw him he was in the act of arranging his cot bed. As he turned to reply in no very civil manner to the intrusive inquiries of the captain, the light fell full on his face, and I could see that anxiety and confinement had left their impress on the last victim of Spanish law. The most alarming stories were set in circulation about the cause of Mr. Price's arrest, without the slightest foundation; the real cause being a desire to discover if I had used any cipher in my communications, or if Mr. Price could throw any light on the means by which I reached the Cuban lines.

On the way to the calaboose, the officer of the guard expressed his regret that I should be subjected to the indignity of being confined in a den which was only a fit abode for robbers, at the same time telling me that as soon as he had fulfilled his duty by locking me in he would go to the governor and protest against my detention in such quarters. This warning prepared me to expect scanty comfort; but, much as I had seen of Spanish generosity in Cuba, I was unprepared for the fate that awaited me. Arrived at length in front of a narrow opening in a blind casemate, it was pointed out as the apartment which I was to occupy during my residence in the Cabañas.

"Impossible!" I said to the officer. "There must certainly be some mistake."

No, much as he regretted the fact, this was my apartment. He considered it shameful to confine anyone but the lowest criminal in such a place, but his orders were imperative. He would immediately see the general commanding and represent the case to him, but in the mean time he would be compelled to lock me in. As the governor had made no preparations to enable me to pass the night, he had ordered one of the soldiers to bring me his hammock and a chair, to which he pointed and withdrew, closing the heavy door of open iron-work behind him, leaving me to my reflections.

The cell in which I found myself was irregular in form, with a low, arched roof, and about twenty feet by twenty-five, half the space being occupied by a sloping wooden bench begrimed with dirt; the roof black with smoke-stains and closely netted over with cobwebs. This place was filled with a sickening odor, proceeding from heaps of ordure which, notwithstanding the hasty cleaning-out, still encumbered the floor. A sickening sensation seized on me, and it was with difficulty that I could prevent myself from vomiting. In order to escape from the deadly atmosphere of this place I took up my position at the grated door, in the hope of breathing a little fresh air; but the well-intentioned efforts of the captain of the guard had cut off even this resource, for the soldiers, after shoveling out the filth which had been allowed to accumulate for I know not how long, had only removed it outside the door, where it remained to poison the air and cut off my only hope of relief. It was useless to complain; so I turned into my hammock, and, covering my head up, tried to save myself from the deadly effluvia of that black hole. In justice to my readers, I cannot enter fully into the description of the foulness of that den, where I was destined to remain for five days, cut off from communication with my friends and abandoned by the representative of my government. Next morning the general commanding visited the calaboose with some officers, and had the impertinence to tell me that he did not find any bad smell, but ordered the soldiers to wash the place out. This order was carried into effect, and rendered matters even worse, as, owing to the superficial manner in which the cleaning was performed, it had only the effect of stirring up the latent stenches, and left the numerous large holes and inequalities filled with viscid water, which, gradually evaporating, rendered the atmosphere of the dungeon most dangerous to health. When it is remembered that the yellow fever was claiming numbers of victims at this moment, the object of the Spanish authorities in pursuing this conduct towards me can easily be imagined. On the second night of my incarceration I was taken suddenly ill with symptoms of fever. So sudden and so severe was the attack, that I at once wrote to Mr. Crawford, the British Vice-Consul here, requesting his presence; but that functionary paid not the slightest heed to my representations. He was even aware of my position in the foul den; but, under the pretense of being refused permission, avoided visiting me, although he was actually in the fort and was informed of my position by Mr. Price, as well as by others. Even the officers and soldiers expressed disgust at my treatment; but the representative of Great Britain, having his own interests to consult, did not care to trouble himself about my state. I was especially anxious that he should come and inspect the calaboose where I was confined; but he took care not to visit me until the day before I was embarked for Spain, when I was in the comparatively princely quarters of Mr. Price. On two occasions he was in the Cabañas; but, under the pretense that I was *incomunicado,* he avoided coming to see the calaboose. In all probability I should have been forced to make the voyage in company with sick soldiers and the offscourings of the Spanish population of Cuba had it not been for the kindness of General Torbert, the American Consul-General. Abandoned by the representative of my government, I wrote to General Torbert, asking him to interpose in my interest with the Captain-General, and obtain permission for me to make the voyage as a saloon-passenger at my own expense. After some difficulty, this request was acceded to, and I was spared many sufferings, mental and physical.

On the evening of the 28th of May I was released from the black hole and conducted to the *boveda,* or casemate, occupied by Mr. Price. It was a pleasant change, and enabled me to pass the last hours of my stay in Cuba in the pleasant companionship of my friend. Mr. Price had learned that the government at Madrid had given the Captain-General peremptory orders to send me to Spain, and had succeeded in conveying the information to me in a small note, which he bribed one of the soldiers to give to me secretly. The man did so very cleverly, although the sergeant of the guard was present whenever anyone came into my cell, to prevent any communication with the outer world.

A few days later the Havana authorities handed me over to the captain of the *Antonio Lopez,* one of the *correos* or regular Spanish mail-steamers, for conveyance to the Peninsula. The voyage was a bright and prosperous one; and the new-found liberty I enjoyed, combined with the influence of the sea, quite restored me to health, and dissipated the gloom and anxiety which had weighed on me during nearly three months' close confinement, rendered the more trying by the constant dread of summary execution.

Night had already fallen when the announcement of land from the lookout sent a thrill of satisfaction through the wave-tossed frames of some hundreds of passengers. There was an immediate rush on deck, and the numerous *ante ojos* that had been drawn in anticipation from among disordered heaps of luggage in the small, dark, uncomfortable *camarotes* of the steamer, were put into immediate requisition by homesick wanderers, eager to catch a glimpse through the night gloom of the iron-bound shores of romantic Spain. For some days the weather had been broken and boisterous, exercising a depressing influence on the homebound landsmen, and preventing the few ladies on board from appearing on deck. Although it was the middle of June the night was cold and raw, and sun and land were covered with dark fog-like vapors that chilled to the marrow despite warm wrappings. In the first eager impulse the damp and the fog and the night were forgotten, and only remembered the joy and the pleasure of arrival.

Most of the passengers were officers, merchants, and soldiers, who, after many years' absence, were returning to their native land; some with acquired wealth and position; others with shattered health and maimed bodies—poor victims of cruel war; yet all were strongly moved when they caught sight of the few glimmering lights and the dark, massive shadows that told them we were almost within hail of *La Vieja España*. But even patriotism was not proof against the chill night air; so one by one the groups dissolved to reunite again in the saloon.

There was at least one man among the company to whom the pleasure of reaching land again was a mixed one. For months a prisoner in Cuba, I had been placed on board the *correo* for conveyance to Spain as a prisoner of state, with the charge of treason hanging over me; but in the enjoyment of the fresh sea-breezes, and so much liberty as can be stowed into a mail-steamer, all gloomy preoccupations had vanished. Although not a good sailor I love the sea, for here alone can we peer without distraction into immensity. To gaze after the setting sun slowly sinking beyond the seemingly endless expanse of waters, and feel the greatness of the Creator impressed with awful and mysterious power upon the soul, has ever been to me the special charm of the ocean. Whether in sunlit repose, spreading out like a golden mirror, or lashed by the finger of God, when the spume-crowned waves rushing with terrific rage dash their plume-like crests in thunderous shock against the bulwarks of the storm-tossed bark, and, shattered into innumerable phosphorescent scintillations, fall back into the sough-tomb, the sea in all its varied phases presents to the mind the truest idea of sublimity.

And under the invigorating influence of the sea I had well-nigh forgotten that I was still a prisoner, but the cry of *tierra* suddenly recalled me to a sense of my position. The prospect of being consigned to a Spanish prison was certainly not pleasing, and as there was no knowing what course might be pursued towards me by the government, my joy at arrival was not extreme.

It was evening when we cast anchor in the port of Santander, and the crowds just issuing from the *toros,* or bullring, poured out on the quays to gaze wonderingly at the ship from the Pearl Island, the Queen of the Antilles. The passengers went on shore, and I was left alone to mope about the ship in utter wretchedness, waiting the orders of the authorities as to what disposition should be made of me. Next morning I was taken on shore by two officers, and the governor of the town, a bald major with a shiny black wig, sent me to the *carcel nacional,* or common jail. It was crowded with Carlist prisoners, murderers, thieves, and all that scum which finds its way sooner or later to the *presidio.* In view of my being sufficiently rich to pay thirty *reales* a month for a separate apartment I was not put among the crowd of common prisoners, but conducted to a gallery which ran round the courtyard, and gave ingress to the second story of cells. The stench of the place was horrible, and there rose a veritable exhalation from the seething mass of unwashed and unkempt humanity below. Fortunately, my stay in this place was very short, as, owing to some cause, the jailer became suddenly very civil, and conducted me to the *sala de audiencia,* or court of examination, and informed me that I would be allowed to occupy it during my stay. As the *sala* included two large rooms and a long corridor, all pretty well ventilated, the change was an agreeable one, and during the fortnight I was detained in the *carcel* I was treated with as much consideration as the rules of a prison would allow.

It was owing principally to the representations made in my behalf by the government of the United States that Señor Castelar had ordered me to Spain; but, unfortunately, when I arrived the Spanish orator was no longer Minister of Ultramar, and the new ministers were so much engaged endeavoring to give stability to the government that they had little time to acquaint themselves with the facts in my case.[*] However, the representations of General Sickles, the United States Minister, induced the government to order my removal to Madrid, where I was permitted to go at liberty under the guarantee of the United States Legation. A few months later Señor Castelar, who was benevolently disposed in my regard,

---

[*]Castelar y Ripoll was minister of foreign affairs rather than minister of ultramar ("overseas territories"), from 11 February to 11 June 1873. Castelar became president of the First Republic of Spain in September 1873.

came into power, and General Sickles, for some reasons unknown to me, withdrew the guarantee of the Legation, and surrendered me to Señor Carvajal, the then Minister of State. Fortunately, the Spanish government did not think well of taking any further steps in my case, and I was permitted to leave Spain without any difficulties being thrown in my way. So ended my expedition to the Mambi-Land.

FINIS

Prologue

Fernando Ortiz

THE MAMBI-LAND narrates a resonant episode in Cuba's Ten Years' War, animated by one of the most picturesque characters of the nineteenth century, whose life was one continuous chain of bold and noble adventures undertaken for the freedom of a nation.

This romantic story will undoubtedly interest everybody who is curious about Cuba's past, presenting, as it does, vivid scenes of the Ten Years' War, sustained with such heroic tenacity by Cuba's independence fighters from Yara to Zanjón.* But there is just as much human interest in the restless character of its roving narrator. When I started to prepare a biographical sketch of its author for the prologue to this volume of the *Colección de Libros Cubanos,* I did not expect to find in the fabric of his life such a vigorous warp of fine intentions, such a tight weft of splendid threads, nor such a knotting of patriotic incidents. The opportunity to visit New York, where I am writing these pages, has allowed me to delve more

---

Prologue translated by Peter Hulme and Jennifer Brittan. In 1930, Fernando Ortiz contributed an introduction to a Cuban edition of James J. O'Kelly's *The Mambi-Land—La tierra del mambí* (Havana: Cultural)—reprinted in a later edition (Havana: Instituto del Libro, 1968). The 1968 edition replaces the original title, "Introducción biográfica" ("Biographical Introduction") with "Prólogo" ("Prologue"), which is the title we use for this first English translation. What follows is the complete text, unmodified except for minor reformatting and silent correction of errors in spelling and in Ortiz's citations, where necessary. The notes are Ortiz's, except where indicated. The original text includes Ortiz's Spanish translation of quotations from sources in English. This translation returns these quotations to their original English, except in some cases where citations are absent or incorrect, as indicated. Notes supply missing citations for quotations, where possible.

*The Ten Years' War began on October 10, 1868, with the "Grito de Yara" ("Cry of Yara") and ended on February 10, 1878, with the Pact of Zanjón.—*Trans.*

deeply into the author's background, to consult private documents and rare publications, and to get to know individuals intimately connected with O'Kelly. These circumstances caused me to extend this biographical essay to an unexpected length, through which I hope to sketch for Cubans the singular figure of that valiant individual who wrote a fine episode in the history of our homeland.

In what part of the world is the *mambi-land?* You cannot find it anywhere today, but in days gone by it was a glorious reality. Cuban readers need no help in remembering and understanding, but foreigners will want some orientation in our historical and ethical geographies before embarking on this book of adventures that reads like something from a novel, but which really took place, part of a vertiginous era of heroism and recklessness, selflessness and crime, martyrdom and atrocity, all happening more than half a century ago in the most beautiful land human eyes ever beheld.

For foreign readers, let me explain that *mambi-land* means the land of *Cuba libre,* free Cuba. *Cuba libre* was the portion of Cuban territory controlled by the army of liberation during the ten-year war of secession (1868–1878). It was therefore the territory subtracted *de facto* from Spanish jurisdiction. *Mambí*—as noun or adjective—was the term applied to the Cuban separatists, especially to those who waged armed struggle to end colonial rule and bring about national independence. *Mambí* is a word of African derivation, specifically Bantu, constructed from the root *mbi,* which has various derogatory meanings. The Spaniards began using the word in Santo Domingo to refer to Dominicans who would not submit to their rule when the Spanish crown re-annexed the territory in the mid-nineteenth century as part of its desperate but short-lived attempt to prevent the renewal of unrest, which it feared on account of a turbulent political and racial situation on the island. *Mambí* meant insurrectionist, bandit, criminal, rebellious, infamous, bad; we find the same meanings in the Congo and elsewhere in Africa, as in the rebellious savannahs and mountain ranges of old Hispaniola.* The Spanish soldiers who evacuated from Santo Domingo when that island reasserted its sovereignty came to Cuba, where they applied the word *mambí* to the Cuban insurgents. This derogatory term then became an honorable name, as has happened on other historical occasions when scorned groups have fought successfully for freedom for themselves and their people, like the French *sans-culottes,*

---

*Fernando Ortiz, *Glosario de Afronegrismos* (Havana, 1916). Another vernacular word from Cuba, derived from the same Bantu root and also very contemptuous, is *mabinga.* See the *Glosario.*

the Belgian *gueux*, and the Italian *carbonari*. Even today the followers of Gandhi in India are called *lice-ridden*.

But even in its most glorious and hopeful days the mambi-land was little known. Perhaps the overseas world knew of the separatist revolution sustained by those islanders opposed to Spanish absolutism, but it was not aware of its importance, its potential, and the huge amount of blood spilled by Cubans to ensure that the adolescent nation could eventually attain its full sovereignty. As our hero himself wrote after the happy conclusion of his adventures: "It is an absolutely unknown land, misrepresented alike by friends and enemies."* To know it, one must journey to that tropical realm.

Who was this explorer of the mambi-land? Simply put, he was a *New York Herald* correspondent who at the end of 1872 and the beginning of 1873 came to Cuba, travelled to the territory occupied by the insurgent troops of Carlos Manuel de Céspedes, and, after various misadventures, succeeded in telling the world about his sojourn in *Cuba libre* and about the heroic efforts of Cubans to achieve national independence. This bold adventurer was an Irishman whose name should feature in biographical dictionaries of Cuba, alongside others of that cultured people who settled on the largest island of the Caribbean. Many of them, who could be called conservatives, were on the side of Spain, such as the celebrated generals O'Reilly and O'Donnell, both military leaders in Cuba; and many were businessmen and soldiers, as well, such as the O'Farrills and the O'Gabans, or members of the professional class such as the O'Connells, the O'Burkes, the O'Hallorans, and the Byrnes.

But other sons of Ireland, or of Irish descent, supported the liberal activities of the Cubans against the absolutist regime of the Spanish colony. Among them was the Irishman Richard R. Madden, a doctor and British government official who lived in Cuba from 1836 to 1839, studying Cuban society, commerce, education, and religion, and in particular slavery and the illicit slave trade. He wrote an extremely well-informed book that is fundamental for an understanding of that appalling human trafficking and the development of Cuban freedom.† Irish names

---

**New York Herald, 9 May 1873.

†Richard R. Madden, *The Island of Cuba: Its resources and prospects, considered in relation especially to the influence of its prosperity on the interest of the British West India colonies* [1849], 2nd ed. (London, 1853). *Trans.*—R. R. Madden also translated and published the only known autobiographical slave narrative from Latin America, by Cuban Juan Francisco Manzano. See Manzano, *Autobiography of a Slave*, trans. Evelyn Picon Garfield (Detroit: Wayne State University Press, 1996).

such as O'Reilly and Kelly were among Narciso López's invading troops, and among the conspirators was John O'Sullivan, a native Irishman and brother-in-law of Cristóbal Madan.* It was the brave Irish colonel O'Hara who inscribed Narciso López's flag with the words "Primus in Cuba!"† Among the fifty shot with Crittenden in Atarés in 1851 were four Irishmen.‡ Years later, *mambises* of Irish blood such as O'Brien and Reeve gave their lives fighting for *Cuba libre*. And among Irish sympathizers with the Cuban struggle must always be remembered James J. O'Kelly.

James J. O'Kelly was born in Ireland.§ According to some, in Dublin in 1845; according to others, in Galway in 1840. A recent biography suggests May 1842. We cannot resolve the discrepancies in place and date, but it is certain that O'Kelly was Irish and not born in the United States, as some people have suggested.¶ The young Irishman belonged to a family renowned for its dedication to the arts. His father was wealthy, both a veterinarian and owner of a coach-building business. On his mother's side James was the nephew of Michael Lawlor, the famous Irish sculptor who contributed to the Albert Memorial that Queen Victoria had built in Hyde Park.** James's brother Charles produced a fine bust of Daniel

---

*See Herminio Portell Vilá, *Narciso López y su época* (Havana, 1930), 77.

†Vidal Morales y Morales, *Iniciadores y primeros mártires de la revolución cubana* (Havana, 1901), 259.

‡Alexander Jones, *Cuba in 1851* (New York, 1851). According to "Letters from Havana" in the *New York Herald* on the very day of the execution, 16 August 1851.

§*James* is an English name that has been translated in various ways into Spanish. The *Enciclopedia Espasa* calls him *Jacobo O'Kelly*. Phonetically, the closest translation would perhaps be *Jaime*, and the purest *Santiago*. *James* is just one of the many forms (*James, Jacques, Jacobo, Jaime, Santiago, Yago, Diego*, etc.) of the same old word. To better distinguish our person of interest, given that every name should provide the sharpest juridical individuation possible for each human being, we prefer to follow the custom of leaving names in their original language, unless common usage or some special circumstance dictates otherwise. In addition, we will always, as in the US usage, employ the initial letter of his second name in order to clearly distinguish him from *James O'Kelly*, an earlier Irish theologian, unrelated to our subject except perhaps via some genealogical link of which we are unaware.

¶Baptismal records for St. Andrews, Westland Row, Dublin, establish that O'Kelly was born on 6 May 1842.—*Trans.*

**O'Kelly's maternal uncle was John Lawlor. Michael Lawlor, also a sculptor, was his cousin. To correct other factual errors in Ortiz's biography, see Peter Hulme's foreword in this edition. Also see Niamh O'Sullivan, *Aloysius O'Kelly: Art, Nation, Empire* (Dublin: Field Day Publications, University of Notre Dame, 2010); Paul A. Townend, "A Cosmopolitan Nationalist" in *Ireland in an Imperial World*, ed. Timothy G.

O'Connell, and his other two brothers, Stephen and Aloysius, were also artists. All this tells us that he must have grown up in a cultured and intellectual environment. O'Kelly had the usual education for a boy of his class, initially in London under the care of his sculptor uncle. But, as O'Connor has noted, he attended a London school where "he learned . . . the scorn that belongs to the child of a conquered race."* Back in Dublin he trained as a blacksmith and, after the death of his father, tried to take over the family business, but with little success. Meanwhile, he studied at the university in Dublin, but, unable to stay in Ireland, sold his remaining inheritance in 1862 and returned to London to study sculpture in his uncle's studio, an apprenticeship he continued at the Sorbonne in Paris.

According to O'Connor, a comrade of O'Kelly's, James belonged to an Irish set of "arch-heretics against the orthodox creed of constitutionalism."† As O'Kelly reached manhood, his compatriots' sole desire was armed rebellion against England. The scandalous treachery of Sadleir and Keogh against the cause of Irish freedom had removed all hope of any peaceful liberalization of government policy, with the younger generation opting for a battle that would turn into a long and bloody campaign for sovereignty over several decades. O'Kelly was always committed to the struggle for freedom. "In every hour from 1858 . . . he had been dreaming and working for Ireland."‡

In 1860, in Dublin, James J. O'Kelly and his school-friend, the also famous John Devoy, joined the military wing of the Irish separatists, then called Fenians,§ so beginning his long involvement with revolutionary activities aimed at liberating Ireland from English sovereignty, and especially from the yoke of the landlords, who maintained shameful and feudal privileges throughout the island. It was O'Kelly who initiated the Fenian movement in London when he moved there in 1862. He gathered together the few scattered members who lived in the city and organized and directed them, increasing their numbers by means of intense proselytizing. In the armed conspiracy of 1867, he was, O'Connor says, "one

---

McMahon et al. (London: Palgrave Macmillan, 2017), 223–44; and Owen McGee, "O'Kelly, James Joseph" in *Dictionary of Irish Biography*, vol. 7, eds. James McGuire and James Quinn (Cambridge: Cambridge University Press, 2009), 601–3.—*Trans.*

*T. P. O'Connor, *The Parnell Movement* (New York, 1886), 353.

†O'Connor, *Parnell Movement*, 354.

‡O'Connor, *Parnell Movement*, 362.

§So O'Kelly said many years later: Robert Anderson, *Sidelights on the Home Rule Movement* (New York, 1906), 158.

of the chief men of the movement."* But before fully committing to the rebellion, and still within the bounds of a conspiracy that needed time and opportunity to mature, the young O'Kelly gave rein to his exuberant and adventurous impulses. With the conspiracy still in mind, he enlisted in the London Irish Volunteers, but after a few months of suffering under British military orders he deserted in 1863 and went abroad to join the French Foreign Legion as a common soldier, serving for several years in Algeria in that aggressive military unit. His blood baptism came in Oran where he fought against the Arabs.

When France embarked on its ill-fated intervention in Mexico, which the United States had to tolerate in spite of the Monroe Doctrine, O'Kelly joined the expeditionary force and took part in the skirmishes that preceded the occupation of Mexico City and the installation of Emperor Maximilian. Before long, the Austrian intruder was executed, his empire collapsed, and the French soldiers were sent home. O'Kelly was wounded in Mien and captured by General Corrales in June 1866, remaining in Mexico as a prisoner of Benito Juárez's troops.† At this point he received a letter from his friend Devoy, informing him that revolutionary action against England would begin the next year and calling on him to join the struggle. O'Kelly decided to return immediately. Escaping from prison, he broke his ties with the French Foreign Legion. After an eventful journey in a crudely built canoe he made himself, some risky encounters with Mexican guerrillas, and the pleading of an old lady for her sons to pardon the gringo they were about to shoot, O'Kelly reached Matamoros and then the United States, from where his uncle helped him to get to London.

Soon after reaching England, O'Kelly learned that the Irish rebellion was due to break out on March 5, 1867. For the first time in his life the young Fenian showed how patriotic ardor, to be effective, must always be balanced by the need to act sensibly. Believing the outbreak to be imprudent and inadequately armed, he opposes it but is ignored: the plot fails ignominiously. O'Kelly then works harder than anybody to reorganize the squabbling Fenians: he insinuates himself into the secret meetings of Irish protestants in order to start a movement in favor of Home Rule; he plots the release of John Devoy and other Fenians imprisoned by the

---

*O'Connor, *Parnell Movement*, 356.—*Trans.*

†In identifying "Mien" as the location of O'Kelly's capture, Ortiz was likely drawing on T. P. O'Connor (see *Parnell Movement*, 354). It is possible that O'Kelly was wounded in the Battle of Santa Gertrudis (June 1866) in Camargo, a border city on the banks of the Río Grande in the state of Tamaulipas.—*Trans.*

British in Chatham, where they were isolated as rebels; he prepares to enter the prison in disguise and everything is ready for the escape . . . but an amnesty renders it unnecessary.

All this would be enough for a colorful life, but we have hardly begun. In 1870, the Franco-Prussian War breaks out. The Irish Catholics show their support for France by sending a fleet of ambulances under the command of Constantine J. MacGuire. Nevertheless, O'Kelly wants to raise a combat regiment and makes his way to Paris. As soon as the French army showed its weakness against Moltke's lightning attacks, O'Kelly's plan was approved, and he, appointed colonel, was entrusted with the difficult mission of returning home and secretly recruiting young Irishmen to form a brigade of volunteers under the Napoleonic flag. O'Kelly accepted the commission and had returned to Ireland to carry it out, but the fall of Sedan and of Napoleon III's empire put an end to his efforts.

After this French fiasco the frustrated volunteer worked in England, according to some accounts, as a secret Fenian agent, charged with acquiring and shipping arms for his country's separatist rebellion. Then, still in 1871 and perhaps in accordance with the needs of the conspiracy, he left for the United States. We believe that his separatist activities were behind this new emigration. The rebellion against England had its most dynamic and extreme organizations in the United States, where thousands of Irish people had gone to escape the famine that struck rural Ireland in 1847. The much-feared Fenian Brotherhood was created in the United States in 1858,* undertaking some audacious, if unsuccessful, actions, such as the armed invasion of Canada and the capture of the frontier Fort Erie on May 31, 1886.

O'Kelly was now an important figure within the Fenian movement and after his move to the United States, he pursued his rebellious actions even more energetically. After the founding of Clan na Gael, the most secret of the rebel groups, O'Kelly was not just a member but also a paid functionary. His constant involvement in the separatist conspiracy was in easy harmony with his new position as a journalist for the *New York Herald*. It is worth recalling that in those days the *New York Herald* was the most famous newspaper in the world, on account of the originality, audacity, and repute of its reports received from the most distant parts of the world and on topics of great general interest. O'Kelly's mission to the land of the mambises was proof that James Gordon Bennett knew how to invest his

---

*This name for Irish separatist patriots was taken from the old Celtic militia headed in the third century by Finn, a semi-legendary figure in Irish history.

money and energy to generate sensational news.* It was the *Herald* that arranged Livingstone's famous rescue by its correspondent H. M. Stanley in the heart of Africa; it was the *Herald* that sent the *Jeannette* to the Arctic; it was no coincidence that in 1898 when Dewey gave the order to fire on Spanish ships in Manila Bay, there was a *Herald* journalist by his side. Oswald Garrison Villard, currently editor of *The Nation* and a man not much given to praise, did not hesitate to declare that, whatever the possible ethical concerns surrounding the Bennetts, father and son, they were undoubtedly the most notable journalists that the United States had produced. The father revolutionized the system of obtaining and reporting news; the son had a talent for acquiring exclusive stories.† In those years the *Herald*'s rivals could not go to sleep after their nighttime labors without first reading, as day dawned, a copy of the *Herald*, always fearful of being surprised by some news scoop of the kind beloved by American popular psychology.

O'Kelly's appointment at the *Herald* was as a substitute reporter, but it coincided with the return from Europe of General Sheridan, who hated journalists. So skillfully did O'Kelly conceal his occupation beneath a soldierly demeanor that Sheridan, the austere military man of Irish background, talked at length with him. In this way O'Kelly succeeded in getting the only interview with the stern general, and, as a result, he was immediately considered a veteran journalist and went on to have a charmed career. Reporters were paid by the column inch, and O'Kelly almost always out-earned his fellow journalists.

There are colorful stories about the ingenious newshound. He hunted buffalo with the famous Buffalo Bill, who always spoke of the Irishman's unsurpassed bravery; he reported on the Indian wars; he practically kidnapped the famous French politician Victor Henri Rochefort after he had escaped from New Caledonia and was crossing the United States by train. O'Kelly kept Rochefort isolated from other journalists while he telegraphed station by station a day-long interview that became a sensation in the United States and Europe.

The *Herald* sent him to Brazil to accompany the emperor on his journey to the United States, and O'Kelly lent his services to Dom Pedro, two

---

*Here Ortiz refers to James Gordon Bennett Jr., who became managing editor of the *New York Herald* in 1867 and inherited the paper following his father's death on 1 June 1872.—*Trans.*

†Oswald Garrison Villard, *Some Newspapers and Newspapermen* (New York, 1923), 273.

of which were much praised: in the bay of Rio de Janeiro he spectacularly saved the life of the empress, and throughout the whole voyage he saved the emperor from other newspaper interviews by only allowing those conducted on behalf of the *New York Herald*. This service must have endeared him to the emperor, who was deeply committed to avoiding the journalist hordes, perhaps agreeing with O'Connor's remark: "Scratch the American journalist and you find a Red Indian, not content to kill unless he can also scalp his competitor."* O'Kelly's success was so bruited that when the imperial retinue reached San Francisco, the Californian newspapers spitefully reported the news in a single sentence: "Yesterday the *New York Herald* reporter, Mr. James O'Kelly, arrived in San Francisco, accompanied by the emperor of Brazil."

While O'Kelly joined the newspaper as a reporter, his keen artistic inclinations converted him into an art critic, where his sharp eye and judgement led him to be promoted to editorialist, and later to membership on the newspaper management committee, a position he filled until 1873.

At the end of 1872, the *New York Herald* sent a correspondent to Cuba on a mission to outsmart the Spanish authorities, find Carlos Manuel de Céspedes, and report on the true state of the separatist rebellion. "The correspondent, Mr. Henderson, was neither courageous nor shrewd enough for such an undertaking."† In fact, he was a liar and a fabricator. The prestige of the great New York newspaper demanded success. Its readers, moreover, wanted accurate and impartial reporting on the situation in *Cuba libre*. To accomplish this triumph of journalism, the *Herald* approached O'Kelly, who gladly accepted the position of "war correspondent." Thus, the intrepid Irishman came to Cuba.

Once in Cuba, O'Kelly abjured hypocritical and underhanded methods in favor of operating openly and transparently. This rectitude may have saved his life. He informed the Spanish authorities of his assignment and requested a safe-conduct for unrestricted travel in the country, including the *mambí* camps.‡ In a letter to O'Kelly dated December 24, 1872, the captain general of Cuba stated that he had allowed the previous *New York Herald* correspondent, Henderson, to accompany Spanish columns

---

*O'Connor, *Parnell Movement*, 356.—*Trans.*
†Carlos M. de Céspedes y Quesada, *Carlos Manuel de Céspedes* (Paris, 1895), 242.
‡Convinced by widely reported statements that O'Kelly would not be executed, Carlos Manuel de Céspedes reassured Francis F. Millen, the *Herald*'s other correspondent in Cuba (*Herald*, 7 June 1873).

and even visit insurgent camps, and yet for reasons unknown to him and despite the consideration afforded the correspondent, Henderson had imputed to the captain general an unseemly desire to sway his opinions and restrict his freedom as a journalist. With Henderson now safe and sound in his homeland, the captain general noted, he could write whatever he liked in sympathy with the "undisciplined hordes of the insurrection." But, the captain general continued, "a second rehearsal cannot be permitted." The letter informed O'Kelly that with his passport alone he could travel the country gathering news of the insurrection from the *thousands* of captured insurgents who "now fight in our ranks or live quietly in their homes," pardoned by the Spanish government. "Understand that any other course you adopt will be *at your own risk*." To conclude his letter, General Francisco de Ceballos clarified that he had been under no obligation to respond to O'Kelly: "I have had the satisfaction to answer your letter, but this condescension I could not repeat, because you already must understand that it is not customary that authorities explain to private individuals, respectable as they may be, the motives of their conduct or the foundation of their opinions."*

O'Kelly chose the path of "personal risk" despite the dangers he could face and the obstacles resulting, whether maliciously or innocently, from the pervasive mistrust and turbulent feelings of a struggle that sometimes assumed the bitterness of fratricidal conflict. The English vice-consul in Santiago de Cuba, Mr. F. W. Ramsden, advised O'Kelly not to cross Spanish lines, but O'Kelly had a professional duty to fulfill and an achievement to claim. He soon made contact with separatist sympathizers and found the path that would lead to the jungle behind whose foliage extended the promised land of the Cubans—*Cuba libre,* or the mambi-land.

O'Kelly left Santiago de Cuba on the afternoon of February 19, 1873, and was heading towards the mambi-land when he was arrested in Palma Soriano. Carlos Manuel de Céspedes wrote of the correspondent's arrival in a personal letter to his wife in New York: "Mr. O'Kelly has contacted the family of one of my officers to obtain information on how to reach our forces. I have given orders for him to be picked up and escorted to Cambute and then on to our camp. I have been informed that O'Kelly has been imprisoned in Palma Soriano and we all wait anxiously for news. The Spaniards cannot possibly welcome such visits, especially now that

---

*The captain general is responding to O'Kelly's letter, dated 22 December 1872. For the full correspondence between O'Kelly and Francisco de Ceballos, see O'Kelly's dispatch, *New York Herald,* 30 Dec. 1872, 3.—*Trans.*

their towns are without garrisons, the volunteers are totally demoralized, and the patriots are on the offensive. Of course the Spaniards would put all kinds of obstacles in Mr. O'Kelly's path so that he gets tired and leaves without fulfilling his mission."

But O'Kelly reached *Cuba libre* at four in the afternoon on February 21, and interviewed Céspedes on March 6, 1873.* He describes his time with the mambises in his book. He must have impressed the leader of the Cuban revolution, who praises his visitor in several letters to his wife. "He handled himself with dignity in our camp," says the leader of the Cuban mambises, "and we acknowledge his great bravery and resolve."†

As Céspedes predicted, the Spanish authorities viewed with distaste the US press's new meddling in the bloody events unfolding in Cuba: a red thread tying together two persistent problems over which they had little control. The *New York Herald* had a permanent correspondent in Havana who relayed details of O'Kelly's adventure to the captain general. Exasperated by the news that O'Kelly was with the Cuban rebels, he pronounced the journalist's behavior a mockery of the laws of the country. The correspondent reported this to his newspaper on March 4. The captain general warned O'Kelly's colleague that if O'Kelly returned from the insurgent ranks, he would be tried by summary court-martial and shot as a spy. Later he softened his stance, stating more circumspectly that O'Kelly would instead face immediate expulsion from Cuba. The *Herald* gave this news the ironic headline "Christian charity softens the official heart of the Spanish gentleman."‡

O'Kelly was with the mambises for about six weeks, and at no point could it be said that he compromised his mission as a journalist. According to a *Herald* report, the officers of the San Quentín battalion saw O'Kelly on horseback during a battle, "waving on the rebels with the sabre of his sire."§ But this was mere fantasy, likely conjured by James Gordon Bennett in an attempt to stir popular emotion. While Bennett acknowledged the report as unfounded, he nonetheless adorned the figure of his correspondent with romantic gestures in line with the Irish gentleman's reputation as a fearless *beau sabreur*. It is believed true, however,

---

*O'Kelly arrived in an insurgent camp on the afternoon of 20 February. See O'Kelly's dispatch, *New York Herald*, 19 March 1873, 7.—*Trans.*

†Céspedes, *Carlos Manuel de Céspedes*, 248, 250.

‡The *Herald* report does not include this "ironic headline." See the *New York Herald*, 12 March 1873, 7.—*Trans.*

§*New York Herald*, 19 March 1873, 6.—*Trans.*

that when O'Kelly observed the mambises wasting scarce ammunition by firing their rifles at close range, he recommended using guns loaded with pellets or other kinds of shot easily obtained around the camps, which would provide better firepower than their Remingtons. They say that the Cubans successfully followed the advice of the astute Irishman.*

With his restless taste for adventure, O'Kelly might have considered extending his stay with the insurgents. But his sense of duty as a journalist prevailed and he was eager to give the press the sensational news of his journey into the very heart of the *terra incognita* he called the mambi-land. Rather than a vague geographical area refusing obedience to Spain, this land of shifting and uncertain borders was more spiritual than earthly. Some heroes had already declared the region a free republic, representing it by symbols burning with hope: a shield with the rising sun and a flag with the morning star in blood-red dawn, illuminating between white bands the blue sky of a beautiful nation.

On March 24, only days after his arrival, O'Kelly separated from Céspedes and embarked on his return journey to Spanish Cuba.† He reached Manzanillo on the 31st, and although he presented himself to the chief military officer accompanied by the English consul, the valiant journalist was escorted to prison. O'Kelly's arrest became his plume of triumph, giving him immense popularity in the United States and among sympathizers of *Cuba libre*. The *New York Herald* had triumphed. The editor and owner congratulated himself and jubilantly accepted the welcome consequences. The military authorities in Cuba all but assured O'Kelly's journalistic success as the intrepid reporter proceeded to make news the world over as a hero, a victim, and a martyr for freedom. Rumors spread that he had been murdered in a dungeon by soldiers angered by this young representative of free opinion, this champion of truth, who came to Cuba to prevent the dragon of tyranny from strangling in its monstrous clutches another sleeping beauty of the American dream, the last maiden daughter of Mother America.

O'Kelly's fellow journalists made his trial about freedom of the press, protesting against the intransigence and absolutism of the colonial government. The *Herald*'s Havana correspondent, Mr. Price, sent telegrams to O'Kelly in Manzanillo; to Mr. Lauten, British Vice-Consul in Manzanillo; to Mr. F. W. Ramsden, British Consul in Santiago de Cuba; and to

---

The Gaelic American (New York), 30 December 1916, 7.

†This is curious phrasing, since O'Kelly spent, at minimum, two weeks with Céspedes. See O'Kelly, *The Mambi-Land*, 141–70.—*Trans*.

United States Consul Mr. A. N. Young, also in Santiago de Cuba. All the telegrams were intercepted and undelivered. Alarm spread among those who understood the ruthlessness of the Spanish volunteers, the swaggering weakness of the captain general who was depicted as a new Pontius Pilate, and the fury of the Spaniards at US meddling in Cuban affairs.

Mr. Price met with the captain general on the morning of April 10 and was informed that O'Kelly had been found in possession of two letters from Céspedes and would therefore be considered a spy. The correspondent reminded the captain general of his promise to expel O'Kelly from the island without further punitive action, but was told that this accommodation was predicated on O'Kelly acting as a neutral rather than as a spy. He added that O'Kelly had worsened his case by refusing to cooperate with judicial interrogations. The Spanish authority "was very harsh in his replies, and arrogant as usual."* Mr. Price submitted the details of this interview to the owner and editor of the *New York Herald*. Mr. A. N. Young cabled *New York Herald* editor Mr. James Gordon Bennett, on April 10, writing: "O'Kelly is in close confinement at Manzanillo. He is in a precarious condition. He asks to be removed to Havana, in order that he may get competent counsel to defend him. He needs all your powerful influence."†

In the beginning, Havana newspapers said nothing of O'Kelly's arrest. When Mr. Price gave them the news on April 10, they replied that they were not authorized to report on it. However, they later published articles full of indignation and sarcasm. The Spanish press in Havana could not keep quiet about the O'Kelly "case" when their colleagues in New York informed them of the *Herald* campaign and the responses of other US newspapers. Since it was impossible to hide what was happening in Cuba, the local press dedicated themselves to ridiculing the insurgents and an austere "Presidency of the Republic that resides in a hut." They distorted O'Kelly's pro-Cuban statements and launched invectives against enemies of so-called "national integrity."

The *Diario de la Marina* dedicated several colorful editorials "to the commissioner of the *Herald*" on April 6, 24, 25, 28, and May 8, 1873, remarking on the reports from its New York editor K. Lendas, especially from his first mention of O'Kelly on March 27. *La Voz de Cuba*, infamous in the annals of the colony for its grimly unwavering support of despotism, printed extensive commentary on April 29 and 30, and May 1, address-

---

New York Herald, 12 April 1873, 7.—*Trans.*
†*New York Herald*, 12 April 1873, 7.—*Trans.*

ing O'Kelly's adventures and dispatches, and responding to reports from New York. Another Spanish newspaper, *La Constancia,* published stories from *Hispánicus,* also in New York, dated April 15, 17, 21, and 24, with special articles on April 24, 25, 26, and 29.

K. Lendas reported on March 27 to the *Diario de la Marina* that Antonio Zambrana had arrived in New York from *Cuba libre* on a mission for the mambises.* He added:

> Zambrana confirmed that O'Kelly arrived at camp "Tempú" on February 25 so sick and debilitated that he thought he was dying. According to Zambrana's calculations, O'Kelly should have an interview with President Céspedes on the 6th or 7th of this month, and he believes that the *Herald* commissioner will be smuggled off the island, which has implications for the character of his future reports. I have the moral conviction that the purpose of O'Kelly's mission has been to carry information to the insurgents, including informing them of filibustering expeditions being planned in this country. He simply continues what Henderson began. Observe how after his interview with Agramonte the insurgents were more active and effective in their operations. Leaving the island is quite easy, but reaching the insurgents presents many difficulties. Only with pretexts like Henderson's and O'Kelly's could anyone get away with bringing advice and military strategy from the United States to the insurgent camps, thereby ensuring coordination between the insurgency and the separatist movement.†

The *Herald* roundly rejected the attack, as K. Lendas noted in a report to the *Diario de la Marina* dated April 8, 1873:

> The news of O'Kelly's arrest, telegraphed yesterday to the *Herald* by their Havana correspondent, and which today comes with further details from Cayo Hueso, has brought the famous *Herald* to the boiling point. It is no surprise that the *Herald* emits greats puffs of steam that will slowly dissipate into nothing. As soon as it heard the news, the Don Quixote of journalism mounted his Rocinante, positioned himself well in the stirrups, gripped tightly his spear, brought his shield to his chest, and with raised voice and arrogant gesture demanded "Do the right thing, you Spanish gentlemen, and release poor O'Kelly at once without touching a hair of his head, or else we will be at war, you

---

*Antonio Zambrana, a member of the Congress of the Cuban republic, had arrived two days earlier with three sailors from a filibustering expedition on the *Edgar Stuart,* after travelling 30 hours from Jamaica to New York in a dugout canoe. See the *New York Herald,* 26 March 1873, 3.—*Trans.*

†*Diario de la Marina,* 15 April 1873, 2.

arrogant giants." The *Herald* holds General Ceballos, the Madrid government, and all of Spain responsible for the safety of James O'Kelly, the valiant, heroic, and reckless "Liberator of *Cuba libre*." What's more, he telegraphed President Grant and insisted that he intercede with the Spanish authorities, indeed that he demand O'Kelly's release. He called us treacherous, low-born cowards, bloodthirsty, cruel, barbaric, and heartless. Foaming with rage, kicking and gesticulating like a madman, he swore to avenge the wrong done by the Spaniards to the *Herald* and its commissioner. But the truth is that the *Herald* is secretly pleased with what is happening to its commissioner, and would even welcome his execution, since then it would be covered with glory, create an uproar, and sell a vast number of copies.*

This bitter and reprehensible commentary reflects the rancor of the opposing sides in this unforgettable struggle.

A New York newspaper and organ of the Spanish colony, *El Cronista*, expressed similar sentiments: "It cannot be denied that the *Herald* has done everything humanly possible to ensure its correspondent would be shot by the Spanish authorities, thereby gaining the glory of having a martyr, a *Herald* martyr! So many sacrifices for this peripatetic and persecuted Republic of Cuba, which seems as difficult for O'Kelly to find as the philosopher's stone was for the ancients!"† Contempt, indignation, and bombast of this kind were typical of a conservative press that was proud but powerless. The *Diario de la Marina* went so far as to evoke the friendship of the Irish for Spain: "At the end of the seventeenth century the Irish were great friends with the Spaniards and this friendship has remained strong. Just as one swallow does not a summer make, Mr. O'Kelly will not make the majority of the Irish people doubt the chivalry of the Spanish people of our time."‡

Overvaluing the friendship between the Irish and Spanish peoples might cause us to misjudge James J. O'Kelly's support for the Cuban separatists as just outrageous heresy, nothing more than an adventurous episode in the life of an extravagantly romantic journalist. But further study reminds us that Ireland and Spain (*Hibernia* and *Iberia*) were once the domain of the same race, that of the Iberians. There was genuine friendship between the Spanish and Irish peoples in the seventeenth century, and even until

---

***Diario de la Marina*, 15 April 1873, 2.

†Ortiz may have been working from an excerpt of the *Cronista* article published (in English translation) by the *Herald*. See 12 March 1873, 7.—*Trans.*

‡"El comisionado del '*Herald*,'" *Diario de la Marina*, 8 May 1873.

the nineteenth century. Stephen Gwynn has recently claimed that no country ever understood Ireland as well as Spain: "Spain's Catholic aristocracy sympathized with and helped their Irish counterparts, recognizing the country's social and military pre-eminence." Just a few weeks ago, the Marqués de Merry del Val gave a lecture in Caxton Hall, Westminster, under the auspices of the Irish Literary Society, with the title "The Irish Regiments in Spain." "A century ago, four hundred Irish surnames took root in Spain, and quite a few of them remain."* The names of O'Donnell and Prendergast appear in high positions in Spanish politics.

It is a fact that for long periods of its history the Spanish army maintained four entirely Irish regiments with their own uniforms and officers. The Spanish military had Irish generals, including O'Donnell, O'Farrill, O'Reilly, O'Neill, O'Hara, O'Mahony, and O'Ryan. But Spain was not alone in having mercenaries from Ireland. France had an entire brigade. Austrian troops also had several Irish generals, while Russia had two Irish marshals, and France had many as well. The Irish presence in the Spanish military was due less to friendship with Spain than an alliance against their long-standing enemy, Protestant England, oppressor of Catholic Ireland. Irish emigration was growing, and Irish aristocrats were welcomed in the Catholic courts of the European continent.†

This explains the arrival in Cuba of Irish nobles and soldiers in the service of Spain, such as the celebrated General Alejandro O'Reilly and General O'Farrill, both of whom established high-ranking Cuban families. General O'Reilly was a good friend of Irish magnate Oliver Pollock, resident of Havana from 1762 to 1765 and financier of the Spanish armies of O'Reilly and Gálvez in North America against the English. At that time, the rector of the Jesuits of Belén in Havana, Father Butler, was also Irish.‡

Irish emigration through military recruitment continued in the eighteenth and nineteenth centuries, with many Irish soldiers sacrificing their lives in the wars for independence in the Americas. We need not go into

---

*Ortiz provides no citations for these quotations from Gwynn and Merry del Val, which he translated into Spanish. We return these quotations to English.—*Trans.*

†Thomas A. Emmet, "Irish Emigrations during the XVII and XVIII Centuries," *Journal of the American-Irish Historical Society*, vol. 2 (New York, 1899).

‡The surname "Butler," which means "housekeeper" in English, demonstrates the difficulty of tracing Irish ancestry. The Irish are known not just by the prefixes "Mc" or "O," since a fifteenth-century ruling by Edward IV required the Irish to adopt British surnames or Anglicize them. Thus, many Irish families were forced to hide their Hibernian lineage, as noted by Edmund Spenser in *A View of the Present State of Ireland* (1596).

detail about the participation of the Irish in the American Revolution.* Many Irish soldiers fought in the South American wars for independence, including entire regiments, from the start of the rebellion in 1810 in Bogotá to its end in 1824 in Ayacucho.† England provided aid and reinforcements to South American armies, settling its score with Spain, who had previously helped the rebel colonies of North America led by Washington. Irish recruitment proceeded so publicly in Dublin that it found an echo in Parliament. Daniel O'Connell's wife sewed, and presented to Irish volunteers, the tricolor flag that they would wave in the Andes. And the austere O'Connell sent to Bolívar one of his sons as "his dearest offering to American independence."‡

During the wars, the Irish cornet Daniel Florence O'Leary became a general and close assistant to Bolívar and his staff, leaving 29 volumes of memoirs.§ He was the Lafayette of South America. General Francis Burdett O'Connor was chief of staff for the victorious Antonio José de Sucre in the decisive Battle of Ayacucho, and his memoirs include intriguing details about the great liberators.¶ Other well-known Irish members of the military elite include Sandes, commander of the Rifle Battalion, who gave the order to close ranks at the Battle of Carabobo; Wright, naval

---

*The following books document the military service and settlement of Irish immigrants in the United States: James Haltigan, *The Irish in the American Revolution and Their Early Influence in the Colonies* (Washington, D.C., 1908); Thomas H. Maginniss, *The Irish Contribution to America's Independence* (Philadelphia, 1913); Edward O'Meagher Condon, *The Irish Race in America* (New York, 1887); Michael J. O'Brien, "The Irish in the United States," in *The Glories of Ireland,* ed. Joseph Dunn and P.J. Lennox (Washington, D.C., 1914).

†While it has been said that foreign soldiers in Bolivia numbered 6,000, there may have been no more than 1,200 at a time. For more on this topic, see the erudite recent book by Alfred Hasbrouck, *Foreign Legionaries in the Liberation of Spanish South America* (New York, 1928). Other useful resources include a pamphlet by Angel María Galán, *Las Legiones británica e irlandesa* (Bogotá, 1919), and a recent article by W. J. Williams, "Bolivar and his Irish Legionaries," *Irish Quarterly Review* 72 (1929): 619.

‡Enrique Naranjo Martínez, *Irish Participation in Bolívar's Campaigns* (Washington, 1927), 4.

§O'Leary's memoirs were translated into Spanish by his son, Simón Bolívar O'Leary, and published in Caracas from 1878–88 as *Memorias del general O'Leary*. Today they are being reprinted in Madrid in single volumes: *Bolívar y la emancipación de Sur América* (1915); *Bolívar y las repúblicas del sur* (1919), etc., up to *Últimos años de la vida pública de Simón Bolívar*.

¶Francisco Burdett O'Connor, *Independencia americana: recuerdos de Francisco Burdett O'Connor* (Madrid, 1915).

and military hero; Colonel Ferguson, Bolívar's assistant, who saved his life during an attempted assassination in 1828; and Doctor Foley, Bolívar's physician. John D'Evereux, the Irish revolutionary who fought against England in 1798, was made a general by Bolívar, and he recruited more than 2,000 soldiers from Dublin, Liverpool, and London for an Irish Legion of lancers and riflemen in the Bolivarian armies. While this general never led his legion in combat, the soldiers of Erin that enlisted in its ranks were brave and effective.

A number of Irishmen were also involved in the establishment of Argentina.* After joining José de San Martín, General O'Brien and other Irish compatriots became liberators of Argentina, Chile, and Peru. Admiral Brown, also Irish, founded the Argentine navy. From Chile, recall the Irish General Ambrosio O'Higgins, viceroy of the country and father of Chilean dictator Bernardo O'Higgins. Finally, we cannot forget the name Mackenna.

Now that Ireland has appointed a historical commission to collect biographical data on Irish people around the world, it will find an abundant harvest in "nuestra américa."† It is clear, therefore, that James J. O'Kelly's allegiances were neither unusual nor contrary to Irish traditions. Generally the Irish nobility sided with Spain, though a considerable number—especially the red-blooded ones—supported South American independence from Spain, not with ill will towards this country, but rather with the sympathy of all patriots for nations seeking liberty. Liberty was likewise a concern for the Irish. England was their Spain, and O'Kelly was a mambí of anti-British separatism.

While the press of these countries grew fat on combative prose, good judgement was not altogether absent. The Spanish correspondent K. Lendas viewed O'Kelly with the philosophical pragmatism of a good Castilian Sancho Panza: "We must admit that no good can come from O'Kelly's imprisonment. No matter the judgement in the case, the *Herald* and other newspapers of that ilk will not stop unleashing complaints against us, even of the most trifling kind."

As alarm grew in the United States, the O'Kelly case became a heated topic. The US press responded, as might be expected, to the captain general's reluctance to provide information: "This demonstrates the weakness

---

*Thomas Murray, *The Story of the Irish in Argentina* (New York, 1919).

†Here Ortiz evokes the Cuban revolutionary, poet, and essayist José Martí and his vision of Latin American nationalism, particularly as expressed in his 1891 essay "Nuestra América" ("Our America").—*Trans.*

of the Spanish government. Only governments that are illegal or stained by injustice demand secrecy of the press."* In turn, emigrant separatists stoked the fires. At this time a new center of Cuban conspiracy formed in New York called the "Sociedad de Amigos de Cuba," echoing Havana's "Sociedad de Amigos del País." Comprised of emigrant *aldamistas*,† the group aimed to bridge divisions within the revolutionary movement.‡ They presented a statement to the president of the United States protesting O'Kelly's arrest.

Though forgotten today, the petition of the "Amigos de Cuba" to President Grant is characteristic of the times, and deserves reproduction in full:

TO HIS EXCELLENCY THE PRESIDENT OF THE UNITED STATES:
Intelligence has just been received from Cuba, by which it appears that Mr. James O'Kelly, the Commissioner delegated by the HERALD to gather facts concerning the war pending on that island, has been arrested by the Spanish authorities and is now liable to trial by court martial. This news has naturally produced a well-founded alarm among the Cuban residents in this country. They understand the spirit that animates the Spaniards in Cuba, and they fear for the life of an American citizen, who, imbued with the free spirit of this great people, accepted the mission of studying and investigating and communicating to the world, through the medium of the press, the facts concerning this war, which for four years has been waged by liberty against despotism.

The citizens of Cuba have had no share in the mission intrusted to Mr. O'Kelly, but when a man with a brave heart, representing one of the great journals of this city, undertook the painful and dangerous task referred to, they could not but feel a deep interest in his undertaking and in his safety. They felt assured from the outset that the result of his investigations would be favorable to them; that the testimony of an impartial witness must and would show the moral and physical resources of the natives of the island, which entitle them to become independent of the Spanish nation.

That nation has never recognized their right to interfere in their own affairs. It has ruled them with a rod of iron for the most selfish purposes and com-

---

*Since Ortiz omits a citation, we merely return this quotation to English.—*Trans.*

†The term "aldamistas" refers to the conservative wing of the separatist movement, named for Miguel Aldama, prominent member of the Havana elite and agent of the Cuban Republic in New York in 1869.—*Trans.*

‡Eladio Aguilera, *Francisco V. Aguilera y la revolución de Cuba de 1868* (Havana, 1909). Key figures included Hilario Cisneros, L. del Monte, Bramosio, General Juan Díaz de Villegas, F. Arteaga, Vicente Maestre, etc. Miguel Aldama declined to be named president of this society.

mitted without hesitation the most flagrant acts of injustice. All improvement has thus been shut out from a people all the more entitled to feel and appreciate the regenerating influence of liberty because of their proximity to this great Republic and their consequent superiority over their oppressors.

The world will then be able to learn and understand that in that island there is now organized and established a republican government with a constitution of unsurpassed liberality and freedom. Proof will be offered, of a conclusive character, showing the existence of armies that are struggling against, and able to meet on equal terms, the best and most experienced troops of the Spanish government; and, above all, and what is most important, the world will be satisfied that it is the determination and unalterable resolve of Cuba to be free and independent.

It is evident that on all these subjects the interests of Cuba and of Spain are diametrically opposed to each other, and that the Spanish authorities in the island will use every effort to drown the voice of Mr. O'Kelly, and to appropriate to themselves all the notes, proofs and memoranda that he may have accumulated; and, as the most expeditious and familiar method that they are acquainted with, applicable to such cases, is the infliction of summary capital punishment, no one need wonder if, under pretended forms of justice, employed for the mere sake of saving appearances, they should resort to that course in the present instance. Nor need any person wonder if the first intelligence that reaches us should apprise us that Mr. O'Kelly has disappeared from this world, a victim of Spanish cruelty and state policy.

Under these urgent circumstances, permit us, Mr. President, composing, as we do, the Directory Committee of the "Society of the Friends of Cuba," to direct our feeble voice to you, the Chief Magistrate of this great people, and respectfully ask your intervention in favor of a man now in great peril, and whose only offence lies in this, that, having been educated and accustomed to the practice of republican institutions, he has undertaken to disclose to the world, after personal investigation and upon positive proofs, the actual conditions of Cuban affairs. The administration will do its duty.

We well know, sir, that Mr. O'Kelly, being an American citizen, active in discharge of a duty of an eminently American character, the government to which he belongs needs no stimulus to urge it to that course which the exigencies of the case so imperatively demand. Of this we are fully convinced, and we cannot remain silent, even if our appeal should be utterly useless and uncalled for. But we desire, at least, in advance, to give some proof of our gratitude to the man who, by the mere public exhibition of the simple truth, will essentially contribute promptly and effectually to stop this terrible effusion of blood and to put an end to the terrible distress and suffering that have accompanied the struggles of a neighboring people on their way to liberty.

J.G. D. DE VILLEGAS, PRESIDENT
FRANCISCO ARTEAGA, TREASURER
HILARIO CISNEROS
VICENTE MESTRE
VICENTE BUENO
JUAN JOSÉ DÍAZ
PEDRO M. RIVERO, SECRETARY*

The vice president of *Cuba libre,* General Francisco V. Aguilera, recently arrived from Paris, was asked about the possible development of events with respect to O'Kelly's imprisonment. He was explicit and unhesitating:

> I differ from the majority of my countrymen in this city, who fear that O'Kelly will be shot or assassinated. I do not (emphatically). From the tact and good sense he has displayed all along, I feel confident that he would not be so imprudent as to carry written dispatches from the Cuban patriots when he presented himself at the Spanish lines. One of the principal objects of the Spaniards in his case is to gain time, and to make his news "flat, stale and unprofitable." . . .
> Mr. Aguilera then continued, after lighting a fresh cigarette—I read the other day in your paper about one of my engineers, named Phelps, an Englishman, who was taken prisoner at Manzanillo shortly after the commencement of the revolution, and that an English man-of-war was immediately despatched to Manzanillo to demand him. I also remember enjoying the joke of the English Captain, who wrote to General Ampudia, who commanded the town, that, as the town was unhealthy at that season, he only intended waiting to two o'clock in the afternoon for the Englishman being surrendered to him, or if he was not on board his ship at that hour he would bombard the town. As you can readily understand, not a moment was lost in hurrying him on board.
> Now, as to the case of Mr. O'Kelly, I consider that there never was a case in which prompt and decisive action was more urgently called for at the hands of this government. Mr. O'Kelly, although, I believe, a British subject, is, by his long residence in this country and as an American journalist, fully entitled to the protection of the Stars and Stripes. Perhaps the British may be too peremptory in their procedures, but it is still energetic. Germany and France follow in

---

*Published in the *New York Herald,* 10 April 1873, 3.—*Trans.*

the same school; but this country has, it seems adopted a peace-at-any-price policy, very different to the days of Jackson and Pierce.

Although I am not a citizen of this country, I cannot help regretting this policy, which is unworthy of the great United States. . . .

They know he is a bold and fearless writer, and will give a truthful and impartial account of what he has seen in Cuba Libre—and that is where the shoe pinches, for they are afraid of publicity being given to the manner in which they carry on the war. In conclusion I would say, as qualified by my long experience of the Spaniards, that they, fearing the powers which will support Mr. O'Kelly, will not venture to hurt him.*

Cubans questioned by the *Herald* reporters believed unanimously that O'Kelly would not be shot because Spain would not make this mistake, given his reputation.†

The *New York Herald* and almost all of its colleagues fired shot after shot against Spanish despotism in Cuba, except for some rivals of that great newspaper, one among them even commenting on the matter, saying that O'Kelly should be left to his fate for having gone where he should not have. But in general, the US press threatened Spain with recognition of the belligerence of the mambises if O'Kelly was mistreated.‡ The *New York Herald* called for the independence of Cuba, saying "The death of O'Kelly would be the end of the domination of Spain in America."§ The *New York Herald* had been and continued to be a supporter of the separatist cause, but never before had it been so indignant. The threat of a reporter's death weighed more on the editorialist than did the prolonged torture of an entire people in their longing for freedom.

Commenting on O'Kelly's report in its leading article, the *Herald* stated:

> It provides the governments and the people of the United States and Europe with the reports they have so long desired but failed to obtain. From it they will see the true state of the insurrection, its weakness and its strength, the scarcity, the shortage of arms and ammunition, the itinerant government that roams

---

*Ellipsis added. This interview appears in the *New York Herald*, 12 April 1873, 7. Ortiz's version is a particularly loose translation that omits brief sections of the interview.—*Trans.*

†We see this clearly in the *Herald*'s report from 8 April.

‡For discussion of the contentious issue of formal US recognition of the Cuban insurgents as belligerents, see introduction, xxii–xxiv.—*Trans.*

§Since Ortiz omits a citation here, we merely return this quotation to English. For similar statements, see the *New York Herald*, 12 April 1873, 7, and 13 April 1873, 8.—*Trans.*

the mountains and hides in dense forests, the painful resignation of men, who, through trials and hardships, demonstrate devotion to the cause of *Cuba libre* and determination to carry forward the desperate struggle for independence.

Below it stated: "If we advocate for the independence of Cuba, we do so based on the sweeping principle of freedom and humanity, but if the Cubans are unworthy of being independent, or if the struggle, however worthy, is hopeless, the *Herald* will announce this to the whole world and will call for the end of this cruel and destructive conflict."*

The *New York Herald* laid out the ideological basis for the right of intervention, as it had done many times before and would do more effectively in 1898: "It becomes more imperatively than ever the duty of the American government to intervene for the purpose of ending a barbarous war waged at our very doors, and prosecuted in a manner hazardous to the lives of our own citizens, disgraceful to a civilized land and destructive of American interests."†

The *Herald*'s thesis wrapped its correspondent in an immunity more inviolable than that of a diplomat. O'Kelly was an "ambassador of truth. Neither Emperor, King nor President could sign the brevet of an emissary in such a case."‡ On another occasion, the *New York Herald* arrived at the idea that O'Kelly could be called upon providentially to intervene in the bitter conflict between Cubans and Spaniards, proposing naively that he be given leave to hold a plebiscite through which the inhabitants of Cuba could decide what form of government would prevail in that country, whether colonial or republican.§

The New York newspaper the *Sun*, rival of the *New York Herald*, provided its own dispassionate assessment:

> There has been some wild talk during the last few days about the case of Mr. O'Kelly who went down to Cuba as a correspondent of the *Herald*. Being in the Spanish lines in the eastern department of the island he applied to the commanding officer for permission to visit the insurgents. This, of course, was refused to him, as it ought to have been. No General in the world would be justified in granting such permission. During our own war it was repeatedly refused to parties having quite a good a claim to it as Mr. O'Kelly, and no

---

*Since Ortiz omits a citation here, we merely return these quotations to English. Many of the editorials from this period express similar sentiments.—*Trans.*
†*New York Herald,* 12 April 1873, 6.—*Trans.*
‡*New York Herald,* 19 March 1873, 6.
§See *New York Herald,* 4 March 1873, 6.—*Trans.*

one thought of finding fault with the refusal. When, however, he found that he could not reach the insurgent camps with the consent of the Spanish commander, Mr. O'Kelly took the business into his own hands; and though warned by the Spaniards that if captured after visiting the insurgents he would be liable to be shot, he nevertheless took the risk and went. He has now been captured, and the Spaniards are considering what they will do with him. It does not seem probable that they will execute their threat, but they have a perfect right to do so, and if O'Kelly is shot or hanged neither the United States nor the English government, of which he is a subject, will have any right to complain.*

But this argument was in fact favorable to O'Kelly because it demonstrated his most extreme audacity in the pursuit of a journalistic service, purely journalistic, carried out with real danger of death.

Other newspapers, however, like the *Daily Graphic,* though no friend of its colleague the *New York Herald,* depicted O'Kelly as a legendary hero, a beautiful *gentleman of journalism:*

"He is remarkably good-looking, with a fresh color upon his cheeks, and an unmistakable Celtic twinkle in his eye. His figure is well-proportioned, inclining perhaps a little to stoutness. He is an agreeable companion, witty and cultured, and a young man of great personal bravery. Mr. O'Kelly, in addition to his other acquirements, is a very fair artist, and indeed comes of an artistic family."† The Hispanophile French-language newspaper of New York, the *Courrier des États Unis,* also tempered the mood, recognizing that O'Kelly was a young and intelligent journalist, a friend of art, and, above all, a charming gentleman, always of good humor and cheerful disposition, "who would soon return to New York with the glory of having had a semi-heroic adventure."‡ The balanced attitude of this French newspaper irritated the Spanish press, unconditional defenders of absolutism.

O'Kelly's success was even more resounding when the public discovered that the interview with Céspedes reported by the correspondent who preceded O'Kelly in Cuba, Henderson, was a sham. Henderson undoubtedly managed to speak with Ignacio Agramonte and the Camagüeyan mambises, but not with Carlos Manuel de Céspedes, who wrote to James Gordon Bennett that the correspondent had left Cuba abruptly, fearing the volunteers of the colonial army after being told that they had killed a

---

Sun, 12 April 1873, 2.—*Trans.*
†*Daily Graphic,* 10 April 1873, quoted in the *New York Herald,* 11 April 1873, 3.—*Trans.*
‡*New York Herald,* 9 April 1873, 9.

poor wretch just for wearing a blue tie, emblem of *Cuba libre*. The *New York Herald* reported this to its readers to rehabilitate its creditability and underscore its success with O'Kelly. The *Herald* stated:

> Mr. Henderson did well enough without resorting to fraud; but, eager to make his success appear complete, he forfeited his honor and palmed off a false story upon the public through our columns. We make all the atonement in our power by this explanation, which will probably impress upon all correspondents the knowledge that our columns can never be made the vehicle for the imposition of false news upon the public. The dishonorable conduct of our first commissioner only serves to enhance the value of the information we are now receiving from the mountain home of Cuba Libre.*

Any defensive measures to rescue O'Kelly fell primarily to the English government, but the English authorities were likely disinclined to make energetic efforts in O'Kelly's case. A Spanish journalist suggested as much, saying: "James O'Kelly was born in Galway, Ireland, in 1840, but, as I understand it, he is in favor of Irish separation and instead of serving in the British Army, he enlisted with the French troops in Mexico during the time of Maximilian. It is therefore unlikely that the British government is in a hurry to claim him."† Perhaps for this reason the English consul did not appear to Mr. Millen to be particularly interested in O'Kelly's freedom.‡ According to the reporter, he said: "O'Kelly put his nose in the business; not only so, but his whole face."§

The State Department in Washington may also have been annoyed by O'Kelly's adventures, as it was not in their plans at the time to have a challenging problem in Cuba stir popular opinion at home, an attitude shared by some New York newspapers that were already disinclined to support a popular correspondent of the *New York Herald*. This is why the caustic K. Lendas observed the following in the *Diario de la Marina*:

**New York Herald, 16 April 1873, 8.—*Trans.*

†Lendas, *Diario de la Marina*, 22 April 1873, 3.

‡Francis F. Millen was the *New York Herald*'s "Secret Cuban Commissioner." He reports traveling to Cuba on the same day as O'Kelly (14 December 1872), spent over two months in the insurgent camps, and was arrested in Manzanillo where he occupied (briefly) the same cell in Fort Gerona as had O'Kelly. For his account, see the *New York Herald*, 30 May, 7; 7 June, 4; 16 June, 3. Millen was a US citizen, a Clan na Gael member, and a spy for the British. See Peter Hulme, *Cuba's Wild East: A Literary Geography of Oriente* (Liverpool: Liverpool University Press, 2011), 61–62.—*Trans.*

§*New York Herald*, 7 June 1873, 4.

It is natural that some newspapers would cover the matter because they have to fill their columns with something, but not all of them do so in a way favorable to the *Herald* or its commissioner. Among those that show a little common sense I could cite the *Evening Express,* which, after satirizing O'Kelly's assignment, ended by saying, "don't go into a well you don't know how to get out of," as well as the *New York Times,* whose reporting from Washington, which tends to be inspired by the State Department, recently included the following: *A great advertisement gone to waste.* The *New York Herald*'s beautiful plan to send a correspondent to Cuba in order to create conflict and entangle our government with that of Spain, has failed utterly. Precisely when the paper most vehemently claims protection under the aegis of the United States, our cruel authorities discover that the person for whom it is invoked is not an American citizen and therefore has no right to such protection. All newspapers that send commissioners of this type should take note of this situation and naturalize their correspondents in advance.*

But at last, the US authorities took action on the matter. One of O'Kelly's brothers, then living in the state of Connecticut, telegraphed Mr. Fish, Secretary of State, and Mr. Thornton, British Minister to the United States in Washington, so that they might intercede on James J. O'Kelly's behalf. The responses of both officials were as follows:

STEPHEN J. O'KELLY, Hartford, Conn.

I have telegraphed to United States Consul General in Havana, A. T. A. Torbert, instructing him that, inasmuch as James J. O'Kelly is a British subject, this government cannot interfere officially, but that he see the British Consul use his good offices, either in conjunction with him or separately, with the authorities to allow the trial of James J. O'Kelly to be conducted in Havana, and expressing the hope that they will deal mercifull [sic] with him.

HAMILTON FISH,
    Secretary of State

STEPHEN J. O'KELLY, Hartford, Conn.

Mr. Dunlop, British Consul General at Havana, is the agent of Her Majesty's government in Cuba. I have no authority over him nor in Cuba.

EDWARD THORNTON.†

---

*Lendas, *Diario,* 22 April 1873, 3.
†*New York Herald,* 13 April 1873, 5.—*Trans.*

The vice president of the United States, Mr. Wilson, also made statements about the O'Kelly case, "inspired by true Americanism and in admiration of O'Kelly's valor."*

The *Herald* took advantage of the proclamation of the Spanish Republic to invoke liberal idealism: "The Spanish Republic has no reason to exist if it absurdly declares itself liberator of its country in Europe and oppressor of its colonies in America."† It was even insinuated by Francisco V. Aguilera that, according to rumors from Spain, Mr. Sickles, US Minister in Madrid, was too friendly with Castelar and the Spanish republicans who governed in Madrid to apply the pressure needed for O'Kelly's release, but the facts proved precisely the opposite.‡

In the end, the *New York Herald* led readers to believe that General Ceballos had been relieved of his post by the government of the Spanish Republic for mishandling the O'Kelly case, and this was repeated ingenuously by Havana's *La Constancia* in a report from New York on April 9, 1873. It is true that General Ceballos's command ended at the end of that month and that he left for Spain, replaced by General Pieltain. This brought more attention to the O'Kelly "case" in Cuba. There is no doubt that Emilio Castelar defended the freedom of the journalist, as he acknowledges in his memoirs. Henri Rochefort, in his memoirs, suggests that it was the declaration of the Spanish Republic that saved O'Kelly.

Whatever the case may be, it is true that in May of 1873 General Sickles, US Minister in Madrid, informed his president that the republican government of Spain had given the order to the captain general of Cuba to transfer O'Kelly to the Peninsula under guard. This was done to remove him from the jurisdiction of the military authorities in Cuba, to emphasize the international nature of the case, and, in short, to end the controversy by freeing the arrested correspondent.

O'Kelly was taken from Manzanillo to the fortress of El Morro in Santiago de Cuba, and from there on the steamer *Villaclara*, destined for the

---

*This is a very loose translation from an interview with Wilson. See *New York Herald*, 13 April 1873, 5.—*Trans.*

†Since Ortiz omits a citation here, we merely return these quotations to English. For similar sentiments, see the *New York Herald*, 11 April 1873, 6.—*Trans.*

‡*New York Herald*, 27 March 1873, 3.

cells of another fortress, La Cabaña, in Havana.* From there, on May 30, he left for Santander on the steamer *Antonio López*. In Spain he was kept in the penitentiary at Santoña before being given provisional release under oath of not attempting to leave the country and presenting himself to the authorities in Madrid.

In the capital, Mr. Sickles offered to facilitate O'Kelly's release, but his liberty arrived in an unexpected manner. It is said that Emilio Castelar, President of the Spanish Republic, and Francisco Pi y Margall, Minister of the Interior, were friends of Ireland who had decided to save O'Kelly.† One day Castelar sent a confidential messenger to O'Kelly, saying: "The president of the Republic knows that Pavia, the captain general in Madrid, has decided to overthrow the Republic and the government cannot prevent him. That is what I am here to tell you. If the Royalists restore the monarchy they will come down hard on you, so you are advised to prepare your luggage and get the United States envoy to accompany you to the Ministry of the Interior to let them know that you, James J. O'Kelly, have withdrawn your word of honor not to escape and are putting yourself at their disposal." This is what O'Kelly did, although Mr. Sickles went reluctantly, not privy to the secret, and when the journalist told Pi y Margall of his decision to turn himself in again and to then escape if he could, the minister cleverly told him: "I cannot force you to change your mind and you will know what is appropriate to your responsibilities. Please return to your hotel until the authorities require your presence." Sickles was wide-eyed. Freed from his word of honor, O'Kelly took the first train for Gibraltar. The following day the Republic would expire in one of those outbreaks of pretorian violence that punctuate the political history of Spain and its former colonies, in this regard so faithful to their parent.

It is therefore clear that O'Kelly was not condemned to death as a spy, as the story was then told, and as today still appears in a small Irish dictionary. Doubtless this rumor, quite credible, contributed to the romantic image of the daring correspondent whose adventure in the mambi-land constituted a picturesque episode in the Ten Years' War. The best-informed

---

*In La Cabaña he was visited by the *Herald* journalist Francis F. Millen, through the mediation of the now elderly Mr. Springer, always a great supporter of Cuba, who at that time (25 May 1873), was an official in the US embassy, as he still is today, 57 years later!

†*The Gaelic American* (New York), 30 December 1916, 7.

Spanish historian of the war recognized the propriety of O'Kelly's action and included an extract from the book in one of his chapters.*

The sensational story continued with the adventure of the *Herald* correspondent in Havana, Mr. Price, who had been actively involved in the O'Kelly incident. As K. Lendas wrote in his Havana newspaper:

> Fortune favors the *Herald*. The O'Kelly sensation was beginning to fade, and with no pretexts suitable for it to unleash one of its thunderstorms, what should happen but the opportune arrest of the *Herald*'s Havana correspondent, Mr. Leopold A. Price. Besides the telegram from the Associated Press, the news was communicated directly by the United States Consul General in Havana, who did not know the reason for the arrest. These two telegrams, and another received from Washington on the same subject, were placed by the *Herald* in a column under the headline "War Against the *Herald*," and then in a feature article on the coup in Spain. The *Herald*'s blustering style and preposterous arguments on all subjects are now so well-known that it is unnecessary to describe the storm the young journalist unleashed over us. If there is a reason, or at least a pretext, perhaps it is not entirely his fault. I said that fortune favored him, as it indeed did, since he was given just the pretexts he needed. From Washington the *Herald* was told that on receipt of the telegram from Mr. Torbert, the government had instructed him to lose no time in obtaining Mr. Price's release and that he should keep the State Department informed.†

The *Herald*'s Cuba correspondents continued to keep Spain occupied. On April 17, a new *Herald* war correspondent presented himself at the headquarters of Carlos Manuel de Céspedes, as recorded by K. Lendas:

> Yet again I find myself with the unavoidable, though disagreeable, task of reporting on the *Herald* and its commissioners. Without any warning, and without priming their readers' nervous systems for the great surprise in store, it presented us last Saturday on one of its entirely typical pages a letter from its third commissioner, who has the wit to call himself F. F. Millen, and to have done exactly, point by point, what those famous emissaries Henderson and O'Kelly have already done on this troubled island. Envoy number three has gone to Cuba, visited the insurgent camp, seen Céspedes, collected letters and messages from the wandering president, returned to Manzanillo, presented himself to the governor, been arrested and imprisoned, spent a few days in

---

*Antonio Pirala, *Anales de la guerra de Cuba*, vol. 2 (Madrid, 1896), 548–54.
†*Diario de la Marina*, 28 May 1873.

the same cell in Fort Gerona that had O'Kelly as a guest, was subject to some verbal advice with consequent consular intervention and protest, was set free in error, returned to Havana, fired off a letter modelled on O'Kelly's, and has set off for New York where he will judge the living and the dead of that ill-starred rebellion in order to complete the work left hanging by O'Kelly's imprisonment. Just look how far-sighted the *Herald* is! It foresaw that "Spanish tyranny" would cut off O'Kelly's communication, silencing half his story, and so sent at the same time another secret commissioner, a silent partner, a duplicate emissary, so that if one got lost or was mislaid, the other could step in, so that readers would not lose the thread! And how quiet were the *Herald* and Mr. Millen about this new tactical and journalistic flourish! What seems likely to me, given the *Herald*'s lack of fuss before and after Mr. Millen's letter, is one of two things: either the third commissioner is junior to his predecessors and has been sent purely as a deputy or substitute (I was going to say spare horse), or that the *Herald* is finally beginning to get tired of all this farce and straight-faced lying. If it is neither of these two things, then we must conclude that Mr. Millen's mistaken release has unhinged the *Herald*'s plan of having a series of martyred correspondents. A case, one might say, of a happy error.

However, despite the insignificance of the third commissioner's letter, just repeating what O'Kelly has already reported, it contains two or three points worthy of mention: I will refer to them in the order in which they appear. Telling of his arrest in Manzanillo, Millen says: "I expected to be thoroughly searched for papers or documents. Ample preparation for that disagreeable process had been made by me days before. My notes, letters from President Céspedes, and other papers were already on their way by the underground railroad. They reached Manzanillo by secure hands other than mine. By the same means my papers were safely conveyed here, and they will not reach my possession until I shall have sailed at least the conventional marine league out at sea, beyond the limits of Spanish waters. Let the Dons [that is what they call us Spaniards] divine how the thing was done. To their credit be it said, however, no search was made of my person, nor was I ever asked for papers."

Mr. Millen relates a curious conversation that took place in Santiago de Cuba between Mr. Hippisley, captain of the English gunboat *Plover,* and Mr. Ramsden, Vice-Consul for Her Majesty's Government. The former said to the latter: "'British influence can do nothing here; you and I, Ramsden, had better take out our naturalization papers and become American citizens.' 'I think so, too,' assented Ramsden. 'Only think of it! That confounded Millen released after two days' imprisonment, and he charged with the same offence as Mr. O'Kelly, who is treated with such rigor; and all because Millen happens to be an American citizen. It is preposterous.'" To which Millen adds: "The fact is that my prompt release was looked upon with great dissatisfaction by British representatives in the island, because they saw in it a proof of American influence with the Spaniards and a sign of wholesome fear entertained by them of the American people."

Mr. Millen then went to Havana with Mr. O'Kelly and found there "another victim of Spanish tyranny," a stereotypical phrase that almost all typesetters have to hand for dealing with Spanish matters. This victim was Mr. Price, who did not know what crime he had committed. Mr. Millen went to intercede for O'Kelly with Mr. Crawford, acting British consul general in Mr. Dunlop's absence. I will convey the result of the visit in Millen's own words, punctiliously translated: "The acting British consul general appeared neither to have sympathy nor pity for the prisoner. He said 'Mr. O'Kelly put his nose in the business; not only so, but his whole face.'"*

O'Kelly's sensational adventure concluded without further mishap. The Cuba-loving Irishman was set free by the Spaniards and returned to New York, crowning his journalistic triumph with the full account of his excursion into the mambi-land, first in the columns of the *New York Herald* and then as a book.

O'Kelly's first report to the *Herald,* dated March 10, was published as a double-page spread with a large map of the eastern part of Cuba and thick black headlines.† The others followed from time to time. The president of the peripatetic republic felt moved to thank James Gordon Bennett for his services to the revolution. On June 17, the *Herald* inserted a letter from Carlos Manuel de Céspedes indicating his gratitude for the mission to *Cuba libre* entrusted successively to Henderson, O'Kelly, and Millen. For the *Herald,* wrote Céspedes, "the boldness of Mr. Stanley, who marched through the deserts of Africa in search of the renowned traveler, Livingstone, was not enough; it was necessary to explore also the mysterious fields of the garden of the American Hesperides, where men more barbarous and despotic than the petty kings of Africa wish to rule

---

*Diario de la Marina, 18 June 1873, 3.—*Trans.* Here Lendas quotes from Francis F. Millen's report, *New York Herald,* 7 June 1873, 4.

†In fact, the *Herald* published the first O'Kelly dispatch it received much earlier, on 30 Dec. 1872 (p.3), dated 24 December. O'Kelly's first dispatch, dated 20 December, arrived late and was published 1 January (p.5). While the *Herald* did publish a map of Cuba on 16 April (p.6), the map Ortiz refers to appears on 8 April (p.5).—*Trans.*

others on whose feet they would put fetters, and drive them to be sold, like swine, in the markets of Cuba."*

Extracts from O'Kelly's reports were immediately translated and appeared in *La Independencia,* which championed the separatist Cuban cause in New York. The English edition was entitled *The Mambi-Land, or Adventures of a* Herald *Correspondent in Cuba,* by James J. O'Kelly (Philadelphia. J. B. Lippincott and Co. 1874. in 8°. 359 pgs). The book had a great and lasting impact among Cubans and *Cuba libre* sympathizers, as demonstrated by the four Spanish-language editions. The first translation, by Nicanor Trelles, appeared in New Orleans in 1876. In 1887, O'Kelly's work appeared again, translated "exclusively for *El Cubano,*" an autonomist newspaper in Havana edited by Antonio Zambrana. It was published serially between May 3 and October 12, and was followed by two brief episodes from the Ten Years' War entitled "The Action at Las Guásimas" and "The Rescue of a Hero." Another Spanish edition appeared in Santa Clara in 1887, translated by Ricardo García Garófalo, which is the one used for this present volume. The fourth was published in Havana, though under a spurious imprint. The cover reads, after the title, "translation by E. C. (Mayagüez, P. R. 1888)." But Figarola Caneda has already said that the edition was published clandestinely in Havana, and not in Puerto Rico as the cover indicates. It is likely that this was the case, although the circumstances are obscure, as a year earlier, *El Cubano* had published the entire text, and it is not obvious why what could be done in 1887 could not be repeated in 1888. And if it could not be done in Havana, it could not have been done in a small Puerto Rican town.

There are three further Spanish translations: one in a Matanzas newspaper; another done by A. Núnez-Parra, which has just appeared in the *Heraldo de Cuba;* and another which we owe to the cultured diplomat and financial official, Dr. Recaredo García Fernández, and which we have unfortunately not been able to use for the current edition. Just a few months ago, a new and much-praised Cuban short story writer, Pablo de la Torriente Brau, drew inspiration from reading these very lines to create one of the most praised stories in his book *Batey.*† This shows the past and continuing interest in O'Kelly's story in Cuba.

We will not say much about the narrative reproduced here. It is as lively

---

*This letter from Céspedes was published alongside another similar letter from Francisco Fornarís y Céspedes, secretary of the House of Representatives of the Republic of Cuba.

†Pablo de la Torriente Brau and Gonzalo Mazas Garbayo, *Batey* (Havana, 1930).

and interesting as an episodic novel: it is saturated with the patriotically liberal, passionate, and restless spirit burning in the heart of a young Irishman who, in the years that follow, would distinguish himself in the Parliament in London defending the character of his captive nation. *The Mambi-Land* is a stimulating book, animated by the emotions of motherland, liberty, and youth. It paints an epoch, a people, a character, and an ideal.

O'Kelly never returned to Cuba, but his adventurous spirit was not sated by the risks he endured in Cuba, and, having left the mambi-land, he never forgot about the fate of this country. Hardly had our intrepid reporter fled from Spain into Gibraltar when he hatched a devilish plan to make an imperial gift to the Spanish crown at English expense: nothing less than the Rock of Gibraltar itself. In the few days that O'Kelly spent in the formidable British possession, he studied the fortress and discovered an abandoned path running across the rock, now used only by smugglers defrauding Spanish customs. Along this path he could send two hundred Irish adventurers by night. With intelligence provided by the numerous Fenians in the two regiments of the garrison, as well as subsequent Spanish support, the success of the surprise attack could be guaranteed. The hatching of the plot awaited the right moment. It is known that several years later O'Kelly returned to Madrid with Dr. William Carroll, from Philadelphia and a representative of Irish organizations in the United States, and they explained the plan to Cánovas del Castillo, then president of Alfonso XII's Council of Ministers, who made them understand there would be no point in Spain taking Gibraltar, since England, navally superior, would shell Spanish coastal towns and annihilate Spanish shipping, resulting in the enforced return of the captured Rock. O'Kelly had therefore to abandon that new plan of attack against despised Albion, but, undeterred, he returned to New York to continue working for Irish freedom. We read that, in 1876, he again took up arms in the United States, as volunteer or war correspondent on a military expedition against the Sioux Indians and their spirited chief, Sitting Bull.

We have already told how from his youth O'Kelly conspired for the freedom of Ireland, not hiding his enmity for his country's oppressors, be they Irish or not. On all his journalistic forays through France, Mexico, the United States, and Cuba, he carried the Irish conspiracy with him. The Gibraltar episode clearly shows his ceaseless antagonism towards Great Britain. In New York, he continued plotting for Irish independence through his active membership in Clan na Gael. William O'Brien tells how his romantic adventures in Cuba as a *Herald* correspondent gave O'Kelly a remarkable influence over US politicians, which he took advantage of to further his plots and propaganda.* From 1870 he had been sending guns from the United States to aid the revolution in his country. "There's no concealment about it," he said years later to the English investigators of his subversive activities, while they showed him incriminating letters from those years, and O'Kelly smiled to himself at the evocation of his romantic youth.†

When the Fenian agitator Michael Davitt went to New York in August 1878 to broker an agreement between Irish revolutionaries and constitutionalists, with a view to ending Anglo-Saxon absolutism, the first person he sought out was O'Kelly, only to find that O'Kelly, along with John Devoy and others, had already prepared the ground for an anti-British political coalition.‡ Indeed an alliance formed, at least temporarily, between the Irish parliamentarians, that is the autonomists under the leadership of Parnell, and the separatists of Clan na Gael headed by the romantic figure of the poet John O'Leary.§ This did not mean that the revolutionaries were giving up. Indeed, in 1878, our dashing Dublin journalist went back to Ireland as a Clan na Gael representative in pursuit of his patriotic ideal. He came to "'organize' Ireland for the revolution," he told the judge, without beating around the bush. "Whatever you want to know about myself personally, I will tell you."¶

While the revolution would come if the parliamentary initiative fell apart, O'Kelly did not meanwhile forget his spills and thrills as a war correspondent. He turns up again in Africa, in the Egyptian Sudan, sending reports to the London *Daily News*. The valiant reporter and soldier of fortune tried without success to get behind the lines of the Mahdi's insurgent troops, but his derring-do on the Upper Nile and in Khartoum made popular news, burnishing his reputation. O'Connor notes that O'Kelly's reports on the Sudanese conflict were the first news that the British public received about the true character and real impact of the Mahdi rebel-

---

*William O'Brien, *The Parnell of Real Life* (London: 1926), 90.

†John MacDonald, *Diary of the Parnell Commission* (London, 1890), 299.

‡Richard Barry O'Brien, *The Life of Charles Stewart Parnell, 1846–1891*, vol. 1 (London, 1898), 164–165.

§Editor of *The Irish People*, this lyrical Irishman, who seared his poems in the flames of patriotic freedom, recalls in his civic passion the figure of José Martí, the great poet and apostle of Cuban freedom fighters.

¶MacDonald, *Diary of the Parnell Commission*, 298.—*Trans.*

lion against Egypt's khedivate, closely linked to England. The judicious observations of the soldier-journalist about the strategy deployed by Lord Wolseley, published in *Freeman's Journal,* caused a sensation. Disaster ensued, just when and as O'Kelly had predicted.*

Despite this account from a reliable source, we have just read in an Irish newspaper another explanation of O'Kelly's Sudanese adventure: "In 1884, O'Kelly disappeared from the House of Commons for six months. Nobody knew where he had gone. In fact he went to help the Mahdi and his desert warriors fight against English troops. Dressed as an Arab, it was none other than O'Kelly who, through the distinction of his military valor, inspired, unbeknownst, Rudyard Kipling's lines about a brave Sudanese warrior."† This explanation may sound like something out of a chivalric romance, but it is not entirely impossible given O'Kelly's lifelong Anglophobia. We do not, however, have any way of knowing for sure the truth of this mysterious episode.

We do know of another version that sounds truthful, on account of its authoritative source, which we must keep to ourselves. It was recognized that O'Kelly had Anglophobic intentions when, voluntarily and promptly, he launched himself into the risks and exhaustion of war journalism as a subject of one of the belligerent parties, and hastened to the Sudan as correspondent for the *Daily News*. He went there with the daring and secret purpose of helping the Sudanese separatists in their struggle against the English, giving them advice and helping them acquire arms, as theirs were primitive and inefficient. O'Kelly made contact with the brave mambises of the Mahdi, gained their trust, and even gave them helpful advice. Everything was set for the audacious Irishman to join the Mahdists' fight against England, but the English were suspicious of O'Kelly's intentions, arrested him in Dongola, and forced him to return to Wadi Halfa, on the banks of the Nile, thwarting his plans. Be all this as it may, O'Kelly's actions in the Sudan are enough to indicate his mettle, his daring, and the temper of his enmity towards the country that had subjugated his native land.

The Sudan had hardly been pacified when England was confronted by the Muscovite government over the frontier of distant Afghanistan, and once again O'Kelly had to entwine his clandestine activities with Russian and anti-British diplomacy. O'Kelly must have felt possessed by great

---

*O'Connor, *Parnell Movement*, 361–62.

†According to *The Advocate*, an Irish weekly published in New York, 21 December 1889. The article is dedicated to O'Kelly.

patriotic feeling around this time, in 1885. In his view, one of his enduring plans—to defeat England by collaborating with its age-old enemy, Czarist Russia—was about to come to fruition. The government in St. Petersburg energetically threatened Afghanistan, the frontier troops had advanced, and all seemed set for armed conflict. With the security of its Indian Empire in mind, the British lion could not allow the Slavic eagle to get its claws into Afghan territory, thereby moving within touching distance of the Indian border. So war between England and Russia was probable, and Parnell let himself be convinced by his lieutenant to carry out one of his devilish plans. The trustworthy O'Kelly was sent by the separatists from London to New York, so that, taking advantage of his great influence in US political circles, he might investigate among them the possibility of—and then organize—an armed expedition prepared on US soil to fall upon Ireland at the opportune moment and rescue it from the English. The plans were highly developed, and received the approval in London for a secret envoy from the Czar. In the United States, 5,000 Irishmen—native-born or descendants, drawn from veterans of the Civil War—had to be enlisted privately without arousing suspicion. When the time came, the volunteers would congregate in a US port, where they would embark on a merchant or privateering fleet provided by the Russians, and, crossing the Atlantic, would land on the beaches of Ireland, proclaiming its independence. O'Kelly was bullish about the plan. He was sure that the famous general, Phil Sheridan, the hero of Shenandoah Valley, would be the leader of the liberating army and he had even arranged for a senior functionary in Washington to ensure that there would be no indiscreet interference that would obstruct the movement of the Russian ships, the Russians being at that time, in M. O'Brien's words, the "favorite sons" of the American people, on account of their enmity towards England. O'Kelly must have made use of his knowledge of the history of Cuban conspiracies and armed rebellions in this plan's development, but this marine expedition for Irish freedom, rather like those of Narciso López, was doomed for failure. It never even got started because Russia changed tack and entered negotiations with its rival.

Now think again about the likelihood of O'Kelly offering military aid to the Sudanese against England. Perhaps O'Kelly fashioned other analogous plans on later occasions when England was under pressure. It is known that Parnell entered into similar machinations during the imperialist war against the Boers, but we do not know whether on this occasion—as could have been the case—O'Kelly also conspired with the South Africans.

Other overt struggles waited for him at home, where he took an active part in liberation movements.* When O'Kelly was in Ireland in 1880 as an agent for Clan na Gael, Parnell invited him to join the parliamentary coalition of all the Irish political forces formed to gain constitutional concessions from the London government. As a soldier, O'Kelly doubtless understood the strategic efficacy of dividing the nationalist forces into two wings, something Parnell openly expounded in a speech in New York.† One wing would operate in the open, with clear constitutional tactics, fighting in the British Parliament for Irish freedoms, explaining the wishes of the people and the real injustices that made a complete change of regime inevitable; while the other revolutionary wing would operate under cover, in the dark, and would carry a threat, ready to act when political insufficiency indicated the need for greater sacrifices. Many people were of the opinion that this was also how the forces for national liberation played out in Cuba, although without the kind of public declaration made by Parnell. But in Ireland, in those years, the collaboration was more deliberately structured than it was among the Cubans. For a long time Fenianism's assets and moral pressure sustained the constitutionalism of Parnell and his followers, while at the same time supporting shock troops. In both countries the relationship between the two wings was reciprocal. Separatism made advisable certain transactions for metropolitan absolutism as a way of avoiding swifter and more radical solutions, and autonomism enlivened national consciousness, guided patriotic sentiment, studied the needs of the country, put the politicians in the limelight, and—at least this was how they saw it—made gains that would facilitate a final victory. As we learn the story of O'Kelly's life, we see one of those complex personalities who not only could understand the dimensions of this strategy, but who, according to changing circumstances, could also operate personally and decisively within both the autonomist and revolutionary wings of the Irish liberation movement, even conspiring with foreign powers against British dominion while energetically and combatively maintaining his position inside Parliament in London.

Thus we see that when the opportunity for revolution had passed,

---

*These campaigns for the liberation of Ireland, as well as the conspiracies within Parnell's constitutionalist movement (O'Kelly played a part in both), can be followed in the recent work by James O'Connor, *History of Ireland 1798–1924*, 2 vols. (New York, 1926). This book does not mention O'Kelly, but it does offer a comprehensive account of the struggles for Irish national independence.

†Cited in James R. Thursfield's entry on Parnell for the *Encyclopaedia Britannica*.

and the parliamentary route to obtaining concessions from England was opened, O'Kelly accepted the opportunistic program as an inevitable and short-lived response to adversity, joining Parnell to advance the right wing of the nationalist cause. O'Kelly thought long and hard about this move, with much cogitation about circumstances and events and their possible outcomes. It also entailed a certain personal risk, given the violence in political life at that time and the mistrust within Fenian ranks that resulted from a series of unexpected betrayals. When O'Kelly—the renowned extremist—voted in favor of the parliamentary pact, he appeared at the decisive meeting under the pseudonym of James Martin.*

For ten years O'Kelly was one of Parnell's lieutenants. By 1881, we already find him influencing the leader's behavior. The Irish conflict was deepening and divisions were hardening. At that time the intrepid soldier's political strategy was for Parnell to leave the country to avoid probable imprisonment and that which would follow—the disorganization and ineffectiveness of the Irish parliamentary movement, due to its lack of leadership, as well as perhaps some violent contingency that could unexpectedly arise.† Parnell took refuge in Paris but returned shortly after. During the nationalist upheaval on October 12, 1881, O'Kelly, Parnell, and other colleagues were imprisoned for several months in Kilmainham for their propaganda in support of the freedom of their beautiful Hibernia.‡

Incarceration did not extinguish his fire; along with Parnell and other companions, O'Kelly continued to conspire from behind bars. However—and let this be a demonstration of the vigor of O'Kelly's personality, governed in all cases by noble and tempered judgment—the fiery political prisoner refused to subscribe to a manifesto entitled "No Rent!" with which the Parnellites responded to Gladstone.§ It was a threatening revolutionary proclamation urging the Irish not to pay rent owed to British landowners, meaning a refusal to remain in their condition of feudal vassalage, subject to the lords of the land. It was the kind of sit-down revolution so often preached by Tolstoy and others, and implemented in proletarian struggles. James J. O'Kelly did not sign and was staunchly opposed to the "down with rents!" manifesto, despite his usual extremism, because, along with other fervent Fenians like Dillon, he understood

---

*O'Connor, *Parnell Movement*, 362.

†T. P. O'Connor, *Memoirs of an Old Parliamentarian*, vol. 1 (London, 1929), 175.

‡Katharine O'Shea (Parnell's wife), *Charles S. Parnell: His Love Story and Political Life*, vol. 1 (London, 1914), 208.

§M. M. O'Hara, *Chief and Tribune: Parnell and Davitt* (Dublin, 1919), 198.

its flaws. They were acutely aware that at that moment an unbeatable force was rising against them, this being the Catholic Church, which in Ireland was and remains all-powerful. The Cuban José Martí explained to us, with his characteristic vehemence, what the Catholic religion was for the Irish, according to his liberal vision:

> The Catholic religion has become the homeland of the Irish, but not the Catholic religion that the servile and ungrateful secretary of Pope Pius VII tried to foist on the Protestant king of England, King George III, when, asking for favors from this relentless enemy of Irish Catholics, he made him see that "The Protestant colonies of America had risen up against their gracious majesty, while the Catholic colony of Canada had remained faithful." Rather, it was that other religion of knightly bishops and poets who, with the golden harp embroidered on their banner, green as their countryside, left behind the venal clerics who came from Rome, stained with the wickedness and vice of an arrogant oligarchy and immorally committed to helping princes from whom they had received donations—using their influence against their vassals and enemies.
>
> The Irish priest was the pillow, the medicine, the verse, the legend, the anger of Ireland. From generation to generation, love for the priest grew in the Irish people, precipitated by misery, and they would sooner have their hearts burned in their pipes than have their love for "Sogarth Aroon" torn from them—their poetry and consolation, their homeland in exile, the smell of their native fields, their medicine and pillow.*

O'Kelly and Dillon clearly understood in those critical moments that a struggle against rent "cannot be carried out without the help of the priests, and the priests cannot support so barefaced a repudiation of debt as this. Rome would not let them."† It was a sterile sacrifice, and therefore a backward step. Privately Parnell agreed with O'Kelly but he let himself be swept away by the impetuous majority and the dreaded manifesto was published. According to R. B. O'Brien, O'Kelly predicted what then followed: "It was condemned by the bishops and priests and ignored by the people."‡ This claim may have been overstated, since the proclamation had great resonance. The large landowners were attacked on the basis of their age-old privileges, and the Cardinal Archbishop of Dublin excommunicated those who, in rebelling against this most abusive prop-

---

*José Martí, "La excomunión del Padre McGlynn," letter to "El Partido Liberal," Mexico, 20 July 1887, in *Obras de J. Martí,* vol. 4, *En los Estados Unidos,* 43.

†John Dillon, quoted in O'Brien, *Life of Charles Stewart Parnell,* vol. 1, 320.

‡O'Brien, *Life of Charles Stewart Parnell,* vol. 1, 320.

erty right, waged a patriotic war. The peasants, threatened from London by English forces and from heaven by ecclesiastical dignitaries, could not respond to incitement from the imprisoned Parnellites. Finally, however, amid increasing fear of government terrorism, secret societies grew, rural lords were murdered in violent reprisals, and, in the following May, Gladstone had to come to a compromise with Parnell, called the Kilmainham Treaty. O'Kelly and Parnell were released and went to London with political haloes around their heads. When the imprisoned delegates reappeared at Westminster they were congratulated and greeted so warmly that their liberation constituted a great political victory for Ireland. A minor crisis in cabinet followed, and more than a few of O'Kelly's former opponents congratulated him on his return.

In 1885, O'Kelly was elected member of the House of Commons for the county of Roscommon. His triumph was the biggest news of that political campaign, not only because O'Kelly was a known extremist, but also because he defeated a dreaded opponent—"the O'Conor Don"—one of the staunchest supporters of the vassalage of the Irish peasantry.* As a member of Parliament he became famous for his pugnacity within the ranks of the Home-Rulers. O'Kelly would say: "It reminds me of what used to happen in the buffalo hunts on the American prairies. The buffalo, after it had received the fatal missile, ran one or two or sometimes three miles, but the missile was there, and it ultimately fell dead. So it is with the Irish party and the Government. They struck the Government the fatal blow many a day ago, and the Government may run for a session or two, or even three, but it is gone."†

Word spread in the corridors and gossip corners of Westminster that some British members of Parliament so feared O'Kelly's sharp language and inflexible attitude that they schemed to avoid appointments on the same standing committees as the steely Irishman, preferring him face-to-face in Parliament than at their side on a committee. O'Kelly was undoubtedly Charles Stewart Parnell's most significant collaborator—that famous political fighter who was called the uncrowned king of Ireland and was a frequent ally of Gladstone in exchange for support for the principle of autonomy in green Erin.

O'Kelly's gifts came to the fore in Parliament: he was cool-headed, calm, prudent, and shrewdly vigilant, all at the service of the irreproach-

---

*Michael MacDonagh, *The Home Rule Movement* (Dublin, 1920), 131.

†O'Kelly, quoted in T. P. O'Connor, *Gladstone's House of Commons* (London, 1885), 337–38.

able principles of a true soldier. T. P. O'Connor, recently deceased (1929), who was the senior figure of the House of Commons and O'Kelly's longtime companion, remarked that "in Parliament, too, O'Kelly has, while little known to the public, been one of the most potent forces in shaping the fortunes and decisions of his party. He has brought to its councils great firmness of will, world-wide experience, a common sense which may be described as ferocious, and a devotion to the interests of his country which is absolute."*

While unquestionably bold in his behavior, O'Kelly's advice was always carefully weighed rather than impulsive or rushed. No rash adventurer, he was a soldier, entirely an old soldier, and a cool calculator of the enemy. You are a "Whig-rebel," his friends told him, because of those seeming contradictions that gave more strength and meaning to his actions. "His large experience of life and the ruggedness of his sense, give to his thoughts the mould of almost cynic realism, and yet he is an idealist of the first water."† His "military appearance and bearing struck everybody.... With his erect, stout figure, in close-fitting, buttoned-up frock coat, his fierce moustache, keen, frank, steady grey eyes, prompt, downright address—but respectful, withal, as of a man who respects himself—Mr. O'Kelly looked every inch a soldier."‡ "Unlike all the others was James J. O'Kelly," says a historian of Parnellism. "He was a typical soldier of the old school—dash and daring and resolution were expressed in his heavy jaw, bristling eyebrows, resolute blue-grey eyes, thick moustache, and not less in his curt and barrack-square style of speech."§

We know little about O'Kelly's oratory. It has been said that, like his obstructionist colleagues, he knew how to speak when he had something to say and also when he had nothing to say,¶ but what most distinguished

---

*O'Connor, *Parnell Movement*, 362–63.

†O'Connor, *Parnell Movement*, 363.

‡MacDonald, *Diary of the Parnell Commission*, 297, 298.

§MacDonagh, *Home Rule Movement*, 140. O'Kelly's figure appears well reflected in the picture we reproduce, a fine gift from Mr. G. Patterson, current Minister of Cuba in London, showing O'Kelly shortly before his death. We would have preferred to include another portrait from 1880, kindly given to us by Aloysius O'Kelly, James's brother, this image being closer in likeness to the man who journeyed through the mambi-land during the most resonant period of the illustrious Irishman's life, but it was too discolored to be used in this book. [This image of the elderly O'Kelly serves as the frontispiece of the 1930 edition of *La tierra del mambí.—Trans.*]

¶J. S. Mahoney, *Charles Stewart Parnell and What He Has Achieved for Ireland* (New York, 1885), 44.

him was his forcefulness and precise use of words, which reflected his character and his tireless persistence in pursuit of his purpose. O'Kelly's oratory in the London Parliament was so biting that several times he was honored with the suspension of his rights. When the Parnellites were accused of being accomplices or instigators of the terrorist campaign waged against absolutism in Ireland, and a member rebuked them on the floor of Parliament, Parnell rose from his seat and replied, simply, "It's a lie!" But O'Kelly immediately got to his feet and began to shout at his accuser "Lie! Lie! Lie!" Repeating the insult, he overwhelmed his adversary for a long time before he was expelled from the hall and had his parliamentary rights suspended for a week. That kind of oratory must have been characteristic of the parliamentary soldier. Referring to the incident, O'Connor adds that he joked with his colleague, telling O'Kelly that one day he would publish a collection of his speeches, a long series of them consisting of only one sentence, "'It's a lie,'" repeated indefinitely, since it was O'Kelly's most common oratorical expression.* Among other initiatives, O'Kelly made the thunderous move of signing a legislative bill declaring the total abolition of the House of Lords, a parliamentary action possible in England where there is no written constitution. O'Kelly even brought this revolutionary initiative to the traditional meetings of the London crowds in Hyde Park. And he made a loud official appeal to Gladstone, asking him ironically if he would not support the anti-senatorial project.†

Nonetheless, it is recorded that in 1883 O'Kelly managed to pass a bill of his own, namely the Reproductive Loan Fund Bill, concerning agricultural credit in Ireland, which lessened the difficult rural situation.‡ He was reelected in 1886 without opposition, but lost in the polls during the parliamentary elections of 1892. He took revenge in 1895, continuing as a Member of Parliament through the vicissitudes of Irish politics, but no longer as a Parnellite, since Parnell had died on October 6, 1891.

In the political struggles for his homeland, O'Kelly did not forget his skills as a journalist. As editor of the radical Irish newspaper *Daily Irish Independent,* founded by Parnell in London shortly before he died, O'Kelly ardently supported and provided wide circulation to liberal ideals of Irish nationhood for several years. Not only an Irish separatist, O'Kelly was markedly liberal and ahead of his time. He was proud to be a friend

---

*O'Connor, *Memoirs of an Old Parliamentarian,* vol. 1, 277.
†Thomas Power O'Connor, *Gladstone's House of Commons,* 203.
‡O'Connor, *Gladstone's House of Commons,* 360.

of radical French republicans, most notably Georges Clemenceau, who has just been lowered into his grave in La Vendée. In 1884 O'Kelly persuaded his political leader, Parnell, of the benefits of establishing strategic contact with radicals overseas, which led him to France. While there, the Irishmen allegedly visited the newsrooms of the red press, astonishing French conservatives who could not conceive of Irish freethinkers, accustomed as they were to thinking of O'Kelly's homeland as "Catholic Ireland."

Word soon spread of these visits to liberal centers, inspiring bitter commentary in Dublin, and particularly in clerical circles, which have always played a significant role in Irish politics. From this point Parnell was considered a dangerous enemy of the Catholic Church in Ireland, with the clergy declaring a war to the death. It can therefore be said that O'Kelly's initiative was fatal to Parnell, causing the clerics' open and unceasing opposition to Parnell's policies. Finally, they defeated him: borrowing Gladstone's strategy, they created a scandal over a love affair involving the head of the Irish group in Parliament. It is not that from this point onward the Catholic clergy were hostile to the separatist politics of the Irish people, but rather that, in representing the interests of the Church, clearly understood and remembered from Rome, the priests of Ireland were against militant nationalisms in their homeland that promoted revolutionary conspiracies and upheaval. The Church needed order, and established and respected monarchical authority, for its work of saving souls. With the unrest in France still fresh, the clergy did not want political upheaval. This unrest had caused serious losses for the Church—not only during the republics, but also under the Second Empire, which in 1870 abandoned the temporal power of Rome for Italian liberalism. As early as 1798, Irish nationalists faced excommunication by their prelates, who were supporters of the ruling monarchy, as were their colleagues in the America of Spain's King Ferdinand VII, who also opposed nationalists on that side of the Atlantic. During the violent tumult of 1866 and 1867 in Ireland, the Fenian rebels were denied the sacraments.* The humble priests were branded nationalists, though they were merely tolerant. Identifying primarily with their parishioners and neighbors, they did not break contact with their flocks. Bishops were already excommunicating, and the archbishops, with the cardinal of Dublin at their head, pronounced anathema against those who refused vassalage to the English king.

---

*Frank Hugh O'Donnell, *A History of the Irish Parliamentary Party*, vol. 2 (New York, 1910).

O'Kelly was never given to religious fervor, nor was he a friend to the clergy. As far as Cuba is concerned, we remember that when imprisoned in the Morro Castle in Santiago, he told a visiting comrade an irreverent and sarcastic anecdote about the archbishop of Santiago de Cuba coming to see him in the dungeon without presenting a calling card, and then eying him "like some natural curiosity."* With haughty contempt, O'Kelly turned his back on the ecclesiastical hierarchy.

Thus, circumstances were such that Parnell—like Butt before him—came to forcefully represent the refusal of the liberal elements of the Irish people to submit to age-old clerical tutelage, a refusal which, before the liberal campaigns of the nationalists, had been embodied in the traditionalist politics of the dour and gloomy O'Connell, who would say that "all human freedom was not worth a single drop of man's blood." Despite his prestige, O'Kelly was criticized, like Parnell and others, for his short-term and "possibilist" deals, such as truces to rest and reorganize forces during periods of weakness. However, his fundamental separatism remained undiminished.

In Ireland, as in Cuba, the yearning for freedom and the different criteria for evaluating situations, tensions, and benefits, led to many shades of difference among politicians—forgers of the country's future. On one hand were those who sided with the privileged, and, on the other, the revolutionaries. At the center were the "possibilists," exploiters of opportunity. In 1870, Isaac Butt founded the Irish party that supported Home Rule, or, in the terminology of Cuban politics, autonomy for Ireland. But even among autonomists, there were those who nurtured a growing Irish movement for a civic future with fully protected rights, and those for whom Home Rule represented merely the final formula for imperial union. O'Kelly, a Fenian and radical, was not one of the latter. He treated Parnellism like one of those athletics and rifle organizations that serve to train the youth in oppressed villages, promoting under the cover of sporting competition and recreation the health and vigor of body and character for the sacred days of redemption through blood. A fellow countryman opposed to O'Kelly called him "that ultra-extremist follower of Mr. Parnell who had consented to come from the representation of the *New York*

---

*Correspondence of Francis F. Millen to the *New York Herald*, 7 June 1873, 4. [Ortiz and Millen refer here to the Castillo de San Pedro de la Roca del Morro in Santiago de Cuba, rather than its counterpart in Havana, called Castillo de los Tres Reyes Magos del Morro.—*Trans.*]

Herald at Cuba to the British House of Commons in order to express his inflexible defiance of the Saxon and Saxondom."*

This animosity toward England kept O'Kelly in contact with adversaries of Albion, in line with the proverb that says, "the enemy of my enemy is my friend." One of his colleagues in journalism reports that "O'Kelly had a provoking way of never affording more than a glimpse of his treasures of romance, in connection with the Algerian and Mexican wars, but he ever loved to construct ingenious schemes of foreign complications, which would bring about the assured downfall of England—if they would only come off."† Parnell had to routinely disillusion O'Kelly, calling his attention to international realities. While O'Kelly contemplated anti-English schemes under pressure from France or Russia, Parnell rejected them. "'Poo!!' [he said to O'Kelly,] 'The United States are the only people that could smash England. They may even be the means of freeing Ireland without the smashing.'"‡

The Irish leader was not completely misguided, at least in terms of the positive influence of the United States in determining the political destiny of old Hibernia—setting aside the fact that Parnell was, according to W. O'Brien, almost American: one half by blood and "five-sixths in sympathy."§ It was not rare at this time for Irish patriots, afflicted by the overwhelming injustice of an absolutism protected by the fortress of Great Britain, and in need of coordinating energies for liberation, to call insistently in their desperation for United States intervention on the grounds of human justice.

O'Kelly's inflexibility was again revealed at the end of 1890, on the occasion of the grave crisis Parnell faced due to Irish conservatism and the attitude, perhaps largely constrained, of Gladstone. At this point, and out of patriotism, the faithful lieutenant had to disagree with his leader and friend. A conspiracy broke out against Parnell in the form of a scandal linked to his trial as an adulterer, and, even though he married his then-divorced lover, he could not continue as head of the Irish Parliamentary Party. The Irish traditionalists opposed him, and Gladstone could not support his ally. For their part, the liberal Irish members of Parliament were forced by the undeniable realities of the political situation to choose

---

*O'Donnell, *History of the Irish Parliamentary Party*, vol. 2, 152.
†O'Brien, *Parnell of Real Life*, 37–38.
‡O'Brien, *Parnell of Real Life*, 39.
§O'Brien, *Parnell of Real Life*, 39.—*Trans.*

between Ireland with Gladstone, or Parnell without Ireland: that is to say, between the fading hope of favorable legislation for Ireland with Gladstone's support, or the sterility of an indeterminate struggle under a leader who had already lost the backing support of English liberals, and who was now the enemy, directly and systematically, of the Irish prelates, due officially to his sinful conjugal life. Weighing Gladstone's support in terms of advantages for their patriotic ideals, Parnell's followers sacrificed their leader.

His lieutenants were deserting him, and some "cowardly," as his grieving wife put it. Parnell esteemed O'Kelly greatly, having worked intimately with him for several years in the conspiracies, even from the United States, and, according to his biographer and loving wife, he felt deeply what he judged to be the disloyalty and defection of his friend. Yet O'Kelly reciprocated his affection, and there may be some exaggeration in the posthumous recriminations of Parnell's wife, since it is clear that O'Kelly stood by Parnell, even when the leader's friends were leaving him and he was on the verge of disaster. Shortly thereafter, when Parnell ran for office and was defeated in Kilkenny on December 13, 1890, O'Kelly was at his side, as witnessed by O'Brien, who describes O'Kelly as "the one personal friend whom Parnell had in the whole party—the one man to whom he freely opened his mind."* As soon as Parnell died O'Kelly went to Brighton and was received in the mortuary chamber—conclusive proof, says Anderson, of his intimate friendship with the uncrowned king of Ireland.† O'Kelly "never deserted his chief," said one who was an opponent of both, being an Irish conservative.‡

O'Kelly's integrity showed in his ethical conduct, which was beyond reproach. When O'Kelly went to Ireland as commissioner of the Clan na Gael, the most aggressive section of the Fenian brotherhood (the Irish Republican Brotherhood), he took with him plenty of money to buy weapons, smuggle them into his homeland, and distribute them among groups of hungry conspirators. This was during sure predictions of famine and misery for 1879, but scarcity was not as great as expected and the rural masses' discontent could not be mobilized for revolution. O'Kelly returned the money entrusted to him by O'Donovan Rossa, who in 1876 had founded the secret Fenian "skirmishing fund."§ On another occa-

---

*O'Brien, *Life of Charles Stewart Parnell*, vol. 2, 300.
†Anderson, *Sidelights on the Home Rule Movement*, 159.
‡O'Donnell, *History of the Irish Parliamentary Party*, vol. 1 (New York, 1910), 458.
§MacDonald, *Diary of the Parnell Commission*, 299.

sion, he had to thoroughly rectify claims made against him when, as had happened to Parnell and others, his intractable absolutist enemies forged false and dishonorable letters that they published in the London *Times*.*

Undoubtedly, O'Kelly's efforts to free Ireland from oppression must have reminded him of the unhappy fate of the Caribbean island that he found so beautiful. Many analogies can be made between Irish and Cuban separatism: such as the insularity of the nations; their proximity to a strong military and economic power; the proclamation of the republics by revolutionaries when they were only bloodstained dreams; constant and intense conspiracies in the United States;† subscriptions of money and volunteers for expeditions by emigrants; extensive and active secret societies at home and abroad; the enlistment of officers and soldiers seasoned by foreign wars; and the hostility of metropolitan liberals, who, while applauding Garibaldi's Italian nationalists or Kossuth's Hungarian nationalists, abhorred their subjugated equivalents in Ireland and Cuba. Ireland even had the problem of racist implications in its struggle against England, as had Cuba with Spain, for it was said of the Celts that they were an inferior race that should submit to the semidivine Anglo-Saxon.‡ And just as here many separatist leaders were children of Spaniards, and even born on the soil of the Spanish peninsula, over there, since the time of Queen Elizabeth, more than a few of Ireland's most exalted patriots have been Celticized Anglo-Saxons—Parnell himself was of genuine English extraction. The social forces were, however, different: in Ireland, nationalists had to stand up to large estate owners with feudal roots, and here the Cuban landowners drove all secessionist efforts towards independence or annexation. But deep-down, Ireland was, like Cuba, a nation eager to govern itself through the republican organization of its social forces.

It is well known that during the last Cuban war of independence, O'Kelly—then a member of Parliament—expressed his unwavering sympathies for our homeland and its attempt at redemption. He established contact and collaborated with the mambises, although we do not know how intensively. We do know, for example, that on July 2, 1896, O'Kelly addressed Estrada Palma, then a delegate of the revolution in New York, by answering a letter from him. The Irish MP found it strange,

---

*Thomas Power O'Connor, *The Home Rule Movement* (New York, 1891), 678.

†This factor, very similar to Cuba, can be understood about that period in the nineteenth century from the works already cited, as well as Philip H. Bagenal's *The American Irish and their Influence on Irish Politics* (London, 1882).

‡See the critique of that false scientific racism in John M. Robertson, *The Saxon and the Celt* (London, 1897).

he wrote (using the letterhead of the House of Commons), that Cubans at war did not use the English coasts for their arms expeditions, where they would have less difficulty than in the United States. He also informed Estrada Palma of a temporary possibility that the Cubans might buy 3,000 German rifles left over from the Franco-Prussian war, at five pesos each. He concluded his letter with a vote of support for *Cuba libre*.*

We have taken some time to give due attention to O'Kelly's frank and tenacious position in favor of Irish separatism because it shows that there was more in the lively Irishman's adventure in the mambi-land than the professional interest of the journalist. While among the Cuban separatists, O'Kelly must have thought about the parallels in the political misfortunes of Cuba and Ireland, and in his pro-Cuban sympathies the heart of the Fenian must have beat, quickened by the oppression of his own people. O'Kelly was one of those energetic, idealistic, austere, tireless, and picturesque figures common in the nineteenth century—that century of national liberation—who fell before completing the full task for which they were destined.

"Born in another country and to other times, James J. O'Kelly might have left a name which his people would not let willingly die."† Of his labors, O'Kelly declared, "my best work was not the showy pages which have caught the general eye, but rather the quiet political work which I have done for the last twenty years."‡ The "gentleman of journalism" continued as a member of Parliament for North Roscommon, fighting both England and the ailments that led to semi-paralysis and the wheelchair he used to attend Parliament until his death in London on December 22, 1916.§ By the time of his death he had already stepped back from political activity because of his infirmity and was living in the dignified simplicity dictated by his adventurous and stormy life, and by the rigid integrity of his ethics.

His body lies in Dublin's Glasnevin cemetery under a monument erected by his political brethren. Someday Cubans will lay flowers there,

---

*This letter is preserved in the National Archive of Havana among the political correspondence of Estrada Palma as head of the revolutionary delegation and is cited in the *Boletín* of this archive (vol. 20, 378).

†O'Connor, *Parnell Movement*, 353.

‡James J. O'Kelly, quoted in O'Connor, *Parnell Movement*, 363.

§See "Full Story of his Life," issued on the occasion of O'Kelly's death in *The Weekly Freeman*, 30 Dec. 1916, and John S. Crone, *A Concise Dictionary of Irish Biography* (London, 1928).

remembering him with affection and gratitude.* Now that his homeland of Ireland is also free, we Cubans could, at the initiative of O'Kelly's professional colleagues—journalists—consecrate a statue or street to James J. O'Kelly, in what would be a rite of thanks and a spiritual bond with the Irish people, that nation which, deprived of arms by its oppressors, knew how to fight and win with only its intelligence and its spirit of sacrifice, leaving us much to learn from its glorious civic fortitude.†

Cuba must not forget James J. O'Kelly's example of patriotic manhood. Remembering his life may be more beneficial than reading his only book, which is dedicated to our heroes.‡ The present edition of *La tierra del mambí* and the biography that ends here seek to interpret that good will.§

We Cubans are indebted to the many who helped *Cuba libre*. And here, where so many public monuments and even grandiose statues consecrate absurd minor figures and self-important figureheads who turned Republican Cuba into a servile sideshow, an immoral morass, or a bowl full of colonial *chocolates,* we must not completely forget the names of those who dreamed of the mambi-land as a free democracy. They loved Cuba without vainglory and at great personal sacrifice.

Fernando Ortiz
New York and Havana, 1930.

---

*See Peter Hulme's foreword in this edition, viii.—*Trans.*

†Claude G. Bowers, "Introduction," *The Irish Orators* (Indianapolis, 1916).

‡Ortiz refers here to the 1930 Cuban edition. O'Kelly dedicated *The Mambi-Land* to "his brother journalists."—*Trans.*

§We would like to express our sincere gratitude for the collaboration so generously given us in terms of information and facilities used for research by Dr. Herminio Portell Vilá, Captain Joaquín Llaverías, and Adrián del Valle, of Havana; Dr. Constantino C. McGuire, notable North American economist of Irish stock, whose namesake was a companion to O'Kelly in the Franco-Prussian War; Miss M. C. Donehu of the *American Irish Historical Association* of New York; Mr. James Reidy, editor of the *Gaelic American*; and Mr. Felipe Taboada, correspondent for *El Mundo* in Havana. And, finally, last but not least, to Mr. Aloysius O'Kelly, brother of the subject, for the favor of providing us with very interesting personal information. Thank you all!

Acknowledgments

PETER HULME and I first talked about a critical edition of *The Mambi-Land* in a café in New Orleans in 2010. We had just met at the annual conference of the American Comparative Literature Association. It was seven years and a move to Kingston, Jamaica, before I broached the subject again. I couldn't have asked for a better collaborator on this project. Peter has been generous beyond description. He shared his own O'Kelly files, including unpublished work, and connected me to his O'Kelly network. He helped solve persistent mysterious, like O'Kelly's birthdate (thanks to Owen McGee), and provided incisive and invaluable commentary on the manuscript. I'm also grateful to Peter for the intellectual and creative might that he brought to our translation of Ortiz's prologue. I would not have had the nerve to attempt the translation on my own. I owe a large thank you also to my talented former student, Gyasi Neil, for his editorial assistance in preparing the manuscript, and for his astute and inspiring observations on *The Mambi-Land*. I was very fortunate to have crucial help from the University of Florida—first from Leah Rosenberg, who put me in touch with experts at dLOC, specifically Laurie N. Taylor, who worked with the Biblioteca Nacional de Cuba José Martí in Havana to secure translation rights for Ortiz's prologue on my behalf. Without Laurie's many efforts I would have been completely at sea. My thanks to Manus O'Riordan for our correspondence and for providing me with a copy of his book. Many people provided support and advice, including Edward Mitchell, Jay Sexton, and my colleagues in the Department of Literatures in English at the University of the West Indies, Mona. A thank you to Fernando Acosta-Rodríguez at Princeton University Library and Matthew Brooke at The London Library for responding so swiftly and graciously to my appeals for obscure items in their collections. I'm grateful for material assistance from the Research and Publications Fund at the University of the West Indies, Mona. Andrew Wildermuth's exceptional work on the manuscript provided considerable peace of mind in the final stages of the project. Finally, a thank you to the University of Virginia Press: particularly J. Michael Dash and Marlene Daut for their enthusiasm for the project, to the manuscript's anonymous readers for their careful attention and sharp insights, and to Eric Brandt, for advising me so thoughtfully, and for shepherding the manuscript through production.

Bibliography

Bradford, Richard H. *The Virginius Affair.* Boulder: Colorado Associated University Press, 1980.
Brittan, Jennifer. "A Foreign Correspondent in the Mambi-Land: James J. O'Kelly's Fugitive Cuba, Fernando Ortiz's Irish Mambí." In "Travel Writing and Cuba," ed. Peter Hulme, special issue, *Studies in Travel Writing* 15, no. 4 (2011): 377–92.
Céspedes, Carlos M. *Carlos Manuel de Céspedes: Escritos.* Edited by Fernando Portuondo and Viñals H. Pichardo. 2nd ed. 3 vols. Havana: Editorial de Ciencias Sociales, 1982.
Chambers, Stephen M. *No God but Gain: The Untold Story of Cuban Slavery, the Monroe Doctrine, and the Making of the United States.* New York: Verso, 2015.
Crouthamel, James L. *Bennett's* New York Herald *and the Rise of the Popular Press.* Syracuse: Syracuse University Press, 1989.
Douglas, George H. *The Golden Age of the Newspaper.* Westport: Greenwood Press, 1999.
Ferrer, Ada. *Insurgent Cuba: Race, Nation, and Revolution, 1868–1898.* Chapel Hill: The University of North Carolina Press, 1999.
Foner, Eric. *Reconstruction: America's Unfinished Revolution, 1863–1877.* Rev. ed. New York: Harper Perennial, 2014.
Greeson, Jennifer Rae. "Expropriating the Great South and Exporting 'Local Color': Global and Hemispheric Imaginaries of the First Reconstruction." *American Literary History* 18, no. 3 (2006): 496–520.
Guerra y Sánchez, Ramiro. *La Guerra de los Diez Años, 1868–1878.* 2 vols. Havana: Cultural, 1950–52.
Guevara, Gema R. "Geographies of Travel and the Rhetoric of the Countryside: Mid-Nineteenth-Century North American and Cuban Travel Writing." *Bulletin of Spanish Studies* 85, no. 1 (2008): 11–27.
Guterl, Matthew Pratt. *American Mediterranean: Southern Slaveholders in the Age of Emancipation.* Cambridge: Harvard University Press, 2008.

Horne, Gerald. *Race to Revolution: The United States and Cuba during Slavery and Jim Crow.* New York: Monthly Review Press, 2014.
Hulme, Peter. "James J. O'Kelly at Jiguaní (1873)." In *Cuba's Wild East: A Literary Geography of Oriente*, 17–72. Liverpool: Liverpool University Press, 2011.
Kaplan, Amy. *The Anarchy of Empire in the Making of U.S. Culture.* Cambridge: Harvard University Press, 2005.
Kennedy-Nolles, Sharon. *Writing Reconstruction: Race, Gender, and Citizenship in the Postwar South.* Chapel Hill: The University of North Carolina Press, 2015.
Lazo, Rodrigo J. "Los Filibusteros: Cuban Writers in the United States and Deterritorialized Print Culture." *American Literary History* 15, no. 1 (2003): 87–106.
Leary, John Patrick. "Four Million Freedmen and One Bronzed Body: Cuba's Ten Years War in US Culture, 1868–74." *J19: The Journal of Nineteenth-Century Americanists* 6, no.1 (2018): 117–45.
Love, Eric T. L. *Race over Empire: Racism and U.S. Imperialism 1865–1900.* Chapel Hill: The University of North Carolina Press, 2004.
Malouf, Michael. *Transatlantic Solidarities: Irish Nationalism and Caribbean Poetics.* Charlottesville: University of Virginia Press, 2009.
Maume, Patrick. "'Cuba, the Ireland of the West': The Irish Daily Independent and Irish Nationalist Responses to the Spanish-American War." *History Ireland* 16, no. 4 (2008): 29–31.
McGee, Owen. "O'Kelly, James Joseph." In *Dictionary of Irish Biography*, edited by James McGuire and James Quinn, 601–3. Vol. 3. Cambridge: Cambridge University Press, 2009.
O'Brien, William and Desmond Ryan, eds. *Devoy's Post Bag 1871–1928.* Vol. 1. Dublin: C. J. Fallon, 1948.
O'Neill, Peter D., and David Lloyd, eds. *The Black and Green Atlantic: Cross-Currents of the African and Irish Diasporas.* New York: Palgrave Macmillan, 2009.
O'Riordan, Manus, ed. *Irish Solidarity with Cuba Libre: A Fenian Eyewitness Account of the First Cuban War for Independence.* Dublin: SIPTU, 2009.
Ortiz, Fernando. "Introducción biográfica." In *La tierra del mambí*, ix–xciv. Havana: Cultural, S.A., 1930.
O'Sullivan, Niamh. *Aloysius O'Kelly: Art, Nation, Empire.* Dublin: Field Day Publications, University of Notre Dame, 2010.
Quesada, Manuel. *Address of Cuba to the United States.* New York: Comes, Lawrence and Company, 1873.
Ramon, Marta. "Shifting Alliances: James J. O'Kelly and the Spanish Government." In *Life on the Fringe? Ireland and Europe 1800–1922*, ed. Brian Heffernan, 101–16. Dublin: Irish Academic Press, 2012.
Scott, Rebecca J. *Slave Emancipation in Cuba: The Transition to Free Labor, 1860–1899.* 2nd ed. Pittsburgh: University of Pittsburgh Press, 2000.

Townend, Paul A. "A Cosmopolitan Nationalist: James J. O'Kelly in America." In *Ireland in an Imperial World: Citizenship, Opportunism, and Subversion,* ed. Timothy G. McMahon et al., 223–44. London: Palgrave Macmillan, 2017.

Wong, Edlie L. *Racial Reconstruction: Black Inclusion, Chinese Exclusion, and the Fictions of Citizenship.* New York: New York University Press, 2015.

CHRONOLOGICAL LIST OF *NEW YORK HERALD* REPORTING

"The Herald Cuban Commissioner—Failure of the Expedition," 1 Dec. 1872, 8; "Life in Central Africa and the Horrors of the Slave Trade," 4 Dec. 1872, 3; "Recruits for Cuba," 4 Dec. 1872, 4; "The Herald and Cuba," 6 Dec. 1872, 5; "Our Cuban Corps," 8 Dec. 1872, 10; "The Colored Men for Cuba," 14 Dec. 1872, 10; "Spain and Cuba—The Freedmen of the United States Rising to the Main Question," 15 Dec. 1872, 8; "The Herald's Second Mission to Cuba—Fighting Still Going On," 30 Dec. 1872, 4; "Fear of Herald Filibusteros," 1 Jan. 1873, 4; "The Vision of Six Thousand Herald Men Agitates the Diario," 1 Jan. 1873, 5; "Secretary Fish on the Foreign Policy of the Government," 8 Jan. 1873, 3; "The Steamship Edgar Stuart at Sea, with Munitions of War, Volunteer Recruits and Arms," 8 Jan. 1873, 7; "Landing of the Aguero Expedition in Cuba," 14 Jan. 1873, 3; "Comments of the Press," "The New Verb, To Stanleyise," 15 Jan. 1873, 5; "The Emancipation Question," 20 Jan. 1873, 4; "The Spanish and the Modocs," 28 Jan. 1873, 6; "The Havana Slave Market," "Exciting News at Key West," "Slavery in Cuba: An Address to the President of the United States by the Cuban Anti-Slavery Committee," "A Special Appeal to the Freedmen of This Country," 1 Feb. 1873, 5; "How We Administer Impartial Justice to Cuba," 1 Feb. 1873, 6; "'To Be Shot as a Spy'—A Piece of Spanish Bombast," 7 Feb. 1873, 6; "Fitting Out a Spanish War Vessel in New York," 9 Feb. 1873, 5; "The Herald Commissioner to Cuba," 11 Feb. 1873, 6; "The Herald Commission to Cuba," 15 Feb. 1873, 7; "The Republic in Spain—Government by the Will of the People—Justice to Cuba," 18 Feb. 1873, 6; "Wild Rumors from African Quarters in Georgia—Five Thousand Negroes Alleged to Have Been Shipped to the Antilles to Reinforce the Republican Regiments," 25 Feb. 1873, 5; "The Herald Commission to Cuba," 1 Mar. 1873, 6; "Civil Rights and Belligerent Rights," 11 Mar. 1873, 7; "The Herald and Its Martyrs," "'El Valiente O'Kelly,'" 12 Mar. 1873, 7; "Independent Journalism—The Causes of the Success of the Herald," 16 Mar. 1873, 8; "O'Kelly's Great Feat of Reaching the Cuban Camp—The Heroes of the Independent Press," 19 Mar. 1873, 6; "'Cuba Libre': Popularity of Mr. O'Kelly—Arrival in This City of a Distinguished

Cuban Patriot," 26 Mar. 1873, 3; "Pedro Rodrigues, the Captain of the Soldiers of the Edgar Stuart Expedition, Tells His Story," 27 Mar. 1873, 3; "Insurgent Cuba," "Views in Washington on the Arrest," 8 Apr. 1873, 5; "President Cespedes on O'Kelly's First Arrest," 9 Apr. 1873, 9; "An Appeal to President Grant by the Cubans of New York," 10 Apr. 1873, 3; "The Work of the Herald Commissioner in Cuba—A Practical Refutation of the Spanish Charges," 16 Apr. 1873, 8; "New York Spaniards Overflowing with Bitterness—Superserviceable Partisans Trying to Make a Case," 21 Apr. 1873, 3; "Cespedes and the Herald's Enterprise—The Attitude of the United States," 17 June 1873, 6; "The Cuban Struggle," 22 June 1873, 13; "'Manifest Destiny'—Free Cuba, Not Annexation," 13 Nov. 1873, 6; "The Revolution in Cuba—Release and Return of Our Correspondent," 19 Nov. 1873, 6; "The President's Message—His Report for the Year and His Recommendations to Congress," 3 Dec. 1873, 6; "Cuba's Claims: The Cuban Republic to the President of the United States," 8 Dec. 1873, 4–5.

CHRONOLOGICAL LIST OF *NEW YORK HERALD* REPORTING BY JAMES J. O'KELLY

"Notes of the Voyage from Gotham to the 'Ever Faithful,'" 30 Dec. 1872, 3; "Excited Cuba," 1 Jan. 1873, 5; "Slavery in Cuba," 9 Jan. 1873, 4; "Cuba by Rail," 16 Jan. 1873, 4; "Cuba," 31 Jan. 1873, 4; "Herald Special Reports from Cuba," 7 Feb. 1873, 7; "Spanish Truculence," 12 Feb. 1873, 7; "Fighting Cuba," 15 Feb. 1873, 4; "With the Rebs," 3 Mar. 1873, 3; "In Cuba Libre," 19 Mar. 1873, 7; "O'Kelly's Dungeon," 14 Apr. 1873, 7; "Cuba: Underground Special Dispatch from the Insurgent Camp," 16 Apr. 1873, 5, 7; "The Prisoner of War," 29 April 1873, 5; "O'Kelly Interviewed," 9 May 1873, 4; "The Prisoner of War," 12 May 1873, 3; "Spanish Dungeons," 13 June 1873, 3, 10; "O'Kelly's Captivity," 6 Aug. 1873, 4; "The Return of Mr. O'Kelly," 19 Nov. 1873, 5.

Recent books in the series
New World Studies

Fictions of Whiteness: Imagining the Planter Caste in the French Caribbean Novel
Maeve McCusker

Haitian Revolutionary Fictions: An Anthology
Edited and with translations by Marlene L. Daut, Grégory Pierrot, and Marion C. Rohrleitner

Rum Histories: Drinking in Atlantic Literature and Culture
Jennifer Poulos Nesbitt

Imperial Educación: Race and Republican Motherhood in the Nineteenth-Century Americas
Thomas Genova

Fellow Travelers: How Road Stories Shaped the Idea of the Americas
John Ochoa

The Quebec Connection: A Poetics of Solidarity in Global Francophone Literatures
Julie-Françoise Tolliver

Comrade Sister: Caribbean Feminist Revisions of the Grenada Revolution
Laurie R. Lambert

Cultural Entanglements: Langston Hughes and the Rise of African and Caribbean Literature
Shane Graham

Water Graves: The Art of the Unritual in the Greater Caribbean
Valérie Loichot

The Sacred Act of Reading: Spirituality, Performance, and Power in Afro-Diasporic Literature
Anne Margaret Castro

Caribbean Jewish Crossings: Literary History and Creative Practice
Sarah Phillips Casteel and Heidi Kaufman, editors

Mapping Hispaniola: Third Space in Dominican and Haitian Literature
Megan Jeanette Myers

Mourning El Dorado: Literature and Extractivism in the Contemporary American Tropics
Charlotte Rogers

Edwidge Danticat: The Haitian Diasporic Imaginary
Nadège T. Clitandre

Idle Talk, Deadly Talk: The Uses of Gossip in Caribbean Literature
Ana Rodríguez Navas

Crossing the Line: Early Creole Novels and Anglophone Caribbean Culture in the Age of Emancipation
Candace Ward

Staging Creolization: Women's Theater and Performance from the French Caribbean
Emily Sahakian

American Imperialism's Undead: The Occupation of Haiti and the Rise of Caribbean Anticolonialism
Raphael Dalleo

A Cultural History of Underdevelopment: Latin America in the U.S. Imagination
John Patrick Leary

The Spectre of Races: Latin American Anthropology and Literature between the Wars
Anke Birkenmaier

Performance and Personhood in Caribbean Literature: From Alexis to the Digital Age
Jeannine Murray-Román

Tropical Apocalypse: Haiti and the Caribbean End Times
Martin Munro

Market Aesthetics: The Purchase of the Past in Caribbean Diasporic Fiction
Elena Machado Sáez

Eric Williams and the Anticolonial Tradition: The Making of a Diasporan Intellectual
Maurice St. Pierre

The Pan American Imagination: Contested Visions of the Hemisphere in Twentieth-Century Literature
Stephen M. Park

Journeys of the Slave Narrative in the Early Americas
Nicole N. Aljoe and Ian Finseth, editors

Printed in the USA
CPSIA information can be obtained
at www.ICGtesting.com
LVHW041928011223
765279LV00003B/264